Becoming Human Through Art

PRENTICE-HALL, INC., Englewood Cliffs, New Jersey

Edmund Burke Feldman

The University of Georgia

Becoming Human Through Art

AESTHETIC EXPERIENCE IN THE SCHOOL

**To my wife
and daughters**

Design by Walter A. Behnke

PRENTICE-HALL INTERNATIONAL, INC., London
PRENTICE-HALL OF AUSTRALIA, PTY., LTD., Sydney
PRENTICE-HALL OF CANADA, LTD., Toronto
PRENTICE-HALL OF INDIA, PVT. LTD., New Delhi
PRENTICE-HALL OF JAPAN, INC., Tokyo

Current printing (last digit):

10 9 8 7 6 5 4 3 2 1

0-13-072363-0

Preface

This book is written during a period of violent change in the cultural and educational climate. Every assumption, every goal, and every technique of education as we know it is being subjected to the most thoroughgoing analysis and criticism. As a result, the atmosphere in which we learn, study, and teach is one of profound uncertainty. It is harder than ever to say anything with confidence about the nature of art, the behavior of children, and the processes of learning. Still we must try.

But a time of uncertainty is also a time of opportunity. Dissatisfaction with past educational practices leads to readiness for new approaches to persistently difficult problems. We can attempt radical solutions, that is, *fundamental* changes in teaching as opposed to minor improvements and modifications in conventional routines. I would be less than frank if I did not confess my desire to exploit the opportunity presented by today's uncertain educational climate: I want to institute radical transformations in what we have been calling art education. It may be that "aesthetic education" is a better term for what I am advocating, but it really is not important which label is used. The reader will quickly see that I approach aesthetic education from the terrain of the visual arts. This book, then, can be regarded as either an art education text with a strong aesthetic bias, or an aesthetic education text with a strong art education bias.

Other motives guided the writing of the book. It was planned to be used by college teachers, college students, school teachers, and, in some cases, school pupils. Hence I tried to anticipate the way each of these groups would respond to what I was saying. I tried mainly to address the prospective teacher but without infringing on those areas of instruction and guidance that would normally be dealt with by his college or university instructor: studio participation, classroom discussion, and teaching internship in the schools. It has also been my purpose to avoid, as well as I could, the sort of jargon that so often intimidates the college student embarking on his professional studies in education. I would rather help him than impress him.

An important innovation of this text, I hope, is an endeavor to use visual learning. Art educators subscribe to this goal in principle, but few books attempt to employ images and book design as instructional media in and of themselves. You will notice that all kinds of reproduced images are used here—not necessarily to illustrate words in the text, but to stimulate insights and idea-image combinations by themselves. This seems to me especially important because general classroom teachers often have little opportunity in their undergraduate preparation to experience art in the varieties of its impact. I want the book to act on them the way art acts. This volume, then, is not just an image-container or a word catalog, but a type of art object that tries to make its own direct appeal to the senses.

The objective of making aesthetic education a central concern rather than a trivial embellishment of schooling has been the aim of all art educators, whether or not they agree with the approach taken here. But in practice, we have been able to influence only a minority of gifted artistic performers. A great deal of the literature in art education endeavors to bring the mass of pupils up to the artistic level of that gifted minority. To be sure, this effort is carried out under the banner of enlarging the creative powers of *all* children. Alas, it often succeeds in convincing many of them that they are inadequate *as performers*. But their tremendous creative potentials as intelligent viewers, perceptive critics, and sensitive interpreters of the arts are left largely untapped.

The mass media, of course, profitably exploit the potential of children for learning creatively through what they see. In school art programs, however, we have tended to confine their learning to what they can make. This limitation is not always imposed; but in general, we ignore the opportunities that exist for learning about man and the world through studying the visual arts *as well as* through the creation of art objects.

The evidence seems obvious and overwhelming that visual learning is an exceedingly rich but untapped resource of education. How to use it? What to do with it? This book tries to give some answers. I have built as well as I could on all the art disciplines: philosophy of art, art history, art criticism, art education, and studio performance. Anthropology, too, has been very useful. Since some of these disciplines seemed to exist in remote and austere isolation from the concerns of teachers, I have attempted to offer a useful synthesis of their findings.

Because I believe that anyone who teaches any phase of art history, theory, or technique is an art educator, no matter what he calls himself, I have become indebted to a considerable number of persons. All these academic and professional people have been my teachers even when a few of them were my students. I caught their enthusiasm about what art education could be and their occasional frustration with what it was not. And I tried to fashion a book to help them. Needless to say, a sympathetic publisher and a perceptive editor played important roles in giving birth to a book so difficult to produce: Prentice-Hall has been more than tolerant of my extravagant requests; Ron Nelson has employed his shrewd editorial eye to keep me honest and occasionally lucid; Vera Timbanard has kept tabs on figures and proofs and has helpfully tracked down elusive illustrations; the book designer, Walter Behnke, has struggled manfully, I believe, to make good our claim that this book is a visual learning instrument; the imaginative layouts were the work of Rita Ginsburg (the text) and Winifred Schneider (the color inserts). Finally, I am indebted beyond words for the loyal support of Lamar Dodd, my chairman at The University of Georgia. Let me express appreciation for the assistance received from this University's Research Foundation and from colleagues, innumerable secretaries, and, not least, kith and kin.

Contents

PART ONE

The Nature of Art

Anyone planning to teach art, no matter at what level, ought to know what art is, or what experts believe it is. It is also desirable, clearly, to have had experience in the practice of art. But a book cannot provide practical experience. Besides, proficiency in the practice of any art can hardly be gained in the time expended on one or two college courses. Consequently, the person who has the responsibility for teaching a great many subjects in addition to art needs a comprehensive idea of the nature of art along with an understanding of the ways art is practiced and studied in schools.

We ought to be realistic about what a book (which is a combination of words and images) can accomplish for the prospective teacher. On the one hand, it cannot provide him with the concrete experience of painting or carving or modeling; it cannot simulate the problems of light and space organization, which are encountered only in actual performance. Indeed, books that claim to do so, or that give directions for carrying out successful artistic operations, are not entirely candid about the complexities of studio performance, and they do a disservice to the reader who is led to believe that he is truly being instructed in art. On the other hand, a perceptive reader can learn a great deal that is useful from a book, provided he uses it intelligently. Verbal language is a distilled and concentrated form of experience. It can communicate insights and conclusions representing a vast amount of empirical, or trial-and-error, effort. Moreover, a creative reader can form analogies between

1

the practical experience he has had and the symbolic experience embodied in the words he reads. And what is exciting about modern books is the opportunity they provide through their reproductions to reinforce verbal description and imagery with visual images that have become increasingly faithful to the original. In addition, today's well-designed art volumes offer access to a quantity and variety of art objects that would be almost impossible to visit in person.

We can say, then, that it is possible to learn a great deal about the nature of art and the teaching of art from the judicious use of books. I do not believe that one can learn to create art from books, although many persons are stimulated by art volumes to undertake serious artistic study. What I hope you will gain from Part I is "the big picture" of art as seen through the eyes of the scholarly disciplines that study the subject. This information will not make you a performer, but it should help you to guide the artistic and aesthetic development of your pupils. I think a conscientious teacher needs the confidence that can grow out of knowing the the broad outlines of a subject, its place in the total educational scheme, and its place in the lives of the growing persons who are his clients.

You will notice that this volume consists of two parallel texts. The first and larger one follows the organization of the table of contents; it carries the principal message of the book. The second text, usually at the bottom of the page, can be read independently although it is related to the main text. It deals chiefly with the visual material, but it also comments further on many of the issues raised by the book as a whole. You can begin to read the book through any of these channels: through the main text, through the secondary text, or through the illustrations. Then by moving back and forth between these verbal and pictorial materials, I hope, you will experience a greater degree of freedom than is usually possible with a textbook. Also, I hope you will discover visual-verbal relationships that the author and designers have not anticipated. That discovery would demonstrate, significantly, a type of learning advocated throughout the volume.

The customary way of beginning the study of art is to define what it is. I shall depart somewhat from this tradition by classifying several definitions of art and presenting what I believe are the principal assets of each type. In this chapter I will discuss the kind of definition that derives from disciplines like anthropology, art history, and archaeology as well as the definition derived from journalism, the mass media, and the general contemporary art scene. You will see that although the definitions differ, they are nevertheless useful because in their sum they create a composite idea of art—one that teachers need in realistically planning their work.

By *definition* I do not mean a particular verbal formulation such as we find in a dictionary; definition here should be understood as an *explanation*. We know, however, that explanations vary according to the person who does the explaining. We can as-

sume that a definition of *work* by a farmer would differ from the definition of *work* by an accountant, a nightclub entertainer, or an economist. Knowing how all three define *work* would give us a more concrete and specific idea of work than a single definition that is abstract enough to apply to all kinds of work. My intention is to offer several concrete and specific ideas of art rather than a single definition that, however valid, tends to promote a false sense of security. That is, you can know a definition of art without knowing what art is. But knowing *how* several kinds of definition are derived may help overcome the inadequacies of committing verbal formulations to memory.

For the teacher of art there are distinct insights to be gained from the work of scholars in anthropology, archaeology, and art history. These disciplines lay great stress on empirical methods of gaining knowledge about art and hence they serve as correctives

1

Anthropological

and Historical Dimensions

to any tendency of the teacher to treat art as a matter of emotion alone. Also, young artists and teachers are sometimes prone to feel that art truly began during this generation, or at most, a generation earlier. This conviction results from intoxication or infatuation with the exciting developments in the contemporary art world; but it militates against balanced judgment and balanced instruction. In addition, we are all often guilty of thinking about art in ethnocentric terms; we think art has been created only by the cultural tradition to which we belong. Consequently, the disciplines that examine art in its widest manifestation in time and space perform a genuine service by helping us to overcome notions of art based on cultural, geographic, historical, and emotional provincialism.

The Definition from Primitive Art

Primitive art is created by people living at a tribal level of organization; it is not *bad* art. The label *primitive* has no evaluative meaning; it is purely descriptive. Normally, it is understood to include the work of tribal

As a result of their contacts with Western civilization, the American Indians learned to ride horses, drink whiskey, and fire guns. Their visual art was also Europeanized: they drew "pictures"—detailed visual narratives recorded on notebook paper sold to them by white traders. The late nineteenth-century artist of the plains could compose in pictorial space; as a nomadic hunter he had to have sophisticated experience with space in depth. But he represented the contours and anatomy of horses better than the figures of U.S. cavalrymen. They appeared to him as uniforms without real bodies inside; the horse is alive while the rider is an inanimate thing. The artist identified with the pursuing warrior—his hero who was, perhaps, himself. The Indian rider really sits on his horse instead of being pasted on the saddle. Apparently the artist's empathy with the warrior was strong enough to break through his inherited representational tradition. In the rest of the picture, he returned to the repetition of a conventional device for drawing a running horse, creating in that way a semblance of authentic action.

The more modern and versatile Oglala Sioux artist begins to show mastery of foreshortening in the horse at the left of his composition. His riders sit on their horses the way they should. They are not stiff and geometrical. As a composer rather than a mere imitator, the Oglala artist varies the angles of the warriors' lances; he is more sophisticated than the ancient Egyptians in representing figures behind each other. He creates variety of surface through the juxtaposition and overlapping of forms. Along with these "aesthetic" concerns, he tries to remain faithful to his sensory experience. Still, there are residual signs of conventional representational formulas in the horses' heads and legs. The artist has not entirely escaped the memory of traditional artistic stereotypes. What happened during the short interval between the execution of these two drawings? The later artist learned to think of himself as a spectator, as someone who could manipulate the technology of optical representation. But as he gained in accuracy of drawing, he lost the ability to identify with his "subject matter." He acquired the capacity to see things at a distance—and with his eyes alone. He became an "artist" in the Western sense. ■

A Dakota pursues five United States soldiers, Indian painting. (The New York Times Studio.)

BATTLE OF THE LITTLE BIG HORN, drawing by Amos Bad Heart Bull. (University of Nebraska Press.)

artists in Africa, South and Central America, Oceania, the Arctic regions, and the Australian bush country. In addition, specialists in this field study the art of prehistoric man, the art of pre-Columbian and North American Indians, Eskimo art, Australian aborigine art, the art of Bushmen—indeed, the art of any group not embraced by one of the great historic traditions, Western or non-Western. Of course, all art has primitive origins, since all civilizations emerged originally from nomadic, tribal social organizations. Western civilization, on which we pride ourselves, is less than three thousand years old. Its Neolithic or tribal phase surely lasted nine or ten thousand years. Consequently, primitive art represents more than an esoteric branch of the total body of art. Indeed, most of the world's art, it is safe to say, has been created by man during the tribal phase of his existence.

For what reasons would a definition of art based on what primitive groups have created be especially valid or useful? First, as noted above, much art has been fashioned under the circumstances of tribal life. Second, sophisticated or so-called advanced art can often be better understood if we know something about its primitive origins. Third, the art of children in some ways resembles primitive art. Fourth, the art of adults who have had no formal artistic training—who remain artistically naive, so to speak—is also called primitive, and it, too, resembles tribal art in certain respects. Fifth and finally, we recognize in primitive art not just an anticipation and preparation for later styles, but an art with its own reality concept,

its own stylistic conventions, and its own aesthetic fascination. In other words, primitive art is legitimate in its own right and not just because of the later, sophisticated artistic traditions that have been built upon it.

Perhaps the most important fact about primitive art, from the standpoint of modern education, is that it is not created to be stored and exhibited in museums. Indeed, it is rarely made just to be looked at. Rather, it is made to be worn, handled, waved, and carried; it functions in a mixed-media context. That is, song, dance, theater, and ritual are the normal accompaniments of tribal art when it is displayed or used. In addition, there is no distinction in tribal life between so-called "fine" art and useful or applied art. These somewhat invidious distinctions are more characteristic of Western than non-Western cultures, and they are of fairly recent origin in the West—as late as the Industrial Revolution, in some instances. Tribesmen, past and present, recognize differences in degree of artistic skill among their carvers, painters, weavers, potters, and metal workers, but each man practices several arts or crafts to some extent. It does not occur to the tribesman who is making something he needs that he is creating *art* in our sense of the term. To be sure, he has standards of craftsmanship, conceptions of form and beauty, and stylistic conventions passed on from the artistic tradition he follows. But these are simply part of his inherited way of making things. They are associated with the magical, cultish, or religious effectiveness of useful objects. Tribesmen are not interested in form as a stage in the historical evolution of style. They do not study art as we do; they make it and use it and often discard it. Art for them is not necessarily precious; hence it is frequently expendable after it has served its purpose.

The attitude of the tribesman toward his art is clearly somewhat similar to the attitude of children toward their art. They, too, discard their creations after they have been "used." The use or function of art for the child may be fulfilled simply by the act of making. Or it may serve its purpose when it is shown to someone and evokes a response. Another similarity to tribal art is that children do not know they are creating art until adults tell them so. They create graphic and plastic forms quite spontaneously, without instruction, because it is apparently instinctive for the human species to form materials and afterward to characterize what has been formed. Finally, children, like tribal artists, do not follow rules governing the exclusiveness or purity of an artistic medium. Just as the Polynesian or African sculptor will encrust his wood carving with a variety of extraneous materials, so also a child will combine common or exotic materials as he sees fit, without regard for notions about the "unity of material" or the differences between sculpture and painting. Permanence, too, is usually a matter of indifference both for the tribesman and the child.

These very brief and simplified observations about primitive art represent the sort of knowledge that anthropology develops with far greater detail and richness of illustration. The essential characteristic of the anthropological study of art is the examination of art objects, technical processes, and formal conventions in the light of the social entity, or organism, called culture. The an-

---

The mask (as illustrated through page 12) is an almost universal type of human creation. Whether in a tribal or a civilized state, man engages in masquerades; he plays roles with and without the aid of devices for disguising his identity. Sometimes the identity of the mask merges so completely with his person that he feels himself to be, literally, the individual it represents. At other times he maintains a distinct awareness of his real self and uses the mask identity for some ulterior purpose. But in order to use a mask even in this ulterior fashion, the mask-wearer has to believe there is some magical exchange between his own being and that of the mask.

What is the meaning of the mask for art education? First, the spontaneous desire of children to make and wear masks is a sign of their psychological kinship with tribal men who use masks in formally ritualized situations. Children, tribesmen, all of us, periodically wish to change our identities. This need is recognized not only in the grotesque portraits and caricatures that children create, but also in their tendency to perceive fantastic and demonic creatures in ordinary or accidental combinations of objects and images. The child or youth who engages in this type of activity is experimenting with a form of instant personality transformation; through the mask or a masklike image he is trying to escape what he regards as the limitations of his own person. Second, children usually attribute superhuman powers to masks and mask images. This is an expression of their need for superhuman representatives and protectors. Third,

Mescalero Apache crown dance. (New Mexico Department of Development.)

the magical power of a mask is not dependent on the quality of its artistic craftsmanship; it depends on the capacity of the mask to express dominion over some aspect of nature. And that power of expression in the mask is governed by its creator. In other words, the child or youth who makes a mask spontaneously has no doubt of its real dominion over some portion of the world. His artistic ability is always adequate for his magical and psychological purposes.

The magical potency of masks and mask images, then, gives us an important clue, not only to the nature of image-making, by children and youths, but also to the conduct of the art program. An emphasis upon picture-making alone is empty and without any personally redeeming value; the magical intention of children's imagery has to be recognized and given a formal role in the structure of each teaching practice. This is to say that we should encourage children and young people to make, assemble, or study images as if these images possessed powerful connections with the real world. Unfortunately, the magical connection between the world and its imaged representation has been severed by our essentially verbal education. We have to restore the connection.

In tribal life, visual art forms—masks, crowns, ceremonial weapons, special costumes, and body decorations—are inseparable from the totality of ritual, as with the Mescalero Apache Indians masked and dressed for the Crown Dance. Art is seen naturally, that is, in a living context. All members of the community participate in the creation of art, either as performers

Ski masks (at left). (Photos by Paul E. Pepe.)

MEXICAN PAPER MASK (below), by Ben-Hur Baz. (Banfer Gallery, Inc., private collection; photo, Geoffrey Clements.)

or witnesses. There is no isolation of sounds from images, of listening from seeing. How close is this experience to that of the museum of fine art—or of the classroom, for that matter?

To be sure, the entire dance spectacle may be a re-enactment for the benefit of tourists as much as for the Apaches. On the other hand, it may be the only device these Americans possess for holding on to their earliest identity—the one they value most. But why is the ceremony so fascinating for modern, industrialized men, the descendants of Western European civilization? Could it be that the tribal dance demonstrates a unification of life with art that moderns have lost and desperately wish to recover?

Designed solely for protection, ski masks appear to be authentic: The wearer is disguised, he seems to enjoy his new identity, and a new creature emerges—part human, part ogre. Modern culture, convinced of its escape from a superstitious past, periodically offers opportunities for the discovery that the magical imagination is always latent—always ready to break through the veneer of scientific empiricism.

The Mexican death's-head paper mask appeals to us for its sensitively modeled surface combined with stark, linear reinforcement. But we are ignorant of, or indifferent to, the original ritual function. Instead, we create our own ritual—aesthetic contemplation, the detached observation of formal qualities and workmanship. Are we missing something?

A modern mask—the working parts of a mechanized doll (p. 10).

"Baby's Hungry" doll, in an advertisement for engineers. (Mattel, Inc.)

With the surface stripped away, we can see the wheels and gears that enable the doll to chew her food, suck on her bottle, and move her eyes—effects created by a three-dimensional cam and "quasi-random motion on both an X and Y axis via two pinned gears driving an integrated linkage."

This is an engineer's image; it represents his reality—the substance he knows is under the humanoid illusion visible when the doll wears its skin. But the technical reality that intrigues en-gineers frightens humanists. We think of biological engineering, of monsters created by self-governing computers or by genetic mutation. Suddenly the mechanical image becomes terribly convincing—more credible than the humanoid illusion. For a moment, this doll mechanism functions like a real mask—say the ancient Gorgon face from Taranto. It assumes magical power for us like the evil-averting tongue of the Gorgon for the primitive Italian tribesman of the sixth century B.C. Through a momentary reaction of dread, we experience the malignant power of art—for tribal men confronting mysterious adversaries, or for modern, urban men hallucinated by their technology.

Widely separated in space and time, each of three images—the Gorgon face, the head from a Mayan incense-burner, and the Iroquois mask—employs the protruding-tongue theme, an evil-averting device often seen in primitive magical art. The materials

Head of Medusa, an antefix from Tarentum (left). (Metropolitan Museum of Art, Dick Fund, 1939.)

Mayan incense burner (below left). (Collection Baronness Lucy de Kerdaniel; photo, Metropolitan Museum of Art.)

Iroquoian wooden mask (below right). (American Museum of Natural History.)

thropologist seeks to reconstruct the customs, values, preferences, daily habits—the entire way of life of a group—on the basis of the artifacts tribal men create and somehow preserve. Why does the anthropologist undergo the personal deprivations and rigors of living with and studying a primitive group, often for years, far away from the conveniences and presumably civilized customs of his university or museum? Because he believes he can thus examine a *total* culture under pure, virtually laboratory circumstances. Moreover, an alien or distant culture affords him a better opportunity to develop perspective or objectivity for viewing his own culture than he could manage through the screen of his own biases. He is committed to the assumption that all cultures are structurally similar, and that he can therefore learn something about all human societies—no matter how large and complex—by examining a relatively simple, isolated group

VALI, THE WITCH OF POSITANO, from the Rochlins' film. (New Line Cinema Corporation.)

and styles of execution are very different, but the magical intention of the heads seems to be the same. Assuming a teacher knows very little about ethnology or art history, how could he use this material in teaching? Do children stick their tongues out at each other? Why? Who taught them to do it? Does this type of behavior offer a clue to the meaning of the art objects? Perhaps there is also a clue to the ugly faces children like to make—in art and in life. When exploring these questions, you (and your pupils) are performing art-historical tasks; but you are discovering meanings and relationships rather than memorizing data. In addition, you are learning to learn.

"Vali, the Witch of Positano," represents a survival of the mask in the form of facial make-up as used in a cinematic fantasy of the Jean Cocteau variety. The beautiful witch who tempts men and then destroys them is an ancient tension-generating device as well as a mythic explanation of the seductiveness of evil. These primordial feelings and ideas are all expressed vividly and directly in the occult markings on the face of a lovely young woman. ■

whose size, innocence, and stability make the scientific observation of its customs and relationships uniquely possible. The anthropologist, then, does not study art for its own sake, but rather for the light it can throw on general "laws" or structural regularities among human groups.

If anthropologists' assumptions about extrapolation from simple cultures to complex civilizations are sound, then primitive art is fundamentally similar to advanced or sophisticated art. That is, our "civilized" art is created for the same purposes, expresses the same anxieties, exhibits the same pride and ostentation, and follows the same kinds of stylistic formulas as tribal art. Differences in artistic appearance are thus superficial, merely reflecting change in the materials or technology of art. Differences in terminology or in discourse about art serve only to conceal the underlying commonalities in the function and purpose of art in all cultures. Civilized discourse about art, or art criticism, the anthropologist might argue, often serves to confound the authentic purposes of art, although he might be willing to study discourse about art as a secondary form of art in itself. Here we might summarize the approach of three disciplines to art: Criticism is concerned with *meaning* and *value* in art; archaeology with the *distribution* of artifacts in time and space; anthropology with the *function* of artifacts in cultures that are distributed in time and space.

Given the anthropologist's approach to art, how in fact does he define it? Art, he might say, is both a type of technology and a type of behavior. It serves as a cohesive force in culture, recording experience, communicating information, perpetuating traditions, displaying wealth, entertaining the community, invoking gods and departed spirits, protecting individuals against illness and catastrophe, promoting fertility, averting death in childbirth, building courage in war, renewing the life of the departed, facilitating passage from one human condition to another. This definition of art is derived from the anthropologist's analysis of the artifacts a primitive group typically creates. It was not until the early part of this century that museums and scholars were willing to regard such artifacts—the art of "savages"—as worthy of study as authentic art. Hence tribal art was relegated to museums of ethnology and natural history. But artists—notably Pablo Picasso, Georges Braque, and Juan Gris—forced the scholarly world to acknowledge the tremendous creative power of primitive art by the inspiration they obviously derived from it in their own work. The result has been a thorough revaluation of aesthetics and the meaning of art history in our time and a reassessment of the worth of art objects that for centuries were regarded as curiosities by the civilized world.

Art education is only beginning to feel the consequences of the revaluation of art from the standpoint of a definition derived from primitive art. In many places, art is still taught as if it were an adornment of gracious living rather than an essential expression of the human spirit. From the viewpoint of primitive art, we are afflicted in our culture

by a separation of art from life. By isolating art in museums and isolating its study in our school programs, we have accomplished what the primitive tribesman might consider the murder of art. The irony of our predicament is that when we recognize the separation of art and life in our culture, we try to reinstate art by artificial means. That is, we encourage the creation of artistic products by children and adults who feel no vital need to make them. Yet anthropology clearly demonstrates that in those cultures where art is integral or continuous with living, it is created because of genuine personal and social urgencies. The occasions are not manufactured, they are presented by the recurring crises and opportunities of daily life.

Anthropology also reminds us of the practical usefulness of art—its role in magic, in primitive medicine, in personal adornment, in the creation of vital symbols, and in the

Hippy car. (Eugene Anthony from Black Star.)

Body painting may have been the earliest type of art, with a person's entire skin serving as a pictorial surface. After all, there is no law requiring that drawing and painting be done on flat pieces of paper and canvas. The Eskimos, for example, prefer to work on irregular and curved surfaces; they start with the unevenness of bones, stones, and tusks. Compare the experience of painting the body of a living, breathing creature with making marks on a homogeneous, disposable material like paper. The living material is exciting—before anything is done with it. But paper and canvas tend to be neutral.

Decorating the human body survives to this day, of course, mainly as facial decoration or makeup, and chiefly for the purpose of appealing to the opposite sex. In addition, some people decorate the skins of automobiles. This, too, is body painting. John Lennon's costly chariot is covered with bouquets of flowers on its sides and signs of the zodiac on the roof. A less expensive, anonymously owned car uses hippie slogans as ornaments; it celebrates, in general, the mind-blown subculture of psychedelia. But are these objects merely ornamented and decorated vehicles? Or is the automobile an extension of our physical bodies, and ultimately of our inner selves? If so, their "decorations" are visual gestures—messages sent out to whoever will listen. They are protests against the stereotyped shapes and surfaces created by mechanical mass production and, at the same time, pathetic assertions of the self and its claims to uniqueness. ■

Aborigine painting a boy's body. (Photo, Charles Mountford, South Australian Museum.)

Beatle John Lennon's Rolls Royce. (Wide World Photos.)

communication of concepts. Thus anthropology refutes the popular notion that art is the pictorial imitation of lovely places, persons, and objects. The social scientist who traces the origin of a type of ornamental motif found in primitive textiles, pottery, or cult objects can show how a visual pattern we regard as beautiful for its own sake may have had a practical and utilitarian beginning. Primitive art continuously presents us with visual and plastic *solutions* to human needs, fears, and aspirations. It helps locate the idea of art at the center of life rather than at its periphery.

The Definition from Contemporary Art

Understandably enough, we are more familiar with contemporary art than with the art of any other era. Our familiarity with this art includes not only its appearance but also the places and occasions where it is encountered, and the personalities who create it. Mass-circulation magazines reproduce work by leading painters, sculptors, and architects from throughout the world, and their subscribers thus have virtually instant access to the latest examples of artistic creativity. As a result, most of us are extremely up to date so far as innovation, experimentation, and popular success in art are concerned.* Journalistic accounts of happenings in the art world often stress the glamorous

*For example, *Life* magazine devoted its entire issue of December 27, 1968 to Picasso, surely unprecedented for a popular publication with a vast general readership.

or exotic behavior of artists, and consequently the public develops a greater interest in artistic personalities than in art. An endless chain of artistic biographies issues from the publishing houses. School teachers encourage their pupils to report on the lives of famous artists, and the children obediently respond with mildly disguised copies of encyclopedia articles about Michelangelo, van Gogh, and Picasso. Museum directors have become skilled managers of public relations; they entice the public into their institutions by the millions where formerly they came only in the thousands. The visual arts are obviously very much "in" with jet-setters, middle-aged suburbanites, young urban sophisticates, the "old money" set and the "new money" set, school children of all ages, corporate executives, social workers, parish priests, prize fighters, physicians —in short, everyone.

The popularity of art and its easy accessibility to the public are clearly happy developments—a source of satisfaction to art educators who have labored for generations to encourage this interest. But success here, as in other areas, raises problems too. The idea of art held by many persons begins to seem too chic, too much a matter of fashion, too superficial. From the standpoint of education, art has become not a source of meaning and illumination so much as a delightful plaything or entertainment. To be sure, educators contributed to this condition by their fatuous books and speeches about art as fun, as recreation, as play, and so on. Nevertheless, the successful promotion of art in our society has resulted in a strange irony: art seems less relevant to life than before it became so popular. The reason for this irony is that by making a spectacle of something called art, we have managed to remove *art* to the outer periphery of our lives and imaginations. We are alienated from art precisely when we believe ourselves to be most in love with it. And that is because our love, in many instances, is infatuation. Just as the disciplines of archaeology, anthropology, and art history are responsible for bringing primitive art to our attention, so journalists, museum directors, gallery managers, art-book publishers, and art educators bring contemporary art to our attention. Their interests in art and artists are not identical, but certain common features of their interest and activity in behalf of art can be identified. From that identification we derive the *definition from contemporary art.*

The first, and possibly most prominent, idea connected with contemporary art is that it is a commodity with a market value. This obvious fact becomes very striking when we consider that art was *not* primarily a commodity in tribal life. It was traded and exchanged for other needed objects, but not as an investment whose money value would hopefully increase. The status of art as a commodity, or as property, or as an investment, inevitably influences the way we perceive art objects and the activity of artists. Only children, in their innocence, are unaware of art's pecuniary value; consequently their behavior with respect to art—giving it away, discarding it, creating "too many" beautiful objects (ignorance of market behavior), using impermanent materials and

techniques—reveals to adults their essential irresponsibility. But as adolescents, children learn that art is bought and sold; hence they cease to create spontaneously and begin to worry about whether their work is "worth" anything, that is, whether it deserves attention as a commodity.

We should distinguish between the modern idea of the artist as one who creates a commodity of fluctuating value and the medieval idea of the artist as a worker or artisan who is paid for work done to order. In the medieval context, quality of materials and workmanship were crucial; in the modern context, market potential is crucial. But market potential does not rely on workmanship so much as it depends on the interest of collectors, which is, in turn, greatly influenced by art journalism, museum and gallery activity, and the availability of funds—usually from successful investments in other commodities. The importance of art as a marketable commodity leads to another feature of the contemporary definition of art—originality.

Whether we think of artistic originality as novelty, innovation, progressiveness, or the conceptual and technical expression of genius, it is probably the single most important factor in contemporary evaluations of excellence. It is certainly so regarded by many art teachers. The dictum of the architect Ludwig Mies van der Rohe—"I would rather be good than original"—becomes heresy in the light of the supreme valuation we place on the new. The term *valuation* here is used to express monetary as well as aesthetic interest. That the two are fused in

Art in a park (right). (Floyd Jillson.)

Sidewalk art festival (below). (Daytona Beach Resort Area Photo.)

the popular imagination can easily be verified from listening to discussions about the latest important acquisition by any of our major museums.

As a result of the emphasis placed on originality, much of our culture is devoted to discovering, nurturing, and rewarding the persons who are innovators or who give promise of becoming innovators. Art in the schools is sometimes regarded as the essence of innovation, the ideal activity for training innovators. It is valuable, not so much for what it signifies or embodies, but for its capacity to demonstrate the young artist's ingenuity in fashioning new organizations of materials, themes, or imagery. We can understand how the interest in innovation leads to an interest in personalities who are original and then to an analysis of originality, that is, identification of the various factors participating in the ontology or make-up of original personalities, and finally to the study of educational practices leading to the presence of factors that induce originality in human personality.

If the contemporary idea of art is first characterized by a fascination with its money value, it ends with curiosity about the mysterious ingredient of originality or creativity in the artistic personality. In this regard, we resemble the collectors of the Renaissance who, Bernard Berenson tells us, were fascinated by the idea of genius as a type of divinity working within the "gifted" individual. The modern counterparts of the Medici, then, are the psychologists of creativity. Unlike the Medici, however, they modestly disclaim expertise in identifying truly creative art and artists; hence their researches must proceed on the basis of provisional agreement among equally fallible "experts" about the identity of creative art and artists. For these psychologists, art objects are not especially important as sources of pleasure or meaning; they are merely instruments that help identify who is or is not creative.

A corollary of the contemporary interest in originality and the personalities that produce it is the interest in stylistic succession. This theme will be discussed in further detail in connection with the definition from art history. For the present, we can say that modern culture is, in general, greatly concerned—even anxious—about the most recent developments or fashions in all realms

---

Art's new accessibility and its familiarity to all classes and age groups—these factors have to change the way we teach. It is no longer possible to pretend that art is encountered for the first time in school.

The outdoor art show has become one of our chief public spectacles—like the Fourth of July parade. It is too easy, however, to be clever at the expense of the exhibitors who are deeply committed to their art although they may not always be creators of a high order. Even the obviously derivative work signifies a search for meaning that is probably unavailable to the artists through other kinds of activity they might pursue. ∎

of activity and thought. It is embarrassing to be found owning, preferring, or talking about a book, film, automobile, vacation place, artist, clothes designer, TV personality, architect, philosopher, or guru who is currently démodé, out of favor. Written and spoken discourse about art now largely concerns itself with the *next* development in artistic style. Style, a term borrowed from art history, is referred to by laymen and not a few artists in the same way that they speak of the changing body design of automobiles or the new models of electric toasters.

The influence of stylistic succession on the art curricula of our schools is often hectic. Teachers and students wish to emulate the most recent technical and expressive developments. Educational magazines often gratify this desire by publishing short, illustrated articles giving directions for simulating the effects that the most innovative gallery artists have been able to achieve. Art teachers engage in a frantic effort to keep up. All of this furious striving seems educationally justified in the light of the supreme value set upon innovation in the culture as a whole and on originality in art especially.

Stylistic succession in modern culture has been unconsciously identified with scientific and technological progress. The contemporary definition of art is therefore unwittingly modeled after the idea of science as a never-ending quest for *new* knowledge. In science, new knowledge supplants and makes old knowledge obsolete. But in art, a new style *does not* supplant or make an old style obsolete. That is, the success of Pop or Op or Ob art does not make Baroque painting as prac-

ticed by Rembrandt and El Greco obsolete. No doubt today's artists do not and should not work in the manner of Rembrandt or El Greco, but the work of these masters is nevertheless significant for viewers even at the present moment. This elementary distinction, however, is lost upon those contemporary artists and teachers whose commitment to the ideology of science is so complete they do not realize that the idea of "progress" has little relevance to the idea of art. We progress, of course, in our modes of teaching art, but such progress does not invalidate the art of eras previous to our own. Indeed, educational progress increases insight and capacity for understanding the creative expression of other times and places.

The definition based on contemporary creativeness also contains the elements of a cultish approach to art. That is, we build a cult of personality around outstanding performers—Picasso is the great example—and we are fascinated by the convertibility of that originality into money. The interest in stylistic succession is also an interest in fluctuating market behavior; it is an endeavor to anticipate changes in the pecuniary value of art and to profit from those changes. It should be apparent that the educational concern with originality is, in part, a reflection of the general cultural obsession with possessing the new as an index of status and as a source of personal advantage in the competitive marketplace.

What does the contemporary definition exclude? It excludes an interest in art as an effective agent in human behavior. That is, we are not especially concerned about the types of visual art that influence daily activity—as in tribal culture, for example. Although contemporary culture excels in the scope and quality of its advertising, communication, information, industrial and product design, these forms of creativity are often disdained as art, tolerated only because of their indispensability, rewarded well but not honored. To be sure, everyday art is glorified in Pop art, which is everyday art "framed," made respectable or museum-worthy. Our indifference to art that "works" may be taken as a sign of idealism, but it is more likely a lingering vestige of an old-world snobbism not yet completely expunged from American culture.

Art curricula are substantially confined to the study and practice of the "fine" arts (architecture excluded) and the crafts. Even where the so-called useful arts, or crafts, are practiced, emphasis is frequently on the aristocratic virtue of unique possession rather than the democratic-industrial virtue of fitness of form to function. In other words, the study of art as the creation and adjustment of form to human use has not been fully accepted, as yet, in contemporary art education. Instead, art objects are still created and examined as if they were avatars of status for their possessors. It should be clear that the ideology prevailing in much of art education is a reflection of the definition of art held in the culture as a whole. The private and personal values of art are stressed out of proportion to their healthy relevance to the social dimensions of democratic life. There is always a danger in a culture which stresses individualism that the energies and attitudes which support social cohesion will be permitted to atrophy. In other words, we overdress ourselves, overdecorate our homes, and overspend on vacations while our roads, schools, hospitals, natural vistas, and central cities fall into decay. This is, in part, the burden of John Kenneth Galbraith's argument in *The Affluent Society* with regard to our expenditures in the public and private sectors of the economy.

Contemporary culture affords numerous unofficial instances of the integration of art and life, but our schools and museums rarely recognize them. In other words, our *official* culture is guided by outdated or exceedingly limited definitions of art. Ours is a time when a fire hydrant or a bicycle pump can be a work of art. This point is recognized and celebrated by some of our most perceptive artists and teachers. But official culture continues to glorify the *behavior* of the artist-as-eccentric; psychological researchers tend to identify art with nonconformity, which for us misses the point: They are interested in the personality traits of innovators whereas we, as art educators, are interested in the connections between art forms and everyday living.

An important educational objective, then, can be derived from the assets and liabilities in the contemporary idea of art. It might be stated as follows: Since art is everywhere around us—in the design of the large-scale and the small-scale environment—teachers should try to enlarge their pupils' concept of art so that they can help bring about its integration—naturally and *officially*—with the rest of our common existence. They must learn to perceive form and meaning not only in pictures but also in every aspect of personal and social life.

The Definition from Art History

Before discussing the definition from art history, I must make an important distinction: By art history I mean the actual events and art objects created throughout time and space by man; by art *historiography* I mean the written and other commentary about art history by art historians. Because historians are human, and because they have critical and philosophic biases like other human beings, their accounts of art history must be regarded as psychologically and philosophically conditioned by these biases. For example, the art that historians choose not to discuss would reflect their biases about a proper definition of art. The styles or chronological epochs or geographic and nationalistic categories into which they place works of art also reflect their biases and methodological assumptions. The implicit assumptions of some art historians about "golden ages" of art and periods of decline necessarily reflect critical biases about aesthetic and other forms of value. It is, of course, essential that a systematic discipline operate on the basis of philosophic and methodological assumptions; my intent here is to make you aware of the inevitable gap between the events of art history and the historical reconstruction of those events.

In line with the distinction above, note that the type of reality called art can be approached through historiography or by directly encountering the works of art that constitute the substance of art history—that is, by viewing the art in collections and museums. As a practical matter, most of us encounter art in both ways—through reading about it and through looking at it. There are two other very important modes of knowing art that the world of scholarship sometimes disdains: We can encounter art by making it and by using it. If you consider that a chair or a poster or a magazine illustration is a form of art, then everyone has had experience with art—even illiterates. Nevertheless, learning about art through studying its written history has considerable value because the written history of art represents the results of a great deal of empirical investigation and reflective thought.

One of the great assets of art historiography lies in its capacity to help us see the *whole* of art history. The art historian studies individual artists and their work in the light of all the art that preceded and followed. Consequently, he is in a position to detect the transmission of influence from artist to artist, from country to country, and from people to people. Just what is the transmission of influence? Usually, the scholar assumes, a particular way of seeing reality, or a technical procedure, or the treatment of a theme is developed in one or more places in the world and then diffused through various kinds of human contact—through trade, conquest, migration, transfer of documents or portable copies, and so on. But some ways of

From kids in the sand…

This is where it begins—the serious work of making and discovering form.

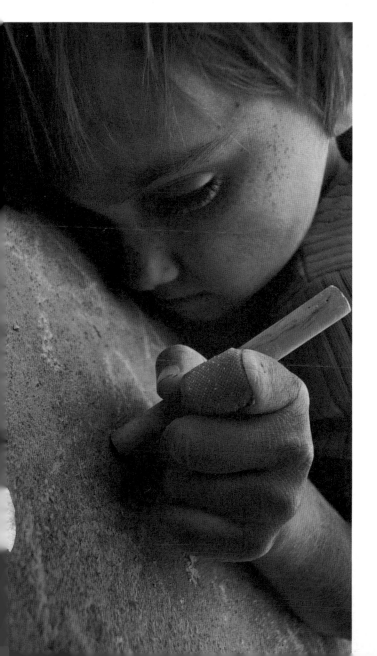

Two photos of children in the sand (above). (Martin Schnur.)

Child with chalk (left). (Johnson & Johnson.)

SKYCOACH (above). ("Der Pelikan.")

MOON VEHICLE (right), by Lamar
Dodd. (Courtesy the artist.)

to heavenly machines...

TWO WORLDS (far left) and THE L.E.M. (near left), by Lamar Dodd. (Courtesy the artist.)

to the moon itself...

and to exalted persons and (overleaf) angels.

PRINCE WITH ANIMALS AND FLOW-ERS. ("Der Pelikan.")

ANGEL
MUSICIANS.
(``Der
Pelikan.``)

HANDBALL (above), by Ben Shahn. (Collection The Museum of Modern Art, New York, Abby Aldrich Rockefeller Fund.)

City sidewalk (right). (Martin Schnur.)

CITY SIDEWALK (below). (University of Georgia Department of Art.)

Back to earth...

Some environments are unaffected by space flight.

and men's problems…

Two views of a Roxbury (Boston) wall mural (above). (Council on the Arts and Humanities, Commonwealth of Massachusetts.)

Manhattan wall mural (left). (Martin Schnur.)

of living together;...

TWO GIRLS (top left). (University of Georgia Department of Art.)

CROWD (bottom left). (University of Georgia Department of Art.)

Three youngsters (above). (Martin Schnur.)

but some are happy.

MY FRIENDS (above). (University of Georgia Department of Art.)

Children building a house in a playground (left.) (Martin Schnur.)

Second-graders' mural (below). (University of Georgia Department of Art.)

painting or carving are invented or discovered over and over again and are not necessarily to be attributed to the transmission of influence. Deciding whether a particular technical, stylistic, or thematic trait was locally originated or whether it was borrowed constitutes a continuing problem for art historians and for associated disciplines like archaeology and ethnology. As a result of his professional habit of seeking out the sources of a particular artistic manifestation, the art historian characteristically studies an art object by asking where it came from, who made it, how it was used, and where its formal or stylistic features originated. The last question is often the most difficult to answer; it constitutes a fascinating cultural puzzle and considerable knowledge, imagination, and intuition must be invoked to find a solution to that puzzle.

Clearly, the kinds of problems art historians endeavor to solve, and the procedures they use, result in a distinctive way of looking at and thinking about art. As mentioned

Huastec figures. (Courtesy Edward Merrin Gallery; photo, Justin Kerr.)

Pre-Columbian art, if discussed at all, is usually "tacked on" to the conventional survey of art history. These examples, created eight or nine hundred years ago, do not fit organically into the chronology of Western art history. Consequently, they are dealt with in passing on to something else, or ignored altogether.

Does conventional art-historical instruction prepare us to relate to non-Western art meaningfully? We wonder how we are supposed to react to work that falls outside the Graeco-Roman tradition. How can we classify it? What can one say about it? It seems so different. There are some options: We can find resemblances to the early art of our familiar Western tradition —archaic Greek art, the Bronze Age fertility figures of Sardinia, Yugoslavia, and Crete. We can note the stylistic similarities—the frontality; the long, narrow waists; the small breasts; the exaggerated thighs; the slightly opened mouths; the weight evenly distributed on both feet. But what do these observations add up to? Should these traits be noted just to classify and arrange the objects? What then? The pertinent educational questions have not been asked. ■

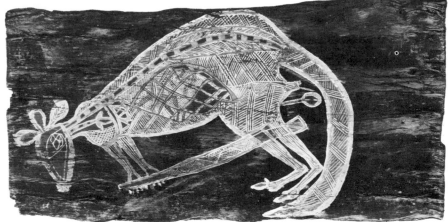

THE SPOTTED COW (above left), by Jean Dubuffet. (Collection Mr. and Mrs. Gordon Bunshaft.)

Diagram (above right) of a Scandinavian rock engraving of a reindeer showing X-ray rendering of internal organs.

Australian aboriginal spirit drawing (right). (New York Graphic Society.)

Dubuffet simulates the naivete of children's drawing in the contour of his animal figure, but he reveals a highly sophisticated mastery of texture in the interior area. The child's painting of cow and calf also yields its greatest interest within the boundaries of the animal shape, as does the Aborigine drawing. What can we learn from comparing these works of art? First, the child employs the so-called X-ray style, in which the artist represents what is inside a house, a vehicle, a person—in this case, an animal: an unborn calf, food, internal organs, bones, viscera, and so on. The X-ray style and its variations have been common in the art of tribal and nomadic hunters from prehistoric times to the present. But what would a child of today share with an Aborigine artist, for example, or a Siberian hunter of the Aurignacian era some 12,000 years ago? The answer is a common inability

24

Animal from a Zuñi Indian pot, ca. 1880, executed in X-ray style showing the "lifeline," a diagrammatic symbol designating the animal's vital organs.

Diagram based on drawing of an animal in the X-ray style, Arctic region, ca. 3000 B.C.

Child's X-ray painting of a cow and calf. (University of Georgia Department of Art.)

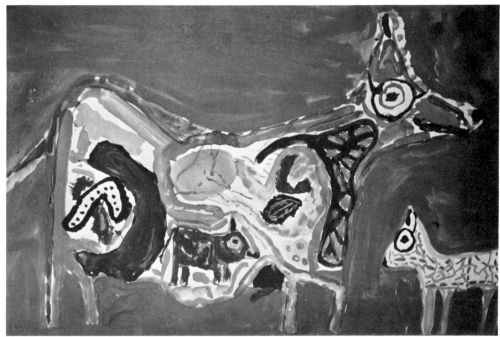

to distinguish between what we call concepts and percepts. It would be a mistake to believe that the child represents percepts— what he sees—in the animal outline, and concepts—what he knows —within the animal's body. This error results from projecting our cognitive patterns upon children —or on primitive men, for that matter. In fact, the child represents his percepts consistently. That is, the child artist, as well as the contemporary tribesman and the prehistoric hunter, makes no distinction between seeing and knowing. They all do in fact "see" what they represent; they possess percepts for the imagery in their drawings. The absence of retinal images does not preclude, for them, the presence of perceptual imagery.

Now we can explain Dubuffet's variegated treatment of "The Spotted Cow." Dubuffet is neither a child nor a tribal hunter; he is

25

a complex contemporary artist. He looks to child art for solutions to his artistic problems—in this case, for imagery that can plausibly contain his textural fantasies. In other words, the contemporary painter deliberately exploits the simplified contours of children's imagery be-cause he realizes that it liberates him from the constraints of optical naturalism and retinal logic. The viewer, in turn, will accept Dubuffet's teeming surfaces when they are enclosed by contours derived from the vision of children. It is the kind of vision that gives the mature artist license to incorporate an extravagant range of colors, textures, and materials in his painting. In a sense, children have done "research" into magical perception, and the modern painter shrewdly applies their findings for his own artistic purposes. ■

above, the historian is inclined to be concerned with the broad sweep of art history. As he sees certain processes or cycles of artistic performance repeat themselves, he may be convinced that there are underlying *laws* governing the occurrence and recurrence of more or less perennial types of artistic expression. Such recurrent types are often called styles; they include common visual, expressive, technical, or thematic features of art. For example, an archaic style may be one in which the human figure is always painted or modeled as if it were intended to be seen from the front; the representation of anatomy is based on a formula rather than on direct observation; the attitude of the figure seems very stiff, almost rigid; a somewhat mechanical smile, always identical, is visible; the eyes are slightly enlarged; weight is equally distributed on both legs. This list could be greatly extended. It is an example of a set of artistic traits that seem to recur together in many parts of the world at many times and that are usually associated with a particular stage of culture. A stylistic label is attached to such a bundle of traits for convenience, to facilitate study and discussion.

Once scholarship has established what might be called the "pure type" of a style, it proceeds to identify and study major and minor variations of it. From the standpoint of the historian's overall view of art history, he believes he sees *development toward* a style, or the evolution of a style. Also, he sees *development away from*, or the decline of, a style. To be sure, the artist who created what the scholar sees did not know he was evolving away from or toward a style, but that was because he lacked foreknowledge —something the historian possesses in a sense because he already knows the outcome of a particular artistic development.

We can now see why the definition from art history is dynamic—that is, we can understand how historical vision emphasizes sequences of art objects moving in particular directions.* Consequently, it is not surprising that the historical definition encourages us to perceive specific works of art as if they were approaching or departing from an ideal type. The viewer's attention is focused on

*Perhaps this explains why art historiography is a scholarly discipline developed and carried to its highest level by Western civilization—a civilization characterized by dynamism in the extreme.

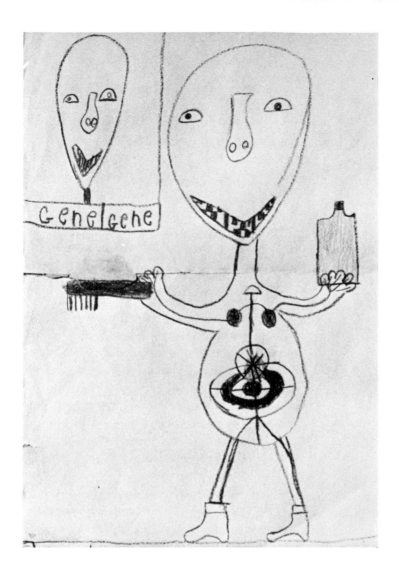

Self-portrait of Gene combing his hair before a mirror. (Courtesy Frank Wachowiak.)

Copied detail from a thunderbird painting, Nootka Indian, ca. 1850.

Gene wrote his name under the mirror twice to make sure no one missed the resemblance between himself and the reflected image. Compare this delightful drawing by an elementary school child with the detail of a Thunderbird painting by a Nootka Indian. Although the Nootka painting exhibits a stylized, somewhat decorative treatment of the bird's internal organs, it derives ultimately from an X-ray type of representation. Gene, too, places great emphasis on his insides. His drawing describes visceral rather than optical perceptions. Although less finished in execution, his work appears to share the Nootka conception of what is real in a living creature. ■

the traits that seem to argue for or against including the work within a certain stylistic or chronological category. As a result, the immediate meaning of the work to the viewer—its existential meaning—may be overlooked. From the standpoint of scholarship, we can see why it is necessary to solve problems of dating, provenience, and influence with respect to art. Such solutions establish order and precision of reference, and they often uncover related knowledge of considerable value for the history of culture. From the standpoint of the education of the layman, however, it often appears that the answers to the scholar's problems are not necessarily answers to questions that the typical citizen asks. Or the answers may tell him more than he wants to know.

One of the unfortunate educational consequences of the structure of art scholarship is the feeling of many art teachers that they must "know" the historiography of art before they can teach the history of art. What teachers ought to realize is that there are many alternative and valid ways of dealing with the actual objects and events of art history. Each of these ways inevitably reflects a *selection* of works of art to be studied. By multiplying the data a teacher or any citizen must possess *before* he can come into meaningful communion with works of art, scholarship often succeeds, unintentionally, in effectively removing the individual from art. This statement should not be construed as advocating ignorance as a preparation for teaching. Rather, I wish to liberate the teacher from fears about the deadly consequences of not possessing certain informa-

tion while assuring him that his teaching effectiveness may grow out of his experience with art as a performer, as a viewer, or as a reasonably alert person living in an environment substantially influenced by art. In other words, the origin of a teacher's knowledge of art does not matter so much as the requirement that it be based on his own experience.

Conclusion

The discussion in this chapter has been devoted to the ideas of art we get from primitive art, from contemporary art, and from art history. There are, of course, other sources for our conceptions of art. Those mentioned here are intended to suggest the varieties of opinion, knowledge, and experience that art teachers must be aware of— both in their students and in themselves— when preparing to teach.

The facts we hope pupils will learn and the skills and sensitivities we hope they will acquire are very closely related to our own knowledge and ability in the realm of art. Therefore, it is most important for anyone who teaches to know what he knows and how he came to know it. Ultimately, we teach out of the ground of our own experience; and in order to be skillful or reasonably effective, we must be honestly aware of what that experience has been and what it means. For example, you ought to know how your ideas or definitions of art are related to the kind of person you are; and you ought to know or have some expectations about what children will learn about art as a result of *your* experience with art and the sort of person they see in you.

One of the truisms of university education is that students often take a course "in" a particular professor. That observation is meant to indicate that the students may learn very little about the ostensible subject matter of the course. Also, it alludes to the unprofessional practice of converting classroom teaching into an exercise in self-disclosure—something more suitable in clinical situations. Nevertheless, there is considerable educational validity in the view that instruction and learning are shaped and organized to a large extent by a teacher's character and knowledge. That is why I have introduced this material about some of the origins of our ideas about art. I hope it will encourage you to examine your working assumptions about art and art instruction. It is not essential that your reading of this material result in substantial agreement. It would be *desirable*, however, for you to accept the underlying premise of the chapter—that there are several intellectually valid and educationally useful ways of learning the meaning of art.

2

The conception of art as a demonstration of originality leads to an interest in artists as exemplars, *par excellence*, of creativity. Hence psychologists and art educators both investigate creativity because they regard it as one of the most important outcomes of the process of education. Indeed, the prediction, measurement, and cultivation of creativity has the educational status today that was once accorded to intelligence, which, in turn, successfully competed with the acquisition of knowledge for the attention of educators.

It is natural for psychologists to study creativity since creativity is thought to consist of a combination of psychologically testable mental traits—traits such as sensitivity to problems, tolerance of ambiguity, originality, fluency, flexibility, and spontaneity. Creativity is also described as a mental process involving a succession of stages called preparation, illumination, incubation,

and discovery. The art educator, of course, is as concerned about the product of creativity as he is with its process. From his standpoint, there is really no way of knowing whether someone is creative or not except on the evidence of the visible things he has created. This attitude is, no doubt, an expression of the folk wisdom encountered in sayings like "Handsome is as handsome does."

The general educator's interest in art within the school is not based on the need to identify and train artists. Such individuals constitute a minority of the school population and although they should be encouraged and instructed, the needs of the entire school population have a higher priority in curriculum planning. Consequently, since all the children in the elementary schools, most in the junior high schools, and a lesser number in the high schools are given some art instruction, it must be for a reason other than, or in addition to, the training of future

Creative

and Psychological Dimensions

artists. In fact, the usual justification for art activities in the schools is the one based on the nurture of creativity. Closely allied to it is the need for self-expression. According to Frederick M. Logan's valuable book on the history of art education,* practical and vocational motives caused the original introduction of the drawing, painting, and manual-training programs that eventuated in contemporary art education. Nevertheless, despite art's early use in vocational training or in the preparation of the middle classes for respectable leisure, today's art programs are mainly intended to develop traits of mental behavior that are considered valuable quite apart from the artistic products that may ensue.

The art educator is understandably annoyed when he finds that art itself is regarded by some educators and psychologists as only an incidental outcome of the nurture of creativity. He would prefer to regard creativity as an incidental outcome of the creation of art. So far as general classroom teachers are concerned, however, it is not necessary to become embroiled in the controversies of psychologists and artists. Certainly both the making and the understanding of art call for the exercise of mental powers we can call creative no matter what qualitative level is achieved. However, it is difficult to see how creative powers can be significantly developed if a pupil is not strongly *motivated* by the anticipation of an artistic or aesthetic objective. In other words, it would be unreasonable to expect

*Frederick M. Logan, *Growth of Art in American Schools*, Harper & Row, 1955.

an individual to organize his thoughts, to expend his energies, to exert himself, and consequently to grow very much just for the nebulous purpose of being creative. A meaningful and reasonably concrete goal strengthens motivation in any sort of activity; the art teacher should remember this point when planning his creative strategies.

Art as Problem-Solving

In the first chapter we attempted to find out what art is by examining the way some scholars study the subject and the way the contemporary art world influences our conceptions of art as a whole. Another approach is essentially psychological, involving an analysis of the artist's behavior. One assumption in this analysis is that there are no fundamental differences between the mental behavior of professional artists and that of amateurs or children. To be sure, the visible artistic results differ markedly, presumably because of differences in technical ability. Whether technical ability can be separated from psychological or mental behavior is an open question, but for the sake of presenting the psychological position, let us assume that they are separate.

A fruitful way of defining what the artist does when he is working is to say that he is engaged in solving problems. In this connection, we are indebted to John Dewey for the conception of thinking as a problem-solving activity. Does this mean that artistic creativity is no different from thinking? The answer must be "yes" and "no." To the extent that thinking involves being aware of a problem, suggesting a hypothesis for solving it, and anticipating the results of trying that hypothesis, artistic creativity is the same as thinking. However, the artist also *acts out* or tests his hypotheses in the form of actual performance, and in this respect creating is different from thinking. Thinking does not require publicly visible behavior, although it may *lead to* such behavior. Consequently, we must look for some other connection between problem-solving and artistic creation.

Let us begin with the origin of the problem that the artist solves. Where does it come from? Anthropology provides an easy answer: Problems arise when a social organism is confronted with a crisis—a threat to the group's existence or to the existence of one of its members. Art objects like funerary urns, totemic sculptures, masks, and portrait effigies are magical ways of manipulating

reality so that the crisis can be overcome or lived through. But psychology as a discipline is interested in the *individual* rather than the collective or social identification of a problem. Therefore, it must account for the individual's perception of a problem. Here we are told that the individual's noticing of disturbance, doubt, disequilibrium, or conflict within himself leads to the awareness of a problem. Of course, such inner disturbance may be caused by an external difficulty such as the type of crisis (shortage of food, sickness of a chief, attack by an enemy) experienced by a tribal group. But it is *felt* by the individual as a displeasing, even painful, interruption in the accustomed order and flow of his experience.

Presumably, art is created in a tribal community when a public crisis generates the awareness of a problem in an individual who then behaves artistically (or magically) to solve that problem. On this point the anthro-

---

These sculptures, which may have been given to barren women, were intended to promote human fertility. They were, in a sense, gynecological devices. Sterility is a serious problem among people whose survival depends on their ability to reproduce at a faster rate than they die off. Our culture solves this problem, if it can, through medical science; but tribal culture employs magical art. As students of art and education, however, we are not concerned with the comparative

effectiveness of the different solutions. We are interested in the fact that works of art can be perceived as solutions to, or as instruments for solving, significant human problems.

Modern culture tends to see the "problem" of art as a problem in the organization of form. But children, like tribal men, cannot separate represented shapes, textures, and volumes from living reality. That is, they do not have rigidly distinct categories for art and life. As a result, form, con-

sidered in isolation, is not a real problem for children. They use and create visual form but they are always thinking about what it designates. Consequently, strategies of teaching that concentrate solely on problems of abstract form must inevitably fail to relate to the genuine interests and concerns of children. The excitement I feel in Numayuk's manipulation of solids and voids is a discriminating, adult response to "Art." The child, however, sees a woman who loves her baby. ■

MOTHER AND CHILD, Yoruba tribe.
(Katherine White Reswick Collection;
photo, Cleveland Museum of Art.)

WOMAN AND BABY, wooden carving by Eskimo
sculptor, Numayuk. (University of Alaska Museum.)

pological and the psychological accounts of the origin of art would agree. But how can we describe art as problem-solving in the case of a Renaissance artist who is commissioned by a churchman or a banker to create a madonna-and-child painting? The problem of the artist working for a knowledgeable patron is different from that of the artist-hunter in a tribal situation. A sophisticated artist living in fifteenth-century Rome or Florence had to consider any work he created in relation to comparable works by other painters, living and dead. In other words, he felt himself part of a tradition in which he had to excel and with which he had to compete. His problem was to paint a madonna and child in a manner that resembled similar works sufficiently to identify the style or tradition in which he was functioning and which also *improved upon* acknowledged examples of excellence. That is a very difficult, a very real, problem.

To move from the primitive tribal artist and the sophisticated Renaissance painter to the child in school, what problem does he have to solve? First, I shall identify some inauthentic problems that the school may create for him. The most obvious lies in the situation in which he finds himself: A certain period or time of the day is set aside for "art" and the child learns that during this period he is expected to make things. He has no particular reason for making things except that his teacher has passed out materials and very clearly would like him to create something. Indeed, *the teacher* is his problem! If the teacher realizes the essential artificiality of the classroom situa-

tion as an occasion for creating art, he may endeavor to *motivate* the child artist. Motivation can be varied and ingenious, and it might take the form of *creating a problem for the child* in using art materials, or in following directions for fashioning an art object, or in making something to display or take home, or in recalling visually a place or event the child has seen. But there is very little assurance that the challenge created by the teacher for the child will be felt by the child to be a genuine problem. So far as he is concerned, it may only be one of the tribulations of getting through the school day. Nevertheless, children are aware of having problems, and it is the task of teaching to show the relevance of art to their public expression and solution. Consequently, we can take it as an axiom of teaching and curriculum development that classroom practices should be based on real rather than artificial problems. And real problems must be brought to awareness through collaborative planning with students —in other words, through dialog rather than *a priori* construction of courses of study.

The real problems of children are those involving their interactions with the social and physical environments. Art is not their problem, it is the *expression* of their problems. To make a problem of art is to add one more difficulty to the child's existence. Besides, he will create art spontaneously if he wants to. The function of teaching, to repeat, is to show the relevance of what children create and admire to their problems of truly perceiving and relating to the world. (The curricular implications of this

Boy wearing African mask at the Bedford Lincoln Neighborhood Museum. (The New York Times.)

Boys with masks. (Photo, Gene Pyle.)

An important museum takes a "revolutionary" plunge: It arranges exhibitions in which the viewers—children—can handle the artifacts. A ten-year-old is photographed wearing a mask. His contact with it is not exclusively visual.

One of the great problems presented by art is what to do with it after it has been created. In museums, the visual encounter with art can often be translated into a "Don't touch" encounter. But we must remember that visual perception overlays a primal foundation of tactile perception. To be sure, seeing is a "higher" type of sensory exploration; it replaces touching and handling. Still, visual perception cannot be rich and profound if it does not build on a generous fund of implied tactile and kinaesthetic impressions. Especially in the case of the tribal mask worn here, physical contact —the awareness of weight and texture—extends and deepens a purely optical relationship with the object.

Wearing face paint and dime-store disguises, two young citizens stand around, waiting to amaze someone. Why is their situation so infinitely pathetic? Because no one notices. The tragedy of boyhood is to reach out for romance, to imagine yourself into an exotic role, and to get no reaction—not anger, not even ridicule, just indifference. ■

idea will be spelled out in greater detail in Chapter 9, *Understanding the World*.)

Now we can leave the question of the *origin* of problems in artistic creation and move to the processes involved in their solution. From the artist's standpoint, solution necessitates performance, that is, physical execution and sensory response to what has been executed. The psychologist has to acknowledge that solutions are not known in advance; they are merely intuited in advance. A solution has to be perceived in actuality, it cannot be reliably guessed at. This means that artistic problem-solving involves real risk-taking as opposed to hypothetical risk-taking. In other words, an artist must do more than think about a solution, he must *accomplish* a solution.*

How does the artist know he has found a solution? The tribal artist receives the reinforcement of magical effectiveness: The sick chief gets well; the frightened warrior acquires courage; the spirit of the unhappy ancestor is appeased; the barren woman conceives a child. For the Florentine artist of the Renaissance, the signs are different: His patron is pleased; his competitors are jealous; connoisseurs of art give their approval; and the artist himself is aware of a special sort of gratification from having taken technical risks that "worked out." So

*To be sure, there is a current tendency among artists to offer the public their "plans" for artistic projects, as if the execution of these plans were a very mechanical, perfunctory matter. This attitude, which is certain to be transient, results from an excessive emphasis, in the analysis of creativity, on inspiration, illumination, incubation, and so on, and a corresponding disdain for the physical act of execution.

far as the child artist is concerned, his problem is solved to some extent in the cathartic act of execution; that is, in artistic effort he releases energies that are in themselves gratifying kinaesthetically and that establish his mastery over small (to him very large) areas of reality. In addition, a child who is somewhat more perceptive than his fellows, needs the social reassurance that comes from his teacher's or his classmates' *acknowledgment of the meaning* of what he has done. I stress acknowledgment of meaning—a critical expression of interest and concern—rather than praise, which is often the expression of indifference. The awareness of a solution comes to the child artist, then, from two sources: (1) He regains a physical and psychological sense of equilibrium mainly from the neuromuscular activity entailed by artistic execution; (2) he receives social confirmation of the meaning, hence the worth, of his expressive effort.

From the very beginning of school, the art teacher must respond to child art in terms of the themes and meanings seen in his work. In this way, the conception of art as communication is developed, the young artist grows aware of visual conventions as vehicles of meaning, the habit of critical discourse is begun, and he begins to appreciate his worthiness as a being who can evoke the considered reactions of other beings.

Art as Expression of the Self

If we define art as self-expression, then we are obliged to ask what it is about the self that needs to be expressed. Moreover, we must ask if there is something distinctive about the visual arts that makes them expressive of the self in a way that speaking, writing, singing, and acting are not. To answer the second question first, there is a popular assumption that verbal language, whether oral or written, is so beset with rules and conventions that its use is frequently inhibiting rather than liberating. But the practice of the visual arts is supposed to be very little influenced by rules, and consequently the individual experiences a sense of freedom when painting that he does not experience when writing a sonnet. This suggests that the answer to the first question above might be: The need of the self for freedom from the constraints of civilized life finds its fulfillment in the act of artistic creation.

. The idea of art as self-expression clearly rests on an essentially cathartic foundation. Everyday life, it suggests, contributes to a build-up of frustrations, an accumulation of pent-up energies. In order to live harmoniously with each other, we repress our instinctual desires, and that repression builds tension, as the aspirin ads say, and thus a psychological problem is created. Artistic activity, then, constitutes a socially acceptable and personally rewarding outlet for those energies. At the same time that the individual solves his problem of tension, he also creates something that is objectively satisfying and aesthetically valuable.

For the school, the attractiveness of this idea of art is readily apparent. Confronted with stubborn discipline problems, and anxious to channel the energies of children constructively, the school seizes upon the explanation of art as cathartic self-expression in a desperate effort to maintain itself as a peaceable community of teachers and learners. The administrative consequences of this idea of art are well known to experienced art teachers: Students who create discipline problems are thought to be more in need of the self-expressive benefits of art than those who have made better adjustments to the school routine; hence "bad" students, slow learners, academically ungifted students, culturally deprived students—all the unfortunate and unhappy and unloved—are assigned to art classes, especially in secondary schools. The irony of the situation is that many an unhappy youngster *has* found himself in an art class. But, of course, the administrative or "guidance" practice described above is a caricature of educational planning; it is a typical stratagem of bureaucracies for doing a sorry deed under the umbrella of a seemingly generous intention.

Let us return to the self which art presumably expresses. If the self is thought to be a fixed, static, hermetically sealed entity whose nature is translated by art into visible form, then the result is a rather rigid and mechanical conception of art or of any symbolic language. But the self is in a continuous state of change. By virtue of the material that acts upon it and that interacts with it, it changes and issues forth transformed. Most important of all, the self is changed in the process of expression by the requirements of the "other" with whom it desires to unite. In other words, self-expression does not occur in a social vacuum. Expression is directed outward, *toward someone*. That someone affects not only the visible form of artistic expression but also the self that is intent on communion with another.

Self-expression then is a completion in the form of *communication*. Self-expression by itself would be a type of human incompleteness. Alone it has no more significance as art than your sitting on a tack and saying "Ouch!" Your exclamation of pain would be a sign or symptom of an antecedent sensation or experience; it is emitted involuntarily, without reflection. There is not enough time for you to interact with that sensation with all the elements of your being. There is not enough time for you to consider the impact of your expression on the persons you wish to influence. Your expression constitutes behavior, but not *artistic* behavior. That is because you have not made or shaped something according to your estimate of the requirements of communication.

GIRL WITH TWO OTHER PEOPLE. (Clarke County Public Schools, Georgia.)

With practice, it is possible to read these pictures as fairly reliable self-images. In effect, the child or adolescent artist is saying, "This is who I think I am." Is there, however, some discrepancy between "who I am" and "what I look like"? Yes, there is, if the visual image is expected to be a faithful likeness of the artist. But if we regard the visual image as a report of the child's self-perceptions, then it is quite honest and reliable. For one thing, the child's personality is defined in the process of describing it visually. In representing himself, the child predicts who he is in process of becoming. To be sure, each artistic medium has its own properties, and these often appear to dominate the child's expression. Tempera paint, for example, seems to preclude precision and delicacy when used by a young child. Pen and ink, chalk, felt-point markers, and wax crayons seem to direct the way they are used—especially by inexperienced persons. But even within the limitations of the various media, a wide range of visual expression is possible. The child is resourceful enough to

SMALL BOY (left). (Clarke County Public Schools, Georgia.)

GIRL WITH JUMP ROPE (right). (Clarke County Public Schools, Georgia.)

make the medium say what he wants it to say. The increased distinctness of imagery as the children grow older is caused not only by greater technical skill; it is also the result of a more definite consciousness, on the part of each child, of his own personality and visual appearance.

The child does express himself; he is anxious to tell who he is; he does need the acknowledgment of his worthiness; and art instruction does make these possible.

"Girl with Two Other People." The important thing is that I have two friends who do what I tell them.

"Small Boy." He has most of his teeth. He knows how to button his clothes. His legs and arms are long. When he stands up, he is bigger than other little people.

"Girl with Jump Rope." Combine a circle with a triangle; add braids, legs, shoes, enormous eyes, and a smile. She is hardly a complex person—just someone who likes to play and knows she is very pretty.

LATIN-AMERICAN GIRL (top left). (International Child Art Center, San Francisco.)

BOY WITH INSECTS (top right). (International Child Art Center, San Francisco.)

YOUNG LADY (bottom left). (International Child Art Center, San Francisco.)

FIGURE OF A YOUNG WOMAN (bottom right). (New York City Public Schools Bureau of Art.)

Why do I say that the self is *completed* in the act of communication, that is, *successful* self-expression? Because I do not know in advance whether someone else will understand what I have made, or said or done. I await a response, I expect a knowing answer; I try to imagine how you will react by conducting a dialog with myself. But my expectations and anticipations are necessarily provisional until they are confirmed in a *real*, as opposed to a conjectured, reply. When you do in fact respond to my expression, you eliminate at least some of my uncertainty. Consequently, if you are a teacher, or a critic, or just another person, you have some control over my feelings of completeness or wholeness. You have the power to withhold your response or to respond inadequately with reference to my expectations. Or you may discover more in my expression than I thought I was saying. From this it follows that self-expression is at least two-directional; that we are responsible —that is, answerable—for one another's self-development; and that self-expression in art is excellent or qualitatively superior only insofar as it exhibits the capacity to evoke excellent responses.

The unanswered expression of a self denies communion to that self and prevents it from becoming complete. The hyphen in the term *self-expression* provides the clue to its real meaning. It implies a self that acts *and is understood.*

There are styles of art—notably Abstract Expressionism—that seem to exhibit a max-

---

"Latin-American Girl." She wears a bonnet, a veil, delicate sandals, bracelets on one arm, and a purse on the other. Her long, wavy hair falls to the shoulders of a lacy white blouse. Those heavily lashed eyes are framed by dark bangs carefully combed forward. The hint of a feminine figure is suggested by the nipped-in waist, but her face is somewhat large for her body and her cheeks are still full. These tell us she is a young girl still—but very anxious to grow up.

"Boy with Insects." You need a net to catch butterflies and you have to be patient if you want to catch any. It is important to move slowly and quietly; when you hurry you make mistakes. Try to take things one at a time instead of plunging into them all at once. If you take the time to look at snails or beetles slowly and steadily, you can eventually learn to like them.

"Young Lady." The artist uses a refined formula for the nose. The shape of the lips has been drawn with attention to their symmetry. Her hairdo is neatly and efficiently indicated, and a real effort has been made to represent the eyes in the "right" size and location. The portrait reveals the girl's concern about propriety and correctness; it also shows confidence in her capacity to meet the social standards of her group.

"Figure of a Young Woman." The artistic level is now preprofessional. This painter can make conscious decisions about the best blend of abstract visual quality and psychological expressiveness. Some of the rounded female forms have been deliberately pressed into semi-geometric, rectilinear shapes. In other words, personality is now revealed through affinity for style. The danger of becoming submerged in a commercial formula arises. But just enough individuality is preserved in the strong representation of arms and legs, chin, mouth, and nose. ■

THE TERRORS OF ALICE, by Jacob Lawrence. (Collection Dr. and Mrs. Herbert Kayden; photo, Peter A. Juley from Dintenfass, Inc.)

Drawing of a young girl by E.J. (Collection of the author.)

Jacob Lawrence has entered the inner world of Alice—a world of terrifying fears. She has been threatened; she has been wounded; her fears are not fantastic. It is not easy for a young girl to be a martyr. But Alice is brave. She will make it to school.

One reason for the effectiveness of this painting lies in Lawrence's ability to incorporate youthful imagery into his composition. Compare his painting of Alice with the drawing of a girl by E.J. Notice in both works the angularity of the body contours,

the small hands, the combination of naturalism and distortion in the head. Lawrence has been very skillful in exploiting the style features of early adolescent drawing in creating the nightmare world of Alice. But most important of all is an act of empathy by the imum of spontaneity and a minimum of calculation and reflective thought during artistic execution. But such styles entail a great deal of personal preparation, philosophizing, and self-stimulation *in advance* of execution. In other words, the appearance of spontaneity is carefully planned. How human it is to make elaborate plans for the purpose of seeming to be governed completely by impulse!

The art of children, of course, is more truly spontaneous. They have had less experience of the world than adults and accordingly they are less inclined to hesitate in their artistic execution. For this reason, the self-expression of children is regarded as more *revealing*, more truly reflective of their inner selves than the self-expression of adults—adults who have learned to dissimulate. To say that child art is *revealing* of the self is not to imply that it is also *expressive* of the self. After all, we reveal ourselves unwittingly by our spontaneous, unreflective behavior. We *express* ourselves when we deliberately attempt to share our feelings and ideas with each other. But our interest as art teachers is not in the exploitation of the child's expression for the purpose of

learning more about him; that is the concern of a clinician who is diagnosing and treating a sick child. The educator's concern is with the *transformation* of the self through art. And by stressing the effect of art as communication, we can help transform the self of the child in the direction of the truly human.

Emphasizing spontaneity in the art of children, then, amounts to encouraging what they do naturally. It is the adolescent or adult artist who is usually timid or inhibited, and who needs to learn to express himself with greater fluency. By encouraging an unreflective approach to art in the child, we are, in effect, asking him to postpone his maturity. We adult teachers of art want him to retain the charm and innocence of child art because, unconsciously, we regret the loss of our own innocence and would like to regain it through the children we teach. No doubt some teachers will violently object to this observation, but I feel, in all candor, that it needs to be made. I should like to make a distinction between accepting child art for what it is and endeavoring to prevent its development into something else. There is a great deal of Romanticism in the ideology of

artist. It is not merely a matter of seeing himself in the place of the girl; he must behold Alice's self as she does. And Alice is his creation! The result is a convincing work of art which could have been only an illustration—an event described from a distance.

A central task of teaching is to imagine yourself into the minds of the people you teach. In this respect, a teacher is like the artist or novelist who enters the existence of his invented characters. Teachers "invent" their pupils, too, continuously correcting their

artificial constructions in the light of what they see and know about them as real people. This artistic element in teaching, with its sensitive perception of the qualities in people, its subtle powers of self-correction, will defy simulation by computer for a long time. ■

DEUX PERSONNAGES (below), by
Jean Dubuffet. (Courtesy the artist.)

Two figure drawings by children
(above). (Collection of the author.)

Child's painting of a man (left).
(University of Georgia Department of
Art.)

art education. By educational Romanticism I mean a desire to escape the unpleasant realities of human development and the unbeautiful features of the human environment. The Romanticism of art education is based on the discovery that the art of children, like the art of primitives, is legitimate in its own right; in addition, this Romanticism, like that of Jean Jacques Rousseau and his noble savage, assumes that the innocence and spontaneity of primitive or precivilized persons represents a truth and reality that are superior —not equal but superior—to the truths and realities of adult, civilized existence; furthermore, the onset of adolescence, which is the growing person's encounter with adult reality—in art and in life—is consequently regarded as an unmitigated disaster. A teacher may hold these views philosophically, but insofar as he acts on them in his

---

Dubuffet has been foremost among modern masters in his consistent and enthusiastic borrowing from the art of children. In the process, he has taught us to see and prize the unique qualities of children's creative expression. For anyone who teaches children, this artist's work is virtually a textbook on child art. But more importantly, he encourages us to find serious enjoyment in a distinctive type of human creativity, and that enjoyment is a wonderful asset for the person who works professionally with children.

Children's art can be collected, studied and appreciated as a separate and specialized artistic genre —like still-life painting, or Japanese woodblock prints, or medieval manuscript illuminations. It possesses characteristic traits that can be fascinating in themselves and not only for the clues they offer to a particular child's development. Clearly, the effect of Dubuffet's work is to call attention to these unique fascinations; he has no ulterior motives.

What are some of the traits of children's creativity that give pleasure, especially the traits Dubuffet, Klee, Picasso, and others have chosen to reflect in their own work? First is the marvelous blend of observation and fantasy; children seem to draw what they hear and feel and imagine as well as what they see. Since optical experience has not been sharply separated from their other sensory experience, children may endeavor to represent visceral and tactile sensations as well as optical effects. The resulting imagery is often richer, in many ways, than that of adults. A second intriguing trait is seen in the child's tentative approach to form. His lines and shapes always seem ready to become something else. There is an exquisitely tremulous quality in some of these forms, as if the artist were conscious of dozens of simultaneous feelings and intentions, and wanted to act on all of them at once. Finally, the strange proportions and irregular contours of child art have a mysterious interest. We get a rollicking, almost disorienting set of feelings from shapes that have been squeezed, elongated, tapered the wrong way, outrageously enlarged, or ignominiously reduced. We seem to be in the presence of a magical world where anything can be something else, and probably is.

Why are these departures from adult reality, and from common sense, felt as liberating experiences? It is because we sense our involvement in growth itself through our participation in the child's intoxicated vision. We know that we are watching a little human being on his way to making sense of the world. And, since adults have made very little sense of the world, we hope the little human being will be more successful. ■

teaching, his position *in a school* becomes anomalous. He is committed, after all, to a professional role in an institution devoted to systematic change, the encouragement of growth, and the achievement of maturity. To some extent, school systems solve the problem of educational Romanticism by the physical separation of elementary and secondary schools. Nevertheless, many secondary schools perpetuate educational Romanticism by conducting elementary-school art programs.

One of the ways of preserving the artistic and aesthetic innocence of children is through limiting their experience with art created by anyone except children. Of course, children "know" that art is also created by adults, but only the qualities of child art are reinforced in their school experience. Consequently, when it is no longer possible to preserve their innocence, when the imagery and space relations of the "outer world" enter their consciousness perforce, they arrive as a paralyzing shock. The art teacher who has been directing the expression of the child's self incestuously back upon itself has succeeded in fashioning a personality that is unfit for the visual adventures of maturity. In practical terms, the adolescent, having lost confidence in his childlike creative powers, ends his artistic career; he ceases to celebrate the poetic world of vision. From now on, his feelings about existence will be expressed in the prose of engineering or accounting.

This unromantic outcome of excessive Romanticism in teaching can be prevented by supplementing the artistic activity of the elementary-school program with liberal exposure to the art of professionals—both contemporary and historical. Practical suggestions for such instruction will be given in Part Four. Here, I may say that the teacher can move a child's self-expression toward communication by deliberately creating encounters between the child and professional art, by directing his attention toward the comprehensive meaning of all types of creative expression, and by setting aside time for examining the child's work in sequence and attempting to identify and interpret to the child his stylistic tendencies. It is especially helpful if the teacher can show examples of work by professional artists that exhibit qualities and style features found in the art of children. Our educational intent is to make explicit and conscious what is implicit and unconscious in the child's self-expression. In this way we accomplish several important objectives: (1) We respond humanly to his work; (2) we help establish the idea of art as communication; (3) we give the child as artist a sense of motion toward an aesthetic goal; (4) we prepare him for the passage into adolescence; (5) we acquaint the child with the larger world he must eventually live in; (6) we provide him with a rudimentary model of critical discourse.

These ambitious goals are possible because of the natural impulse toward self-expression in the child and because of his human curiosity about the meanings of artistic signs, symbols, and configurations. I do not claim that their achievement is easy; and working toward them *does* take time. But that is why teaching is an art.

Art as Perfectionist Impulse

Any treatment of the nature of art must deal with the human interest in form and in the organized appearance of things. We have to account for one of the curious features of man's forming activity—his persistence in working materials *beyond* the point where they are physically useful or functional. It almost appears as if the artist has a built-in program that tells him how long to tinker, refine, embellish, simplify, and correct the forms he has brought into being. I call this activity "the perfectionist impulse" not because it necessarily leads to excellence in art, but because it implies the idea of *completeness* that seems to belong to every artist, no matter how unskilled, inexperienced, unoriginal, or unknown.

Why do children or adults make things when there is no apparent social or practical need for their artistic production? One reason lies in our human biological equipment, especially our hands and eyes. Our opposable thumbs and remarkable fingers and our binocular vision and depth perception—these clearly predispose any human being to form materials in the light of what *he sees in them*. A second reason is man's symbol-making and sign-reading capacity, his ability to interpret sense data, to endow objects with semantic value. Third, of course,

are man's residual forming capacities and drives inherited from hundreds of thousands of years as a tool-making and tool-using animal. Even in the absence of an immediate need to fashion tools or symbolic objects, then, man *cannot help* creating forms just for his personal—what might be called his aesthetic—gratification.

The biological case for art is made by the fact that children form things instinctively and without external reinforcement. For the educator, this means that the original human material we are given to work with already possesses a powerful impulse toward form and forming. The educator *must not* forget that there are two sides to the coin of form: One is the artistic and one is the aesthetic. That is, making is always undertaken *in the light* of a desired result. The goal or result or formal objective may be exceedingly nebulous and vague at first, but it is modified and grows more precise as the work progresses. The important point is that no matter how primitive or immature the level of forming activity, it is never a purely mechanical or manipulative phenomenon; there is always a simultaneous reading of meaning and an anticipation of the visual outcome. In other words, you cannot separate making from understanding.

Prehistoric art provides the best evidence for assertions about the role of form and forming in man's existence. The earliest known Paleolithic paintings and sculptures—about 20,000 B.C.—already exhibit the capacity to convert sense data into meaningful forms and configurations. Even before he

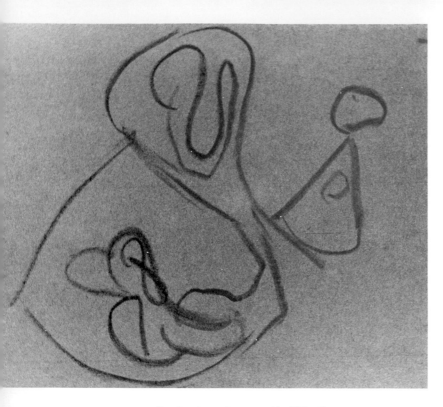

Drawing by a four-year-old child. (Collection of the author.)

SHAME, by Paul Klee. (Permission S.P.A.D.E.M., 1969, by French Reproduction Rights, Inc.; photo, Paul Klee Foundation, Museum of Fine Art, Berne.)

could plant seeds, raise animals, or build his own shelter, man was able to fashion images that gave him a measure of magical control over reality. This same need to master reality is recapitulated in the spontaneous art of children. Without the representation of reality—without artistic form, in other words—the world would be too terrifying for man to endure. That is, it would be too terrifying to endure by man *as man*; he would have to revert back to a prehuman condition.

Now we can begin to understand why human beings carry their artistic efforts beyond the requirements of satisfying a practical need: The *act* of forming, or creating, builds the individual's confidence in his human—that is, symbolic—control over reality. Like the Aurignacian hunter of the Old Stone Age, the child through his art asserts his dominion over what he can represent artistically, and thus he dissipates his fears by converting *its* magic—the magic of its being and reality—into *his* magic. That is why the child repeats over and over again the same configurations, the same schematic

At first, the child's drawing appears to be simple—a random arrangement of lines. But that simplicity is deceptive. For the child, the drawing represents a hard-won victory: The image in his drawing has just barely emerged from his scribbles; it constitutes form; it has the power of designating a human being. In the continuous line which repre-

representations of the objects and persons sharing his psychophysical living space. Each day brings with it the burden of new and potentially fearful realities, hence their terrifying content must be exorcised daily. The repetition of imagery by a child is directly proportional to the fund of fear that is aroused by the realities symbolized in his artistic imagery.

If the statement above explains why children or prehistoric men repeat their imagery over and over again, does it also account for the persistence of more mature or sophisticated artists in refining and embellishing the formal qualities of their art? Can we say that it is fear which makes them reluctant to change or finish their work? To some extent there is a component of fear behind the art of later tribal men—men who are settled in villages, who live in huts, who raise crops—Neolithic men. Their art often exhibits what is called *horror vacui*, a fear of empty spaces. Their more advanced way of life, their more elaborate structures of language and custom, have simultaneously equipped them to per-

ceive a greater number and variety of dangers in their psychophysical living space. It is a situation like that of the rich and propertied man who has more to worry about than the poor man who owns nothing.

The perfectionist impulse, then, manifests itself in primitive and child art as a result of the fear that raw, unadorned reality presents to the unsophisticated person. The child's art acquires a somewhat obsessive quality when he uses it to exorcise demons he cannot otherwise cope with. Contemporary artists, too, attempt to find in the reiteration of certain forms and themes a kind of personal salvation that life somehow withholds. We can see such motifs in the persistent whiplash curve of Aubrey Beardsley's graphic art (see page 50) and in the repetitive convolutions of Jackson Pollock. The artist seems unable to forego the singular gratification of repeating what is essentially the same formal statement. Carried to an extreme, his work becomes a clinical manifestation, a symptom of fear rather than a self-expressive drive toward communication.

---

sents nose, mouth, and both eyes, we can see an astonishing formal invention. It is a creation a modern master might envy. Yet it was not taught, it was not copied. Still, the total image was no accident: It was willed, fought for, wrested from myriad possibilities of formlessness.

Klee's drawing line also has a quality of randomness, because it is consciously derived from the drawing imagery of children. Clearly, he has studied the struggle of the child to create visual form and has then based his work on that struggle. Here he tries to simulate the characteristic perception and small-muscle uncoordination of children. He even shows the figure evolving from a geometric scribble—a triangle that **also acts as a house for his little image. In this way, a mature artist can build expressive qualities into his work that would be inaccessible to him otherwise. We, in turn, gain a unique insight into the emotions of childhood because the lines that create Klee's imagery are simultaneously expressive of the child's instinctual drive toward form. ■**

The whiplash curve, obsessively repeated in Beardsley's art, became one of the most characteristic features of the Art Nouveau style. For other artists and designers, it may have been a decorative motif; for Beardsley it was a psychological necessity—the symbolic expression of his sublimated erotic longings.

The mature artist may disguise the devices he uses to exorcise his fears or forbidden wishes. Or the meaning of certain forms and configurations may be hidden even from himself. In any event, once he has embarked on the voyage of artistic execution, it is exceedingly difficult for the artist to prevent unconscious or latent material from asserting itself. Indeed, the artist may work and rework a composition repeatedly, until it seems to "feel right," although an observer may have seen no reason for dissatisfaction with an earlier version.

The process of execution has a function apart from its visible result: It enables the artist to purge himself of very disturbing feelings—feelings that often cannot be named but which nevertheless contribute to a special sort of unhappiness. It is very likely that the habit of purging the self of depression or guilt through artistic activity begins quite early in the lives of some children, and that these children are the ones who must, perforce, follow artistic careers. If not, some other symbolic activity must perform, for them, the function of dissipating accumulated tensions and fears. ■

THE PEACOCK SKIRT, by Aubrey Beardsley. (Fogg Art Museum, Harvard University, bequest of Grenville L. Winthrop.)

For the contemporary, sophisticated artist, the perfectionist impulse also represents the perception of aesthetic opportunities in artistic form. That is, the incomplete or the almost completed work of art is under continuous inspection for its potential sources of visual pleasure. How can each square inch of surface be exploited maximally for sensory delight? The educator should see in this question the precise opposite of the question asked by the tribal artist: How can the threat present in each sensory datum be averted through artistic action?

Here we encounter the difference between the child's motivation to create art and that of the adolescent or adult. The adult has learned that art can be a positive source of gratification *in itself*, apart from its magical powers. But the child delights in art only because its magic rids him of fear; his pleasure is not in the art object but in his own feelings—in his narcissistic enjoyment of the sense of being responsible to no one as a result of the freedom from fear which artistic execution provides. It is normal, of course, for the child to seek to persist with an art of self-gratification. But the teacher's function is to convert the concern with self-gratification into the pleasure of human understanding and communication. In other words, the child artist has to learn that his creative expression is a type of transaction with someone else, not just himself.

In the mature person, perfectionist effort is undertaken for the purpose of entering into a meaningful relation with a special public, a general audience or another person through the medium of art. Such an artist's pleasure in his own work is always colored by the anticipation of its effect on others. His formal and technical drives are predicated on the existence of interested viewers. Such "other-directed" concerns are natural and healthy so long as they do not result in paralyzing inhibitions leading to the inability to create. Creative inhibition is caused, in my judgment, by instruction that is excessively oriented toward liking, preferring, and admiring artistic products instead of understanding what they mean. If a student believes that the goal of artistic effort is to arouse his teacher's admiration, he is likely to end his effort when he has secured that admiration or give up his effort if he fails to do so. It is too easy for the teacher to say what he likes or dislikes—too easy as criticism and too easy as human response. If the teacher sees himself as surrogate for the learned and adult community, then he should know that his answer to a student's artistic statement must not be given casually, automatically, apathetically, *unresponsively*. Like self-expression, the perfectionist impulse is incomplete without a loving answer, that is, an answer which also expresses concern about the self that seeks embodiment in artistic form. Art instruction involves more than a single climactic episode in which a student is congratulated by a teacher. It is rather a *series* of events, a process in which a variety of changes in the content and perceptiveness of the pupil's self are observed and interpreted by an art teacher. This activity of the teacher confirms the student's growth. It is the answer to the question he has been asking.

Having considered the meaning of art in the individual's existence, let us now examine art as it affects groups and communities. Of course, a group is a collection of individuals and it possesses no organs, no nervous system, no anatomy and physiology in the same way that persons do. And yet, organized groups often behave *as if* they possessed organs of perception and expression; they act *as if* they have an anatomical structure and a nervous system. Certainly we refer to social groups *as if* they have needs, interests, and requirements. Statesmen and politicians have been known to speak of the "character" and the "destiny" of a national group. To be sure, these terms are metaphors—implied comparisons with human beings. But the law can create "legal" persons, as with the corporation, and corporations have rights; they "pay" taxes; they "borrow" money; they "invent" new products; they "patronize" artists. Clearly, groups —legal or otherwise—have many of the attributes of living organisms.

A community is a group bound together by similarity of interest and, usually, of physical location. The common physical location may even account for the similarity of interest among the members of a community. Art is obviously related to the physical community since all structures and spaces have been designed—for good or ill—to facilitate the life of the group and, hopefully, to express the group's values and aspirations. Because art is responsible, through architecture, for shaping what we see in the environment and how we move, assemble, and meet each other, it plays a very crucial role in the life of a community. And in architecture we encounter a social art in pure form: The architect designs a building such as a school, a store, a library, or a theater, only for a group. The shape of the structure is conditioned by *collective* requirements

3

Social

and Cultural Dimensions

for circulation, work space, illumination, comfort, privacy, access, safety, and so on. Furthermore, architecture usually involves collective creation: several persons are involved in the design of a building, including its engineering and financing; and many more are involved in the actual fabrication of its structure.

Art education has not, until recently, devoted much attention to physical and communal forms of art. Artists and art teachers tend to be fascinated by personal, more-or-less private kinds of artistic expression. Indeed, when elementary-school children are engaged in making a mural, their art teacher usually guides the project with scrupulous care lest individual pupils be submerged in the collective effort. Such well-intentioned concern reflects the enormous value placed upon self-expression as well as the desire of schools to conduct their instruction according to democratic models. But it is possible to misconstrue the application and relevance of democratic ideals to learning—in the arts or in other areas of instruction.

What are some misconceptions about the relationship of art education to democratic life? First, art is not necessarily a democratic product; it has thrived under the most autocratic and authoritarian forms of government. Second, one does not gain any insight into the democratic process by pretending that all youngsters are capable of equal levels of artistic or other achievement. Third, children are much tougher psychologically than many imagine, and they will not be bruised by the discovery of differences among them in ability and desire so far as artistic creation is concerned. But more important, it is necessary for teachers to understand the true relevance of the democratic ethos to cultural effort: A democracy is not indifferent to excellence; it does not ignore distinctions of quality; instead, a democracy tries to facilitate the access of all its citizens to excellence and it tries to give its citizens an equal voice in the determination of what they will prize and enjoy. That is why the aesthetic component of art education is so vital for the functioning of a democratic society. Because of our form of political organization, it is possible for insensitivity, brutality, conformity, apathy, violence, and know-nothingism to become dominant social and aesthetic values. Such qualities are occasionally visible in both the fine and the popular arts. To the extent that they exist, they indict our schooling, and especially our art education. The citizens of a democratic state must learn that there are alternatives— many of them—in the realm of artistic and aesthetic value. That is, they must become skilled in deciding what is excellent among the many qualities and things a democracy makes available in such enormous numbers to everyone. But such critical and decision-making skills will not be acquired if children are encouraged to believe that everything is as good as everything else.

The social dimension of art also deals with the public expression of ideas and feelings. That is, it presents us, through the arts of information and communication design, with a tremendous amount of visual material designed to influence our lives. This material is so pervasive, so skillfully organized, and so varied in its ultimate objectives that the individual who is unable to understand it and respond to it selectively cannot truly be called educated. Consequently, this chapter will begin by describing the manner in which art helps to establish group norms by functioning as a visual persuader.

The Determination of Group Norms

Many of us have been accustomed to think of pictures as objects of admiration and contemplation. We believe our commerce with visual art is ended after we have finished looking at it. But if this were true, great corporations would not invest huge sums in the creation and display of visual imagery intended to interest the public in the corporation's products and services. The managements must surely believe the influence of this imagery persists long after the

Harlem wall mural. (© Peter Polymenakos.)

Graffiti are, of course, timeless and universal. They have a special meaning, however, in the lives of poor people. Finding themselves alienated from much of the mass media—especially that enormous segment of the communications industry directed toward affluent consumers—they employ walls and sidewalks to carry messages, display decorative impulses, and generate a sense of social cohesion. Artistic level varies greatly, and there is little pride in authorship or ownership. This is public art, collectively created without supervision, generously shared, viewable at all hours, and with no charge for admission.

The outdoor mural, whatever its degree of craftsmanship, is rarely intended as a defacement, although it may occasionally seem to defile genteel notions of aesthetic value. Its first intention is to make the outdoors indoors— that is, to convert walls that shut out people into walls that enclose them. The sociopolitical mural may begin as an effort to generate class feeling and racial pride; but after its slogans have been absorbed and its literal message digested, it becomes an aesthetic and humanizing device. The anonymous and impersonal walls of urban structures are transformed into friendlier surfaces. Architects might well pay attention. ■

Roxbury (Boston) wall mural (above). (Council on the Arts and Humanities, Commonwealth of Massachusetts.)

Manhattan wall mural (left). (Martin Schnur.)

Pro-Mao poster (above). (Pix, Inc.)

Cosmetics poster (left), by Tsuneji Fujiwara. (Arthur Niggli, Ltd.)

"Strike against Liu until he smells. Stone Khruschev to death."

The intensive use of visual art as propaganda by revolutionary and autocratic regimes constitutes striking evidence of the vital importance they attach to the power of visual imagery in mobilizing the sentiments of the masses. The relatively stable societies of the West also employ art as propaganda, but in considerably subtler fashion. They can do so because our populations are more literate and sophisticated, because all media of persuasion are not in the hands of a single, centralized authority, and because our media encourage, chiefly, the varied delights of consumership as opposed to the bloody goals of militant revolutionaries.

From a design standpoint, the Maoist poster is interesting for its easy integration of Chinese literary characters with simple pictorial images. Our Western letters are more likely to support phonetic than visual perceptions; consequently, Western designers are faced with a more difficult problem when they seek a powerful unity of word and image. Also noteworthy is the way each character and image crowds the space allotted to it in the Maoist poster; this adds to the stridency of the message. It also contributes to a sense of urgency in the viewer: Large, black forms seem to ad-

Family-planning poster, Delhi. (Raghubir Singh for Nancy Palmer Agency.)

viewing is done—long enough to produce the desired sort of behavior. Whether we enjoy the arts of visual communication or not, we must concede that they are effective. Not only do they influence our behavior in a thousand ways, but they also constitute a substantial portion of our visual environment—whether as great posters outdoors or as the small-scale imagery of television and direct-mail advertising at home, paperback book covers in the drugstore, or magazine illustrations in the dentist's waiting room.

Where do our citizens get their guiding ideas about interpersonal relations, about how to use leisure, about what is worth owning, about manhood and womanhood, about what the good life feels and looks like? Clearly, from advertising. By compari-

vance upon him; they "crowd out" other considerations; there is nothing to do but act decisively and quickly.

Family-planning poster in India. Moslem women in India are largely motivated by the ideology of an old, tribal, nomadic culture, although they presently live a substantially urbanized existence. Consequently, they contribute to a birth rate higher than that of India's general population. Therefore, the problem faced by national policy planners is to create an attractive image for the small, Moslem-but-modern, family. The poster illustrated represents an effort to communicate that im-

age tactfully, boldly, but without offending the sensibilities of a tradition-oriented people. Compare this poster with the fertility art of the tribal peoples shown on page 33. It is easier to appeal to the instinctual drives of people (an art of greater emotional impact is created) than to offer images of substitute gratifications if they will but redirect those drives. Still, this poster manages to raise a delicate question in simple and positive terms. Verbal language could hardly have said so much so economically.

Japanese poster advertising cosmetics. Whether to buy a beauty aid or not seems a less vital issue

than taking political action to crush a counterrevolutionary, or making a personal and social decision to limit the size of one's family. But in advanced economies, questions about what to buy or enjoy replace many fundamental questions affecting national and personal survival. Artists and designers have to create images that can successfully advertise the delights to be enjoyed because of the economy's creativity. The social role of art shifts as society moves away from the problems of establishing itself and toward the problems of cultivating the pleasures of a complex civilization—describing the varieties of goods and services that can be acquired and, at the same time, promoting the high levels of consumership that mass production and distribution require. In this respect, American production, marketing, and advertising strategies lead the world. Our art lies in creating art that sells things. We have carried this art to the point where it is possible to generate new needs through visual-verbal incantation. Nothing like it has ever been seen.

Although older societies resent the aggressiveness and the blatancies of American marketing techniques, they seem anxious to enjoy the fruits of American-style mass production and distribution. They are confronted with the question of whether it is possible to enjoy the benefits of a high standard of living—low unit costs of production and popular access to a wide variety of goods and services—

without a marketing system that force-feeds the social organism. In any event, visual art in our kind of society is inevitably drawn into the production-distribution apparatus. This type of art has to be studied if it is to be controlled. Art and aesthetic education devoted exclusively to the handicrafts or the "fine art" of the museums is bound to be irrelevant. ∎

---

son, the schools holding class during the week and on Sundays are minor distractions. But it is not our purpose in this section to complain about this state of affairs, or to moralize about the corrupting effects of mass persuasion through the electronic and printing media. Instead, I want to continue the extended definition of art, and surely the information and communications arts (a polite label for the business of advertising and public relations) constitute a substantial portion of the products of human creativity during the latter half of the twentieth century. How, then, do these forms of creativity actually influence our ideas of what is good and true and beautiful?

Perhaps Marshall McLuhan is the most perceptive analyst of the communications media in our time. Surely his "probes" and insights constitute highly suggestive hypotheses for explaining not only the media but also vast areas of popular perception and feeling. With respect to advertising, McLuhan feels that its trend "is to manifest the

product as an integral part of large social purposes and processes." This is accomplished, he believes, because "any expensive ad is as carefully built on the tested foundations of public stereotypes, or 'sets' of established attitudes, as any skyscraper is built on bedrock." He asserts, in addition, "It is obvious that any acceptable ad is a vigorous dramatization of communal experience. No group of sociologists can approximate the ad teams in the gathering and processing of exploitable social data* Here McLuhan pays tribute to the highly competent social and psychological researchers engaged by the advertising and communications industries to ensure the acceptability and effectiveness of their messages. They identify and "dramatize" communal experiences. He seems to believe that group norms have a prior existence which it is the business of social research to discover and exploit in the interest of effective communication and control.

*Marshall McLuhan, *Understanding Media: The Extensions of Man*, McGraw-Hill, 1964; paperback edition, Signet, 1964, pp. 201, 203.

In other words, advertisers first find out what people's desires are *and then* claim that their products are the most satisfactory answers to those desires. But it could be maintained that industry first decides what it can make *and then* employs marketing and advertising experts who conduct social research to discover the best ways of persuading people to want what industry has to sell. McLuhan has been misled, I believe, by the spectacle of social science in the employ of market research into reversing the order of priority in production, market research, and advertising. The media do not follow; rather they *lead* public taste and aspiration.

What is the relation of production and marketing strategies to art? It is simply that the creation of an ad, as McLuhan and others have pointed out, is a highly elaborate art form. And its verbal material, as we have been aware at least since 1912, when Picasso began to create newsprint collages, is converted into sensory data rather than cognitive or semantic meanings. In other words, Picasso taught us to view an area torn from *Le Journal* as a texture—gratifying because of its visual arrangement rather than its verbal import. As a visual art form, the ad possesses certain creative or innovative properties: It is not merely the reflection of public desires; it is also an anticipation of what the public *will want*. This is because visual art is effective by virtue of its magical relation to the viewer's tested needs. Art compels assent; it does not merely ratify an already existing agreement between buyer and seller.

If this analysis is correct, then advertising design is tremendously influential in the determination of group preferences and norms. But the "magical relation to the viewer's perception" needs further explanation: How does looking at a visual arrangement of words and images *compel* assent? Here it is necessary to say something about aesthetic perception. The shapes, colors and textures in a work of art cannot really be perceived if they are merely registered on the viewer's retina. The viewer must expend energy—more energy than is needed to transmit the optical data to his eyes—in order to "make sense" out of what is registered on his retina. Is the expenditure of that energy controlled by the art object or by the perceiving organism? The answer is that the art object can initiate and dominate the process of perceptual expenditure. This is especially true for individuals who are tired, who are easily distracted from their own concerns, or who lack aesthetic skills—the ability to organize and interpret their perceptual responses. In other words, once the perceptual process has been "triggered" by the art object, a series of transactions between the object and the viewer takes place which the viewer *is unable to prevent*. Short of stuffing his ears, closing his eyes, or leaving the scene, there is little that an untrained person can do to avoid the influence of the object. The viewer *is obliged* to expend energy in the process of perception. And he is obliged to expend his energies according to a pattern substantially governed by the visual design of the art object. To the extent that the object is organized according to the laws of visual perception,* the viewer's investment of energy will be either increased or diminished. But it cannot be cut off. It is the involuntary participation by the viewer in the perception of advertising art which I call a "magical relation." Perhaps this process is best illustrated by our virtual inability *not* to hear or *not* to see something we would prefer to ignore. Consequently, the compelling, or magical, quality of advertising art should be attributed, ultimately, to factors of visual organization rather than of social research. For example, if a manufacturer knows that middle-income housewives prefer heavily scented bath soap, he will, no doubt, add perfume to the soap he tries to sell in their market. But this knowledge will not cause middle-income housewives to pay attention to his advertising. It is necessary for his advertising to make the housewife *realize* that she prefers heavily scented soap. Art makes her aware of a need she did not know she had. What she has told an interviewer or market researcher is merely the answer to questions the researcher has asked. Research does not elicit behavior but art does.

The capacity of art—whether advertising art or another kind—to elicit or compel behavior is not especially surprising if we remember the magical function of art in tribal culture. Why else do primitive men often refuse to look at certain visual representations? There is no question of the compelling power of art for the tribesman.

*According to Gestalt psychology: regularity, or good continuity; balance, or symmetry; and unity, or closure.

Likewise, there should be no question of the compelling power of advertising art for modern "tribesmen." What is the role of education in the sort of situation described here?

First, I think it is necessary to take information and communications art seriously *as art* and not as an inferior or debased mode of expression. Today, it would be quite possible for the objective and detached scholar to characterize the art of the galleries as "commercial" and the communications arts as vastly more significant from the standpoint of human creativity and influence. Our textbooks and our teaching, in failing to recognize this point, are perpetuating eighteenth and nineteenth century aesthetic categories—the aesthetics of detachment and disinterestedness. Second, we must learn to make intelligent discriminations among examples of communications art, neither condemning nor accepting everything, but recognizing the wide range of quality in this type of art as in conventional painting, sculpture, and architecture. Third, we should study the outstanding examples of communications art the way we study masterpieces of prehistoric art, tribal art, classical art, sacred art, the art of kings and princes, bourgeois art, peasant art, and so on. Finally, students should be taught to enjoy information communications art as a mode of human creativity quite apart from the specific practical behavior it is supposed to promote. This is one of the most significant services the art teacher can perform for pupils, because it is a way of liberating them from automatic obedience to the imperatives of commercial culture. Remember that it is possible for us to admire African tribal sculpture without believing in its medical efficacy. We can also convert the compelling magic of advertising art into a source of aesthetic gratification; it is a matter of invoking the critical techniques (to be discussed in Chapter 12) which we normally employ when studying art which has been conveniently "framed" for us by art museums, art books, art galleries, art professors, and collections of lantern slides.

Tools for Everyday Life

According to La Fontaine, "we make a fuss over the beautiful, we despise the useful." Chairs and tables, coats and hats, spoons and pitchforks, plates and shovels— all serve practical purposes and owe their shape to the requirements of the work they do. But not entirely. When these implements are not being used physically, they are often being used visually. That is, we look at everything and desire that everything be pleasing to look at. Hence, the spoon ought to balance easily in the hand and fit conveniently into the mouth and *also*, it should "look good." Art is involved, not only in the "good-looking" aspect of a spoon, but also in designing it for fabrication, for storage, for cost, and for use. Art cannot afford to despise the useful; if it does, then engineering will supplant it in the design of everyday objects, with the result that the separation of art from life will become even greater than it is.

What happens to human culture when useful objects are separated from art? Such a divorce results in an intensification of interest in painting, sculpture, and architecture as the sole vehicles of "beauty." That is precisely what occurred in Western culture from approximately 1740 to 1910—from the beginning of the Industrial Revolution to the early days of modern industrial design. An almost neurotic obsession with the decoration and embellishment of surfaces set in because the fine arts were thought about in essentially negative terms: The distinguishing feature of art objects was their uselessness. Hence they were encrusted with ornament and overladen with vestiges of deceased styles so they might seem to have significance and value. But the entire effort was unavailing because it existed in a vacuum; the "fine" art object seemed to have no serious reason for being. Consequently, the objects brought into being by the honest craftsman or even the engineer became the truly valuable artistic expression of their culture because they were conceived positively—in terms of their relation to realities like fabrication, cost, storage, appearance, and function. And out of these considerations in the design of useful objects we can derive the dimension of meaning.

Is it possible for knives and forks and refrigerators to be aesthetically expressive? Of course it is, provided we do not expect them to be *pictorially* expressive. On the other hand, one does not expect a picture to be convertible into an eating utensil. Obviously, different artistic types serve different sorts of purposes. The art of the de-

Nineteenth-century wooden molds for making machine parts (at right). (The New York Times Studio.)

Ironwork cooking accessories (below left). (Courtesy Henry Francis du Pont Winterthur Museum.)

Jar mart in Tunisia (below right). (Allyn Baum.)

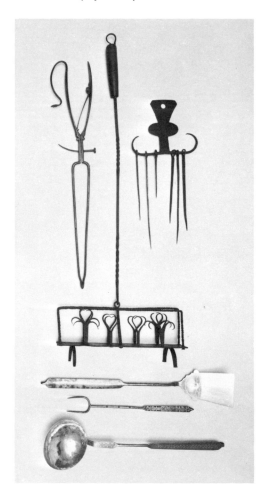

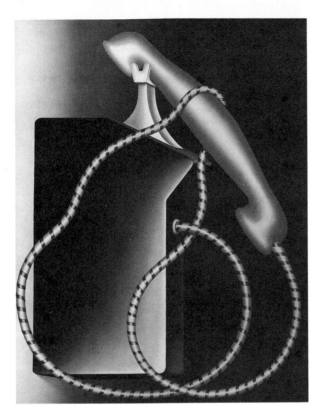

LE BAISER. by Konrad Klapheck. (Private collection, N.Y.; courtesy Sidney Janis Gallery, N.Y.; photo, Geoffrey Clements.)

signer consists precisely in understanding that purpose of an object so well that he can shape and fabricate its materials with a high degree of efficiency and clarity. Why efficiency? Because art often consists in the perception of the *right amount* of effort for a particular effect—the harmonious uniting of means and ends. Why clarity? Because we have a right to expect that a useful object will visually express its practical function. It should look as if it were made for the purpose of its actual use. Any conflict between appearance and use strikes us as somehow dishonest—an example of our tendency to use ethical judgments about matters of form and function.

All of us recognize that there can be beauty in the fabric and cut of our clothes or in the line and shape of our automobiles. Why, then, do we refuse to accept fabrics or automobiles as art objects? Because we have been greatly influenced by the tradition of

Men have always prized their tools for beauty as well as utility. But it has usually been yesterday's tools, not today's. Present utility seems to drive out thoughts of the beautiful. And some are put off by the commonness of mass-produced utensils, the widespread possession of objects identical to those they may own. They prefer to use or look at objects that are one-of-a-kind; uniqueness is more important than quality or design. To be sure, the Tunisian craftsman tries to make his earthen jars as much alike as possible. Their basic shape has long been established and he sees no reason to change it. But he is a man, not a machine; so he cannot help it if minor variations creep into each jar. And we, who have many other containers for our needs, value his clay jars for their "art"—their minor flaws and variations, the very things he would eliminate if he could.

The appeal of eighteenth-century kitchen utensils lies mainly in their form and craftsmanship—the artisan's ability to exploit wrought iron for a maximum of strength and utility with a minimum of material. In other words, he pursues a functionalist goal and achieves beauty indirectly. The form of these tools is not seen in a vacuum: We mentally grasp and use the implements; we imagine their weight and texture; we experience dozens of feelings because of the slender, almost calligraphic shapes of these useful objects. They show that it is possible for practical objects to "rise above" their humble origins.

The nineteenth-century wooden molds are patterns for reproducing cast-iron machine parts, but they are themselves handcraft objects of aesthetic value. Like the cooking accessories, they relate the viewer to the design decisions of the craftsman. Notice how the requirements of reproduction in another material have affected the craftsman's forms. Working in wood, but thinking in iron, he has to anticipate the effects of the casting process; he has to defend against the brittleness of cast iron; and he must learn to take advantage of the dimensional stability of cast iron. These are not just abstract shapes (although they appeal to us as abstract shapes); they represent real solutions to real problems. That is why they are expressive—even beautiful.

A telephone is a convenience that extends our ears and voices. It is also a remarkably shaped tool when you consider how it is held, how it rests, and how it manages to provide facilities for speaking and listening in the same economical form. For the painter of "Le Baiser," the phone is a kind of creature, alive enough to be loved by its cord. Their connection is more than mechanical and electronic, it is erotic. This love may be absurd, but it has a logic, and the artist has found it out.

Each of these tools or objects owes its existence to a distinct type of logic that can be studied, learned, and enjoyed. If you hope to enjoy a logic of expression or of beauty, you often must learn a logic of utility or practical problem-solving. You have to learn how and why the forms "got that way." Then you can understand art from the inside, instead of learning about it verbally. You begin to be visually literate. ∎

art as an *imitation of reality*. Hence, we enjoy pictures *of* a girl, *of* a peach, *of* a tree. But a fabric imitates nothing except itself. Its appearance is the result of the way its threads have been arranged. And an automobile does not look like anything else (although car designers occasionally introduce semi-abstract versions of shoulders and breasts and thighs). In general, our useful objects owe their form to their materials and processes of making and the particular operations they are expected to perform. To enjoy them aesthetically, it is necessary to recapitulate visually those processes and purposes. That is, you must be able "to see" the action of a hatchet in its blade, the drape of a fabric in its weave, the comfort of a chair in its shape, and the tactile sensation of a spoon from its bowl. Perceiving the relation between the visual qualities of an object and its use can be a very satisfying experience. For this reason, some persons collect useful objects only for the purpose of looking at them. No doubt that is why museums exhibit antique furniture, including chairs on which one can no longer sit.

One of the false distinctions about art that causes mischief for art education is the one between handcraft objects and machine-made objects. In schools, this distinction is often, and regrettably, institutionalized in the form of separate subjects or departments of industrial arts and fine arts. Errors are consequently made on both sides of the fence that education has artificially erected. Art should be concerned with *the entire realm* of making and forming; the fact that an artist or designer works with hand tools or machine tools does not affect the status of the object created. Neither does it matter whether the created object is one-of-a-kind or one of thousands. As a distinguished museum director, John Cotton Dana, once said, "Beauty has no connection with age, rarity, or price."

Students have to learn that there is a type of excellence of form in a toolmaker's calipers or a farmer's scythe which is no less beautiful for having grown out of a solution to the problems of measuring or cutting. It is exceedingly difficult to design tools; they are not primarily examples of self-expression. The teacher who believes art is only self-expression may experience some difficulty in perceiving the beauty of useful objects because his expectations are chiefly of the self as it is revealed or explained through art. Such a teacher will miss the intellectual element in form—its emergence as the result of a designer's analyzing an operation and discovering the appropriate materials and shapes for performing that operation. But tremendously exciting possibilities for learning are overlooked if this dimension of art education is left unexplored. What could be more challenging and rewarding for a child than to study the form of eating utensils, common articles of furniture, mechanics' tools, household hardware, objects like mailboxes, fire hydrants, utility poles, traffic lights, doorways, street signs, and gasoline pumps. Only by subjecting these commonplace objects to critical scrutiny do we create the possibility of improving their appearance, or, at least, of seeing them as sources of visual interest.

In a mass-consumption society such as ours, improvement in the design of useful objects depends on a combination of the efforts of manufacturers, designers, retailers, teachers, and consumers. An appetite for excellence in the design of everyday objects has to be created in the schools so that industry will not succeed easily in marketing trashy products. And because models and styles and products change very rapidly, it is not possible or desirable simply to indoctrinate pupils by telling them authoritatively which objects are excellent and which are not. Instead, pupils must be taught ways of deciding these matters for themselves. If making an ashtray or a pair of earrings truly affords the child an insight into the nature of form in objects *other than* ashtrays and earrings, then the project is worthwhile. If the teacher can do the job better by the critical examination of a variety of objects made by good designers, then that is the approach to follow. The determining factor becomes the ability of the student to extrapolate from his classroom experience with making or studying to his existence away from school. The art educator cannot be doctrinaire in this matter, insisting that insight into form qualities is gained *only* by one approach and not the other. Perhaps there is a useful analogy in the experience of foreign-language teachers. Some claim their subject affords the student insight into the culture of the people whose language he studies. They also claim that a student gains a better understanding of *his own* language by studying a foreign language. But the research on transfer of learning tends to support the view that the benefits claimed by the foreign-language teachers are in fact experienced by students only

Lumber trucks. (University of Georgia Department of Art.)

We encounter the automobile as a sculptural object, as a symbol of the human body, as a temporary home, and as part of a swarm of machines constituting a lethal environment. Children in their early years encounter autos, trucks, and trains as toys—that is, as tiny objects they can manipulate. It is only later that they learn these vehicles are dangerous. Even so, it is difficult for them ever to forget those early perceptions of the automobile as a beautiful machine, instantly responsive to their fantasies of speeding effortlessly through space. As adults, we learn slowly and reluctantly that our favorite machines can be de-

structive. That is the ironic lesson of Rosenquist's painting; he has tried to build a little drama of absurdity around the gentlest meeting of two polished metal giants: Their merest touch is a crushing event. Automobiles are constantly showing how easy it is for them to tear each other apart. Still, an automobile driver has to remind himself, repeatedly, that the huge machines are very vulnerable, and that he is vulnerable too. Traveling in great herds, automobiles occupy our best spaces, poison the sweetest atmosphere, and maim or kill the nicest people. But these ugly facts cannot really dislodge our earliest perceptions

of the car as a wonderful space ship. So there is a tension in our culture between opposed perceptions of machines, and of technology in general. Art lives in that region of tension. The aesthetic education of children, then, should enable them to feel this sort of tension, to express it through some language, and to hope for a humane synthesis of man and machine. Art humanizes when it helps us to examine and respond to what is new, unknown, contradictory, or frightening. As educators, we have to believe we can deal with a problem if all its dimensions are confronted and made visible. ■

Traffic on Belt Parkway, New York City (above left). (New York Daily News Photo, Tom Gallagher.)

ULTRA-VIOLET CARS (above right), by James Rosenquist. (Leo Castelli Gallery; photo, Rudolph Burckhardt.)

Automobile (at left). (University of Georgia Department of Art.)

when a teacher deliberately plans his instruction with these benefits as objectives. In other words, there is no automatic and inevitable transfer of learning simply by virtue of teaching a certain subject.

So it is with art. No doubt many subtle insights are unintentionally generated by art instruction. Such unforeseen dividends for the learner, however, should not be the central objectives of teaching; art teachers cannot confidently rely on the operation of chance to bring about discriminating perceptions of form in their students. Moreover, learning a maxim such as "form follows function" is not especially valuable, not in its abstract, verbal formulation. Knowing who first said it—Louis Sullivan—does not enhance the individual's ability to use the idea for his own growth and perceptual enrichment. The validity of this idea, *and its limitations*, have to be discovered in concrete situations in the perception of real relationships, in the exercise of what Ortega y Gasset called "vital reason"—that is, by using one's mind to uncover the correspondences between the world of visible form and the world of logical necessity.

So far as the physical tools of everyday living are concerned, the art educator must view them with the same ardent hope as the designer. He must see in an ugly refuse container on the street a fragment of unredeemed reality—matter unredeemed by art and therefore a summons to imagine a form that might be better.

The Shape of the Environment

By now you have seen that much of our environment is man made and that its quality—for good or ill—is the responsibility of art. We should not let the enormous scale of man's architectural and engineering efforts obscure the fact that we occupy and move through spaces shaped by designers. The difficult question raised by this fact is: Does education have any relevance, any responsibility (apart from the training of designers) for the shape of the environment?

Those who are acquainted with the education of designers, architects, and engineers would agree they are very able. Indeed, they are capable of building better physical communities than we permit them to build. Consequently, the problem becomes one of a social strategy in whose formulation the schools are necessarily involved. That is,

Three views of man shaping his environment. The open-pit copper mine in Utah is overwhelming for the eye and mind because it shows man hollowing out a mountain on the same gigantic scale as the forces of nature that built it.

The rice fields show man in the intimate and beautiful cooperation with nature that he has practiced for several thousand years. Cleveland's lake front tells what happens when high concentrations of men build, use, and discard at a rate that makes their pattern of life poisonous.

The African village, its tiny huts dominated by trees and terrain, reveals a different world view: Nature is not there to conquer; we live in her bosom. ■

Open-pit mine at Bingham Canyon, Utah. (Kennecott Copper Corporation.)

Pollution on Cleveland lake front. (Plain Dealer Photo.)

Rice fields in California. (Wide World Photos.)

AFRICAN VILLAGE. (International Child Art Center, San Francisco.)

schools need to develop in pupils the sort of awareness of the man-made environment that they develop respecting personal hygiene, for example, or the conservation of natural resources. Children and adolescents, particularly, need to learn that communities are not part of the natural order, but the arbitrary creations of man.

It is not necessary to propose the addition of one more subject to the already overcrowded school curriculum. Instead, we have to identify the study of large-scale design as an integral part of the art education program. Now let us spell out what this means.

What are the educational objectives of instruction in environmental design? What do we want pupils to know about the shape of the environment? We want them to understand that the physical community is a form of art organized, according to Le Corbusier, to facilitate four functions: living, working, recreation, and circulation. Therefore, we have to study the form of communities by asking how their buildings and spaces are shaped to promote these four functions. Children must learn to see the connections between environmental spaces and the needs of people who use them. In Chapter 9 some specific teaching practices dealing with large-scale design will be suggested. Here, I wish to elaborate on the idea that a complete definition of art must include the shape of the community.

One of the criticisms sometimes made of architects and community planners is that they conceive of the community as large-scale sculpture, forgetting that these "sculp-tures" are also containers for human beings. Presumably they are more interested in their beautifully executed scale models than in the coming and going and living and dying of the members of a community. If this charge has some foundation in fact, then it could be made just as well, presumably, against art educators who are concerned only with the visual qualities of urban areas. We too might be accused of being more interested in texture, shape, and expressive form than in the "real" problems of the human inhabitants of the forms which fascinate us. But if the charge is examined more closely, it reveals a hidden assumption that there is an inevitable conflict between the social requirements of a community and the aesthetic requirements of architectural form. Such a conflict arises if we assume that visual form is responsive only to its own laws—that it has a great deal to do with subjective preference and very little to do with utilitarian function. That assumption is grossly in error, but the fact that many intelligent persons make it suggests the size of the task art education has before it.

If the study of form in useful objects (as suggested in the previous section) were conducted seriously and systematically in the schools, we could expect educated persons to know that the determinants of form are a good deal more rigorous than the transient impulses of a sculptor. Even knowing Le Corbusier's definition of the art of community planning (designing for the functions of living, working, recreation, and circulation) should exempt this art from the charge of arbitrariness and social indifference. On the contrary, it is aesthetic indifference in some of our great public housing projects that seems to suggest the "packaging" of people. The dreary structures erected according to the rather unimaginative building formulas of social agencies reflect exceedingly uncreative approaches to the problems of communal living; and the resulting dwellings would seem to be ideal centers for the cultivation of self-contempt and hopelessness.

The solutions to the problems of urban rapid transit, of pedestrian safety, of automotive circulation and storage, of the location of utilities, of zoning for commerce, industry, recreation, and residence, are partly contingent upon the possession of a great deal of information—much of it technical. But this information is ultimately put to work in the light of guiding ideas about space and light and surface and movement. Art teachers may not have the time nor the resources to solve the technical problems of urban design, but they *can* conduct their instruction in the form of organized inquiry into appealing and functional arrangements of light, space, volume, and texture. They *can* create the foundation of experience with sensory immediacies without which traffic surveys and revisions of building codes are largely irrelevant. At some level of his education, a citizen has to acquire some meaningful convictions about living space. If he becomes a lawyer or an engineer, these biases will hopefully become intelligently operative. At present, unfortunately, persons charged with decision-making responsibility for the shape of our environment must gain an understanding of the aesthetics of urban space on a very haphazard basis.

In autocratic states, the decisions of emperors and kings about the shape of the environment are translated without question into visible form. For good or ill, the vision of a Napoleon or his agent confers unity and cohesiveness upon a city which might otherwise exhibit the chaos of competing individualisms. In a democracy, we tend to admire individualism and its cultural expression. But a democratic state must also have the means of arriving at decisions that can confer a provisional unity upon those structures which will simply collapse if surrendered entirely to the free play of personal expression. Our urban places are presently at the point of collapse—largely because for several decades they have been arenas for the acting out of personal drives to express the self on a gigantic scale; because of commercial avarice; because rapacity is often an attribute of the businessman's style; because of megalomania in high places and egotism even among persons of moderate station. We have not as yet developed a way of creating unity and harmony in the physical community without sacrificing what many regard as the essential prerogatives of free men in a free society.

Our problem would seem to be political. But it is also aesthetic. Political difficulties arise because aesthetic alternatives are not vividly seen and firmly grasped. "Where there is no vision, the people perish." By the time a man is mayor or head of a planning board, it is too late for the cultivation

Home Office of the Northwestern Life Insurance Company (above left), designed by Minoru Yamasaki. (Courtesy the Company.)

Midtown Plaza, Rochester, N.Y. (above right), designed by Victor Gruen Associates. (Midtown Holdings Corporation.)

Sculpture by Isamu Noguchi at Marine Midland Building, N.Y. (at right). (Skidmore, Owings & Merrill; photo, Ezra Stoller.)

Southeastern Massachusetts Technological Institute, designed by Paul Rudolph. (Courtesy the Institute.)

Habitat, designed by Moshe Safdie. (Canadian Consulate General; photo, Central Mortgage and Housing Corporation.)

Business and commerce often foster better environments for working than communities do for living. Bankers, merchants, and industrialists seem willing to employ the architects, commission the sculptors and designers, and allocate the funds to create great soaring spaces—indoors or outdoors—for their employees and customers. But the builders of tract housing and so-called middle-income apartment buildings are unable, or insufficiently imaginative, to create comparable aesthetic values for their projects. Noguchi's huge, delicately balanced cube, surrounded by a great deal of expensive space, makes no statement about the bank or its managers. It is merely a magnificent demonstration of poise. It constitutes the sort of anonymous, generous gesture that even the Medici were incapable of making.

Apartment houses and collegiate buildings need not be drab, monotonous, prison-like, as Habitat and the Southeastern Massachusetts Technological Institute demonstrate. Dramatic and exciting architecture is possible: We have the design talent, the technical skills, the organizational ability, and more than enough wealth. But do our citizens know about these possibilities? Where can they learn how the man-made environment might be changed?

Some of the most exciting architectural forms in our environment are created as technological structures: power-generating

ALL THAT IS BEAUTIFUL, by Ben Shahn. (Kennedy Galleries, Inc.)

Nine-Mile Point atomic power plant, Oswego, N.Y. (General Electric.)

plants (see General Electric's atomic power plant), space-launch buildings, waterfront loading and storage facilities, housing for radar and space-monitoring devices, oil refineries, grain elevators, astronomical observatories. Of course, these structures shelter people only incidentally; they are primarily designed to house and move complex equipment, or vast quantities of raw materials, chemicals, or agricultural commodities. Still, their engineering forms inspire architects, artists, and poets; they also constitute much of the landscape of twentieth-century man; they symbolize our dependency on large-scale technology; and they generate confidence in human technical ingenuity. We wish that ingenuity could be directed toward the solution of some of our social and interpersonal problems. The artist cannot solve them—not directly. But he keeps searching the forms as if they had some secret he can discover. Perhaps he will find it.

The urban environment is constantly being torn down and rebuilt. Ben Shahn contrasted linear patterns and, by implication, life styles. The solid, homely masonry structures below are being replaced by lacy steel-and-glass towers above. Old, run-down neighborhoods, where children played and grew up, give way to corporate mansions populated by junior executives and swinging secretaries. Shahn could imply all these things with texture and shape; a sensitive designer, he would not let himself be a decorator alone. The social statement is always there. ■

of vision. The task must be undertaken much earlier. And the schools would seem to be the logical place to begin.

Conclusion

I hope you have gained from this chapter some idea of the tremendous range of art, both in its size and variety and in its influence on our lives. We have seen that art is involved in everything from the design of a teaspoon to the shaping of a whole city. And in the several information and communications arts, there is a visible and psychological force of immense power and influence.

For a teacher of art, the task of dealing adequately with a phenomenon so vast and varied may on occasion seem staggering. Consequently, the job of organizing what is taught and learned about art—in other words, designing the art curriculum—becomes a separate task which is, in itself, exceedingly difficult. This volume treats problems of curriculum construction in Part Four on the assumption that a teacher should first gain some comprehensive ideas about art and about education before planning strategies and sequences of art experience. Sometimes the weaknesses of an art program result from too narrow an idea of what is included in art as a subject of study. As teachers, we can reach more students, and reach them more successfully if we realize that our subject extends throughout the entire range of human needs and interests.

Some final comments about the cultural value of art need to be made. The term *culture* has been variously explained, but here I should like to define it as the totality of meanings, ideas, and values learned by an individual from all sources—family, school, church, the media, work, play, travel, and so on. One of the conventional justifications of art in education is its *cultural* value. This presumably means that looking at great works of art affords the individual access to ideas and images which somehow make him a richer, better, more *cultured* person. For some reason, however, *creating* art has not been considered as cultural as looking at it. Perhaps that is because it is possible to see a great many more works than it is possible to create. Of course, there is no reason why the individual cannot do both, and many do. Nevertheless, there is some validity in the notion that serious acquaintance with art helps to make a person more *interesting*— to himself as well as to others.

The cultured person is not, as middle-class opinion would have it, someone who has visited museums, who can identify artists, who can relate anecdotes about art travels, or who knows something about the comings and goings of the world of art. Even when such knowledge rises above the level of specialized gossip, one does not discern in it any quality different from the common discourse of engineers or physicians, who know a great deal about very technical matters. On the contrary, the cultured person is someone whose thought and discourse have been lifted by art out of the prose of the workaday world and into the

Garbage in Atlanta during collectors' strike (at right). (Wide World Photos.)

THE SUBJECT IS GARBAGE, advertisement for television program (below left). (WNBC-TV.)

Painted garbage cans (below right), by Alexander Calder. ("Art in America," 1964.)

The Subject Is Garbage.

HELP, I LIVE IN A SLUM. (Martin Schnur.)

poetry of heightened thought and feeling. For such a person, art is an instrument for leading a richer spiritual existence than would otherwise be possible. His traffic with the world of art has led, not necessarily to better judgment about whose work to buy, but to greater discernment of ideas and feelings embodied in art and elsewhere. He may find the noblest of ideas expressed in a suspension bridge or an Aborigine bark painting. But this is not because he is a connoisseur of exotic art; it is because he is cultured, that is, free of slavery to the *status* of objects and open to the complete reality of their being.

The cultured person, then, is free in a special sense of the term. His inner life—his life of mind and feeling—is selectively dependent on what the world has to offer. He is not always in the position of reacting to the estimations and interpretations of others;

Garbage is the question—not just the technological question of what to do with it, or the design question of how to fashion attractive containers for it. We need ultimately to answer the moral-aesthetic question: Is the pattern of living that produces these mountains of refuse morally and aesthetically defensible? If the sanitation men did not go on strike periodically, and if city dumps were not rapidly filling up, and if trash cans were not occasionally overturned, we would not, presumably, be very aware of the enormous quantities of waste we generate. If garbage, like poverty, is kept invisible, can we forget about it?

Just as weeds are flowers that nobody wants, garbage represents material that nobody understands or knows how to use. Artists have been attracted to garbage since the beginning of this century; often they deliberately created art that looked like garbage. They seemed to be interested in discovering the aesthetic value of what had been disposed of. Now engineers and ecologists realize we must recycle our wastes; designers realize we need to employ reusable rather than disposable containers. It is not just the survival in our culture of New England puritanism or of Great Depression frugality that rebels at waste. Something in man resents the desecration of the earth's natural abundance. When we encourage sensitivity toward the destiny of natural materials and man-made objects, we begin to see our environment in a new light. Garbage is not merely ugly; it represents a failure of imagination. ■

he is not obliged to run as fast as he can in order to "keep up" with fashionable, or slightly unfashionable, opinions. He has the option of finding delight where it has not been found, of revising his judgment of the value of things whenever he wishes. These are some of the advantages of a cultivated existence; they are earned, however, not conferred. It can be hoped that teachers are, or will become, cultured persons, and that schools are places where children can begin to sense that subtle and quietly exciting sort of freedom.

The greatest asset of a cultivated person is his ability to perceive the wholeness of life in particular fragments of it—fragments such as art provides. The idea of the macro-cosm in the microcosm is not less true for being very ancient, but, like all great and true ideas, it necessarily lacks concreteness. This is the concreteness some persons find in great art. That is why art is, for them, like food. The habit of searching for the largest possible meaning of a work of art is not currently fashionable since it is thought to divert energies away from pure and unalloyed sensation. But all human beings are possessed by a drive toward large and comprehensive meanings. Without it, they are seriously frustrated. That is why their learning, as children and as adolescents, must be organized around this powerful drive— toward meaning, toward comprehensiveness, toward freedom.

PART TWO

The Character of Learning

A person may be an artist or may know a great deal about art, but there is no assurance that he can also teach. On the other hand, he may be a keen student of teaching. Still, if someone knows a great deal about teaching, there is no assurance that he can teach art. If he knows about art and teaching, he may still have difficulty teaching art to children. We do not teach in a vacuum. We teach certain kinds of people—let us say children; in a particular place—let us say an elementary school; within a particular program—let us call it a curriculum. Hence the people we teach, the kind of place where we teach, and the curricular context of our efforts influence the character of children's learning in general.

In this section, we have to examine the relations between learning in general and learning through art, or aesthetic education. Two approaches are taken: In Chapter 4, the school is discussed as a place where knowing and doing—knowledge and performance—are combined to foster learning. In Chapter 5, the ethical development of children through artistic and aesthetic experience is discussed. In both chapters, the school and its curricula are kept in sight even when they are not explicitly mentioned. In that way, we can defend against the perils of advocating a program for people who never were, in schools that never will be. To be sure, theoretical positions and ideal teaching situations have to be explored in education, but they must be tempered by an authentic grasp of human and institutional realities.

The main reason for undertaking an analysis of the general character of learning is, of course, to make room for the type of learning fostered by the arts. Aesthetic education has not yet secured its place in school curricula, and that is probably a result of the excessive emphasis we place on the mastery of facts and concepts. But the complete and fully human development of children requires more than cognitive mastery, important though it is. That is why this section is devoted to the aesthetic component of learning.

Ever since Socrates became convinced that being good would result only from *knowing* the nature of goodness, organized education in Western culture has had a strong bias in favor of knowledge. Up to a certain age, we say, children do not *know* the difference between right and wrong. How, then, can they be expected to behave properly? If they spend some time studying goodness or the rules that generate good behavior, we can be reasonably sure they will know the difference between right and wrong and we hope they will choose to do right. St. Paul, despite his Greek education, realized that knowledgeable men often do *not* do the right thing when he said "That which I should have done I did not do"—an observation employed by Ivan Albright as the title to one of his most mysterious paintings. Knowledge of the good, Paul understood, is no guarantee of good behavior or excellent morals; it is not an enemy of morals either. But I wish to stress that it would be naive to believe that knowledge in any field necessarily leads to intelligent application in the form of right action. Knowing what causes nuclear fission does not necessarily lead to right decisions about the production of atomic energy or the development of nuclear weapons.

Education need not be organized as the pursuit of knowledge. Instead, it can be devoted to training young people to behave as the community feels they should. No doubt the Spartans spent very little time explaining to their young the principles upon which their rules of conduct were founded. Armies and regimented societies, in general, waste no time on speculating about the intellectual assumptions that guide their organization and procedures. Indeed, such speculation may be regarded as a threat to the goals of loyalty and obedience a proper military establishment insists upon.

4

Knowledge and Performance

Authoritarian societies favor social arrangements that result in highly predictable behavior. The trouble with training people to be good, however, is that they will not know how to behave when confronted with a situation which was unanticipated by their early training. Human freedom presupposes the need to respond in an original fashion to new situations.

If knowing what is good does not necessarily equip people to behave the way they should, what are schools supposed to do? Presumably we could organize schooling to accommodate both policies; that is, children could spend some time in acquiring knowledge about all sorts of things, and they could spend some time in developing a variety of appropriate behavior habits. This is what, in fact, schools seem to be doing. In theory, and often in practice, schools are devoted to transmitting knowledge, inculcating attitudes, and developing skills. Unfortunately, the knowledge, attitudes, and skills that are officially prescribed are not always the knowledge, attitudes, and skills that children and adolescents learn.

There are many reasons why the learning that takes place in schools is not always the learning educators, parents, and the community in general desire. Contrary to popular belief, however, *more* pursuit of knowledge and *more* training in right behavior will not necessarily lead to the educational goals so ardently desired by the community. In order to achieve these goals, we have to change the way we go about developing free citizens who are both moderately wise and reasonably good.

So the fundamental question for education becomes, "What can be done or practiced or listened to in schools that will result in better progress toward those modest and estimable goals the schools are established to pursue?" Without claiming omniscience or the possession of a panacea, art educators believe that their approach to learning meets some of the objections to the mere accumulation of knowledge or the stultifying practice of moral indoctrination.* They believe art is a mode of both knowing and performing. And they think it is conducive toward the kind of learning that is fitting for free citizens in a free society. Moreover, the modes of knowing and performing advanced by art are not the same as the modes of knowing we encounter in other types of learning—in science, for example. But lest these claims for art education seem extravagant, an analysis of art as knowledge and performance is offered below, hopefully in support of the art educator's position. First, however, it will be necessary to discuss the role of knowledge and performance as

---

*The strongest case is made for this position by the late Sir Herbert Read (*Education through Art*, 2nd ed., Pantheon, 1949, p. 272) in his paraphrase of Plato: "Plato meant exactly what he said: that an aesthetic education is the only education that brings grace to the body and nobility to the mind, and that we must make art the basis of education because it can operate in childhood, during the sleep of reason; and when reason does come, art will have prepared a path for her, and she will be greeted as a friend whose essential lineaments have for long been familiar." To be sure, Read has earlier (p. 7) defined "art" as "all modes of self-expression, literary and poetic (verbal) no less than musical or aural." Consequently, he can say (p. 11), "The aim of education is therefore the creation of artists—of people efficient in the various modes of expression."

they fit into the context of the school as a whole.

Knowledge, Performance, and the School

The most obvious feature of educational effort is that it is usually conducted in groups, in structures called schools, and under the auspices of boards representing community, state, or church. Notwithstanding the possibility that in the future much learning will take place in the interaction of a child and a machine, it is still reasonable to expect that most school instruction will continue to take place in the interaction of children and teachers. The groups into which a school is divided have a great deal to do with the way teachers teach and also with what they teach. Here we can examine the way schools characteristically perceive the

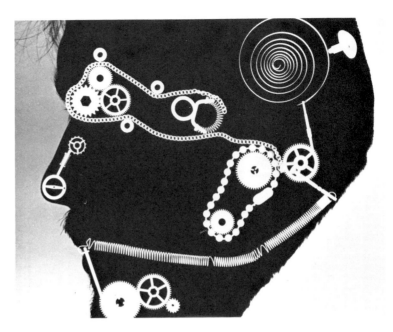

Experimental photograph by Lawrence Melkus. (Scholastic Magazines, Inc.)

By superimposing two negatives and printing them together, a high school student seems to comment visually on prevailing notions of cognition and mental life. Some teenagers realize, perhaps intuitively, that mechanistic schemes do not adequately explain the way people think and learn. An image of this kind may reflect the resentment felt by a perceptive teenager toward his schooling. These days, young people listen to a great deal of rhetoric about learning, much of which must sound to them like directions for acti-

vating a five-dollar watch. In the photograph, notice the mechanical linkages between mouth, eye, ear, and brain. Does it represent the act of knowing in the manner of "scientific" advertisements diagramming the action of a nasal decongestant, or of a superior aspirin doing battle with an extraordinary headache? What sets the parts in motion? What kind of maintenance do they require? Who keeps them oiled? What is the relation of that container—the head —to those chains, wheels, gears, sprockets, and springs?

Machinery, in general, is offensive to organic substances. That is one of the themes of Siegfried Giedion's book, "Mechanization Takes Command." When the activity of our most distinctively human possession—the mind—is compared to a machine (and a cheap one at that), we are either insulted or painfully amused. Of course, this sort of image does not represent the true state of affairs inside our skulls, but it is a truthful image nevertheless, because it truly describes what many people believe. ■

functions of knowledge and performance and the roles they are assigned in the education of the young.

So long as possessing information is the most prominent goal of educational effort, we can expect the school to be organized physically and programmatically for the systematic transmission and storage of facts and the testing of pupils' ability to recall and use those facts.* Progress in school and status in life after leaving school are thus considerably influenced by an individual's ability to store, recall, and use the knowledge he gained as a student. In a complex culture such as ours, knowledge often has a status value that is independent of its practical utility. Indeed, knowledge that is false or out-of-date or merely inert may be prized by society even though it is counterproductive for an individual's life goals. He finds himself imprisoned within the intellectual walls of his earlier education, unable to cope with new experience because he has been accustomed to react to events according to obsolete facts or obsolete models of knowing, feeling, and thinking. Whitehead says,† "Knowledge does not keep any better than fish. You may be dealing with knowledge of the old species, with some old truth; but somehow or other it must come to the students, as it were, just drawn out of the sea and with the freshness

*See the section on "Knowledge as a Taxonomic Category" in Benjamin S. Bloom, ed., *Taxonomy of Educational Objectives: The Classification of Educational Goals. Handbook 1: Cognitive Domain*, McKay, 1956.

†Alfred North Whitehead, *The Aims of Education*, paperback edition, Mentor, 1949, p. 102. First published in 1936.

of its immediate importance." The negative consequences of possessing incorrect or useless knowledge might be compared to the results of taking harmless medication for a serious illness: The medication causes no further illness but since it causes no cure either, it postpones effective remedies and thus prolongs the illness.

On the other hand, we believe that reliable, up-to-date knowledge is useful, indeed indispensable for dealing successfully with reality. Hence, schools endeavor to pass on reliable information of all sorts. This fundamental activity of our schools and school systems is based on a hidden assumption that requires further scrutiny: Reliable or correct knowledge, if appropriately applied, can solve the problems that reality constantly presents to individuals. Clearly, sound knowledge is of little value if it is not used in relevant situations. Now some important educational questions arise: How do we "know" we are using our reliable knowledge in a relevant fashion? Secondly, if we know our knowledge is adequate for our present needs, how do we modify it or add to it so that it will be adequate for future, unanticipated needs? Finally, is there some way for the school to manage the acquisition of knowledge so as to facilitate its relevant application in all circumstances?

From the discussion so far, it might appear that I am attempting to denigrate a most sacred endeavor—the pursuit of knowledge. But in fact I wish to show that we have a serious problem to solve in dealing with knowledge in schools, namely how to acquire and use knowledge in a manner that does not repeat the ingestion of harmless medicines for real illnesses.*

The school is the official place where knowledge is acquired. Its characteristic routines and procedures give form and style to learning. Although the school perceives its function as the transmission of information that authorities assert is reliable, there is a strong likelihood that children are mainly learning a style of acquiring and using knowledge. At the present rate of production in the knowledge industries, most information acquired in school will be shown false or will be substantially modified by the time each student graduates. Hence what resides with the graduate is the mode or fashion in which he gained his learning. Or, if his obsolete knowledge remains with him, he learns through frustrating experience that it is not very helpful in gaining his ends. And this idea that the *style* rather than the content of learning is retained finds confirmation in the typical reminiscences most of us have about our school days. We talk about the "characters" we knew, hilarious incidents in class, the way a teacher dressed or spoke, athletic celebrations—everything except the cognitive contents of instruction.

If it is true that a style of learning is an important product of schooling, then we should be as concerned about ways of learning as we are about what is learned. The aesthetic mode of learning becomes relevant: It is characterized mainly by its style, which is to say, by its *affective** manner of connecting the elements of perceiving, doing, knowing, and sharing. Instead of separating knowledge from the living, organic situations in which it is acquired, the aesthetic unites all the features of experience by endowing them with a single, pervasive quality. Art synthesizes whereas science analyzes. You can see how important this style of learning is for elementary education: Children are not ready to encounter the world in the form of an endless succession of isolated entities; as their fantasizing and myth-making activities suggest, they seek a *comprehensive vision* of reality. Educators implicitly recognize this need by postponing the departmentalization of learning until the secondary school years. In grade school, our principal emphasis is on the wholeness of experience, the unity of knowledge, the integrity of learning.

In view of this emphasis on wholeness and unity in elementary education, how do we introduce the vital elements of growth, change, and innovation? Western culture is not disposed to linger very long over the mythic unities of childhood. We encourage curiosity, we institutionalize the spirit of investigation. What is the relevance of the

*Jacques Barzun makes this point in discussing pedantry: "It is intellectually right *not* to try to know or tell more than a subject contains of significance; or in still other words, knowledge is not an absolute homogeneous good, of which there cannot be enough." *The House of Intellect*, Harper & Row, 1959, p. 219.

*The term comes from the German word, *affekt*, meaning feeling, emotion, or desire. Among educational psychologists it tends to be used in contradistinction to *cognitive*. But some are well aware of the cognitive components of affective learning. See D. A. Krathwohl, B. S. Bloom, and B. B. Masia, eds., *Taxonomy of Educational Objectives: The Classification of Educational Goals. Handbook II: Affective Domain*, McKay: 1964.

aesthetic mode of learning to the dynamic intellectual drives that begin to make their appearance during the upper elementary years? How do we satisfy the child's desire to know what makes things tick? By teaching him how to *interfere with ideas and things.* You may say this is the province of science and experimental method. Perhaps it is. But art claims a very ancient right—older than alchemy—to rearrange things, to transform substances, to call new forms into being. In other words, aesthetic education implies taking things apart and putting things together *in the light of an affective idea about what they might become.* This curiosity presides at the birth of new knowledge *and feeling.* The elementary school is a place where children *do something* to ideas and materials in order to find out who they are and what the world is like.

Performing with Ideas

The school has been defined as a place where we do something to ideas and things. It is obviously possible to alter the shape of clay or plaster, but can one *do* anything to an idea since it has no palpable or physical existence? However an idea acquires a home, a physical location, as soon as a person begins to deal with it seriously. We can "handle" it, that is, twist and stretch and shape it with the aid of sensibility and imagination. When we think about the origin and function of an idea or of its possible connection and combination with other ideas, we are clearly treating it the way a sculptor treats his modeling clay. The educational question now becomes: How do

Studio performance, 1901. (Pennsylvania Academy of the Fine Arts.)

we know we are dealing with an idea seriously? The answer is: When we use that idea to alter a portion of our inner or outer environment. How do we alter the environment with ideas? By predicting or anticipating, by guessing what would happen, what meanings would emerge, if certain ideas were introduced into new situations that happen to interest us.

In dealing seriously with ideas, it does not matter whether we handle them as if they were embodied in the tangible materials of art. What does matter educationally is that the result of our handling of ideas has a public existence. In this light, the school can be defined as a place where ideas are *publicly* handled. Children, then, should spend their time in classrooms learning what happens to ideas when people do things to them. For this purpose, teachers function like the much-maligned gym instructor whose main work consists of rolling a volleyball into a cluster of youngsters who proceed to kick it around. Perhaps kicking or punching a volleyball is a way of venting aggression; but it is also done for the sheer fun of finding out what will happen to it after it leaves your toe and careens off somebody's elbow. A good gym teacher goes further and organizes a game; *any* good teacher organizes a game.

One of the games played in school is called art. For example, we might try to find out whether a convincing representation of bottles and fruit on a table can be made by drawing the shapes of the empty spaces between the objects. A teacher organizes that game because pupils will not, most likely, have thought of it themselves. Then they make a discovery not entirely unanticipated by the teacher—that forms can be defined by what they are not as well as what they are. That is a fairly sophisticated idea. How do we know that the pupils have really

---

Academic training in art assumed a very close relation between knowledge and performance. The prospective painter or sculptor could not represent objects "correctly" unless he knew anatomy, perspective, and proportion. In addition, he needed to know the principles of good composition. To be sure, technique was also vital; but the artist would not succeed unless his technical skills rested on a sound knowledge of the structure of the things he was trying to represent. A painter like Eakins could advise his students: "Strain your brain more than your eye." Eakins had almost a surgeon's knowledge of human anatomy; and perspective was for him a demanding and exact science. Other artists, who painted landscapes or seascapes, had a practical understanding of geology and patterns of vegetation; or of tides, wave motion, and the effects of light on different kinds of moving water. The varied information artists possessed, however, was rarely pursued for its own sake. It was acquired naturally in the course of searching for the most truthful way to represent visual reality. Unlike many intellectuals artists as a class do not pride themselves on the accumulation of recondite information; on the other hand, like most thoughtful men they are interested in ideas and the life of the mind.

The emergence during the twentieth century of abstract and nonobjective art did not exempt artists from the pursuit of knowledge, but it did change the character of the information they needed. Instead of concentrating on the objective traits of what they saw, abstract artists grew more interested in the processes of perception within the viewer. They also became keen students of every detail of the act of artistic execution. In many cases, the abstract work of art deals only with itself; that is, it points to the way it was made as compared to the way other works of art have been made. Consequently, the spectator is expected to know what a work of art is being compared to. The artist, in turn, has to know how knowledgeable his viewers are. Many artists even feel they need to know how critics think and what they are thinking about. In other words, artists often know a great deal, although they may not always know the things that schools consider important.

These remarks may imply that schools ought to reconsider the cognitive materials children are obliged to learn. Or it may suggest that aesthetic education offers, in many instances, a better way for children to learn what they need to know. In that case, the advocates of aesthetic education have to state clearly what it is, and demonstrate convincingly how learning, as they define it, is advanced. This latter requirement calls for substantially new modes of educational research: We have to develop much more sophisticated techniques than are presently available for dealing with cognitive and affective learning through art. ∎

---

learned it? Their work, the public result of their performance, constitutes a type of evidence of what they have learned. The bottles and fruit will not appear, will not be visible, unless the student has indeed brought them into being by altering shape, color, or value relationships around them on his previously unmarked drawing paper. But suppose the student is merely following directions and does not really "know" what he has done. In that case, it is up to the teacher to press the student until he exhibits what he "knows" in an altered context—a matter of teaching tactics. The important point about this hypothetical game of art is that the student is obliged to institute changes in ordinary materials in order to generate new visual relationships and hence new meanings among them. The function of the teacher is to plan the activity in which the student engages and then to make certain the student grasps its meaning.

At this point, we have to make an important observation about the relation of knowledge to performance. It is possible to do something, to engage in an activity, and yet not learn anything; it is also possible to be told something and to commit it to memory and yet not to "know" it. In other words, we do not always realize the implications of what we do or the applications of what we know. Education can become the ritualistic repetition of what we have done or been told without our possessing knowledge that is in any way our own. Consequently it is necessary to combine intellectual effort with performing effort if something worthy of the name learning is to result. It is ultimately up to teachers to organize classroom behaviors and school environments so that combinations between knowing and doing occur. A good rule for teachers might then be: When pupils are engaged in an activity, be certain that they draw inferences from it in the form of ideas; when they are engaged in an abstract symbolic or verbal effort, make certain they apply their experience in a concrete and publicly demonstrable form.

This combination of intellectual and performing effort in all of a school's learning activity is more time-consuming than the present practice of stuffing pupils with knowledge. But multiplying the facts and concepts that schools must handle and pupils must "know" does not especially enhance their education. As Whitehead says, "So far as the mere imparting of information is concerned, no university [school?] has had any justification for existence since the popularization of printing in the fifteenth century."* Remember that it is a *style of learning* that remains with the individual; and it is a style of learning that facilitates further learning under altered cultural and institutional circumstances. Consequently, the tendency of schools to add material to their curricula without pruning the dead branches of the educational tree needs to be resisted. It would appear that the multiplication of learning materials reflects a type of panic on the part of school boards and school administrators; they believe, quite properly, that unsolved social problems require a better-educated citizenry. But they err in thinking that the best-educated citizen is the one who is most completely stuffed with facts. It is what he can *do* with facts and ideas that matters. Consequently, school curricula (which are fairly arbitrary selections of experience anyway) can and ought to be pruned so that teachers can devote more time to perfecting the *style* of student learning and the refinement of their teaching practices. Then, hopefully, each learning sit-

*The Aims of Education, p. 97.

uation will be fully used, its intellectual and performing opportunities fully exploited.

Art as Knowledge

What does a person know as a result of looking at a work of art or as a result of creating an art object? Let us concentrate on the first case—looking. Of course, we know we have seen the work, and we may know who created it, where it is located, and when it was made. Such knowledge is not very useful, not especially interesting, and not likely to lead to further growth for the knower. But with a certain amount of instruction, and the assistance of intellectual tools like books, we may learn to know the purposes for which the work was created as well as the social and cultural circumstances surrounding its creation. Such knowledge begins to be important because the work then serves as a portal to realms of meaning beyond itself. We learn, for example, that an ancient king caused a statue of himself to be erected so that his spirit could inhabit the statue after his body had died. Such knowledge, at the very least, raises interesting questions about one's own mortality; it encourages speculation about what a man is and what part of him can survive. To be sure, we do not know with certainty that there is a human spirit that can survive after death even if magical arts are invoked. What we *do* know is that men try to rise above natural processes and that they may use art for the purpose. This type of knowledge represents one of several inferences that can be drawn from looking at a Pharaoh's *ka* figure. It is humanistic knowledge because it deals with a problem that is common to the human condition; in one form or another, this knowledge must be gained by all men, no matter where or when they live.

There are many valid observations we can make about an Egyptian *ka* figure. That is, there are many things we can say about it that are true or confirmable through observation and sound scholarship. And we can oblige pupils to "know" one or several of the many possible valid assertions about a work of art. Especially if the work is a masterpiece, the fund of meaningful statements one can make about it is virtually inexhaustible. Of all the assertions that can be made and presumably "known," however, which are the ones we actually choose to make? What factors influence our knowledge of art when we are observers of it?

Clearly, the persons or circumstances that call a work of art to our attention have some influence on what we come to know about it. Scholars, critics, journalists, and teachers know something about art that they often seem anxious to communicate. But the reading public or the pupils in a classroom will not necessarily "know" what teachers tell them about art—or about science or history, for that matter. Pupils may be persuaded to memorize and recall what they have been told or what they have read; and they may give evidence of such recall by writing correct answers to examination questions. However, such "knowledge" of art is not especially impressive so far as the cultivated person is concerned. Here again, Whitehead is most instructive: "Culture is activity of thought, and receptiveness to beauty and humane feeling. Scraps of information have nothing to do with it. A merely well-

---

The portrait statue of Pharaoh Khafre and the Congo effigy jar exemplify art that tries to deal with the mystery of death. Both were intended as permanent containers of a human spirit. Knowing the original functions of these art objects is important, especially if you are interested in the beliefs different peoples have about immortality. Young children, however, do not believe that death, as modern adults understand it, exists. The Egyptian ka figure would make more sense to them than it does to us. They might

even see the logic of a jar as a spiritual container; they might be willing to accept the idea of the soul as a liquid substance, as many tribal people do. These speculations, however, deal with the possible outcomes of teaching in a program of aesthetic education; first, it is necessary that children see in the objects a specific connection between forms and ideas. Fortunately, children already believe that visual forms convey meaning; that notion has not been trained out of them. Their teachers need to share the same assump-

tion and be prepared to act on it. We want the child to be able to "read" or interpret the effigy jar; his teacher can help, not by disclosing the "facts," but by pressing his pupils to support their interpretations with concrete observations of the visual properties of the object.

If you think about it, this sort of teaching is not really very new; we do it with oral and written literature all the time. Now we must try to do it with art—what Bartlett Hayes calls "visual literature." ■

Two views (above) of Pharaoh Khafre (c. 2600 B.C.). (Hirmer Fotoarchiv, München.)

Pottery effigy jar (left), Mangbetu, Congo. (Baltimore Museum of Art, Wurtzburger Collection of Primitive Art.)

informed man is the most useless bore on God's earth.''* We are interested in the kind of knowledge that grows out of the pupil's own perception of art objects. Not that the information communicated by teachers and scholars is false; rather it does not necessarily lead to the sort of knowledge that is distinctive to what may be called aesthetic education. Perhaps Peter Schrag overstates the case which can be made against professors or teachers who regard themselves essentially as sources of information: "What do the professors know that isn't accessible to anyone who can travel, read, turn on the tube? Yes, they can deal endlessly with technical questions, or with remote matters of scholarship, but can they apply their disciplines to say something valid about the human condition?"† I think professors are entitled to pursue knowledge disinterestedly; there will always be plenty of others who are interested in the applications of research. Still, Schrag calls attention to the dimensions of learning which concern us in aesthetic education, especially in elementary schools: Facts do not automatically relate themselves to humanistic concerns; they must first be perceived in an affective context. Perceptual energies must be focused on *the structure* as well as the cognitive content of instructional material. We want the pupil to know something about an art object because *he has seen that knowledge embodied in the form of the work.*

Here an objection may arise. You may say that it is possible to see a color, a shape,

or a texture, but it is not possible to see "knowledge." The fact is, however, that you do not "see" a color or a shape either; it is only easier for several observers *to agree* about the existence of a particular color or shape, about the label or designation for a particular sensory stimulation. Just as we agree that a particular area is red, so also we can agree that we see fire or love or the sun. We say that the figure of the Pharaoh is vital, optimistic, vigorous, and so on. These adjectives may be regarded as inferences we have made about the form of the work. It is also proper to say that we see vitality, vigor, and optimism *in the form of the work*, because in looking at the sculpture we have been obliged to simulate with our own bodies the feelings designated by the words called vitality, optimism, and vigor. A teacher may have given us the words, but it is our own bodies that provide the feelings —that is, the perceptions. So far as I know, there is no other way to gain understanding or knowledge of matters like vitality and optimism except through feeling them with one's own total organism.

Learning that the figure of the Pharaoh Khafre is optimistic, *by being told that it is*, does not constitute knowledge in the same way as seeing optimism in the figure. In one case, the pupil commits a verbal formulation to memory; in the other case the viewer makes himself *feel* optimism in order to *see* optimism in the work of art.

A question raised above still remains: On what basis do we select what we need to know from all the possibilities of knowledge that are latent in our encounter with art objects? Here, of course, teaching becomes

*Ibid., p. 13.
†*Peter Schrag*, "The End of the Great Tradition," *Saturday Review*, February 15, 1969.

a crucial factor. A teacher, being older or more experienced than his pupils, has seen certain works of art before his pupils have, hence he "knows" something about them which, he suspects, may be relevant to the interests of his students. But a teacher may not know what interests his pupils; if he is a "real" teacher, he should try to find out. Also, the teacher does not know in advance what his pupils are going to learn about a particular work. But it is the uncertainty about what pupils will learn or discover that makes teaching interesting, and it would be foolish to structure the teaching situation so that this uncertainty is eliminated or even minimized. In fact, the teacher ought to be interested in learning something about his students from the fashion in which they employ their freedom to discover new meanings in particular works of art. How then does the teacher's prior experience and knowledge of art become relevant to instruction? The answer lies in the teacher's selection of works that will be studied; his planning of the sequences in which works will be seen; his disclosure of relevant historical and critical data about the works under scrutiny; his estimate of the interest his own insights about art would have for children. Clearly, our pedagogical instincts are brought significantly into play when making curricular judgments of this type. If teaching is an art, then we are continuously making estimates concerning strategies of disclosure; we elicit cues through questioning, and we press for responses that are weighted toward description, analysis, interpretation, or appraisal of art objects. In surrendering complete control over the substantive knowledge gained from art, teachers do not surrender control over the classroom tactics and strategies for reaching the intellectual goals of their instruction. But they *do* gain dividends in the freshness and contemporary relevance of what is learned in their classes.

Art as Performance

Before attempting to derive the educative values of artistic performance, let us examine what it is that the artist does. Consider an artist painting a picture, ignoring for the moment questions about his age, critical reputation, stylistic preference, subject matter, technical approach, and so on. What is immediately apparent is that he is involved in mixing pigment; applying it to a surface; brushing, smearing, scraping, and scratching paint; adding and changing and eliminating; and also refining and reworking passages that are apparently complete. Superficially, he seems to be engaged in a variety of manipulative operations. And unfortunately some persons have drawn the superficial conclusion that art consists solely of manipulating various kinds of material. But it must be apparent to anyone that the muscular performance we see is comparable to the relatively small part of an iceberg visible above the ocean's surface. There are a great many mental or psychological operations that *precede, accompany,* and *follow* any manifest artistic activity.

What is the character of the mental operations that surround the visible portion of artistic performance? It would take more than one volume to reply with any com-

Student building a tower. (Donald O. Williams, Supervisor, Los Angeles City School District.)

Drawing by Mark von der Heide. (Courtesy the artist.)

pleteness. In summary fashion, it is safe to say the artist engages in complex processes of decision-making. You can imagine how vast an array of choices he must range over before making the decisions that are finally evident in his performance and in the visible appearance of his work. To complicate the matter further, there is always the real possibility that he has fallen into artistic "accidents" that have either been judged bad and hence eliminated or found satisfying and hence permitted to stand.

Is there any difference between the decision-making engaged in by artists and the decision-making carried on by scientists, business men, politicians, or engineers? There is considerable research to the effect that the exercise of creativity in decision-making is similar among a number of differ-

Obviously, the boy building a tower enjoys what he is doing. The question is whether he is learning anything. A great deal of the answer depends on what his teacher thinks is being accomplished. The activity the boy is engaged in can support a variety of legitimate objectives if his teacher knows how to handle the situation. But there is a tendency of teachers to entrap themselves in educational slogans—wordy substitutes for genuine planning and analysis. That is, a teacher may write or recite some fashionable phrases from a syllabus about materials, light or space and thus convince himself that the

student has made a significant discovery. Perhaps he has, but how can we know?

We must find out what the student thinks he is doing. The tower itself is handsome, and the boy is right to feel proud of it. Still, we must learn how he sees the tower—not just in metaphoric terms—but how he believes his specific purposes are embodied in the tower's shapes, spaces, and materials. It does not matter if the student "invents" relationships after the fact. Such invention is a type of creativity too. In an educational context, however, the artist has to share his discoveries, not only by showing what he has ent professions. But, of course, the subject matter of these decisions—creative or not—varies greatly. This variation in the themes of decision-making is tremendously important for education because it establishes the grounds of the several disciplines we study. That is why we study art *and* literature *and* economics *and* medicine *and* law; otherwise, it would only be necessary to study creativity. The fact is, what is common to the process of creative decision-making in various disciplines is not as important, educationally, as the variety of themes, materials, or subject matters we must make decisions about. Indeed, if I were sick, I would much prefer to be treated by an uncreative physician than a highly creative lawyer.

So far as art is concerned, what subject matter does it afford for decision-making and why is that subject matter educationally important? First, it should be plain that the physical materials the artist uses constitute critical issues. That is, their actual and potential sensuous effects pose problems of choice for him. The more experienced he is, the more potential effects he will be aware of, and thus his decision will be more difficult to make. Second, the use, purpose, or function of the art object he is making seems to cast a shadow in advance of making it. The artist's knowledge of the way similar objects have been employed or seen or admired enters into his present consideration, especially of design or planning. Third, the pervasive effect of the work has to be thought about in several ways: (a) The imagined or hoped-for effect, (b) the immediate effect of the work in progress, and (c) the approxima-

---

made, but also by declaring his intentions, his plans for next time, the problems he has not yet solved, potential sources of new ideas, and possible connections with what he has seen or done.

Naturally, the entire classroom community can take part in the process of bringing to light what a student has learned. Naturally, verbal language will be used. Of course, we know that verbal language is not a substitute for, or an equivalent of, the tower. It happens to be another way we communicate with each other. This stage of a teaching practice is art criticism—talk about art. It is a way of making public and fairly explicit some of the things a student has learned. It is a way of converting performance into knowledge—that is, of translating symbols that exist in space into symbols that are ordered in time.

When Mark von der Heide drew these pictures, he and his parents were getting adjusted to living in a new house. Mark turned out a steady flow of drawings describing the different rooms and explaining his relation to each of them. He appears, in person, in the bedroom, but he describes the bathtub as a spectator. An exceedingly intelligent child, Mark would worry about a room or its furnishings unless he knew its special name and how its equipment was supposed to be used. In his art work, Mark employs words, images, and diagrams wherever he thinks they are necessary. He is no purist when it comes to telling it "like it is." . . . .

For Mark, artistic performance is analogous to the Navy's shakedown cruise on a new ship: Does the equipment work? What is it like to live in the quarters? Are any special instructions required for the crew? Is the ship seaworthy? Mark satisfied himself on these questions, and his parents were able to accept the house and go ahead with their plans. ∎

tion of (b) to (a) or to some alternative pervasive effect.

Pervasive effect is extremely important to the artist, and in today's context of creating art without commission or patron, it may absorb the major portion of his energy. He has to think of himself as a surrogate for the public to whom his work is addressed, and this imaginative effort requires that he speculate about the potential meanings or communicative power of the work in progress. Consequently, an area of paint becomes for him much more than an area of paint: It becomes a vehicle of ideas and feelings— ideas and feelings that are familiar or original, pleasing or displeasing, clear or ambiguous. But the artist has no certain way of knowing that meanings which are clear to him will be clear to someone else. Thus he must estimate how close his own responses are to the responses of others. Consequently, it is very likely that the great artist is great because he possesses self-knowledge in high

degree *and also* knowledge of others in high degree.

From this account of artistic decision-making, certain educational conclusions seem warranted. The most obvious concerns the alleged distinction between experiencing art as an observer and experiencing art as a creator or performer. Both modes of experience call for a complex psychological performance. Both require empathic behavior —that is, bodily imitation of and psychic identification with what is seen—in order to feel and to understand the impact of visual configurations on oneself or someone else. We cannot say that only artistic performance is creative, or that only art appreciation involves one's knowledge and mind. On the contrary, all our serious encounters with art require that we organize our feelings *and* ideas, our motor *and* intellectual responses.

Most of us believe that the difference between creating art and looking at it lies in skill. Presumably, skill is required for artistic

High-school students examining art by Roy Lichenstein. (The New York Times.)

Part of the pleasure of a museum visit is due to the museum environment; it is so different from that of the school. Especially at the Guggenheim! Very few children fail to be happily excited by the combination of grandiloquent architecture and skillfully installed works of art. Teachers may also be surprised to discover that children really do enjoy art which is slightly or not at all recognizable. After recovering from the surprise, they face the problem of how to

Children examining figures by Alexander Calder. (Wide World Photos.)

Socializing at the museum. (New York City Public Schools Bureau of Art.)

make the best use of the experience.

As a rule, museums cannot greatly help teachers of small children because, although museums want visitors, their personnel do not really know why the children are there. They work up descriptive labels and packages of information about the collection; they furnish guides or docents who relate true stories about the art objects; and they try desperately to appear friendly. Perhaps

that is all one can expect. Still, few museums know how to design an exhibition so that it makes a statement visually. Consequently, each teacher has to create the strategy that can relate the museum and its collections to the over-all objectives of the school art program. That is, you have to establish connections between what the children are making, studying, or thinking about and the objects displayed in the museum.

The best thing children can do

in a museum, or a gallery of modern art, is to learn how to look at real—not reproduced—art objects created by professional artists. That means walking around sculpture, touching it when permitted, examining paintings closely and from a distance, experimenting (as the little girl is with the sculpture) with angles of vision, watching other people look, reading labels only after looking at the work, not sketching, coming back to a work a few times after seeing other

Boy in museum (left). (Alan DuBois, St. Petersburg Museum of Fine Arts.)

Viewing the Jackson Pollock retrospective at the Museum of Modern Art (right). (Friedman-Abeles, Inc.)

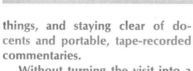

things, and staying clear of docents and portable, tape-recorded commentaries.

Without turning the visit into a junket, you should try to forget the seriousness of the occasion and the monumentality of the place. You can hope that the theatricality of the museum will not destroy the child's notion that some works of art can be found in the outside world and that he and his friends create art too. Finally, you can hope that pupils will begin to speculate about why the objects have been preserved and displayed, why they are arranged as they are, where they originally came from, and what each work is trying to say to him.

Jackson Pollock probably painted the pictures on display at the Museum of Modern Art one at a time. Their installation shows them in the order of their execution and the relatedness of their themes. You can see the paintings in the museum's order, or your order, but not in Pollock's order. That is, he may have lit a cigarette, or taken a trip, or watched television between pictures. Exhibitions create the illusion of a false continuity among works of art; they have to. But you cannot recapitulate Pollock's unhappy existence as you stroll among his logically arranged canvases. Indeed, you should not try to do so.

When visiting a retrospective exhibition, there are four kinds of time to be considered: the artist's time, museum time, the art object's time, and your time. Your two-hour visit is the equivalent of about twenty-five years of the artist's life. You can read about his life after you get home. Spend your museum time with the space-time of the paintings; work out an equation between their space-and-form-time and your present breathing-in-and-out-time. The best tribute to the departed artist is to take his work seriously; that is, to revive his paintings in your own experience, leaving the biographical details to the fellow who wrote the catalog. ■

creation but not for aesthetic creation. In fact, however, both activities call for skill. In any random group there would be wide variation in aesthetic skill—the skill required for the meaningful apprehension of a work of art. Another widely held notion is that artistic skill is exclusively sensorimotor in character.* But it should be plain that the sensorimotor skills of artists are well within the range of all physically normal persons. Artists are not athletes of the senses. Their art consists of their capacity for directing and organizing their sensorimotor activity, and that directing and organizing capacity is also exercised by competent art critics. Looking at art is a type of work involving skills similar to those used in creating art. Although this work is different from the artist's observable performance, comparable skills of organization, discrimination, choosing, prediction, and inference are involved. One of the components of artistic skill is knowledge of what can be done with materials; such knowledge is usually gained, and perhaps is *best* gained, by working directly with materials. Still, we should not preclude the possibility that knowledge of materials can also be gained by looking at what has been done with them. Consider

*"The technique necessary to paint a picture is not restricted to the hand alone. The hand cannot be separated from the eye and brain. Broadly considered, the technique of creating a picture includes skilled use of all the abilities involved in the process. It includes skilled vision, skilled imagination, skilled planning, criticism, and concentration of energies. [Academic training] fails even to realize that there is such a thing as the technique of artistic perceiving and imagining." Thomas Munro, *Art Education: Its Philosophy and Psychology*, Liberal Arts, 1956, p. 105.

how connoisseurs of prints, for example, can make exceedingly fine technical discriminations without having been printmakers. The fact is that various sorts of snobbism have obtained in art and art education, directed back and forth among performers, scholars, critics, theorists, connoisseurs, and so on. This snobbism appears to exist in a vacuum of knowledge about the operations actually performed by artists and viewers of art. It would be well, therefore, if we did not make invidious distinctions among the competencies of the several professions centering upon art. Studying art from the standpoint of a single discipline is not unlike the situation of a blind man describing an elephant after touching only one part of its anatomy.

Conclusion

Art is not so much a *subject* in the school curriculum as it is a way of learning. To be sure, art has its distinctive subject matter, as does history or geography. But it is to the credit of art education that it has perceived in art something of value beyond the unquestioned worth of its subject matter, the art objects themselves. Educators have discovered in the act of creating and perceiving works of art a mode of learning. It is a mode of learning that naturally and organically unites knowing and doing; creating effects and judging their meaning; taking chances and calculating the consequences; erecting hypotheses and looking for confirmation; interfering with ideas and suggesting alternatives.

5

In a book about education we are not primarily interested in an abstract discussion of the connection between theories of art and theories of moral behavior. Instead, we want to know whether instruction in art has any bearing on the development of human decency or good character in children and adolescents. As Buber says, "Education worthy of the name is essentially education of character.* Today especially, the development of human character is of crucial concern because men literally possess the means of destroying their species. Those who teach children must realize that they are engaged in building the foundations of adult character which, in the national or international aggregate, determines the survival of humanity.† Consequently, we have an urgent reason for conducting our inquiry—as urgent as the inquiries of zoologists into the innate destructiveness of the human animal, or of anthropologists into the origins of human cooperation, or of theologians into the primal guilt or innocence of mankind.

The argument for the connection between aesthetics and ethics is very simple; it requires little space to set it out. Dewey put the matter concisely when he said: "Imagination is the chief instrument of the good."** The problem for the teacher is how to *act on* this observation. In other words, if we agree that the ability to imagine the consequences of behavior is necessary for making moral

*Martin Buber, "The Education of Character," in *Between Man and Man*, Beacon, 1955, p. 104.

†Writing toward the end of his life, Freud said on this subject: "The fateful question of the human species seems to me to be whether and to what extent the cultural process developed in it will succeed in mastering the derangements of communal life caused by the human instinct of aggression and self-destruction." *Civilization and Its Discontents*, Doubleday Anchor Books, 1958, p. 105. First published in 1930.

**John Dewey, *Art as Experience*, Minton, Balch, 1934, p. 348.

Ethics and Aesthetics

choices, how do we apply this wisdom to ordinary classroom teaching? Moreover, how is the teaching of art and the whole process of aesthetic education implicated?

My extended answer to these questions is presented in the following pages. In summary, I believe that we can observe the ethical development of children in their aesthetic behavior. That is, their artistic expression and their aesthetic appreciation reveal emerging conceptions of what seems to them good. The function of teaching, then, is to elicit the child's aesthetic behavior, to make it public, and to acknowledge its ethical import by engaging in a dialog with the child and his peers—a dialog that centers on the values expressed in his artistic and aesthetic activity. When we talk about art with children, we talk about alternatives of feeling and doing; we talk about the possible meanings of what they have done and said. That is how we can establish a model of ethical discourse. Without becoming involved in the frequently counterproductive business of adult admonition and moralizing,* we can meet children on *their* ethical grounds—the grounds of their creative choices.

What follows, then, is a presentation of the stages of ethical development as re-

vealed in the creative and aesthetic behavior of children. We are going to look at children and their art as the representation of an emerging capacity to imagine relationships: with the self, with others, with nature, with the man-made environment, and with the idea of society.

The Primal Self

The Real and the Possible

According to Kant, the difference between human beings and animals lies in man's ability to distinguish between *real* events and *possible* events. Man's glory, as well as much of his pain, derives from the same source—the capacity to conceive of a different way, of another outcome to his encounter with reality. But men were not always able to imagine alternatives: Prehistoric and tribal men saw themselves substantially at the mercy of a reality they were unable to change—unable to change, that is, because they had only the weakest powers of conceiving how reality might be different. This weakness in the imagining of possibilities in the world is also characteristic of children. Not that they lack the ability to fantasize. Rather, children do not distinguish very clearly between fantasy and reality. Their behavior seems to result from an immediate conversion of instinct and impulse into activity. Small children act because they have inherited the psychophysical equipment that makes human action possible. But they spend very little time on the calculation

---

*Buber has a very subtle appreciation of the resistance of pupils to outright moral indoctrination. He tells a story: "I try to explain that lying destroys life, and something frightful happens: the worst liar in the class produces a brilliant essay on the destructive power of lying. I have made the fatal mistake of *giving instruction* in ethics, and what I said is accepted as current coin of knowledge; nothing of it is transformed into character-building substance." *Between Man and Man*, p. 105.

Three children's drawings. (Collection of the author.)

The human image begins to evolve from rudimentary scribbles and quasi-geometric formulas. You can see reversions back to the scribble as the child struggles to conserve the circles and triangles that maintain his hold on visual reality. Try to imagine the enormous effort a child must make in order to align the eyes on either side of the head's center axis, his triumph of placement with the nose and mouth, or his problem of locating the body under the head. While fighting to keep his small-muscle movements under control, he must also focus his perception on the correspondence between inner and outer images; resist stray motor impulses; screen out sensations that do not relate to his work; and persist in seeking the goal he started with—if he can remember it.

Klee and Miró, on the other hand, create elegant and seemingly effortless images based on those early childhood struggles. Klee's casual geometries, or his calculated meander in the girl's hair, reveal the expressive potential present in the same visual elements employed by the small child.

Miró pretends to see as a small child does; but, of course, he thinks like an adult. Childlike forms are present, but the element of struggle is absent. Looking at these children's drawings is like watching the birth of a human mind; looking at Klee and Miró is like watching the activity of a mind that remembers its origins with pleasure. ■

of alternatives, the estimation of consequences, or the judgment of the worth of their acts.

We speak of the innocence of childhood precisely because duty, responsibility, and guilt (those dread words of moral philosophers) are substantially absent from a child's thoughts about his own behavior. Instead, children exist in a realm of pure action—a realm in which there is no gap between what is and what might or ought to be.

So far as art is concerned, it is precisely because of the child's inability to distinguish between reality and possibility that his work has fascination for us: It is created as an act of pure will and invention. It is not inhibited by considerations of how it departs from a possible model in reality. It reveals a world

GIRL WITH DOLL, by Paul Klee. (Collection of Chris Schang.)

Detail of a poster by Joan Miró. (Museum of Modern Art.)

—the same world, presumably, that adults occupy—peopled exclusively by fantastic creatures and objects that are nevertheless real, that is, real to the child. The child artist does not know how to dissimulate, he makes no distinction between appearance and reality.* Children do not believe that more than one reality exists. "I am," "I make," and "I want"; for them there is no other reality.

The world of action and desire expressed in the form of child art is the same world in which the ethical behavior of children takes place. It is a world in which there is as yet no alternation or rhythm between freedom and restraint. Freedom is all; restraint is inconceivable. Looking at the painting of a preschool child, we see the result of pure will in action—will unfettered by rules, concern for an audience, desire to please. But by the time a child is five or six, this world begins to be invaded by the supervening reality of the adult world; and by the time of puberty, the child's world of pure act is almost completely demolished. Fortunately, but also tragically, children then prepare to enter the Copernican universe of adult reality following the ruin of their much-beloved Ptolemaic world of autonomous action and ego-centered moral freedom.

During the period when children pass from a world of spontaneous action to one of hesitation and incipient self-control, the school assumes the role of moral midwife. That is, the school repeatedly asks the child to consider what he is doing, and thus assists in the birth of ethical reflection. The concept of right and wrong answers to all sorts of questions is introduced. The claims of other children are given a hearing as if these others really existed. The child learns that his sexual impulses fall into categories—the permissible and the impermissible. The imperiousness of every sovereign self is gently hedged about with restrictions established by a collective entity, the group. This subtle but steady erosion of the child's control over his psychosocial space is attended by an enlargement of his concept of physical space and, of course, by endeavors to represent this new space in his artistic expression. As new space in the physical sense begins to occupy the child's consciousness, he becomes aware of a staggering number of possibilities for emotionally satisfying action. At first, this freedom is exciting, but by the time he reaches puberty the choices before him appear confusedly numerous and far-reaching. Against his will, he has been thrust by biological and intellectual changes into a maelstrom of indecision. Any one of the new feelings and things he can now conceive of would have been sufficient to absorb him completely when he was small. He finds himself confronting the vastness of an immense world with many of the reactions and precedents established during his earlier, provincial existence. The result seems to be a confrontation with chaos. This is the experience of the older child as

*The difference between reality as we "know" it, and as it *appears* to an artist, as it is *represented* in his work, constitutes one of the most important instruments of art-historical and critical analysis. On the basis of this difference we draw many of our inferences about influence, style, and expression.

he becomes aware of a universe organized according to its own rules rather than his despotic whims and desires.

But so long as childhood lasts, the possibility of evil or wrong-doing does not exist, for a child invests his whole mind and body in everything he does. He withholds no part of himself from his behavior because of ethical reservations about its rightness. We regard the child who cannot act wholly and spontaneously as ill, but not as immoral. To be immoral, a child would have to entertain alternative possibilities of action, and this he cannot do insofar as he is a child. That is why the teacher concerned with discipline—in art or in life—should not regard the violation of rules by a young child as moral perversity but rather as a confusion between the sovereignty of his own pure acts and a sovereignty-of-the-group which he has not yet learned to recognize.

Artistic Emergence of the Self

The preschool child first expresses his awareness of his body and its powers of movement by more or less random scribbles. He takes delight in making marks; they are the visible record of his hand in the world. But he tires of these marks quickly. His main interest is in making them rather than looking at them. The scribble, in other words, testifies to the child's graphic expression as an extension of his body; but the scribble has little or no status as an object outside his body.

The inability of the small child to acknowledge the existence of his scribbles as objects *outside* his body has an ethical import. It means that he has as yet no concept of a self which is separate from things.* The scribble has the same status as an infant's toes: He cannot tell whether they do or do not belong to him. What seems to be "selfish" behavior in a very young child, therefore, is really his incomplete idea of himself; he doesn't know where he begins and ends.†

With increased muscular control, scribbles become more defined and regularized, more obviously spiral or circular. The child attends to them for a longer time; he perceives his spiral scribbles as things. The things are given names, but not necessarily because they resemble anything. What has happened? The child has begun to distinguish between the self and its products. The child's graphic products now become precious, not as art, but as evidence of the existence of the self. The self does not exist as an object that the child can contemplate *until* he can conceive of objects outside his body. Consequently, the act of making something as trivial as a scribble has contributed to the child's emerging awareness of himself as a person. By the time he is three or four years of age, he has acquired the concept of things that *belong* to him but are not part of him. These scribbles have names! They have a provisional existence; that is, they are what they are because the child says so. And,

---

*"The child . . . begins by confusing its self with the world and only gradually comes to distinguish the two terms from each other." Herbert Read, *Education through Art*, p. 171.

†See George Herbert Mead, *Mind, Self and Society*, Univ. of Chicago Press, 1934, p. 172.

1. (Above) A hairless person emerges, virtually hatched from the egg. (All photographs collection of the author.)

2. (Below) Solitary man with hat and pipe. Eyelashes upside down.

3. Early man, Neanderthal type. Silly hat. Probably father.

4. Self-portrait with other persons and unidentified flying objects.

5. Primitive cooperation. Helping by watching.

6. She begins environmental studies. Nothing touches anything else. The tree has apples.

A survey of the stages in the drawing development of a child. ■

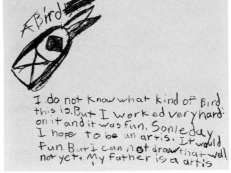

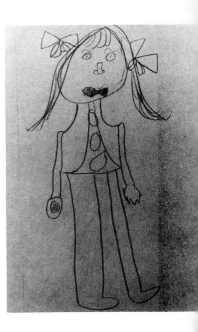

7. Family walk. Pipe followed by grandpa and others in order of importance. Space assigned democratically. Klee influence. (Spaziergang stage.)

8. (Above) Decides on career. Artistic achievement surpassed by literary production.

9. (At right) Acquires linear confidence. Matisse still eludes her. Lips replace mouth.

10. (At left) Designs a robot. Geometric period. First serious fling with science.

11. (Below) Returns to direct observation. Tries perspective in chair legs. Own legs very dainty. (Incipient ladyhood stage.)

12. (At left) Puberty approaching. First experiments with chiaroscuro. Picasso unafraid.

13. (Below) Gives up the figure. Switches to still life. Braque dies at 81. Strong interest in bottles. Morandi dies at 74.

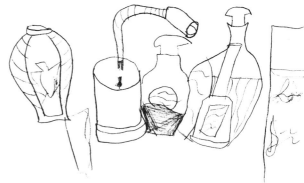

of course, he can change what they are because, like a god, he made them.

Once again, an ethical change is apparent. The child has acquired the power of naming things, hence of governing the existence of objects outside himself. This is a prerogative which was in primitive and ancient times reserved to powerful chiefs or aristocratic tribes descended from chiefs. In other words, the normal development of a child entails the appropriation of the right to control the identity of objects in his environment. This right, moreover, is perceived by the child as an outgrowth of his ability to control his scribbles, to repeat them, to give them a loose but distinguishable visual quality.

Up to this point, the child's graphic expression has served (1) to consolidate his notion of selfhood and (2) to extend his control over anything he chooses to give as a name to his scribbles. We might say that the career of the self, until now (the third or fourth year), has been an uninterrupted success story. Although he has not as yet developed any representational skills, the child has managed to combine his innate motor impulses with exceedingly rudimentary forming capacities, to achieve a gratifying dominion over anything he can think of.

The Emergent Person

A radical transformation of the scribble takes place during the early elementary years. The random or controlled scribble is recognized as bearing some resemblance to things the child has seen, felt, or knows about. The resemblance is probably accidental, but the significant point here is that the child has developed a new concept—that of correspondence between what he can make and the structure of reality. And he has the ability to replicate, deliberately, that correspondence or resemblance. He does so repeatedly. His repetitions become a formula that can be invoked whenever he desires the presence of the person or object symbolized by the formula. To be sure, this is a gratifying power he has discovered; alas, it also anticipates the end of his absolute control over the environment. That control now begins to depend, at least partly, on resemblance—on the child's ability to imitate a world that changes as his experience of it is enlarged.

The desire to control the world through graphic expression and naming persists, but the child is now too sophisticated to accept arbitrary scribbles as adequate symbols or effigies of reality. His work must more nearly correspond with his sensory experience of objects and places. Here it is necessary to stress the principle that *the child's artistic skills are almost always adequate for the visual representation of his experience.* A serious discrepancy (to the child) will not appear until puberty. Consequently, it is unwise, from a teaching standpoint, to direct instruction toward the correction or adjustment of his representational imagery. It takes care of itself.

What has happened to the self in the course of the child's discovery that he can imitate the world through his artistic expression? First, he surrenders his arbitrary control in return for a contingent control over persons and objects. That is, he is the master of these phenomena only to the extent that he repeats the "correct" formula for representing them. You can recognize in this reliance on formulas or stereotypes the recapitulation in the child of the tribal artist's magical aesthetics. Second, sense data now compete more effectively with innate mental and instinctual equipment as an influence in the development of the self. Third, children begin to fall into two main groups according to the method they employ for dealing with their sensations and feelings through art. That is, we see the beginnings of the polarization of style that is visible throughout the history of art: the classic-romantic, visual-haptic, perceptual-conceptual, impressionist-expressionist duality. By the time he is seven years old, the child's artistic expression reveals him as falling more on one side than the other of these pairs. He has a "style" of expression. It is very important to realize that, from the standpoint of one's style, other styles are wrong. This is our ethical inference: The polarization of the child's self in terms of his artistic expression results in his acquiring a type of personality that accepts or rejects experience according to its stylistic content. And that personality will now exhibit its stylistic affinity in every dimension of the child's behavior.*

*Stephen Spender makes a very perceptive observation about the ethics of style in reviewing a book by George Kennan: "A style, of course, has *no tolerance* of another style, except in so far as a certain charity (this happens with Mr. Kennan) is part of the style." [My italics.] "Man of Distinction," *The New York Review of Books*, April 24, 1969, p. 16.

At this stage of the child's development, his aesthetic behavior becomes a more ponderable factor. His personality has emerged with a consciousness of style not only in his own artistic expression but also in the expression of others. If the child's personality is polarized toward the visual, perceptual, or sensory end of the stylistic continuum, he may have difficulty in accepting haptic, romantic, or abstract modes of expression—not only in visual art but in other creative languages. As the saying goes, the style is the man. Hence there is an imperceptible leap from aesthetic preference to personal and social attitudes. Seen in this light, a child's style—both as performer and appreciator—extends beyond questions of liking or disliking in matters of art. To the degree that his personality is oriented toward one or another of the aesthetic poles, the child's conception of what is good is already substantially determined.

The Ethics of Space Representation

The evolution of the preschool child's imagery is in the direction of single object representation. This is understandable enough in view of his need to establish the existence of external objects in order to gain a separate idea of himself. But with the development of formulas or stereotypes for the representation of people, houses, natural objects, and so on, the child acquires a repertoire of images which he must order *in relation* to each other. Ultimately, he must learn how objects are or are not connected to each other; he has to learn the official space relationships of his culture. This knowledge is not innate.* Many types of play and many modes of artistic and aesthetic behavior contribute to the process of learning these relationships. But it is clear enough, from the artistic imagery of very young children, that they have virtually no space conception at all.

The animal art of Paleolithic hunters is, once again, instructive. Their exceedingly accurate representations of bison, reindeer, mammoths, and other creatures are almost totally unrelated to each other in space. Sometimes they are executed on top of each other. No horizontal or vertical axis is implied in the representation of several animals

*Most theories of art assume that visual imagery *reflects* prevailing space-time concepts. We may entertain the idea, however, that cultural concepts of space and time reflect the stage at which the aesthetic development of most persons in the culture has been arrested.

together. All of the Stone Age hunter's remarkable powers of observation are focused on the representation of his sensory experience. The young child, of course, does not possess the sensory acuity of a Stone Age hunter, but he does share the same idea—or lack of an idea—of space. Still, by the time he is six or seven years old, the child has established a base line or ground plane on which he stands, together presumably, with all the people and things in the universe. He has taken the first step toward acknowledging some sort of community—a common earth, a shared space—among animals, objects, and persons.

The ethical implications are clear. The early-elementary child *has to* provide for the space these others occupy together with himself. He does this not necessarily out of altruism but because a *logic of space* needs to be asserted. The intimate space that he

It is conceivable that many abstract sculptures started their careers as living things which their creators disguised in some way—by simplifying organic shapes, by enlargement or exaggeration, or by forcing the shapes into geometric patterns. We cannot recognize the real origins of the forms, but children often do. In other words, children do not need the identifying details of scale, shape, color, and texture that adults require. When playing with their parents, for example, children easily believe that shoulders and

hips, arms and legs are parts of the landscape: mountains, tree trunks, valleys and canyons, stone outcroppings, and soft, spongy swampland. With these man-made sculptures, however, the imaginative process is reversed and the forms are converted into greatly enlarged specimens of the human anatomy. Clambering over them delights children as a continuation of family romps in bed, on the rug, in the water, or on the sand.

Each child has to make the transition from the familiar safety of his parents' bodies to the

menacing strangeness of the great mechanical and architectural structures outside the nest. Large outdoor sculptures help. They are devices for humanizing the environment. Similar, though less professional, structures can be built by the children themselves—as alternatives to their picture-making and small-scale modeling activities. In that way, a foundation for studying the architectural environment is created, and the school helps the child in his passage from home and family to community and society. ■

Model of playground sculpture by Colin Greenley. (Corcoran Gallery of Art.

Playground equipment (both photos below). (Pepsi-Cola Company.)

Animal sculpture at Henry Street playground (above). (Photo, Ken Wittenberg.)

originally shared with his mother was intruded upon, first by his father, then by brothers or sisters, and now by other children in the school and playground. The child's graphic arrangement of people and things along a ground plane is not only a sign that he recognizes gravity; it also represents his desire to stake out the terrain *they ought to occupy*. Usually, the objects on the base line do not touch; they do not overlap. In effect, the child is saying that if he cannot have all the space there is, then everyone else should stay within the space envelope he assigns them through his drawing and painting activity. For the seven-year-old child, his drawings and paintings, which are now *compositions*, function like the map that accompanies a property deed. Through his work he states, over and over again, who belongs where.

The Socialization of Imagery

The capacity for designating objects through a visual formula, together with the base-line device for ordering objects in two-dimensional space, leads to the ability to arrange and compose pictorially. The older elementary-school child, therefore, has the means of reporting his social and environmental experiences. He can perceive paper, for example, as an arena for action, as a place where he can recount events visually with as much fluency as he recounts them verbally. His artistic expression now deals with collective activities in which he is involved with others—not just representations of himself, in his own surroundings,

with his own possessions. In addition to being a *composer* of pictures, the child is now capable of adapting his imagery to what he believes are the expectations of those who will see his work. Consequently, there may be a difference between work he does only for himself and work done in school, that is, work carried out in connection with teacher-sponsored activities.

The social factor now present in the child's artistic expression is also associated with imitation and copying of the work of others. Imitation in art can be attributed partly to the desire for approval, but it can also be seen as a type of borrowing from a more skillful child for the sake of effective communication generally. The young child does not perceive his expressive work as "Art," with a premium placed on its originality and technical accomplishment. These values, however, do become conscious considerations for preadolescent children. They are aware of differences in representational ability and consequently they copy in order to compete more equally with, or to earn the approval of, their peers.

Unfortunately, some art educators view imitation and copying as a type of moral lapse, as an almost criminal act similar to stealing. They may do so because their own artistic preparation placed an extravagant value on originality. But imitation has always existed in art, and it is certainly not to be suppressed during the preadolescent years. This is the time when children develop a group consciousness based on sex, neighborhood friendships, personality affinities, and so on. They have leaders and heroes whom they consciously imitate in speech, dress, and total life style. Their ego-ideals are forming and these ideals play a role in their socialization—their adaptation to the standards of their peer groups. Teaching strategy, therefore, should focus on the expressive content of the child's work rather than its innovativeness in form or technique.

The aesthetic behavior of the upper-elementary child is also a function of his group consciousness. He is capable of grasping the meaning of the *situations* represented in art whereas he formerly tended to notice only isolated details. In some older children, the contextual quality or the pervasive quality in a work of art begins to be perceived as a factor equal in importance to its subject matter. Particularly because of his steady diet of television and cinema narrative, the child is capable of reading examples of visual art as events in a space and time continuum. That is, he can grasp a situation or perceive a mood in a work of art with reference to what followed, preceded, or surrounded it. I believe television influences children toward the spontaneous perception of contextual fields because its imagery con-

Boy modeling a dragon. (Anita E. Unruh and Florida Art Education Magazine.)

The boy modeling a dragon needs to know what the others are doing while forging ahead on his own work. The artistic activity of every member of the group is part of each child's creative situation. Comparison, competition, imitation, leadership, followership— these are inevitable ingredients in a social setting. Art has always been created with the artist's awareness of onlookers, present in the flesh or imagined in the mind. Moreover, originality is a quasi-mythical virtue greatly overestimated by dealers. If artists working alone are rarely original (in a pure and undefiled sense), how can children placed in a collective atmosphere be expected to keep themselves free of one another's influence? Of course, outright copying ought to be discouraged, but it is unwise to attach moral and ethical significance to the sort of imitation that only reflects admiration. ■

sists of many fragments in motion. They have to be put together continuously if the viewer is going to make sense of the whole. As a result, a contemporary child looking at Georges Seurat's *La Grande Jatte*, for example, uses a different kind of perceptual intelligence from that of the child brought up on still images a few generations ago.

The fact that today's children can read contextual cues, often with incredible sophistication, leads to an appetite for visual complexity such as television satisfies, but their own imagery does not. In other words, the upper-elementary child begins to be dissatisfied with his own visual expression. There are a number of reasons (to be discussed below) for the emergence of a self-critical attitude in older children. The factor mentioned above—habits of perception developed by the electronic media— seems especially significant for today's pre-adolescents. In any event, the child has now arrived at the adolescent terminus of the willful and confident journey he began as an infant. The images he creates, and the images he contemplates, have drawn him into the great world beyond his home and neighborhood. Like a baby thrust out of his mother's womb, he cries.

The Adolescent Conflict with Civilization

Adolescence is prolonged and institutionalized in our culture, and the schools are the chief agent in the process. We do not acknowledge puberty as the time when a person begins to assume adult responsibilities and prerogatives. Instead, we initiate through the schools a lengthy period of serious academic and technical study while the family continues the adolescent's condition of economic and moral dependency. He is clearly caught in a conflict between biological capacities and appetites on the one hand, and social constraints and expectations on the other. This conflict might be described in different terms as a prolonged confrontation: The instinctual drives of the individual confront the accumulated culture of men in what we are pleased to call civilization. There results a long and usually painful process of adaptation—not necessarily one-sided—during which many of the individual's innate drives are blunted, repressed, or redirected.

Sensation versus Representation

So far as artistic imagery is concerned, the adolescent's work now reflects two contending influences: a persistent desire to express with fluency and fidelity his sensory and affective experience, and an increased effort to represent reality as he believes adults see it. But these motives are incompatible. The fluency of a child's creative expression is based on the absence of adult standards of imagery and his inability to engage in serious self-criticism. Both of these (adult standards and self-criticism) make their appearance at puberty. Consequently, the smooth, virtually uninterrupted process of perception, feeling, execution, and aesthetic delight, visible in the art of young children, yields to a considerable amount of agonizing in the creative work of adolescence. Also, the polarization of aesthetic types leads frequently to a loss of confidence on the part of haptic, or non-visual, personalities. The visual types, on the other hand, are somewhat frustrated by their inability to meet their own, now highly developed, standards of optical realism. As both types move further into the adolescent phase, their work tends to rely less on purely sensory experience and more on the *representation of concepts*. This is to say that adolescents now have the capacity to *perceive ideas as if they were things*. That is the only way these concepts can find their way into visual expression.

A certain amount of mischief has been created for art education by the notion that children and adolescents represent what they *know*; their inaccurate or distorted imagery is supposed to reflect ignorance or incomplete conceptual knowledge. But this is an error. What adolescent art reveals is a *new type of consciousness*—both biological and social in origin—a consciousness of *the qualities* of ideas held in the mind. Hitherto, the child was conscious only of the qualities of *things* perceived by his senses. Now, as an adolescent, he can "taste" ideas, so to speak; he becomes aware of their shape and texture.*

*In *Education Through Art*, Herbert Read reminds us (p. 250) that the original meaning of wisdom was the "knowledge of the way or shape of things, and not so much judgment in matters relating to life and conduct." This reinforces the point made in Chapter 4 that a school is a place where we learn to treat ideas like the materials of a sculptor. When a youth becomes "wise," he begins to handle ideas with bravado, as if he knows his way "around" them.

The individual who has passed through adolescence without some impairment of his capacity for dealing directly with his sensations is remarkable—a rare exception. Perhaps van Gogh and Bonnard were persons of this type. But civilization damages such people in other ways—ways that are not necessarily visible, although the damage to van Gogh *was* tragically visible. It is during adolescence that confidence in one's unmediated sensory experience begins to fail. So far as aesthetic feeling is concerned, this failure represents the loss of childhood innocence. It is the price civilization asks every person to pay in return for the ability to deal with the world through ideas and abstract symbols.

Fragmentation of the Self

The desire to imitate adult behavior during adolescence leads to a loss of spontaneity in artistic expression and a general lessening of self-esteem. Many adolescents —the majority of them—conclude that they have no real expressive ability. In the past, teaching strategies for this age group usually entailed the following: (1) providing intensive training in representational and technical skills to overcome the student's disappointment with his expression; (2) designing artistic problems that involve abstract and nonobjective styles so that representational skills will not be required; (3) waiting patiently until the student "outgrows" his disillusionment with himself and his work. Obviously, these strategies are evasive and temporizing. They do not get at the root

BIRD IN FLIGHT (above left), by Robert Vickrey. (Collection Mrs. Louisa d'A. Carpenter; courtesy Midtown Galleries, N.Y.)

PLAYGROUND (above right), by Paul Cadmus. (Collection of Mr. Merrick Lewis; courtesy Midtown Galleries, N.Y.)

GIRL JUMPING ROPE (at right), by Ben Shahn. (Collection James Thrall Soby.)

Iron lung as moon rocket. (The New York Times.)

of adolescent malaise because they are based on a hidden assumption, namely, that the fluency of artistic expression in childhood is a norm from which the adolescent has temporarily deviated.

What in fact has happened? The adolescent has lost the unity, or integrity, of the self that he felt so confidently during childhood. When he was very young, art served to consolidate his notion of selfhood; now it reminds him of a childish dependence on sensory experience and an inability to deal with the world through reason—like an adult. In addition, the emergence of sexual —that is, genital—feelings tends to heighten his awareness of a mind-body split. Adolescents have not yet experienced sex as an intense although temporary unification of personality. Consequently, sexual promptings are felt as an evil diversion of energy and attention away from the unity of the person. *All* of the adolescent appetites and urgings, and especially the sexual, are first encountered as threats to the gratifying harmony of body and mind that prevailed throughout childhood. For this reason, evil is identified with the new appetites instead of the temporary fragmentation of the self,

Kids growing up, coping with their loneliness, improvising fun, discovering dream stuff near at hand: Shahn and Cadmus capture the pathos of urban adolescence— the effort to be graceful when your body is clumsy and your surroundings nondescript. Vickrey shows how a still, private place combined with sunlight and yearning enables a boy's spirit to fly without machinery. The youngsters and the iron lung are really sculptors; they convert one thing into another through fantastic thinking and practical performance —working the bellows of the lung machine. Each of these examples illustrates human imagination trying to transcend the here and now. They show the real raw materials of art—what you work with in addition to paint and paper and paste. ■

which is the real source of dread in adolescence.

We know it is more difficult to be good after puberty than before. The activity of the senses and the appetites is felt more vividly and distinctly as separate from mental life; hence young people easily fall into the habit of regarding their character as divided into upper and lower selves. The various types of uncoordination that the adolescent experiences—physical, emotional, and intellectual—are attributed to the malevolent influence of his lower self, that is, the self identified with the physical life of the senses and the appetites. And, unfortunately, the morbid imaginings of some young people are often reinforced by popular folklore. During this period of crisis, many adolescents develop a distrust of their sensorimotor activity with such intensity that they will not be able to cope adequately, as

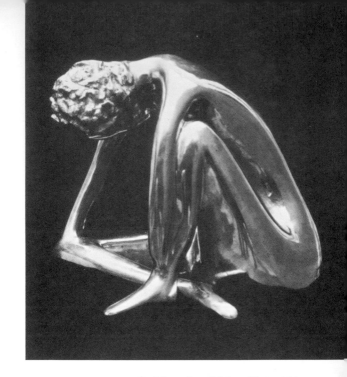

Sculpture by Helaine Blumenfeld. (Chapman Sculpture Gallery.)

GIRL IN CHAIR, by Giacomo Manzù. (Joseph H. Hirshhorn Collection.)

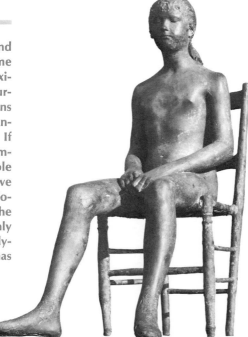

The biological feelings associated with puberty and the introspection that follows range from sensuous anticipation in Pascin, to serene calm in Manzù, to morbid fear in Munch. Because of its intensity or its emotional candor, this art has the power to contend successfully with popular culture for the attention of adolescents. The body curled up or crouching, the knees and elbows felt so prominently, the pudgy flesh that lingers from childhood or the thin chest not yet filled out—these speak to the young about their condition with immediacy, compassion, and dignity. Nudes do not become easily dated; they mirror the anxieties of adolescence without surrendering to the cheap emotions and oversimplified dilemmas manufactured by the mass media. If we wish, we can establish common ground with young people through these visual forms. Or we can pretend the crises of adolescence do not exist, letting the youngsters believe that their only allies live in Nashville and Hollywood, that the world of art has nothing to say to them. ∎

LE REPOS (at left), by Jules Pascin. (Collection Mr. and Mrs. Peter Gilbert.)

THE THINKER (below left), by Karl-Heinz Krause. (Courtesy of the artist and the Grace Borgenicht Gallery, Inc.

PUBERTY (below right), by Edvard Munch. (Nasjonalgalleriet, Oslo.)

adults, with physical and sensuous modes of experience. The moral consequences of separating the intellectual and the sensuous dimensions of personality during adolescence are clear: The individual is prevented from facing life as a whole person. He incurs a burden of guilt as he is inevitably forced to acknowledge the existence of his body and what he may regard as its ugly functions. This guilt becomes self-contempt which is then manifested in behavior designed to provoke punishment.

In primitive or tribal culture, the period of adolescent self-doubt is greatly reduced or nonexistent. But that is because puberty and initiation into adult responsibilities occur at almost the same time. In other words, adolescence is not so clearly institutionalized. We, on the contrary, have a special type of institution—the junior high school—in which students undergoing the severest symptoms of adolescence are segregated. Many of these students would be happier in high schools where they could witness and emulate reasonably attainable models of youthful individuation. As it is, we establish a period during which achieving wholeness and integrity of the self is deliberately delayed.

What are the artistic consequences of adolescent fragmentation? First, the distrust of sensory experience leads to a more geometric type of visual expression in some pupils—an apparent regression back to early, stereotyped representations. Second, both visual and nonvisual personalities tighten up; that is, they make smaller, more detailed images than formerly. They seem to think of images as visual inventories of what they know about objects, persons, and places. Although the adolescent is conscious of the qualities of his concepts, he has difficulty in representing them. Hence he builds up detail with the hope that detail, in the aggregate, will convey the pervasive quality of his experience. But most students do not succeed, and they become discouraged. At this point some teachers provide the adolescent with an artistic device, or a set of devices, to help him out of his difficulties. Such devices are often sophisticated beyond the student's capacity to invent by himself. But the student may nevertheless seize and exploit them, and make them his own. Such a student may well enter preprofessional study of art. Other students will use the teacher's devices mechanically and will achieve a gratifying result. But the result does not testify to anything the student has learned authentically. That is, he has made no discoveries about qualitative form; he is merely following directions. In the absence of his teacher, such a student usually applies devices indiscriminately, unfeelingly. This student has been deceived by his instruction. Sometimes he knows it, sometimes he does not.

It is a tribute to the perceptiveness of most adolescents that they refuse to accept as their own what is clearly the discovery of someone else. (Children, on the other hand, do not make such ethical distinctions.) It is difficult to persuade adolescents that they are expressing the quality of their experience when in fact they are copying a teacher's formula for their experience. Small children copy a great deal. Adolescents borrow from each other, but are reluctant to accept direction from "the enemy"—parents and teachers. Consequently, we do not bring about a unification of the student's personality when we arrange for his "successful" expression. As education, this practice is spurious. We are not dealing with the real roots of the student's "loss of nerve." As teachers, we have to distinguish between the training of craftsmen and the liberal education of young people in our kind of culture. That is why upper-elementary and junior-high-school art education programs must devote increasing amounts of time to the aesthetic behavior of students.

What role does aesthetic behavior perform in the fragmented existence of the early adolescent? It is clearly a mode of integration. Everyone knows that adolescents become intensely involved in music, dance, cinema, theater, and popular and serious literature. Their interest in the visual arts—especially contemporary art—is very keen and often highly discriminating. They are obviously looking for modes of activity that can overcome their feelings of fragmentation. It is natural and logical, then, that they will seize upon the arts—that is, aesthetic experience—as a mode of personal integration. We must, therefore, examine the aesthetic integration of the self during adolescence, with special reference to its ethical consequences.

Cultural Integration of the Self

Adolescents, of course, do not know or say they are seeking aesthetic integration. But their hunger for qualitative experience is very intense. They are looking for embodiments of vivid feeling—the type of experience that can echo the stressful character of their inner lives. It is a mistake, however, to conclude that adolescents are interested merely in thrills and excitement. The pursuit of excitement is a symptom of the *failure* to find aesthetic resolutions for their problems of personal fragmentation. Family life and school studies do not as a rule satisfy their strong desire to experience vivid emotions in connection with "real" life. Consequently, the adolescent typically seeks it symbolically through the mass media.

Here we can advance the idea that art serves as a vicarious substitute for the genuine and intense involvement with life that is withheld from adolescents by our culture. To be sure, that is not the role of art for all young people, but it does serve such a purpose for most of them. They perceive the reluctance of society to admit them as full-fledged members. They see in art and the mass media a mode of experience that is both a preparation for maturity and an arena for the immediate exercise of their senses and emotions. This would explain the teenager's exaggerated response (according to adult sensibility) to singers and instrumentalists whose performance stresses powerful expression of basic emotions through unsubtle musical styles.*

At the adolescent stage of personal development, the so-called generation gap makes itself felt. That is, the differences between adult and adolescent sensibility serve to accent comprehensive differences in life style. The same popular art forms function differently for fathers and sons, mothers and daughters. It is difficult for adults to understand the role performed by aesthetic emotion in the psychic economy of a young person. Similarly, adolescents cannot understand parental indifference to experiences they perceive as almost painfully beautiful. Obviously, there are powerful biological as well as cultural factors at work in the aesthetic life of the adolescent. Through art, the culture attempts to compensate its youth for having delayed their maturity beyond the time of their greatest physical strength, emotional intensity, and sexual desire.

*I realize that the Beatles have appealed very successfully to teenagers while using quite sophisticated musical forms; but this appeal *followed* their initial acceptance, which was based on a blend of simple American styles derived from Afro-American and Appalachian folk traditions.

Here we can discuss two differing conceptions of the meaning of culture and the way they affect schooling: For adults, culture is the totality of values in which they have confidence and which they wish to see transmitted to the young; for adolescents, it is a collection of art forms that appear alive or dead, valuable or useless, for the requirements of self-integration. Ideally, the same works of art can serve both purposes. In fact, adolescence has its own distinctive subculture. School curricula often try to include the best (most acceptable?) features of the adolescent subculture. However, the popular media of entertainment, which play a central role in creating the culture of adolescence, change too quickly for the school culture to keep apace. Consequently, students are frequently indifferent to the form and content of secondary school programs in art, music, drama, and literature. These programs are not truly compensatory for the adolescent so far as his delayed maturity is concerned. He finds himself compelled to deal with symbolic forms that seem almost totally removed by style, medium, or history from his urgent concerns about how to be a man or a woman.

Adolescence heralds the arrival of social concern, here expressed in two ways. The pictorial treatment of the peace marcher is essentially descriptive, neutral; it presents a painterly approach to a contemporary subject. But the lettering on the signs jumps out of the composition; from a visual standpoint, it spoils the picture. Clearly, the young artist feels strongly about the great issues of war and peace, but he does not trust his skill as a painter (which is quite adequate) to convey the intensity of his feelings. This is a problem that the professional artists of our time have also encountered; their artistic language seems to them insufficient for expressing the emotions they experience in connection with contemporary life. And they are right. The Napoleonic invasion of Spain motivated the magnificent "Disasters of War" etchings of Goya. The Nazi bombing of a Spanish town

WARS BRING BLOOD. (New York City Public Schools Bureau of Art.)

HIPPIES. (Clarke County Public Schools, Georgia.)

led to Picasso's "Guernica." But the wars and social catastrophes of recent years have not found expression in comparable monuments of visual art.

The hippie painting exemplifies the theme of adolescent infatuation with style. The couple in the picture are not authentic hippies; they wear costumes—including dark glasses, beard, and long hair —that enable them to participate in the life of a style, a style that is colorful, exotic, and controversial, but fundamentally harmless. A style can support the reputation for nonconformity at the same time that it constitutes a uniform. It is a remarkably convenient social device. The painting attends to standardized details of costume more than individual traits of personality. The peace marcher, too, does not emerge as an individual. In both pictures, people are identified by a pattern of highly visible behavior. ■

We can see that the school sincerely wishes to devote the junior and senior high school years to the work of adolescent self-integration. Moreover, the school correctly perceives study of the arts and humanities as the best way to do the job. But this crucial objective of the school is pre-empted by popular culture. The media of popular culture are more fascinating than the media of school arts programs.

How, then, can schooling participate effectively in the self-integration of the adolescent?

First, it can end the practice of employing the educational techniques used in the early elementary grades during and beyond the stage of puberty. That is, the upper-elementary program can begin to shift its emphasis from artistic performance to critical appreciation. Second, the types of literature, music, and art that are studied in school can include a substantial amount of contemporary subject matter. Especially when working with poor children, it is essential to select thematic materials that reflect at least some elements of their everyday experience. Third, teachers can build connections, wherever possible, between the themes and styles of popular culture and their analogs in the "official" culture of the school curriculum—the culture derived from the world of history and scholarship. In this way, school learning will cooperate with popular culture instead of competing with it. The adolescent will then have a better opportunity to experience the unity of learning and vivid perception that the school should provide.

The Ethics of Art Appreciation

For modern teenagers, one of the most crucial concerns of life revolves around the question of what to like. Adolescents classify each other by what they "go for." Along with their strong drives toward conformity, there is a concomitant tendency to condemn those who do not share their tastes and life style. The adolescent finds it difficult to believe that someone who prefers Lawrence Welk on the one hand or J. S. Bach on the other is entirely normal.

If you think of adolescence as a term of apprenticeship in the business of acting grown up, then you can see the beginnings of adult social and ethical practices in teenage aesthetic behavior. For example, art can be used as a device for sorting out people. Teenagers like to be exclusive: Whom shall they exclude? On what grounds? If they dislike certain persons on dishonorable grounds, how can those grounds be rationalized?

Aesthetic factors constitute the basis for most types of adolescent social discrimination—their decisions about which traits of a person qualify him for inclusion in a gang or a clique. English gentlemen are said to have a similar, more or less intuitive feeling about whether or not a man is "clubbable." Wherever it occurs, snobbism can be subtle or crude; but it relies ultimately on the perception of a person's style. Many faults will be forgiven, when playing the vicious games of teenage social life, provided that an individual exhibits certain desired qualities of personal style. Adolescents, therefore, are avid students of style, for they realize that their social objectives are crucially dependent on whether they can perceive style qualities and can successfully incorporate them in their behavior.

Because of their social striving, adolescents have a more vivid conception of the connections between art and life than professors who conduct experiments in psychological aesthetics. Studies of aesthetic preference in teenagers are frequently confined to measuring student ability to distinguish between masterpieces and mediocre works of art (the distinctions having been established in advance by "experts"). Such studies seem to be based on the belief that the goal of art appreciation is to learn what it is correct to prefer—an extraordinarily naive assumption.* Adolescents do not expect to gain status among their peers by learning to

*This assumption *does* make sense for those élites whose preferences in art are realistically related to decisions to purchase art commodities which will be used for investment or for enhancing one's personal environment. Carol Anne Davis describes a typical study of this type as follows: "Studies by Irvin L. Child deal also with preferences for good or poor works of art. Child has utilized the procedure of selecting works of art through a system of calling upon art experts (those with knowledge in the field of art) to make such selections. The works were paired (good and poor) and shown as slides to undergraduate students. Each student was to select the slide he preferred. The results of these selections, according to whether or not there was agreement with the art experts, gave an indication of the aesthetic sensitivity of the students." "A Study of Controlled Attention to Aesthetic Qualities in Works of Art by Ninth-Grade Students of Differing Socioeconomic Environments," *Studies in Art Education,* vol. 10, no. 3, Spring 1969, pp. 51–52. Miss Davis cited the study by I. L. Child, "Personal Preferences as an Expression of Esthetic Sensitivity," *Journal of Personality,* XXX, 1962, pp. 496–512.

recognize masterpieces. Instead, they want art to help them develop skills in the perception of qualities useful in the games of life; they need art to make them aware of the range of feelings it is possible to have; finally, they need art so they can study it together and thereby have the opportunity to display their *styles of appreciation* to one another.

During adolescence, the individual is quite consciously building the materials of the self. He identifies himself very strongly with a pattern of aesthetic preference, that is, a combination of preferred styles in eating, dress, speech, posture, and attention to the arts and the mass media. The principal ethical outcome of this aesthetic identification is intolerance of alternative patterns. The source of much racial and ethnic antagonism in our culture may well lie in patterned aesthetic intolerance established during adolescence. The processes of cultural exploration that the teenager needs in order to establish his self-identity are at the same time the cause of his profound distaste for persons or groups he associates with alternative styles of aesthetic behavior. As the adolescent becomes more completely individuated, his patterned aesthetic preferences are felt so deeply as to seem instinctive. Aesthetics then becomes the source of invidious distinctions that have the potential for tearing apart our social fabric. Moreover, the development of invidious aesthetic and ethical distinctions during adolescence appears to be virtually inevitable in our culture. Clearly, schooling should strive to make that development less inevitable.

Overcoming Cultural Invidiousness

We know that adolescents relate to each other, imitatively or disdainfully, on the basis of aesthetic qualities—qualities of style that they perceive in each other's behavior. How is schooling involved in this process? First, the school provides an arena for the significant display of social behaviors. Second, through its teachers and rules of conduct the school advocates an official sort of life style—a model to imitate or rebel against. Third, the school provides an opportunity to examine alternate life styles through the study of symbolic forms in the arts and humanities. How can these activities generate a sense of community among adolescents rather than feelings of exclusiveness and mutual contempt?

First, the adolescent needs to learn that liking something does not necessarily imply a corresponding dislike of something else. We can enjoy an experience for its own qualities and meanings. We do not need the assurance that our pleasures and interests are better, rarer, or more costly than the pleasures of others. Second, many interests can be shared even by people who do not have similar life styles. This sharing of interests and meanings often takes place in the presence of significant works of art because such works rely more often on human similarity than human difference.* Third, teachers should try to generate a classroom

*See Theodore M. Greene, *The Arts and the Art of Criticism*, Princeton Univ. Press, 1940, pp. 461–467. I take Professor Greene's discussion of "breadth" as one of the preconditions of artistic greatness to be a confirmation of this point.

environment in which a premium is placed on the creation as well as the recognition of aesthetic qualities and values. In other words, students should be encouraged to compete in the discovery of new meanings by learning to generate original contexts for familiar events. This final point raises questions about teaching strategy—questions that are discussed more thoroughly in Chapter 8, *The New Creative Situation*. Here I can try to show some of the connections between teaching strategy and the aesthetic and ethical development of adolescents.

Teenagers bring to the school a disposition toward invidiousness and competitiveness—a disposition encouraged by the commercial culture that has invaded their home and community life. In addition, the development of an integrated personality during adolescence predisposes the individual toward a heightened awareness of differences in life style especially as it affects patterns of consumption. Unfortunately, the culture of the school often reinforces these tendencies. The individual teacher, however, can function as a countervailing influence. He does so by encouraging students to relate to aesthetic values as if they—the students—were responsible for creating them instead of choosing among them. "Selecting values" describes the orientation of a consumer. A consumer orientation implies that we have to choose what we like from the array of values already determined by a particular market. A productive or creative orientation implies that we can influence, shape, or invent the values we wish to enjoy. The sense of community among young people, indeed, begins with the recognition that what they have in common is creative capacity or freedom with respect to values. It is not so much freedom to choose, but freedom to make.

So far as aesthetic and ethical development is concerned, our main teaching error has consisted of emphasizing the problem of choosing among the allegedly fixed values presented by works of art. Instead, the teacher can stress the individual's responsibility for creating these values in cooperation with the formal qualities visible in the works of art he studies. In other words, the student should learn that we do not admire someone because of what he likes; we admire him because of what he can make or do with what he likes.

Invidious feelings are generated among adolescents because they are encouraged by their culture to compete with each other as consumers of values. Unfortunately, schooling often encourages the process by emphasizing the role of students as passive perceivers and learners. Aesthetic education is subject to the same failing to the extent that teachers regard appreciation as a passive mode while only performance is recognized as a creative mode. If most students are regarded as choosers and consumers of values, they will tend to invest their creative freedom in the discovery or manufacture of spurious differences among themselves. This is to say that patterns of consumption are simply insufficient as a foundation for classifying human beings in some ethically meaningful sense—especially in a society that has not yet succeeded in distributing its wealth equitably. Only creative capacity and achievement constitute a defensible ground for classifying human beings significantly,

and in this respect almost all personalities possess some endowment. Of course, our society operating through its schools must help develop that endowment. Then the real or alleged differences among human subgroups will become irrelevant; it would be better to attend to individual creative achievement than speculate about collective potential. The interest in *potential* values is what the market exploits. What school pupils need, however, is the opportunity to demonstrate their individual capacity to generate real values. That will arm them against our culture's singular pathology—building false distinctions where real differences hardly exist.

Love and Learning

Love is rarely discussed in studies of education and yet it is what most of us are concerned about, what all of us need, and what every community must attract to itself no matter how large or small and no matter what the purpose of its existence. Obviously, I am not referring solely to erotic love, although that form of love constitutes a powerful motive in human affairs and is therefore never very far from what is planned and done in education. We must consider the love that children feel for their teachers and for each other; the capacity for affection that we hope students will possess in full measure as married adults; the generous love that the citizen feels for his civilization and its distinctive values; and, finally, the love of learning that motivates scholars and scientists—a special sort of passion that nevertheless needs to be cultivated in the schools of any modern society intent on survival.

Love has to be a dimension of everything that education means and does because of the crucial role it plays in bringing about wholeness of human character. Whether love is an instinct or a type of spiritual reaching out, it is nevertheless the force that generates all human effort, especially educational effort, striving always to bring about oneness among the things it touches. The love between persons is the best available model for the unity we seek between learners and knowledge, between artists and art, between the individual and the materials of his self. We have to think about schooling as an enterprise established for the purpose of seeking culminations in manifold forms of love—the love of the citizen, the artist, the scholar, the parent, and the husband or wife. If love embarrasses us, then our work as teachers or students will inevitably be inauthentic and artificial; we shall find ourselves in the position of trying to bring about enthusiasm for learning and commitment for values without possessing any motive force that can effectively manage the task. Indeed, if love is not a ponderable factor in the work of education, I am convinced that very little learning of value can be expected to take place.

The Eros of Learning

In Greek mythology, Eros was regarded as somewhat irresponsible. The son of the love goddess, Aphrodite, and Hermes, he

LOVE, by Robert Indiana. (Multiples, Inc.)

Children's love mural. (Photo, Ken Wittenberg.)

Plexiglass love box. (The New York Times Studio.)

symbolized a type of sexual passion that was thought to be destructive of orderly social relations. For us, too, erotic love is less respectable than the kinds of love that more obviously bind together the diverse personalities, the varying conditions, and the uneven talents and energies of the individuals constituting a community. Nevertheless, Eros is inevitably present as a factor in human affairs and especially as a source and catalyst of energy in the lives of the children and adolescents undergoing schooling. The ethical dimension of their erotic natures has already been discussed. Here I wish to show how Eros plays a role in their encounter with ideas.

Erotic drives that manifest themselves in the search for pleasure or in the effort to preserve and reproduce the self are obliged by civilization to come to terms with a wide variety of symbolic and cultural materials. These materials, in the form of the organized subjects we normally study in schools, do

Our civilization's difficulties with love are ironically portrayed by two geometrical devices and a children's mural. Robert Indiana has simply constructed sharp-edged metal letters for the word "love," which he breaks in the middle. Then, by tilting the "O" he fastens our attention on the negative shapes between the letters—antiseptic spaces that say nothing about warmth or affection. Clearly, he is offering us a commercial image. Neal Small has built a pyramidal container for photographs and rested it on a platform where "love" floats in bright pink letters. The human content lies in the photographs of people taken with a mechanical device. But the object constructed by the artist is substantially devoid of any clearly identifiable feeling— if we exclude the letters and their connotations. The cost of the item is $1000.

The children's mural is typical except that it is painted on a cinder block wall in an anonymous part of a city. Someone has painted in the word "love" with the significant addition "me." The youngsters have made the usual inventory of their surroundings. They are in the mural and they can stand off from it and see that they are part of the place it represents. The place, too, is part of them. It is as if someone then said, "It's not a great place, and maybe I don't amount to much . . . but love me anyway." ■

not so much oppose or blunt love as they beguile it with the promise of richer fulfillments if present pleasures are postponed. Even the child who has not yet arrived at genital expression of his longings is partly governed by the erotic component of his personality; and he, too, finds himself persuaded by civilization to forego immediate gratifications in the interest of earning greater pleasures later on. Consequently, there must be in every encounter with the signs and symbols of culture a residual fund of erotic energy—not a neutral or ambiguous kind of energy like the voltage carried by household current—but an energy whose natural destination is something other than the recognition of facts and logical relationships. Whenever we are engaged in the effort to learn or to know, therefore, we participate in an effort partly conditioned by erotic longing—a longing that seeks communion with another person or thing in order to fulfill its own nature. From the standpoint of education, this means that the *process* of learning an idea or acquiring an attitude or skill must inevitably reflect some of the features of the learner's psychosexual motivation and purpose. That is, in coming to know an idea, we try to do with it what we would do with someone or something we love.

So far as the erotic component of learning is concerned, is there a radical difference between our coming to know ideas and things and our coming to know persons or each other? That is one of the fundamental questions raised by Martin Buber's immensely important little book, *Between*

Man and Man. According to Buber, it is possible to have what he calls an I-Thou relationship with forms and ideas as well as with persons. Furthermore, one can have an I-It relationship with persons as well as things. The determining factor in these relationships is not the person or form we want to know or understand, it is the *attitude* with which we encounter that person, idea, or form. To the extent that we encounter persons and things with an attitude of openness, and to the extent that we respond to them with the fullness of our being, we establish an I-Thou relation. But if we regard persons and things as objects to be used or controlled, as permanently *other* from us because we observe them and our reactions to them from a distance—then we estrange ourselves from virtually everything valuable in their reality and we have only an I-It relationship with that reality.

It should be clear that the attitude of openness toward persons and things is a product of the whole or integrated personality that has been described earlier as the foundation of healthy character. Moreover, wholeness and openness are preconditions for the capacity to love and be loved. Now what is the connection between capacity for love and ability to learn?

You can get a glimpse of the interdependence of love and learning if you consider the attitudes it is possible to have toward an idea: You can observe an idea, describe it from a distance, learn its name, use it to practical advantage, and even congratulate yourself on your intellectual mastery of it; or you can identify with that idea, including it within yourself and letting it interact with the other elements of your being. Thus you cause an idea to become part of yourself, organizing yourself in and around it. The first attitude toward an idea embodies an I-It relation; the distance between the knower and what he knows becomes permanent. It is the kind of relationship to knowledge that sets mastery or control of reality over the completion and wholeness of the self. The latter attitude toward an idea embodies an I-Thou relation. It is a loving relation; it virtually eliminates the distance between the knower and the known. Hopefully, it represents the sort of relation that teachers have toward people and ideas and one they are anxious to instill in pupils. Indeed, the teachers children most admire are those whose outward manner and appearance seem to have resulted from their personal integration around a single, vividly perceived quality. Their pupils wish they could emulate such persons—not necessarily to know what they know, but to possess their wholeness and unity of being. Most people strive to exhibit in their own character and bearing a similar correspondence between the public person—the one who is heard and observed—and the private self—the one who is known and understood.

When learning means the ability to recognize, store, and recall information, it can be greatly advanced by machines—not persons —and love has little to do with it. When learning means the reintegration of the self through successive encounters with ideas, forms and pervasive qualities, love is its essential ingredient. In effect, love determines what is worth learning by governing what a person can incorporate into himself and thus truly know of another person or thing. The purely cognitive requirements of institutions and bureaucracies can be satisfied by the schools. But the process rarely entails a learner's self-transformation. So long as cognitive materials are organized from outside the span of a child's relationships, his learning will reflect the structure of institutionalized knowledge rather than personally felt longing. Authentic learning, then, has its source in the longing of a self to overcome the isolation that the human condition imposes on us—after we are born and before we die. Learning is joining the self with an other.

Art and Eros

Art, like erotic energy, also participates in the process of learning and maturing, of becoming a person. But to understand this process, we must set aside the rather restricted notion of art that many persons have, namely, that it is only a matter of drawing or painting or modeling. We should try to think of art, in the present context, as an instrument or tool for dealing with human situations that call for expression. In the course of growing up there are thousands of events and experiences, whose meaning we want to share. It is not a matter of exceptional generosity or lack of self-control that makes children want to divulge their experiences; being human, they *have to share*, they cannot *help* sharing, the meanings of their lives. It is the human need

THE KISS (right), by Edvard Munch. (Sarah Campbell Blaffer Foundation, Houston.)

Mother and child (below), drawing by a French youngster. (International Child Art Center, San Francisco.)

The love of mother and child and the love of lovers: Do they offer any kind of model for our work as teachers and learners? In the French work, the mother's body envelops the child as it did before he was born. He lies in his horizontal position, dependent but secure. The mother, aligned on a vertical axis, is fiercely alert, totally committed to protection and love.

According to the geometry of this picture, the child is separate from the mother, but she resists the separation and tries to retain him as part of her body.

In the Munch image, man and woman lose their distinct identities: A strong contour describes the single form resulting from the merger of their formerly separate persons. Theirs is the unity of Eros to communicate with other people that is the foundation of art in education, not the need to use art materials that happen to be furnished by school systems.

Sharing and exchanging the contents of their lives is what helps children grow into mature social beings who can function normally in communities, make friends, work productively, and develop confidence in their powers of human understanding and expression. This sharing and exchanging takes many forms—of physical acting out, or theater and dance; of vocal and rhythmic gesture, or music; of spoken and written words, or literature; of graphic and plastic image-making, or art. From a human and educational standpoint, it is not correct to say that the individual sets out to create music, art or literature; rather, he is moved or impelled to say something and art is the result. Consequently, when we plan the education of children, it is a mistake to divide their instruction and hence their expressive lives into separate categories called art, music, literature, and so on. Not only is this

contrary to the way children think about the sharing of their experience, it is also contrary to the way artists—especially today— approach their work. At present, artists combine media of expression; they are reluctant to recognize boundaries between painting and sculpture, between two- and three-dimensional expression, between music and theater and opera and cinema and architecture and sculpture and industrial design. Whether he knows it or not, today's artist seems to be seeking the tribal artist's freedom of access to all media and types of expression. Obviously, the need to make a statement, to share experience, to evoke a response, takes precedence over the "rules" about categories of artistic expression.

The tribal experience of man has absorbed by far the greater portion of his time on earth. And the education of children corresponds in many ways to man's prehistoric and tribal experience up to and including the Neolithic Revolution. Man's subsequent agrarian and industrial experience occupies much more of *written* his-

---

—a temporary unity at best, but still the goal of endless human striving. According to Munch, the price of erotic union—and human solidarity, too—is paid in loss of selfhood.

Children, not long separated from their parents' bodies, do not fully realize their aloneness. When they do, much of their energy is devoted to overcoming their feel-

ings of fragmentation and recovering the sense of wholeness they remember and yearn for. Human culture is the symbolic substitute we offer them. It is not the same as being with the mother or uniting with another person in physical love. But learning offers wholeness nevertheless— the union of mind with the entire cosmos. That is why all men

felt a temporary sense of self-transcendence as astronauts from this planet walked on the moon. When we learn to see the human adventure whole, we increase our powers of identification; we learn to feel the lives of all men in our own existence. It is very much like the sense of security felt by a child who loves and knows he is loved in return. ■

tory, but we should not conclude that mankind invented classical civilization or the Renaissance, with their infinitely complex modes of behavior and expression, suddenly and without long and extensive preparation. That is, we should not start the education of children by training them to behave like the full-blown products of high civilization. Flourishing ages of civilization are preceded by patient ages of cultural incubation. Similarly, the sophisticated achievement of the mature artist is preceded by slow and often painful mastery of the tools of his artistic language or languages. So far as education is concerned, this means that we must devote our principal efforts in elementary schools to the task of helping children to become human and to master the human tools of communication and expression. Hence, I repeat the definition of art given earlier: It is a tool for dealing with human situations that seem to call for public expression. As an expressive and communicative instrument, art fits perfectly into the agenda of elementary education. But as a highly differentiated and specialized mode of behavior it belongs more properly to secondary and professional schooling.

The distinction between elementary and secondary education is in many ways the distinction between primitive and civilized life, although the analogy must not be pushed too far. But it is safe to say that primitive or tribal life is often characterized by free and open sharing of experiences and possessions, with only rudimentary division of labor and specialization of occupations. If primitive life corresponds to the elemen-

tary stage of the incubation of humanity, then elementary schooling ought to be guided by those features of tribal experience that have had so much to do with the development of man in general and of children in particular. Art is certainly integral to all other phases of tribal existence. Can we not draw the implications of this fact for the purposes of organized schooling? Art—meaning here all forms of human creativity and communication—is the natural expression of Eros in children. It is their generalized mode of giving and seeking love before they have discovered the principles of specialization and division of labor as applied to the realm of the erotic. We can make it possible in schools for children to practice all or any of the arts spontaneously—not merely as exercises in mastery of technique, but as adventures in extending the self, combining and exchanging it with the selves of others.

Freedom and Maturity

The attainment of manhood in Western culture is at the present time a difficult task. Manhood is no longer, if it ever was, the inevitable consequence of physical maturation and the passage of years. Now it is beset by perils from the changing family structure, the changing character of work, alienation from long-accepted values, the insurgence of women into formerly male enclaves, and the institution of almost impossibly high standards in many of the activities and professions men customarily practice. Education from kindergarten through the university endeavors to foster the development of manhood but it also contributes to the stresses and strains on the structure of male maturity. If only because most teachers are women at a time when a boy needs male models for identification and emulation, the school adds to the burden of attaining the appearance and actuality of manhood. Girls suffer indirectly but just as severely because they cannot become women unless boys become men.

From outside the school, young people are profoundly influenced by the patterns of popular culture, most of which hold up dubious models of adult performance from the standpoint of either an honest representation of reality or the portrayal of idealized versions of maturity. Consequently, the capacity for the responsible enjoyment of freedom is exceedingly difficult to develop. If freedom means personal autonomy, the ability to make decisions, unrestrainedly, on the basis of rational consideration of alternative styles of living, then it is also a product of moral and aesthetic education. Realistic life styles have to be encountered and studied *somewhere* if the prospective adult is to function adequately in a world of complex decision-making, conflicting value patterns, and spuriously attractive life options.

The development of maturity has always faced perils; and one way of dealing with them educationally has been to isolate the school, its personnel, and its programs from the mainstream of contemporary life. Presumably the individual is better equipped to cope with adult responsibilities if he prepares for them in an artificially simplified environment. Even if there were some merit in such an approach to education, however, it would not be practicable today. Physical isolation no longer isolates. Our media of communication are too cheap, too ubiquitous, too tempting to be shut out or long resisted. Consequently, it must be taken as an axiom that *all education, whatever its location, purpose or level, takes place in an environment conditioned by the mass media of communication.* Moreover, education is in many instances a competitor of the media. For most children and adolescents, the mass media constitute the first and primary mode of learning; schooling is second and secondary. Presently, schools must decide whether to ignore the media, succumb to the media, cooperate with the media, or resist the media as a countervailing force.

The mass media of communication influence the development of character and the fact of freedom more than any other institution in our society. Only manhood—considered now as the quality of maturity in men *and* women—can respond vigorously and autonomously to the media and the environment they create. Anything less than manhood will be swallowed up in the ocean of conformity the media can create. Intelligent and mature persons, on the other hand, have the capacity to convert the media into the greatest source of community and the most powerful force for cultural freedom the world has ever known.

We return, then, to the schools as the place where manhood can be nurtured, where the contents of the various media can be confronted honestly as the primary source of experience which, in fact, they are. The schools have to fashion men and women who are in the habit of choosing their own thoughts, forming their own inferences, making their own values, expressing their own feelings. This work the school can now do more effectively than ever before because, ironically, the media liberate the school from its age-long task of dispensing information. It is no longer justifiable to expend time and energy in schools learning data that are stored in textbooks or easily retrievable through information-storage systems, or continuously and directly fed to pupils (in updated versions) by the mass media themselves. *By building* on the media, the school can immediately transcend its difficulties incurred by functioning as if the media were not there.

Maturity is a matter of poise, inner poise.

An outward poise, uninformed by a mind prepared to act for itself and for others, is only arrogance. The kind of school that simulates poise by deliberately cultivating confident manners is really cultivating arrogance and in the crises and dilemmas of a free society arrogance does not serve well. To be genuine, poise must grow out of the manly feeling of having met, understood, and honorably dealt with one's experience. Ultimately, then, poise is an attitude toward experience and it is gained when the individual feels himself adequate to deal with unknown possibilities because his education has been a succession of transactions with possibilities, qualities, meanings, forms, and events. Such an individual—the truly poised individual—has matured because of his schooling rather than in spite of it. He has the capacity for enjoying freedom.

PART THREE

The
Creativity
of Children

The most important point to make about the art of children is that it is created independently of adults. Children make art naturally and spontaneously with manufactured or improvised materials, indoors or outdoors, for themselves or for others, at home or in school. It would be difficult to prevent children from creating art, about as difficult as preventing them from singing or dancing. Art is unlike conventional subjects—subjects that the child is unlikely to learn without formal instruction. You need to understand this point at the very beginning: Art is not a subject like other subjects; it is a way of learning. For that reason it is possible to speak of something called art education.

Art education is a total, a comprehensive, approach to teaching and learning. Its aims are not different from, but the same as, the aims of the rest of the curriculum; but these aims are pursued with different tools and by different methods. The resources available to the art educator include the entire history of art, art appreciation and criticism, and the artistic activity of children. In the elementary grades especially, children's artistic activity is so rich and free and easily stimulated that much of art education in these grades is taken up with child art. But we should not imagine that drawing, painting, modeling, constructing, and print-making are, or ought to be, the only art-educational activities in the elementary school. Neither should we believe that, as art educators, our objective is the training of artists. Our objective is the development of each youngster into a fully human person. Whatever else art may be for the museum curator, the collector or connoisseur, the art journalist, the historian, the dealer, or the artist—for teachers it is a tool, an instrument for doing a better job of liberal and humane education.

These preliminary remarks are intended to introduce the specifically educational context in which you, as a teacher, must deal with child art. After all, there are other contexts in which child art is a feature: the psychiatric context in which the emotional difficulties of children are diagnosed; the therapeutic context in which ill or handicapped children create art to recover their health; the recreational context in which children at camps and clubs use art to occupy their leisure time; the professional context in which artistically gifted children prepare themselves for careers in the arts. In these and other contexts, child art is created in connection with specially defined objectives. Often such objectives are similar to, or overlap with, the objectives of art education in the elementary school. Often they do not. Consequently, it is especially important that the elementary teacher not confuse humanistic objectives with those of diagnosis, therapy, recreation, or professionalism, since in every case, there are other institutions and other professionals better organized and trained to carry out those functions.

If children create art spontaneously, and without instruction, why is it necessary to devote time in the classroom to what they would do by themselves? The answer to this question is very complex and will be taken up in detail in the following chapters. Here it is necessary to say only that some art educators do not have a very clear idea about why this question is raised. They are often content to repeat slogans about the psychological benefits of self-expression, creativity, experimentation with real materials, and so on, without having distinct conceptions of what these phrases mean operationally—especially for the child in the classroom. As a result, other teachers, and some parents and administrators, become skeptical about the value of the whole realm of art education. They know that art activity is somehow a good thing; they know children enjoy it; they know a good school should have child art work on display in its halls and classrooms; they admire the art teacher who can manage a classroom in which several art activities take place at once; they realize that the one-to-one instruction of the art teacher is valuable and unique. Nevertheless, it is often difficult for them to distinguish between real learning through art and rather aimless play with materials.

Learning—whether through artistic or any sort of activity—takes place inside the learner. Overt behavior, spoken and written language, tests and measurements—these constitute only external signs of learning that is alleged to have taken place within an individual. Art educators claim that artistic products (as well as artistic processes) also exhibit evidence of learning or growth in a variety of dimensions. But one must know how to interpret and evaluate such evidence of learning. Moreover, it must be demonstrated theoretically (and empirically, if possible) that changes in artistic production reflect changes within the individual that can justifiably be called growth. If we can do so, then we can properly point to the evidence of child art as evidence of the intellectual, social, and emotional growth that elementary schooling seeks.

In view of the educational questions raised by children's artistic activity—in or out of the school—it would be useful to examine the theories that endeavor to account for child art. Therefore, I shall attempt to summarize the most common and influential explanations of the artistic expression of children. You ought to know these theories since they often constitute the foundation of curriculum construction and teaching method. After this summary of theory, we will see why we require a new theory embracing many types of artistic and aesthetic activity in the education of children. Finally, and with the utmost fear and trembling, I should like to advance what I call "a humanistic theory of art education."

Any theory of child art has to account for the fact that children's drawings do not closely resemble what we see. And this problem raises many questions: Does child art resemble what *children* see? Does child art reflect difficulties in handling materials such as crayons and paint? Does it reflect incomplete neuromuscular development and coordination? Does child art reflect immature powers of thinking and knowing? Do a child's sensory perceptions explain his forms of representation? Are his representational efforts always adequate for his intentions or for the content of his perceptions? And finally, is it certain that children attempt to *represent* their optical experience? Perhaps they prefer to *invent* forms which they afterward claim are replications of what is out there to see.

These are some of the fundamental questions that theories of child art try to answer. You can see that psychologists and others interested in the nature of human thinking and perceiving find these questions fascinating.* Aestheticians and philosophers of art are also concerned, because insight into the nature of child art activity would presumably throw light on the work of mature artists.

*For an early and still useful statement about the theory of child art, with an excellent chapter on its connection to folk and primitive art, see Helga Eng, *The Psychology of Children's Drawings: From the First Stroke to the Coloured Drawing*, Harcourt, Brace, 1931. Miss Eng makes the following interesting statement: "The unquestioned parallels which can be shown between the drawing of primitive man and that of children—formalism, transparency, turning-over, spacelessness, want of synthesis—are based on features common to the psyche of the child and primitive man, on the want of firm voluntary attention, of penetrating analysis and higher synthesis, on the weakness of the power of abstraction and of logical and realistic thinking. When we find these features of children's drawings repeated again in primitive art, we may conclude that their executants were similar in their psychic make-up" pp. 213–214. Helga Eng's statement confirms the view expressed here in earlier chapters that the study of tribal or primitive art is an essential prerequisite for understanding child art. Certainly it is crucial for theorizing about child art.

6

The Theory of Child Art

The educator is concerned with these questions because of his interest in the systematic growth of school children and in the normal parameters of child behavior: If the child's perceiving, thinking, feeling, and representational activity can be understood, perhaps that understanding can be applied for the purpose of deliberately organizing teaching and learning.

Cognitive Theory

Cognitive, or intellectual, theories of art are best described in the common observation that a child draws or represents what "he knows" rather than what he sees. Distortions of size and shape in a child's art are presumably due to lack of knowledge or inadequate concept development about the "correct" or "real" sizes and shapes of things. It is assumed that correct knowledge about reality is the basis of the accurate representation of reality in art. Increased experience with the world will enable the child to modify his faulty or inadequate early conceptions of things so that they are brought more into line with objective reality. According to such theories, the child's eyesight is as good as that of a healthy adult. And his motor control is not a serious handicap in the representation of his experience. In other words, there is no optical or physiological reason for his distortions or oversimplifications in artistic representation. His retinal images are the same as an adult's. But in the act of representing what he sees or recalls, the child does not trust his sense data. He remembers or thinks mainly about the name of what he is representing. He responds only to an intellectual or conceptual understanding of objects—an understanding which is, of course, defective because of the child's relative unfamiliarity with the real world and the things in it. As the child learns and matures, he will build more and richer concepts for dealing with his experience. These richer concepts will find expression in his art, in more detailed, complex, and accurate imagery.

Such a theory seems to explain the simplicity of early forms of child art and their lack of correspondence to what the rest of us see. It also explains changes in the artistic expression of children as they increase their contacts with their environment. But it does not explain, for example, the marked discrepancy in the imagery of older children who have what appears to be similar intelligence, experience, and powers of observation. It does not explain the differences between artistic and inartistic children of similar intelligence. Perhaps the cognitive theorist would argue that differences in artistic imagery reflect differences in intelligence that are not identified by other modes of measuring intelligence, a contention that is difficult to prove or disprove.

The trouble with cognitive theory is that it ties the child's art too closely to his verbal knowledge and powers of concept formation. It does not sufficiently recognize that concept formation necessarily depends on *and follows* sensory experience. It does not realize that representation must involve the creation of a visual image or percept that

CHRIST CHILD IN CRIB. (Henry Jaffee Enterprises, Inc.)

GIRL WHEELING BABY CARRIAGE. (International Child Art Center, San Francisco.)

How do we account for the baby floating above his bed in each of these pictures? A cognitive theorist would say that the child artist knows there is a baby in the crib although he cannot see the baby when viewing the crib from the side. Presumably, the artist has learned a baby-in-the-crib concept. That concept takes precedence over his purely visual experience. Therefore, the artist attends to what he "knows" intellectually. A perceptual theorist would maintain that the artist has many virtually simultaneous percepts of the child and the crib.

His problem lies in ordering or choosing among them. He has to organize his percepts in order to represent them artistically. The artist has percepts of the baby seen from above and of the crib or carriage seen from the side. He has to decide which ones best satisfy his feelings about the quality of the situation as a whole. He solves the problem by representing two sets of percepts simultaneously. A child can do so because he has a weak concept of the lapse of time entailed by moving from one viewpoint to the other.

The evidence of prehistoric art supports the existence of a principle of simultaneity in primitive representation. The development of a time concept follows, and is based on, a foundation of momentary sensory stimulation and two-dimensional space perception. Until a time concept develops (that is, a linear concept of time such as we understand in Western culture), events that are widely separated in space can be represented in the same visual frame—as if they were occurring next to each other and simultaneously. ■

can satisfy a present or a recollected set of sensations. It does not see in the child's expression the influence of his artistic materials and the perception of these materials as he works.*

For the young child, especially, immediate sensations are of vital importance for artistic expression. Consequently, his preference for circles in the representation of people and things may appear to be a departure from his sense data. Cognitive theorists believe these circles are representations of intellectual concepts—in other words, abstractions. But this preference cannot be understood as a precocious ability to create abstractions and symbols instead of visual imitations of what the child sees. Visual imitation *is* the child's intent—not optical imitation but the imitation of the qualities of the things he sees. The simple circles and straight lines he actually uses constitute the best graphic representation he can make of his percepts. Abstraction and symbol-making, on the other hand, are very advanced types of expression—much too advanced for the lower-elementary-school child. In the history of art, Neolithic abstraction follows Paleolithic naturalism. In primitive states of awareness (such as that of small children), the impact of sensation has the highest claim on consciousness. The child's problem is to manage these sensations in the form of a representational device. And the circular and straight line forms he uses are the best solution he

*In general, cognitive theory, with its emphasis on concept development, represents the survival in education of Plato's theory of knowledge, i.e. contempt for sense knowledge and perceptual activity, and a somewhat mystical belief in the existence of unchanging essences or ideas.

can achieve. The fact that they predominate in the early art of the child cannot therefore be explained as the possession by children of common concepts or generalizations about the shapes of things. They constitute common ways of organizing and representing visual percepts.

Developmental Theory

From empirical study of many children's drawings it is possible to identify distinct changes in modes of representation as the individual grows older. Beginning with scribbles during the nursery and preschool years, a child moves on to the use of circular, ovoid, and stick-like representations of people and things; to the creation and repetition of basic representational formulas that seem to him adequate during the lower elementary grades; to the gradual addition of detail to the basic formula, including representations of space and motion; to increasing degrees of visual correspondence to the shape, color, and spatial location of objects during the upper elementary years; and to a proximal if awkward realism at about the time of puberty. These changes in artistic expression have been identified as *stages of growth* accompanied by development in a variety of other dimensions, notably in the work of the late Viktor Lowenfeld.* He

*Viktor Lowenfeld, *Creative and Mental Growth*, Macmillan, 1947. See also by the same author, *The Nature of Creative Activity: Experimental and Comparative Studies of Visual and Non-Visual Sources of Drawing, Painting and Sculpture by Means of the Artistic Products of Weak Sighted and Blind Subjects and the Art of Different Epochs and Cultures*, London: Routledge and Kegan Paul, 1939.

maintained that changes in visual expression correspond to intellectual, emotional, social, perceptual, physical, aesthetic and creative changes within the child. He named the *artistic* stages and the ages of children typically going through them as follows:

Scribbling stages	2 to 4 years
Preschematic stages	4 to 7 years
Schematic stage	7 to 9 years
Dawning realism	9 to 11 years
Pseudorealistic stage	11 to 13 years

It is clear that by connecting so many modes of growth and development to each type of representation, Lowenfeld attributed enormous importance to the change from stage to stage of artistic expression. Other developmental theorists may differ about the precise chronological ages of children during each stage. But there is general agreement that children draw approximately the way they are "supposed to" in Lowenfeld's typology. More serious disagreement centers on the influence of instruction or other forms of external stimulation in the deter-

mination of the child's imagery. Lowenfeld realized that *all* children do not uniformly enter and pass through each stage of artistic development. He did, however, seem to regard the stages as norms, so that very wide discrepancies between chronological age and a child's developmental stage in art would suggest some mental or emotional difficulty, if not retardation. If a child persisted in repeating an early (that is, early for *his* stage of development) representational formula or stereotype, some emotional, social, physical, intellectual, creative, or other type of maladjustment was indicated.

What, according to developmental theory, causes a child to move from stage to stage of artistic expression? Lowenfeld seems to have believed that it was mainly change of affective relationships to people and things in the environment. That is, change in the emotional and intellectual importance of things tends to govern representation. The size of objects in a drawing, for example, is determined by their importance to the child rather than their actual bulk. This view can

---

If the Dubuffet painting were the creation of a child, it might be explained by a developmental theorist as follows:

"The imagery in this picture is characteristic of a child who is still in the pre-schematic stage of development although he may be about seven or eight years old. He has not yet developed a healthy concept of space interrelations; the figures seem to exist independently of each other. They have no common base line; they appear to be floating. Although there are several paths in the picture, the child experiences difficulty in relating himself to them emotionally and physically. Also aesthetically and socially. Because the figures reveal no perceptual relationship, the child can be diagnosed as not yet ready to perform tasks requiring cooperation.

"A pathway in the center of the picture leads to a symbol for a house at the top. It is made up of a group of rectangular shapes enclosed by a single line. The rectangles are abstractions of doors, shutters, and windows; the enclosing line symbolizes the

MENUS SOUCIS, by Jean Dubuffet.
(Findlay Galleries, N.Y.)

emotional quality of the home. Each figure stretches out one or two hands toward the house, suggesting its important emotional significance for the child. Perhaps he is afraid of the house. Also, two of the faces are shown in front view and two are in profile. Now we realize that all of the figures, including the one that is cut off at the knees, belong to the same person. The child is representing several successive events in the same picture space. The picture expresses the child's anxiety about entering the house. His anxiety when he thinks about the house leads to his inability to experience space kinaesthetically and to develop active knowledge of the ground plane he walks on. Therefore, the human figures are represented by rigid symbols and the symbol for house also lacks detail and richness of form.

"The teacher can help the child overcome his schematic rigidity and slight space hysteria through appropriate art stimulation. It is recommended that the child engage in representational activity showing groups of children pushing, pulling, and lifting things." ■

be seen as a variation of the cognitive view that concept development is tied to artistic development. Presumably the child's concept of his mother would make him draw her larger than his father, because the idea of the mother is more important than the idea of the father. However, Lowenfeld contended that artistic expression could govern, or at least strongly influence, concept development: A child's concept of his mother or father may originate in many kinds of interaction with them; but through appropriate types of stimulation and motivation resulting in artistic representation, the child's concept of his parents could be changed. By changing size relationships in his drawing of persons, for example, the child can be induced to change the way he thinks about them because importance, for him, is represented by size.

The *reason* for changing a child's concept of a person or thing would arise in the above-mentioned discrepancy between his chronological age and his developmental stage in art. So far as the teaching of healthy or "well-adjusted" children is concerned, developmentalists would have a strong motive for stimulating them to create imagery appropriate to their chronological age. If, in addition, many significant types of growth are tied in with a child's stage of artistic representation, then art instruction becomes crucial for advancing the child's maturity. In fact, the purpose of art instruction in the elementary school here receives its definition according to the developmental point of view: It is to stimulate the child to represent his experience according to scientific

findings about the norms of artistic expression at every age level.

One of the difficulties with the developmental theory—especially the teaching practices associated with it—is the apparent priority given to psychological, clinical, or therapeutic goals over purely artistic goals. Some educators would not object, of course, to the primacy of psychological goals. Others would see no conflict between therapeutic goals and any other goals that might be defined. Moreover, there is no *theoretical* reason why stimulating children to create according to developmental norms cannot also be productive of qualitatively excellent art work. Still, the practical consequences of instruction based on developmental theory often seem to be work of exceedingly modest quality as art. In other words, developmental theory seems to encounter difficulty when making the transition from the descriptive realm to the normative realm— from describing children's art to telling what ought to be done about it. The cause of the difficulty lies in the fact that a theory setting forth the normal stages of artistic development *contains no inherent justification* for teaching. Such a theory seems better designed to identify departures from its norms. It equates artistic expression with a pattern of development that would occur just as well in the absence of teaching. Consequently, the teacher who is guided by developmental theory experiences some confusion about his role; but usually he tends to perceive himself as diagnostician and therapist. At the same time, his pupils are behaving on the assumption that they are creating art, i.e. meaningful and satisfying representations of their world. In the final analysis, the developmentalist is not wrong in what he knows about children's art, but his assumptions about the purposes of art are not the same as those of the school and its pupils.

Psychoanalytic Theory

It is not possible, of course, to explore at this time the vast subject of psychoanalysis, interesting though it would be for the light it can shed on the general nature of creative activity. Here I shall attempt to discuss only a portion of psychoanalytic theory that might explain child art.

Fundamental to psychoanalytic thought is the concept of the unconscious, the portion of mental activity we are aware of only vaguely, if at all. The unconscious is not the name of a place; it is a word that designates certain activities of the brain and neurological system. These activities are electrochemical, and they go on at various levels of intensity as long as the individual lives. The unconscious is affected by metabolic processes in the brain, that is, by the same conversions of energy into work that occur throughout the body. And, of course, the unconscious reflects changes caused by the breakdown and rebuilding of brain cells. In addition, the unconscious acts as the repository of the individual's heritage. It is not a storehouse of ideas, images, and feelings so much as a set of tendencies to revive or re-enact exceedingly ancient experiences

of man and even his prehuman ancestors. Of course, the cerebellum, or old brain stem, is probably the physical center of the phylogenetic heritage carried by each individual. That is, the coded genetic material that biologists have discovered in every living cell probably becomes operational—so far as mental life is concerned—through the old brain.

Unconscious activity such as dreaming and forgetting takes place continuously and without our deliberate control. It is influenced, however, by the processes of perception and by conscious or intentional acts like remembering, concentrating, imagining, guessing, and repressing. If psychoanalytic theory is right, and if unconscious activity is always taking place, then no mental act escapes the influence of the unconscious. That is, our thoughts, emotions, perceptions, sensations, and intuitions are all, to a greater or lesser degree, influenced by unconscious mental processes.

So far as child art is concerned, we are especially interested in the psychoanalytic view of the relationships between perception and representation. Psychoanalytic theory suggests that representation is *the product* of unconscious material rising to the surface of consciousness where it can influence present perception and artistic representation. (The physical and manipulative aspects of representation can be set aside for the moment.) The unconscious materials influencing a child as he draws, models, or paints would include his archaic heritage, his repressed experience, his remembered experience, and his present sensations and percepts. And the discrepancy between objective reality and the child's representations, according to psychoanalysis, would reflect unconscious processes of symbolic organization operating almost independently of the child's optical experience. Although children do not set out to create symbols, they nevertheless *do* create symbols because of the human mental equipment they inherit. We shall see, later on, that Gestalt psychology also affirms the existence of organismic (also unconscious) processes that structure perception and representation according to autonomous laws—laws operating independently of those that govern the structure of external reality.

Why do unconscious processes of organization cause a child to represent a human

---

Resemblances in the art of a modern painter, a primitive survivor of the Stone Age, and a contemporary child living in a tribal setting. Of course, Klee's "Battle Scene" exhibits considerable conscious borrowing from primitive sources of form. The aborigine painting, however, grows out of its own graphic and mythological tradition; and the African child's painting reflects the universal tendencies of adolescent art, encouraged, no doubt, by a strong teacher. All three works lend themselves to the psychoanalytic account of artistic creativity.

Man hunting a beast is the common theme. Virtually all the peoples of the world cherish a myth in which a dragon, a snake, or a sea monster is subjugated by a god or hero. By vanquishing the monster, a god-hero pacifies the oceans, prevents terrible floods, puts down chaos, and establishes order and regularity in nature for the sake of mortal men. Of course, the man in the African painting may be hunting only for food.

Nevertheless, we can see from his weapons that he expects to encounter a large animal—a powerful adversary. Killing with a spear is a very personal act. Compared to a rifleman, the spear hunter has much more need of his bodily powers to subdue his prey; he needs an archaic sort of courage. On every hunting expedition, therefore, he recapitulates spiritually the heroic feat of a primordial hunter-god who successfully battled with the enemy of all men, pacified the universe, and brought good fortune to his people.

According to psychoanalytic theory, the child artist unconsciously invests an everyday event with mythic significance. His hand is guided, so to speak, by memories and impulses that he barely understands. Why are the size relationships similar in each of the works? Because primitive people as well as adolescents perceive man as small in relation to the universe. The hunter may have a companion—another man or a dog—but he must perform his

feat alone. The monsters are enormous supernatural creatures from the depths of the sea or forest. They have to be creatures that man instinctively dreads because of their size or mode of fighting. In the African painting, we see no monster, but the vegetable forms in the foreground are huge and menacing; the young artist has anticipated the size and dangerousness of the prey in representing these ordinarily harmless forms. The well-observed trees, with their intertwined snakelike branches, can be seen as disguised serpents, with hands or talons waiting to seize the hunter. Finally, we see no trace of muscularity—of physical strength—in any of the hunters. Each of them is small and frail, but seemingly unafraid. This trait tends to confirm the hypothesis that the artist perceives his protagonist as a godlike man—one who possesses an invisible spiritual power. He will overcome the beast, Leviathan, or devil because his victory is ordained; it is part of the universal design. ∎

HUNTER WITH SPEAR, CLUB, AND DOG (above left), drawing by an African child. (International Child Art Center, San Francisco.)

Aboriginal bark painting (above right). (Australian Museum, Sydney.)

Battle scene from the opera "The Seafarer" (at left), by Paul Klee. (S.P.A.D.E.M.; photo, Paul Klee Foundation, Museum of Fine Art, Berne.)

BULLFIGHT, by Joan Miró. (Musée National d'Art Moderne, Cliché des Musées Nationaux.)

RHINOCERUS + BOY, drawing by a Swedish child. (Henry Jaffee Enterprises, Inc.)

RED BULL. (University of Georgia Department of Art.)

Two confrontations with the beast—in Miró's "Bullfight" and the drawing by a Swedish child of a boy and a rhino. In another animal painting, we see the type of childlike imagery from which Miró has occasionally drawn. Although most scholars and critics are hugely entertained by Miró, the meaning of his paintings tends to elude them. The works are usually described by terms like fantastic, poetic, symbolic, miraculous, fabulous, Orphic, Surrealistic, and so on. Perhaps psychoanalytic interpretation can carry us beyond these evasive adjectives.

Miró has exaggerated the size of the bull's horns (only one of which is pointed) and the prominence of his genitals. The matador on the right, wearing a black cloak, is on his way out of the picture. A ridiculous dog-like creature at the left seems to be departing too. Oddly enough, the bull's face belongs to a cat, with standard whiskers and bared teeth. In like manner, the rhino in the Swedish boy's drawing does not have a rhinoceros-type face; he, too, has a mixed identity. To mystify matters further, the horns of the bull, the matador's hat, and part of the dog seem related by shape. Finally, eye-shaped forms appear in several places randomly. (Perhaps they represent the spectators.)

Now, what can all these rollicking signs, symbols, and shapes mean?

A clue comes from Sweden: The boy and the beast seem to be

figure, for example, as a circle with two stick-like legs attached? Why does the child "forget" the existence of neck and body and sometimes the arms? Cognitive theory tells us that the child simply has no concept, as yet, for the omitted parts of the figure. He has not yet learned *to differentiate* the parts from the whole in his concept of a person. But this view is patently unacceptable: A child surely *knows* of the existence of his bodily parts, especially of that part of his body which announces hunger or a stomach ache. In other words, the child surely "knows" more than he represents. Developmental theory would maintain that the body is omitted because the child attaches more

emotional importance to the head and feet during the preschematic stage of growth. This explanation is also unacceptable because there are no findings which establish that the stomach has less affective value for the child than his head, arms, or legs. Psychoanalytic theory points in another direction: It suggests that the child is representing a proprioceptive, or inner image—an image organized by unconscious forces. The unconscious dictates the representation of a circle because of powerful symbolic drives which the child cannot consciously control; for instance, circle equals womb, mouth, breasts. These unconscious forces within the child (who has, after all, very little experi-

---

on excellent terms. The rhino's face is human, it appears to be smiling. The rhino's deadly horn is rounded, like one of the bull's horns. In the imagination of the child, the rhinoceros is a kind of house pet who will let people approach and stroke him. This suggests that the ferocity of Miró's beast, too, may depend on the attitude of the creature that happens to be facing him. The dog brings out the cat in the beast; he chases off the dog, who departs with the signs of a bull imprinted on him. The matador challenges the bull's courage or virility. This annoys the bull who has apparently tried to toss him skyward. The matador is seen in the upper right corner of the picture, running or flying, wearing the signs of the

bull—horns and genitals—in his hat.

Nils, the boy-hero from Sweden, may be giving us, unwittingly, a Scandinavian re-enactment of the Roman story of Androcles and the Lion, or of the biblical myth of Daniel in the Lions' Den. Thus psychoanalytic interpretation uncovers an ancient myth in which gentleness and innocence change the heart of a murderous beast. Both ancient tales tell us that the behavior of a terrifying creature can be governed by the character of the person he encounters.

This type of interpretation may appear to be far-fetched. Even so, it seems preferable to stringing together adjectives that do little more than state the obvious. We can appreciate the endeavor to

arrange a number of seemingly unrelated images into a coherent scheme of meaning. But the teacher may well ask whether psychoanalytic interpretations, assuming they are valid, can be usefully employed in the classroom. It would seem they are impractical for the on-going tasks of instruction.

Psychoanalytic explanation, however, offers us some insight into the potential depth and complexity of child art if we wish to undertake a penetrating investigation of it. Certainly theoretical research, which often disdains depth psychologies, might well entertain more imaginative hypotheses—of which this is an example—than it has hitherto employed. ∎

ence in the external world) are perhaps more responsive to ancient memories carried in his brain cells than to the organizational structure of his visual sensations.* In other words, internal biogenetic forces influence the child's imagery more than external forces and circumstances.

Later, when the conscious portion of the child's personality has had an opportunity to develop, the symbolic content of his art will diminish and his drawings will become more truly representational. That is, the child will attempt to respond more to the external, visible world and less to his internal, symbolic world. When he discovers that his representations do not correspond accurately to what he sees, he will try harder to suppress unconscious suggestions during the act of artistic execution. Those who succeed in effectively suppressing unconscious suggestions during their artistic effort develop good powers of visual representation; they learn to respond to their retinal sensations with a high degree of precision. In the history of art, they are responsible ultimately for the development of "realistic" or naturalistic styles. Those who cannot manage to suppress unconscious suggestions develop symbolic and nonrepresentational types of artistic expression. Or, they withdraw from artistic creation. They are not able, or are unwilling, to isolate their visual sensations from the rest of their experience. In the history of art, they are responsible for the development of abstract and nonobjective styles. In this manner, psychoanalysis would explain those children who "cannot draw" as well as the dual tendencies of the history of art toward abstraction or realism, geometric or naturalistic art, expressionism or impressionism, haptic art or visual art.†

Gestalt Theory

The fundamental position of Gestalt theorists is that we do not see objects as the sum of directly observed parts; we see perceptual wholes, or total images structured by the brain on the basis of retinal impressions *and* the basic requirements of the perceiving organism. These requirements of the perceiving organism are common to all viewers and hence are expressed by Gestaltists as laws, that is, *needs of the organism* for completeness, closure, or unity; regularity, continuity, or rhythm; and balance, similarity, or symmetry. The perceiver *works on* his sensations; he makes something with the sensory excitations focused in his eyes and transmitted to his brain. It is a mistake to believe that human perceiving is completely like the action of a camera. You and I can

---

*The work of artists like Klee, Miró, and Dubuffet resembles the art of children partly because these adult artists resemble children in their ability to draw upon unconscious and archaic sources of imagery. In this connection, see Ellen Marsh, "Paul Klee and the Art of Children: A Comparison of Their Creative Processes," *College Art Journal*, Winter 1957.

†See Lowenfeld, *Creative and Mental Growth*, p. 151. Also, for a more elaborate treatment of the bipolar tendencies in art history and, by implication, in the art of children, see Arnold Hauser, *The Philosophy of Art History*, Knopf, 1959.

see the picture created by light rays focused on the photosensitive film in a camera, but our brains cannot "see" the images on our retinas as if we were looking at photographic film. Instead, our brains organize and restructure the electrochemical impulses received from our eyes. Consequently there are varying degrees of difference between the retinal images in our eyes and the perceptual images organized within the brain. There may be pictures (retinal images) in the eye, but there are no pictures in the brain.

If there are no "pictures" in the brain—just patterns of electrical excitation—how does the viewer conceive of the objects he is looking at? He conceives of them as patterned relationships, more or less generalized images that have a *structural* or qualitative resemblance to the object. He knows, understands, or recognizes this structural resemblance as the "feeling" or the "look" of an object. (Notice that for the Gestaltist, knowing and perceiving are very closely connected.) But he does not possess in his brain an optical duplicate of the object; he possesses its more or less distorted and modified electrical image.

So far as a child and his art are concerned, the problem is to find the type of visual organization that can adequately represent his perceptual imagery. When working from memory, he conceives of objects and persons as sets of percepts; he thinks with percepts, that is, with residual sensory images. Then, when he tries to represent his percepts, he has to manipulate an artistic medium so that the image he makes on paper or with clay will correspond *structurally* (in the relations among its formal elements) to his percept of it. As a result, there are two types of imagery involved in the creation of child art: the intracerebral imagery embodied in the child's percepts and the external publicly visible imagery embodied in the child's artistic expression. Both of these types of imagery correspond structurally or qualitatively to the objects they represent, but they do not duplicate these objects optically. Therefore, we can understand the difference between what the child sees and what he draws in view of the opportunities he has for modifying or distorting his retinal sensations: First is the modification caused by the conversion of optical sensations into intracerebral percepts; second is the modification of these percepts in the process of finding adequate representational imagery for them; third is the modification of representational imagery by the technical processes of the artistic medium; fourth is the limitation of artistic possibilities due to limitations in the child's neuromuscular coordination.

According to Gestalt theory, the child's early representations are not symbols that he has invented through mental processes of abstraction—that is, through eliminating what is (to him) unessential detail. (Obviously, to do this, the child would have to possess a Platonic idea about the "essence" of the object he is representing.) It is fairly clear that the child knows more about an object (has more percepts of it) than he

TWO PEOPLE. (University of Georgia Department of Art.)

Fragment of a Peruvian painted hanging. (The Solomon R. Guggenheim Museum.)

Some scholars attribute the employment of geometric shapes in art to habits developed in the mastery of new Stone Age techniques like weaving. Presumably, the artist persists in using geometric forms even when they are not required by his materials and processes—as in the illustrated Peruvian painting on fabric. In the child's painting, the tendencies toward geometry cannot be attributed to experience with weaving; the forms have a psychological origin. The rectangularity seen in the heads, and the firm, heavy outlines in the torsos result from an effort to establish conscious control over form, to escape the vagueness of the scribble. The child who favors angularity over curvilinear form is asserting his desire to dominate reality. Like the Peruvian artist, he is unwilling to exploit the freedom of the painting medium. Unbounded shapes make him uncomfortable.

In order to convey the disturbed character of his subject's inner life, Cuevas has borrowed from child-art imagery—especially its tendency toward twisting of form. Symmetry is not easily

CRIME BY CUEVAS (at left), from a portfolio of lithographs by José-Luis Cuevas. (Graphis Gallery, N.Y.)

Crayon drawing of a head (below). (Collection of the author.)

achieved by children, particularly when they are anxious to respond to all the traits of a living person. Here the child's wavy, wriggling line represents his effort to express the motion and vitality of an individual he is observing directly. The line is also responsive to his kinaesthetic experience in the presence of another person. Cuevas has attempted to exploit some of these stylistic traits by adapting them in the features of his subject. But the head would have been more effective if it did not form so perfect an oval. The egg-shape sacrifices some of the nervous, disquieting feeling established through the asymmetry of the features. This is a case where the child's spontaneous expression creates an effect that is more powerful than the calculated adult effort. ■

represents. For this reason, estimates of the child's intelligence based on an inventory of the visual detail in his drawings cannot be considered reliable.* But the child's simplified (to us) and distorted (to us) drawings do reflect his effort to organize or give structure to his perceptual imagery. And we have seen that his perceptual imagery is a distortion of his retinal imagery. As the child matures, he grows in his capacity to maintain a close correspondence between his perceptual and his retinal imagery. But even so, he experiences difficulty in maintaining correspondence between his representational effort and his perceptual imagery. It is for this reason that adolescents are so dissatisfied with their artistic expression: They have managed to gain a larger measure of control than children over their intracerebral percepts; what they perceive corresponds more closely to what they "see." But what they draw or represent does *not* correspond closely to what they see.

The psychoanalytic view that the imagery of child art expresses the content of the individual unconscious or of the archaic heritage of the race is incorrect according to Gestalt theory. Gestaltists would argue that unconscious meanings and symbols in child art reflect the perceptual imagery of psycho-

*In this connection, see Dale Harris, *Children's Drawings as Measures of Intellectual Maturity,* Harcourt, Brace & World, 1963; Florence L. Goodenough, *Children's Drawings, A Handbook of Child Psychology,* Clark University Press, 1931; Florence L. Goodenough, *Measurement of Intelligence by Drawing,* World Book Company, 1926; Betty Lark-Horovitz, "On Learning Abilities of Children as Recorded in a Drawing Experiment," *Journal of Experimental Education,* IX, No. 4, 1941.

analysts. In other words, these perceptions belong to Freudians and Jungians but not to children. In defense of psychoanalysis one might reply that there is an extraordinary amount of similarity in the representational forms used by children, regardless of time, place, or culture. Is this to be explained as the operation of the same laws of perceptual organization, no matter whether the child is working from the object or from memory, no matter whether he is drawing a man, a tree, the sun, a cloud, or an animal?

It may be possible to reconcile the Gestaltist view that the child's imagery is organized by autonomous laws of the organism with the psychoanalytic view that the child's imagery is modified by unconscious factors affecting perception. Perhaps both schools would agree that "laws of the organism" and "unconscious factors" require an agency and a medium through which they can operate. According to present knowledge of brain physiology, the agency is electrical current and the medium is brain and neural tissue. The Gestaltists recognize that their laws of closure, continuity, and balance are statements about the result of a long phylogenetic development. The Freudians and Jungians recognize that the archaic heritage and the collective unconscious are terms that also represent the result of a long phylogenetic development. Perhaps each school describes a different aspect of the same phenomenon—Gestalt theory stressing the way electrical currents tend to distribute themselves during perception while psychoanalysis stresses the persistence of meanings and images in those same electrical patterns.

Conclusion

Each of the theories of child art presented here so briefly is, to some extent, plausible. Despite flaws of one sort or another, each theory offers a reasonably convincing explanation of *some aspect* of the phenomenon of child art. But as teachers we are naturally interested in their implications for classroom practice. Here we encounter a serious difficulty, as with all theory, not in the adequacy of the theories for explaining child art, but in the nature of their relevance to the practice of art education. The reason for the difficulty is clear: Any theory of child art *describes* what happens when children create their typical imagery; but art education

THE TREE OF HOUSES, by Paul Klee. (Pasadena Art Museum, Galka E. Scheyer Blue Four Collection.)

HOUSE AND TREE. (University of Georgia Department of Art.)

Klee has built his picture on the child's obsession with trees and houses, combining the two themes to create a new symbol of extraordinary fascination. This work has been copied and reproduced thousands of times during the past fifty years. Its popularity may testify to an archaic dream of living in trees, or of trees giving birth to houses, as, in a way, they do. ■

157

needs to foster human development through the art a child *sees and studies* as well as the art he creates. Even if child art could be completely explained, the question would still remain: What does this have to do with the education of children through art so that they will become complete human beings? The fact is that a total program of art education cannot be built on the foundation of theories of child art alone.

It is easy to confuse the "is" of theoretical investigation with the "ought" of educational practice and morality. The fact that children normally create artistic imagery of a certain type, at a certain stage of their development, does not mean that the art education curriculum should be mainly devoted to encouraging the production of such imagery. It only means that children need the opportunity to paint and draw and model and build. It is also clear that the connection of a child's art with any social or personal difficulty he may have is demonstrable but really outside the province of art education. But the most serious error we make in building art education curricula on admittedly sound theories of child art emerges in *the isolation of the child's image-making from the social and human matrix of artistic creation.* In other words, we do not give children good reasons to make art.

Because of a convincing theory of child art, a teacher may be persuaded to entrap children into creating images because it is supposed to be good for them. In practice,

we often *force* a child to create art in the absence of any compelling reason *of his own* to do so. The work that emerges may reflect the characteristic imagery of children. But it rarely reflects an authentic, a *genuinely felt occasion* for artistic expression. As a result, children use materials and create images under the auspices of the elementary school largely because they have to.*

What conclusions can we draw from these remarks about the theory of child art and its connection to art education as a whole? First, we must recognize that child art is the inevitable rather than the forced product of normal human development. Second, we have to understand the creation of imagery by children as being natural in the context of *their* needs but not necessarily of ours. Third, we must not entrap children into creating art so that we can use their imagery for purposes of diagnosis or mental measurement. Fourth, we have to design curricula in which the creation of art is *one of the outcomes* of a teaching practice rather than its sole objective. Last, we must sadly (or gladly) abandon the notion that a child's intelligence can be trained or enhanced by stimulating him to make images according to pre-established conceptual or developmental norms.

*Herbert Read raised much the same question when he said: "We have to recognize that expression is also *communication*, or at least an attempt to communicate, and the question we are asking, therefore, is why does the child desire to communicate?" *Education Through Art*, Pantheon, 1945, p. 163.

In art education as practiced in our schools there is a tremendous variety of activities performed by teachers and pupils. Studio performance includes drawing, painting, modeling, carving, casting, photography, printmaking, collage, ceramics, jewelry, and metalwork, and various combinations of the crafts, assemblage, and informal construction work. Outside the studio areas, there are art appreciation, art history, art criticism, and artistic biography (learning stories about the lives of artists). In addition, there are a number of interdisciplinary activities involving art, such as the employment of artistic skills in collaboration with stage and costume design for dramatic productions, or the execution of murals and illustrations in support of concurrent school work in social studies, language arts, natural science, or history. Every experienced art teacher is also acquainted with the wide variety of extracurricular requests or even *claims* that are made on the art education program—preparation of posters for school events, illustrations for school publications and bulletins, decoration for PTA meetings, beautification of bulletin boards, as well as other quasi-professional or nonprofessional tasks in the realm of "art services." Many elementary school art specialists conduct classes for emotionally disturbed children or slow learners or low academic achievers. Some teachers also offer classes for especially "gifted" art students.

In studio performance there is tremendous pressure on the teacher to introduce pupils to the newest and latest media, materials, and techniques developed by the ever-fertile minds of art material manufacturers and by American technology in general. The gallery and exhibition world displays an astonishing inventiveness in new media; and reasonably alert teachers feel obliged to include these media and proc-

7

Toward a New Theory

esses in their programs for the sake of enlarging the artistic opportunities of their students and in order to be "up to date." Where the so-called fine arts program is combined with the industrial arts program, the range of equipment and tools and graphic processes is truly staggering. It is a matter of some regret that funds are less frequently expended on art books, slides, reproductions, projection equipment, films, and film strips. Many an art teacher builds his own collection of reproductions to be used in support of his teaching. But happily, this situation is changing; funds and equipment for books, slides, films, and reproductions are becoming more generally available.

I mention the wide range and variety of activity in the art education programs of our schools to convey some idea of what a teacher confronts—whether a general classroom teacher working in the self-contained elementary classroom; an art specialist, consultant, supervisor, or resource person who roams from school to school or from class to class within a school; or an art specialist who is blessed with one school in which there is a well-equipped art room where pupils come for their instruction. It is easy for the new and even the experienced teacher to be at first dazzled and then thoroughly confused by the plethora of activities and tools and goals and projects and services that are normally considered within the art education program in the elementary school.

Art teachers, then, need a theory—a way of thinking about art education—which can help them see through and beyond the maze

of activity that seems to be art education. They need to develop some ideas about priorities, about means and ends, about the impingement of the outside world upon the substance of art education. They need to place child art in its proper relation to the total creativity of children. Only then will it be possible to organize an art education program intelligently. Only then can we talk about specific classroom practices with reasonable confidence that we shall not lose sight of the integrating center of any educational program—the child and his need to become a human person.

The Changed Environment of Art Teaching

It must be obvious to any sensitive student of contemporary affairs that our world has changed radically during the past fifteen or twenty years. Our wars, our technologies, our economics, our social relations, our politics, our sports and recreation, our communications media, our sexual attitudes and practices—all have undergone transformations of considerable depth and breadth. There is, no doubt, some continuity amid all of these changes, but no one would deny that the changes are real. Consequently, the educational priorities and practices that were adequate at the time of World War II, for example, may not be adequate in the light of recent revisions in social structures and personal attitudes.

Education in general, and art education in particular, is especially affected by changes in the physical, social, and attitudinal environment. These, for example, are some of the social and environmental changes that must inevitably change the children we teach and hence the *way* we teach: Our population has grown much larger and most of it is located in cities. We literally see more people wherever we go and we are daily thrown into closer contact with more and different kinds of people. More people means more frequent, more varied, and more intense human interactions. For the art educator this implies changes in the density, texture, and vividness of social experience. It means that growing children are subject to types of human stimulation which in their force, variety, and frequency are unprecedented in human history.

The increasingly urban character of our society causes population centers to be in a continual process of reconstruction—the tearing down of only recently outmoded structures and environments and their replacement with gigantic, gleaming, and often very original constructions. Children no longer grow up in the same comfortably familiar physical settings of an earlier generation. They are assaulted on every side by almost total transformations of their living space. Their parents change homes frequently so children may have to adapt to several regional environments, themselves in process of alteration. For the art teacher this means working with youngsters who have had new experiences with space, with physical permanence, with age and old things, and with the physical shape of the large-scale environment.

The influence of the mass media—movies, magazines, radio, advertising, records, and especially television—is brought to bear very early in the lives of children, often before they begin to attend school. They are subjected to very skillful and intensive sensory excitation almost continuously. Certainly they have developed some capacity to read man-made images before they get any formal schooling. The art educator who wonders why American children are often indifferent about keeping their own drawings and paintings, or why they cannot long sustain attention and interest in their own artistic efforts, might well consider that American youngsters have been accustomed by the media to radically new rhythms of perception. Children in other, less affluent countries undoubtedly listen to a different drummer; their environment is not nearly so saturated with every manner of sensory stimulation. Our youngsters have had to speed up the tempo of their perceptual activity compared to children of earlier generations and other cultural environments. That they devote large blocks of time to watching the images on television screens —more than they spend watching films or reading books—should raise at least some questions in the mind of the art teacher who would have her pupils paint still-life compositions or carve bars of soap.

The almost complete mechanization of transportation and the steady reduction in the cost of air travel have altered conceptions of time and space and motion based on simpler modes of transportation. Children are accustomed to seeing the world

Sidewalk artist. (New York Daily News; photo by Jerry Haynes.)

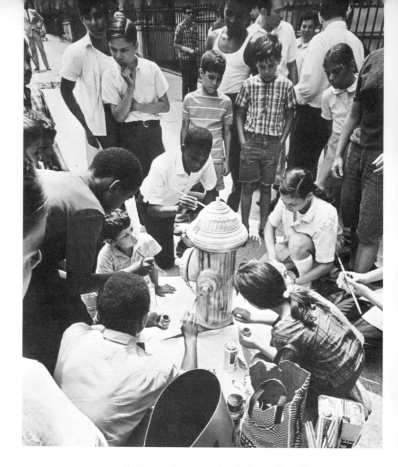

Children painting a fire hydrant. (The New York Times.)

Some exotic environments for exercising creativity. A guardian of the law expresses interest; fascinated kids watch; a curious crowd gathers (anything draws a crowd in New York). Can this be art education? Should children or adolescents be encouraged to express themselves so freely on public property?

What is happening is very healthy. These activities demonstrate transfer of learning in concrete terms. Perhaps the fire hydrant will not be greatly en-hanced as an art object; no doubt the sidewalk mural will be obliterated. Nevertheless, these students have learned, somehow, that the impulse to redesign objects or embellish surfaces need not be confined to school buildings and classroom walls.

Years ago, a few art teachers persuaded the merchants in their communities that vandalism during Hallowe'en could be reduced if school pupils were allowed to paint and decorate store windows —in effect sanctioning and organ-izing their desire to "paint the town." That practice has become a well-established tradition. But its educational meaning has not been understood. The curriculum—in or out of school—should try to be more than a harmless outlet for pent-up energies. If art education is taken seriously, it entails the systematic transformation of the environment; good design should extend beyond schools and text-books. Perhaps children have learned this lesson better than we realize. ■

at higher speeds and rates of acceleration than their parents. If they have traveled in jet aircraft they have altered ideas about the time needed to cross great spaces, and the earth certainly presents itself through a different set of images. Schematic generalizations about the child's representation of the earth and sky are based, of course, on a terrestrial point of view. No doubt these representational schema are changing just as the perspective and three-dimensional space and heliocentric universe of Renaissance man changed from the flat space and geocentric cosmology of medieval man.

The school as a place and as an institution used to be an extension of the home and the church. Art educators wanted it to be —in part, at least—an extension of the Renaissance workshop, or of the Beaux Arts atelier, or of the garret studio of the nineteenth-century painter, or perhaps of the New York East Side loft of today's swinging painter-sculptor-actor. But the media are about to deny these wishes. The school is increasingly an extension of the TV studio and the motion picture theater. It cannot remain a model of the country chapel or the farmhouse before rural electrification. If the school environment continues to be radically distinct from that of today's electrified, automated, and mechanized home (which has been substantially assimilated to the purposes of the media), then children will become increasingly unmanageable. The most perceptive teachers realize that if they are not to be swallowed up by the communications industries, they must absorb the imagery of popular culture into their teach-

ing and use it for their own, hopefully humane, purposes. For the art teacher, this means searching for kernels of meaning and sanity in the environing glut of electronic excitation. It means seizing fleeting images and visions of health and playing them or showing them large, loud, and clear. Although the classroom need not become a sedate version of the discothèque or the command room of the military chiefs of staff, it cannot much longer be modeled on classrooms in medieval monasteries where only the teacher possessed a book. It has to be a place where teachers can compete on reasonably even terms with the fascinations of electronic stimulation.

Clearly, we cannot manufacture spectacles in the classroom—spectacles potent enough to distract or amuse children already turned on by the media. The idea is not to turn them off, either. We should try, therefore, to build something decent and valuable on the foundation of their perceptual habits, their consciousness of the world, and their desperate (if unspoken) desire to make sense of the noisy, image-strewn, mind-blowing, everything-for-sale environment.

The Changed Mode of Perception and Learning

The effect of the electronic media on tempos and patterns of perception is naturally important because looking at art, as well as creating art, is crucially influenced by perception. Many observers, from a variety of disciplines, appear to believe that

New York Parks Commissioner August Heckscher visiting an alley turned into a parklet. (The New York Times.)

Boys pitching bottle caps on street drawing. (The New York Times.)

The devil figure drawn on asphalt shows that children do create art without formal instruction. Furthermore, this street imagery is functional: The children have a good reason for making it; its generous scale reflects the requirements of their game; their canvas—street space—is made of a material that is plentiful and inexpensive; and everyone "pitches in." As a combined arts activity, however, there are disadvantages; the performance is often interrupted by automobiles. These boys must adjust their art to the uneven rhythms of city traffic instead of the regular rhythm of a school buzzer announcing changes of period. Still, there are creatures at the seashore, Rachel Carson informs us, who live their lives according to the cycles of the incoming and outgoing tides.

The children's mural is in a lower East Side neighborhood of New York City, once designated "Mugger's Alley." It used to be littered with garbage. Now the place tries to say it is dedicated to life and growth instead of crime, dirt, and degradation. It seems that in its extremity the city calls on children and art—on children for their innocence, and on art for its power of symbolic transformation. Who knows whether these symbols can, in fact, transform the inner city? Officials like New York Parks Commissioner August Heckscher clearly hope so. ■

we are presently passing through one of those historical watersheds when comprehensive and deep-seated changes in thinking, feeling, and knowing are taking place. Certainly the attention given to the utterances of H. Marshall McLuhan these past several years suggests a somewhat vaguely defined but nevertheless very widespread consciousness of fundamental alterations in the way we see.

The physiology of perception has not changed, however. It is rooted in relatively fixed biological habits. But a changed "mode" of perception refers to a different way of *attending to* one's percepts. It is a different way of "processing" sensations, of managing the interaction of one's percepts and ideas. People can choose or will to see as they do because of very persuasive influences in their culture. Here the record of art history is most instructive. As Heinrich Wölfflin believed, art history is the history of changed modes of seeing. That is, while the physiology of seeing remains the same, the visual content and hence the spiritual or psychological content of art *does* change. For Wölfflin, changes in artistic representation reflect fundamental changes in modes of perception. These changes, when visible as art, are not caused merely by the desire to express new ideas or because artists "know" things their predecessors did not know. The changes are not signs of "progress" either. They are really and truly changes in perceiving—in the way we handle the raw materials of sensation.

How can we determine what and how people perceive? It is plain that the reports of adults about the way they see are necessarily very subjective and hence not too reliable. Children are even less able to tell us how they manage their sensations and perceptions. We must therefore employ an indirect method, one that enables us to study *public* evidence about the nature of subjective processes. This turns out to be the evidence offered by aesthetic form. If the theoretical discussions in the previous chapter are dependable, then the formal organizations we see in visual art reflect the internal organization of percepts by artists. To go one step further, the *common qualities* we see in many kinds of aesthetic form are visible because they have succeeded in capturing the attention of many viewers. In other words, these visual qualities correspond with the feelings or the internal organization of percepts in viewers. This point is especially true of the forms of the mass media because of the close connection between general acceptance of an aesthetic effect and its survival in the costly world of popular communication. To be sure, the impresarios of advertising or television can impose on the public their own modes of perception for a time. But in the end, those who shape the material communicated through these media either succumb to popular preference or they win the public over to their ways of feeling. For our purposes, both cases amount to the same thing: Aesthetic form, especially as manifest in the popular arts, reveals contemporary modes of perception.

Contemporary modes of perception are substantially similar for adults *and* for children. That is, the aesthetic effects visible in the fine and popular arts provide a common denominator of form, whether in material prepared for children, adolescents, or adults. Concessions made to the sensibilities of children are made in the area of theme or subject matter. But, with respect to *form*, material prepared for children is frequently very sophisticated. Often it anticipates—as in comic strips, animated cartoons, pop music and lyrics—aesthetic effects that will subsequently be accepted in serious art forms intended for adults.* Many observers have commented on the seepage from youth culture to adult culture. What I maintain here is that the artists, designers and performers who create the cultural materials consumed by both children and adults operate as if there were a common foundation of perception and aesthetic preference.†

The Evidence of Aesthetic Form

Perhaps the most obvious feature of aesthetic form today is the reduction of psychic distance—the steady elimination of the gap between art and life. Children and adults look at popular art and élite art forms without performing the mental operations that distinguish them from reality. In other words, we deliberately see art as reality and reality as art. It is for this reason that so many youngsters are masters of the put-on. They can behave seriously or unseriously toward any experience almost at the same time, perplexing those adults who are accustomed to fairly rigid distinctions between the real and the artificial, subjectivity and objectivity, the false and the genuine.

Nonobjective art, which seems so fantastic and remote from everyday life to older adults, appears to be entirely real to children and adolescents. They have no difficulty in accepting geometric abstraction as existing in a perfectly credible world—the same world they themselves occupy.** Theatrical performances that spill out of the proscenium, in which actors mingle with the audience, in which "spectators" carry on dialog with the "performers" *as integral parts of the drama*—such performances clearly reflect the viewer's changed perception of himself and of the artistic events he is looking at. Happenings and environments represent the evolution of painting and sculpture *away from* the detached observation of fixed three-dimensional objects and painted simulacra. Art forms increasingly invite participation. As we know from Gestalt psychology, the law of closure always implicates viewers in the completion of an experience initiated by the organization of the art object. The more incomplete or unstable the formal organization of the art object, the more

---

*"[It is] a law of cultural history that the vulgar amusements of today are the highbrow art of tomorrow." Ignatius G. Mattingly, "Some Cultural Aspects of Serial Cartoons," *Harper's*, December 1955.

†See my article on this subject, "The Artist and Mass Culture," *College Art Journal*, vol. XVIII, no. 4, Summer 1959.

**This point is well made by Milton Klonsky: "A generation, born since World War II, for whom science fiction has become science, can hold no truths to be self-evident, no speculations too far out." Quotation from "Mc²Luhan's Message or: Which Way Did the Second Coming Went?" New American Review, no. 2, New American Library, 1968.

effort and participation will be required of the viewer to achieve closure. Contemporary art favors formal instability because contemporary viewers favor greater personal participation in perception. McLuhan attributes this to the "low definition" of such "cool" media as television, jazz, the telephone, and so on. Rather than being annoyed or disturbed by seemingly unrelated, distorted, vague, indistinct, highly abstract, unbalanced, asymmetrical, turbulent, and anonymous visual forms, contemporary viewers prefer them. Instead, they are put off by precision, explicitness, balance, naturalism, predictability, and regularity in art.

A second quality of the contemporary perception of aesthetic form is its phenomenological character. Young people today are better able than previous generations to experience *the object itself* and *the object alone*. Today's viewers spontaneously bracket out the ideas and associations that were formerly considered essential for the cultivated perception of art. Especially, our viewers bracket out history. They do not see an art object as an example of a long evolutionary development; they do not see it as the product of forces initiated remotely in time and space. They are more impressed with the immediate impact of form, which is to say with its sensory character. When a perceiver concentrates on sensations, he tends not to be aware of symbols, semantics, and cultural context. The capacity for interpretation and iconographic analysis tends to be weak in moderns because analysis and interpretation of what we see is a time-consuming activity, and the modern viewer is too beset with multisensory stimuli to pause for the purpose of reflective thinking. Yet one mark of an educated person is the capacity to pause and to sort out and reflect on his experiences. Consequently, the phenomenological character of modern perception exhibits certain tendencies that run counter to classical notions of the educated person.*

By bracketing out history in his perception of art, a viewer refuses to see the art object as a *product of time* and sees it instead as a *creator of time*. That is, he perceives aesthetic form as a device for intensifying and extending the duration of his sensations. Motion pictures are the most common example of this effect: They enlarge imagery and extend its impact upon the senses by lengthening the time required to witness an event or by bringing the viewer much closer to objects than he is accustomed to be. The loss of literary and historical association brought about by modern perception finds compensation in the capacity to experience sensations for longer periods of time. Not only that—more *kinds* of sensation are experienced; hence the tremendous movement toward combined-arts forms. These represent the attempt to stimulate perceivers through several senses at once. Simultaneity in art has been a Romantic goal since at least the late eighteenth century. Now, modern technology makes it feasible. Also, one

*Consider the success among intellectuals of Susan Sontag's *Against Interpretation* (Farrar, Straus & Giroux, 1966). Miss Sontag is clearly the spokesman for the "new sensibility" among the young, which is to say, for the primacy of incongruous sensory excitations in art as opposed to art that embodies ideas already familiar and waiting to be uncovered by academic explication.

should not minimize the influence of superior health and physiology among today's larger, better-nourished children and adolescents. They seem to have greater physical capacities for experience than their parents, although some have suffered hearing impairment because of high-decibel rock. It is conceivable, however, that traditional art forms and traditional modes of perception simply do not exhaust their somatic potentials for feeling and learning.

The interest in form as a source of sensation rather than as a vehicle of history results in a veritable explosion of effort to escalate the sensory potentials of color, light, movement, texture, shape. Witness Op art and its use of shape arrangements to induce altered states of consciousness. Also in this category are experiments with shifting colored light projected on moving bodies—the so-called psychedelic art forms. (Of course, experimentation with projected colored light, with "color organs," is at least forty years old.) It is easy to see in these new experiments the influence of drug culture, that is, the attempt to alter consciousness, to extend and intensify sensation through one or several avenues of perception. Body painting, automobile body tattooing, and fashion design reflect the endeavor to make the human figure and its more personal extensions sources of extraordinary sensory stimulation.

There is an extraordinary resemblance between the figures in the contemporary Theater of Light imagery and those in the rock paintings created by Neolithic herdsmen in Africa and Old Stone Age Aborigines in Australia. The resemblance is not fortuitous; it reflects a growing convergence between contemporary and tribal modes of perception. All three sets of figures exhibit a similar attenuation; all the heads tend to be small in relation to the stretched-out torsos; all strongly emphasize frenetic bodily activity; and all of them present the figures as if they were floating in space. We need not conclude that there is a necessary correlation between the life styles of Bushmen, contemporary Aborigines, and avant-garde artists. Nevertheless, the resemblances in their modes of representing the human figure are too strong to be ignored.

The question that needs to be asked is: Why do these qualities —accelerated motion, fleeting and unstable imagery, strenuous action, stretching and floating—appeal to the sensibilities of young people today? The most obvious place to look for an answer is in the electronic imagery of television— especially in its intermittent distortions of form, its flickering light intensities, its geometric interruptions and displacements of shape, its reversals of light and dark pattern, and its multiplying and dividing of proportion when we tinker with the controls. The present generation has been very intensively conditioned by this sort of image manipulation. Today's children see electronic images of things before they see the real objects those images represent. Stone Age men, of course, had no contact with television. But the acuity of their vision was exceedingly important, especially their perception of shapes. As hunters, they had to be able to read changing shapes very quickly. They became very good at remembering shapes after original sensory stimuli had been extinguished. Paleolithic cave art testifies to this achievement. But later Stone Age men, who combined stock-raising with hunting, were less dependent on the accuracy of their sensory recall, and so they began to stylize their imagery.

Copy of an Australian Aboriginal rock painting.

Copy of an African Bushman rock painting, ca. 5000–3500 B.C.

TRIP IN HEX, kinetic composition. (Theater of Light, Jackie Cassen-Rudi Stern; photo, by Roy Blakey.)

They were in a position to attend to images for their qualities of sinuous rhythm, pleasing contour, and elegant proportion. These "aesthetic" qualities became important for their own sakes—apart from the traits of the real objects they were supposed to represent. And so it is with televised and photographic images. They become primary sensory and aesthetic data; our manipulation of this data reflects our feeling of superiority over Old Stone Age man. Similarly, our children see us as troglodytes—cave dwellers who eat roots, pick berries, and hunt with pointed sticks—whereas they are in the pastoral stage, keeping herds of tape recorders, movie cameras, transistor radios, and portable television sets. ■

169

The abandonment of history and of literary association as means of integrating the sensory excitement in aesthetic form has created a vacuum that is being filled by eroticism. Many contemporary performances in art are simulations of the emotional properties of sexual experience. That is, the flashing lights, blurred shapes, and intense colors of artistic expression as varied as nonobjective painting, kinetic sculpture, fabric design, and popular dancing are often slightly abstract and stylized versions of the culminating stages of sexual intercourse. Children, of course, witness these art forms quite innocently. Still, they perceive color shape, motion, and light relationships that owe their existence to a new permissiveness about illustrating and celebrating erotic feeling and activity. But if children are not consciously aware of the genital implications in contemporary aesthetic form, they do experience the integration of their feeling and sensations under the auspices of an essentially erotic organizing center. As a result, there is a type of unity or closure in their aesthetic experience which is denied to that generation of adults whose early training was deliberately aimed at suppressing any perception of erotic feeling and especially of genital activity.

Several factors mentioned above suggest a kind of neo-primitivism in our contemporary modes of perception. The classical ideas of unified form—beginning, middle and end; dominance and subordination—are being abandoned. Today's visual art forms, like jazz, can be cut off at any point without losing their meaning. They exist in a new continuum between art and life. They are not isolated replicas of the visual world, they just represent temporary shifts in the medium of the artist or the attention of the artist or the attention of the viewer. The cognitive modes of tribal men and today's youth are, moreover, heavily dependent on sensory stimulation and vividness of sensory recall. Early encounter with erotic art and erotic behavior are characteristic of primitive life and increasingly of modern life. Anti-naturalism in art is another trait we share with Neolithic tribal culture. Some other features are also present: totemism, shamanism, mythical thinking, smoking to inhale the vapors of mind-altering drugs, a weak sense of historical time, and a growing disinclination to represent deep space in graphic art. It is unlikely that these features of modern sensibility constitute transient developments. Neither should they be regarded in an apocalyptic light. A fundamental change in perception is accompanied by all sorts of cultural excitement and drama, but it does not herald the end of civilization. It does, however, admonish us, if we are engaged in education, to think in fresh ways about what we are doing and how we do it.

The Changed Role of Art

It could be maintained that the distinctive role of art is to prepare people for new modes of perception largely induced by changes in technology and the media of mass communication. So far as art employs the new media, it is itself an agency of perceptual change. To the extent that it employs the traditional media, it announces changes which have already taken place. This view of the role of art has vastly more potential for education than the conventional notion that art is a permanent storehouse of beauty. It opens up the possibility that works of art can be regarded as sources of insight into whatever questions or difficulties currently beset us. The problem of education is to learn how to get at the insights that art potentially offers. Hopefully, you will find a practical approach to this problem in Part Four of this book. In addition, the method of interpreting works of art, as developed in Chapter 12, will be useful to the teacher who needs a critical technique for finding out how specific works communicate their meanings to the viewer. Here are some of the changes in the role of art today that affect what we can do with art in education.

First of all, young people are less inclined to view art as a type of commodity, a form of property, an item of interior decoration, or a species of household furniture. They are beginning to realize that art *does something* to the people who look at it. It forces them to adjust their ways of seeing in order to make decisions about the value or meaning of what they are looking at. As people begin to realize that art is the man-made environment and the environment is art, they cease to see it chiefly as a kind of object or ornament *in* the environment. In the classroom, then, we no longer think of creative activity exclusively in terms of making adornments for the school room or the school corridors or for the walls and shelves at home. We think of artistic activity as the solving of problems with the tools, materials, and conventions of a particular medium. As Santayana said, "Any operation which [thus] humanizes and rationalizes objects is called art."* Accordingly, the responsibility of a teacher is to help the child to identify the problems he feels the need to solve, hoping that their solution will contribute to the humanization of life. The artistic solutions children create may ultimately adorn a classroom or school corridors, but they are not created for that purpose. They are created because a teacher and her pupils are able to agree that there are things they want to do and say through the language of visual form rather than some other language.

The notion that art is a commodity—something people buy and sell for profit—is educationally irrelevant if not positively harmful. It prepares children to view their creative efforts as potentially ownable and saleable, hence subject to what are, for them, the mysterious standards and requirements of a market. Certainly this is true of older children, those approaching adolescence. And the official art world encourages this commodity-idea of art. But art education—especially in the grade school—is a powerful countervailing force, if the idea is planted early in the child's experience that art is a mode of expression before it is something to own.

The importance of this concept cannot be overemphasized—for the child, for the teacher, and for democratic institutions. Today we are beginning to see the role of art more truly and authentically as the promotion of discourse and the exchange of

*George Santayana, *Reason in Art* (vol. 4, *Life of Reason*), Scribner's, 1954, p. 301.

Psychedelic jeans. (Photo, Look Magazine; © 1968 by Cowles Communications, Inc.)

feelings among the citizens of a free society. That is also its role in the organic cultures of primitive men. The commodity-idea of art develops and reaches its peak during the sickness—that is, the decadence—of a culture. By placing immense pecuniary values on art objects, a sick society makes it virtually impossible for people to regard their ordinary human interactions as potential sources of aesthetic value. Then the probability of a rich common existence approaches zero. Our most vivid and precious values repose in physical objects instead of the human relationships that generate them.

What enables people in general and children in particular to perceive the changed role of art? First, as mentioned above, is the kind of elementary-school art education that stresses the *process* of making and understanding art rather than the value—pecuniary or otherwise—of the product. Second is

Fabric designers are exceedingly alert to changes in the perceptual environment. They watch developments in the arts very closely, and when a distinct visual trend emerges, they modify it according to their needs and rush to be first in the market with the latest look. Designers work under the pressure of limited time, widespread copying, and intense price competition. As a result, they are not usually able to generate fundamentally new visual ideas; they must rather apply all their energies to the creation of dazzling adaptations—visual statements that identify themselves quickly and yet convey a feeling of novelty.

From a designer's adaptations, one gets a hint—but only a hint—of the new ways of feeling and thinking that seem to concern avant-garde artists. Of course, not all artists are immune to the designer's professional impulses, that is, the desire to stay up to date by adapting and paraphrasing what important artists are saying. The number of artists who are genuine form-givers is always small.

One of the functions of art history is to establish where an important form concept or motif originated. This task often entails lengthy and difficult investigation. From our standpoint, however, the priority of a visual idea is less important than its relevance to the way students feel, see, and think. Psychedelic jeans, therefore, tell us something about what the public has been persuaded to like. If you can read visual form, you can learn as much about young people from clothing and fabric design as from pop song lyrics, afternoon TV dramas, or fan magazines. ■

the virtually complete capture of our imaginative life by the mass media. The physical forms of the media are inexpensive and ephemeral. It is hard to say, really, who owns them. We relate to them as sources of experience rather than as permanently graspable containers of value. In other words, we have to look at a mural painting or a sculptured frieze according to the habits of looking at films or television. We do not really care who owns the film projected in a theater. We rarely know the author of a television script. In this respect, we approach the condition of people who worship in a church without knowing who designed it or what it cost to build. Such a situation may be scandalous to the traditional scholar or the unimaginative art educator; for us, it is a delightful development.

The inexpensive reproduction of traditional and contemporary "fine" art has the effect of changing the context in which it is first and most frequently encountered. We see art more often in books, magazines, slides, and films than we do in museums, palaces, churches, and princely mansions. As a result, the most famous and precious monuments of art history are assimilated by the media that communicate their images. And from the other side of time, so to speak, the work of children and contemporary artists is also reproduced and communicated by these same media. Imagine this: The ordinary citizen may see Michelangelo's *Pietà*, Picasso's *Guernica*, and reproductions of child art in the same book or periodical or slide lecture. His attention is drawn to their character as images created by and through a particular medium of communication. While a lecturer or author drones on about emperors, popes, and generals, Michelangelo's neo-Platonism, Picasso's loyalty to the Spanish republic, or the child's expression of size relationships, the viewer is steadily bombarded by light reflected from a beaded screen, or clusters of colored dots resting on glossy paper stock. The teacher, lecturer, or writer often labors to reconstruct these visual simulations in the form of some distant place, event, or idea. But this effort runs counter to the viewer's perceptual activity: The viewer is actively engaged in reorganizing the form or structure of what he sees so that it will be compatible with his present organismic requirements. The modern viewer is already habituated to perceive art as a type of immediately apprehended meaning or expression. To confound or interrupt his processes of perception and apprehension is to annoy and frustrate him: Either help him to grasp what he experiences with his senses, or get out of the way.

From what has been said above, you can see that art education is affected by the way teachers and pupils perceive the role of art *outside the school*, as well as the way they perceive its role within the classroom. But the walls between inside and outside are being penetrated. The distinctions between making images and interpreting images seem less important now as we become aware of the underlying processes of creativity they have in common. The mass media have forced us to recognize that understanding what we see is hard but necessary work: We must learn to do it in order to navigate in this world. Artistic activity of certain types may be obsolete, such as making one-of-a-kind ceramic ashtrays when automated industry produces ashtrays by the millions. But other types of artistic creativity retain their relevance—not because they artificially revive handicraft modes of production in an automated civilization, but because they promote the natural expression of feeling in an increasingly depersonalized world.

A Humanistic Theory of Art Education

What is meant by humanism? "Except God, Man is diminutive to nothing," said John Donne. Describing humanistic education, Professor J. H. Billington speaks of "a continuing celebration of life. Both the subject and object of humanistic study are the whole man—where mind and passion meet, where creativity and criticism interact. Humanistic studies—history and philosophy, arts and letters—directly involve man in the anguish, achievements, and aspirations of other people, and in enduring human questions of artistic form, moral value, and personal belief. These questions, dealing with the quality of life, are relevant to everyone —and not merely to departmental specialists."* Of the other meanings generally in use, the following definition establishes the foundation for the theory of art education offered here: Humanism is the doctrine that man and his works are worth study without

regard to any practical or vocational purpose.† I take this statement to mean that any discipline, any technique we use to learn who and what man is, can be regarded as a form of humanistic study. Such education extends throughout the life of an individual, starting before and continuing after he has learned how to gain his livelihood. But the absence of a professional or vocational objective does not prevent the student of humanism from deriving, indirectly, considerable practical benefit from his studies. His central focus, however, is the phenomenon of man. A statement by Andrè Malraux is especially pertinent here: "The basic problem is that our civilization, which is a civilization of machines, can teach man everything except how to be a man." When humanists examine technology, languages, social and political institutions, science, art, and religion, it is for the purpose of finding out what light they can shed on man and the problem of being a man. It is time for art education to reconstitute itself as the study of man through art.

From a humanistic standpoint, then, the artistic creativity of children and adolescents is seen in a new light. It ceases to be primarily a technical enterprise. Instead, the emphasis in teaching is on the humanistic reasons for creating art and the humanistic purposes that art serves. A child's artistic activity is not regarded, primarily, as evidence of psychological development. A teacher does not so much "motivate" him

*James H. Billington, "The Humanistic Heartbeat Has Failed," Life, May 24, 1968, pp. 32–35.

†See Moses Hadas, "Humanism: The Continuing Ideal," The Journal of Aesthetic Education, vol. 2, no. 3, July, 1968.

to create art as help the child discover a *good reason* for creating art. Let me sharpen the distinction: Motivation in practical terms has usually meant the employment of tactics by a teacher—persuasion, stimulation of memories, holding out promises of rewards or grades—so that the child would create artistic products. The main goal has been to get the child to make something, hopefully to become enthusiastic about his work, especially the process of making. Once the child was "hooked" on art, so to speak, he would continue to make it and thus enjoy the benefits which accrue from self-expression: mental health, identification with artists, creative power, respect for the work of others, and so on. The difficulty with this strategy lies in the fundamentally artificial and arbitrary situation it fosters for the creation of art under the auspices of the school. The situation bears no relation to the creation of art in any living culture that we know about. It is difficult to believe that even small children do not perceive in such an arrangement a kind of trick played by adults (teachers and administrators) for mysterious purposes of their own. Even the fulsome praise and encouragement given by teachers for a child's art activity must appear somewhat strange if not insincere. We arrive eventually at the point where children realize that at a certain time of the day or week they are expected to make for their teachers something called ART.

The humanist would cause art to be created indirectly and incidentally, as it is created in the organic cultures of primitive men, for example. And in such cultures, we are fond of saying, there is no artificial separation between art and life.* People simply become aware of personal or social needs that art can satisfy. In our much more complex civilization, therefore, we have the task of *uniting* art and life—at least in the subculture of the school. There have to be "good reasons" as opposed to calculated and essentially artificial motivations, for the creation of art in schools. What are those good reasons? Or, more specifically, how should teachers develop these good reasons in dialog with their pupils?

A "good reason" for creating art has two essential features: *personal authenticity* and *teleological design*. The former refers to the individual's genuine need to express himself to another person, the latter to the awareness of society's conventional expectations about the functions art can perform. To be sure, children do not know the definitions of these terms. But they do know when they *really need* to say something; that is, they *can* behave authentically without knowing what "authentic" means or that it is common, later in life, to behave inauthentically. The teleology of art, however, must be learned. The fact that human communities have a practical interest in the creation of art—even by children—is not self-evident to children. They have to learn that what they create implicates them in the world in particular ways. That is, they have to learn that their creative efforts are not merely the products of transient impulses. Their art can be fashioned according to the require-

*See Herbert Read, *The Grass Roots of Art*, Wittenborn, 1947.

Fifth-grade class mural. (Athens [Georgia] Daily News.)

A mural of black and brown faces.
(The New York Times.)

ments of the functions it is intended to perform. There is a dialectic in the creation of art: As soon as we say a child's creative expression is art (and it is), we are saying that it is shaped by all the forces of reality that nature and society have set in motion. These natural and social forces constitute teleological design—the purposes of art.

The failure to see the dialectical nature of art and therefore the purposes and functions of art in the world has created considerable mischief for art education. It has caused theorists and teachers to concentrate on the modes of children's perception and representation too exclusively. Perceptual theory tends to ignore the character of the child's art as a reaching out to the universe. And especially, it does not recognize the ritualistic character of all human creativity—its function as symbolic confrontation with reality. The nature of art as ritual and confrontation stands at the heart of a humanistic theory of art education; now it needs to be spelled out in greater detail.

Art and Crisis Ritual

Anthropologists have frequently observed and described the rituals developed by cultural groups around such crucial human events as child-bearing and birth, puberty and initiation, marriage and procreation, illness and death. Because the individual undergoes considerable psychological tension at these events, and because any society has a keen interest in the individual's successful transition through them, their associated practices and conventions have been

---

Murals are often remarkably sensitive barometers of the pervasive feeling in a group of children. Here one of them reflects the search for identity of children who feel themselves abandoned. Its images appear separate, bleakly unrelated, together only in their isolation. Another mural expresses the optimism of its largely middle-class creators—their belief in natural beauty as something that really exists. Flowers can be closely observed, carefully drawn, transferred and painted, and exhibited with pride.

We can draw these limited inferences about a teaching environment because classroom murals are a type of collective art. They do not belong to anyone in particular. Consequently, they must emerge as a result of some sort of consensus. In addition, a mural contradicts today's dominant notion of art as a highly personal product that has a certain monetary value for its owner. Teachers often try to strengthen the collective character of a mural by making certain that each child in the class plays a recognizable role in its creation. The result may suffer artistically, however, unless some provision for a minimal type of unity has been made. Sometimes that unity grows out of the dominance of a few artistically strong pupils, the organizing role of the teacher, the stylistic similarity of the children, or their common theme and outlook. What matters most is that the children relate to the mural as a part of the environment they have created. It represents their planning, their work, and their discovery of form and meaning. They must live a large part of their classroom lives in its presence—against its pictorial space and among its visual symbols. Few adults can make a claim to live so intimately with art. ■

called crisis rites or rites of passage. These rites entail the creation of what we would call art—often in an "operatic" or combined-arts context. They have the function of dissipating individual anxieties (as well as arousing them within established limits), restating and consolidating group values, and stabilizing the relations between the individual and the group at a time when the fabric of society needs reinforcement. These crisis rites represent the conventional moments when individuals, supported by their group, confront reality—that is, when they *do* or *make* or *witness* something in order to come to terms with existence. This kind of doing and making and witnessing is the foundation of all human creativity. The forms that emerge owe their existence to a dialectical process—a tension between the individual and the conventions of the group, on the one hand; and a dissipation of that tension as the individual and his group engage in a collaborative ritual of making and witnessing, on the other. The art objects then created are inseparable from their ritualistic purpose. From the standpoint of a humanistic theory of art education, they exemplify personal authenticity and teleological design at the same time.

It would be a mistake to believe that crisis rituals are characteristic of primitive cultures alone. We, too, have our initiation and puberty rites. They are often highly formalized and we do not usually perceive

---

Roszak in "Rite of Passage" endeavors to represent the experience of a man performing a ritual act. He is a contemporary artist trying to bridge the gap between cultures. What we see is the result of an industrial man creating art out of a primitive man's religious behavior. The viewer is invited to empathize with Roszak's theme, to imagine or to feel what it would be like to engage in a magical act. But the sophisticated form and technique of the modern sculptor inevitably interposes distance—a psychological barrier—between the viewer and the act that the sculpture seeks to represent or symbolize. The problem is very difficult to solve unless the artist can separate himself, somehow, from his roots in a scientific culture and from his knowledge of the history of art.

Children's art, on the other hand, does not encounter these difficulties. Children do not easily perceive the distance between actual events and their artistic representation. For example, a child can celebrate a wedding when she draws a picture of it. The little girl who drew the wedding picture shown here is not just a spectator, she is a "member of the wedding." Stated simply, she is the bride. She is adorned with hearts and flowers; her groom smiles because he is happy and he loves her.

Lorraine Connor's painting is ostensibly her representation of an event she witnessed on television. Or she may have seen a newspaper photograph of the funeral service. But in the act of painting the picture, she attends the service and shares the grief of Mrs. King. Lorraine is older than the little girl of the wedding picture. She knows the difference between an event and the artistic representation of an event. Still, she apparently wanted to paint this picture. Why? Because her feelings about Dr. King's death could not be ritualized adequately through reading newspaper accounts or viewing television coverage of the tragedy. She had to make her own image. That was the best way to confront the crisis, to deal with her feelings, to sort out her emotions and carry on with her own life. ∎

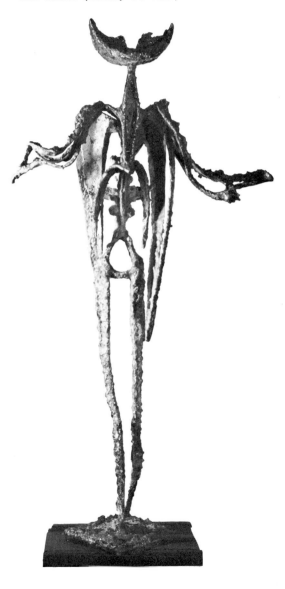

Child's drawing of a wedding (at left). (Collection of the author.)

Mrs. Martin Luther King attending her husband's funeral (below left), painting by Lorraine Connor, a Harlem child. (The New York Times.)

RITE OF PASSAGE (below), by Theodore Roszak. (Courtesy the artist.)

their role in the creation of art. But that is because we do not exploit the crises and confrontations of life as opportunities for aesthetic expression. We do not ritualize our anxieties. Or we ritualize them through empty forms. Still, we have ritualistic needs. We need to confront reality when it seems to threaten us. If we are unable to express our ritualistic needs we may eventually suffer one or more of the maladies that high civilization so abundantly creates; alienation, anomie, affectlessness.

In addition to the fundamental life crises (birth, initiation, death), high civilizations like ours elaborate new types of crisis that every person must eventually confront. This is another way of saying that life becomes more and more complex. We have new problems, often generated by new technology, for whose confrontation a traditional, ritualized expression does not exist. We are placed in the position of having to confront these new crises again and again and of creating original rituals to deal with them. Children are not sheltered from the impact of new social and technical challenges; they also have to confront reality when it appears to them in the form of a problem or a threat —a strange feeling, a new fear, a mystery that cannot be explained.

Now the role of art education in the life of a child may begin to emerge more clearly, for making and looking at art is an indirect consequence of identifying crises and trying to deal with them creatively. The authenticity and usefulness of the child's response becomes visible in the forms of writing, drawing, acting, singing, reciting, or dancing that he employs to ritualize his feelings of confrontation.

What is confrontation? It is a type of meeting or encounter. It is, first, the awareness of a break in the congenial flow of experience—the consciousness of a concern —and a disposition to do something about and with that concern. Arnold Hauser recognizes the creative act of the child as the result of a confrontation when he observes: "To the child, drawing means gaining power over the figures represented, a way of doing good or evil."*

From this standpoint, the child's visual expression is more than artistic representation, it is a type of moral activity, one of the earliest opportunities a person has for acting like a moral agent. This is precisely what the tribesman does with his concern about illness or fecundity or about identifying a new member of his group. He names and actualizes—that is, gives form—to his hopes and fears and thus comes to terms with them. And that is what we have to do in schools: to help children to face life by showing how its substance can be managed creatively.

The Categories of Humanistic Art Education

Part Four of this volume proposes an art education curriculum based on humanistic theory. Each chapter title is a statement of one of the major purposes of the curriculum. Those title statements, in turn, are derived from the categories into which a humanistic theory of art education can be divided.

*Arnold Hauser, *The Philosophy of Art History*, Knopf, 1958, p. 111.

Perhaps the accompanying diagram of their relationships will be helpful, along with the following explanatory statements about each category.

Categories of the Theory	Curriculum Exemplar: The Purposes of Art Education
Cognitive Study ◄——►	Understanding the World (Ch. 9)
Linguistic Study ◄——►	Learning the Language of Art (Ch. 10)
Media Study ◄——►	Studying Varieties of the Language (Ch. 11)
Critical Study ◄——►	Mastering the Techniques of Art Criticism (Ch. 12)

COGNITIVE STUDY

This category is normally understood as the realm of facts, information, or knowledge about art. It is sometimes thought by art teachers that a discipline such as the history of art constitutes the most complete and useful organization of knowledge about art. Certainly this is true if art history is supplemented by anthropology and relevant material from the social sciences. But from the standpoint of a humanistic theory that must be applied in an educational context, we are interested in much more than facts about art, especially facts that have to be learned in chronological order. In this theory, cognitive study means acquiring facts, information, or knowledge *about man* through art. You can see that there is a difference between gaining knowledge about art and gaining knowledge about man through the evidence of art and our own creativity.

If we claim that art education is a *comprehensive* approach to teaching and learning rather than a subject, we must be able to show that a child can learn much more than the names and dates of artists, monuments of art, art styles, the names of artistic media and materials, facts about the transmission of influence, iconological symbols, and so on. Although this information is important in certain contexts, a teacher has to give priority to cognitive learning about people and places, individuals and the community—the personal, social, and physical dimensions of the world made and occupied by man. Therefore, cognitive study, which is here called "understanding the world," aims at learning something about the nature of human personality, social groups, and man-made environments.* In studying persons, groups, and physical communities through art, the pupil will make incidental or concomitant discoveries about art as a subject. And that is the best way to acquire the cognitive materials of a discipline—by learning them in clusters which are functionally related. But we cannot seriously maintain that knowing the difference between tempera and oil paint or knowing who painted the Sistine ceiling is humanistically significant in and of itself. Committing this kind of information to memory is an unintentional parody of serious study of art. Such cognitive data are the *residue* of humanistic *study* —the residue that some persons may recognize as having a connection with genuinely important questions. Unfortunately, teach-

*These subcategories are treated in greater detail in my book, *Art as Image and Idea* (Prentice-Hall, 1967), under the following headings—The Functions of Art: *Personal Functions, Social Functions,* and *Physical Functions.*

ing becomes trivial when teachers do not know or cannot remember the reasons for asking the questions whose answers they expect pupils to know. That is why cognitive study begins with the questions: What are people like? How do groups behave? How does man shape his environment? To get the answers we have to look at art that others have made or we have to create art ourselves in order to share our discoveries about man and to disclose feelings we have about our universe.

There are indirect dividends accruing from the curricular questions about individuals, groups, and the environment. In order to answer them with aesthetic evidence we may also discover that art—no matter who makes it—leads to three kinds of knowledge: (1) knowledge of the different kinds of feelings and ideas people have and express to each other; (2) knowledge of the formal organizations and relationships that make objects pleasing, appealing, or desirable; (3) and knowledge of the uses of art in the physical environment. Those who are familiar with the work of Charles W. Morris will recognize parallels in these three types of knowledge to the three types of signs described in his semiotic theory* (science of meaning): semantic signs, which designate the relation between a collection of signs (or a work of art) and what the signs express; syntactic signs, which designate the relationships *among* and *within* signs (or among the forms in a work of art); and pragmatic signs, which designate the relations

*Charles W. Morris, *Signs, Language and Behavior*, Prentice-Hall, 1946.

between a combination of signs (or an art object) and the people who use it. In cognitive talk about art, we discuss the following: individual personality and the expressive meanings of art; groups and the social functions of art; places and things—the practical uses and the aesthetic effects of art.

In summary, the cognitive phase of art education finds us trying to study man and his works as a primary objective. But in the course of the journey we inadvertently gain insight into the *structure* of art. To be sure, it is the structure of art regarded as a typology of meanings. In other words, in cognitive study we try to convert the formal and sensory qualities of art into conceptual knowledge. However, through linguistic study, media study, and critical study, we shall acquire other kinds of insight into the structure of art as a subject or discipline— all the while pursuing man, according to Alexander Pope, the proper study of mankind.

LINGUISTIC STUDY

As the title of this category suggests, we also teach art as a language or vehicle of meaning. In relation to instruction in other languages, this aspect of art education corresponds to the study of grammar, syntax, and usage. It is not a very popular type of instruction and there is considerable division of opinion about it in art education. Some teachers believe the fundamentals of art, the "building blocks" of art, are the formal, or visual, elements: line, shape, color, texture, light and dark, space, volume, and, perhaps, motion. They maintain that

The impulse toward the sensuous and the beautiful:

Some children develop a strong affinity for rich color
and elaborate texture.

THE TREE (left). ("Der Pelikan.")

THE SUN MAKES THINGS GROW
(above). (University of Georgia Department of Art.)

Different ways to achieve sensuous effects:

The painting of a church reflects the child's steady, methodical build-up of color and shape—always under linear control. Like an oriental rug, the painting depends on the cumulative effect of many small, brightly colored, carefully placed details.

BYZANTINE CHURCH. (Henry Jaffee Enterprises, Inc.; photo, John Pitkin.)

TURKEY (right). (University of Georgia Department of Art.)

MAGIC BIRD (below left). (University of Georgia Department of Art.)

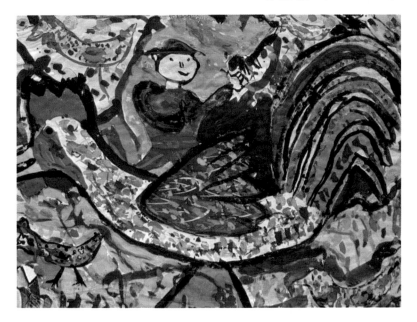

A more direct approach:

Color, shape, and texture are created more spontaneously. A highly charged paint surface compensates for the sacrifice of precision.

Butterflies. (Courtesy Oliver Coleman.)

Decorative abstraction during late adolescence:

The older student can decide, intellectually, on the degree of naturalism he wants. Having made his decision, he feels free to explore and enjoy a variety of interlocking color and shape relationships, and combinations of line with transparency and opacity.

Color composition.
("Der Pelikan.")

Decorative design.
("Der Pelikan.")

Child and paper-bag mask (left). (Globe Photos, Inc., by Michael Austin.)

Two masks: papier-maché and egg carton, and papier-maché and scraps (below). (University of Georgia Department of Art.)

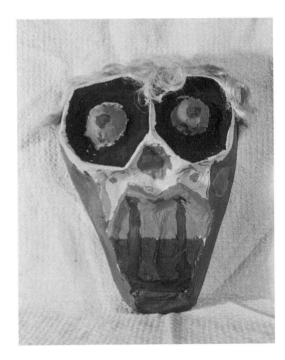

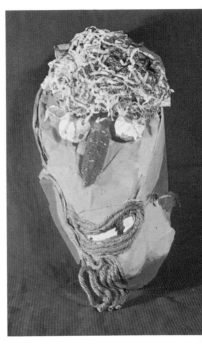

HAMBURGER WITH PICKLE AND TO-MATO ATTACHED, by Claes Oldenburg. (Collection Carroll Janis, New York.)

Painted sculpture—from masks to hamburgers:

Sculpture that is used—living art—is rarely monochromatic. If the artist is a child, he combines color and form because he thinks of the object as real—not as an exercise in shaping materials. If he is a mature artist, like Claes Oldenburg, he may want to narrow the gap between art and reality. The results, therefore, are surprisingly similar.

The container and its contents:

Sometimes an artist paints what is within, sometimes what is outside, and sometimes both. He
might also adorn a surface with little signs of
what is underneath.

MATERNITÉ (above), by Marc Chagall.
(Stedelijk Museum, Amsterdam.)

COW AND CALF (left). (University of
Georgia Department of Art.)

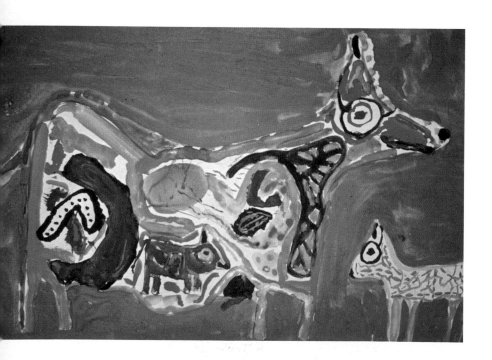

Papier-maché animal. (Courtesy Oliver Coleman.)

FAMILY CAR. (University of Georgia Department of Art.)

Fanciful surfaces and forms:

More painted sculpture—fantastic papier-maché creatures that resurrect the bestiaries of ancient and medieval times.

Papier-maché animals. (Courtesy Oliver Coleman.)

these elements are fundamental whether one is creating visual form or looking at form already created. Other teachers believe that the visual elements constitute intellectual abstractions, that one becomes aware of these elements only by separating them artificially from the living, organic reality of a work of art. If they teach the formal elements at all, it is in the junior or senior high school. They feel that elementary-school children care too much about expressive meanings to be interested in dissecting art into its constituent parts.

As with so many dual views of a controversial issue, there are in reality alternative positions that can be taken. If possible, we would like to be able to study visual art as a language without killing the thing we study. Here, I believe, the humanistic bias helps. We should study line, shape, color, and so on, as man actually encounters them rather than as definitions or as diagrams that hopelessly imitate the real qualities of visual experience. In addition, a humanistic theory recognizes two other aspects of the study of language: style and aesthetics. In the light of art-historical research into art styles and psychological research into perceptual processes, a theory that deals only with formal elements is incomplete.

The purpose of studying style, to state the point negatively, is *not* to learn the labels for artistic movements or the order in which styles normally succeed each other. This latter question is interesting, but from a *linguistic* standpoint we are more interested in the formal and affective characteristics of a style. That is, what does a particular style look like? What arrangement of the formal elements leads to the inference that a particular work *belongs to*, can be classified under, a particular style? Secondly, how does the presence of certain stylistic features in a work influence our perception of it? What accounts for the capacity of certain styles to arouse our feelings in certain ways? The answers to these questions call for attention to the linguistic features of an artistic medium.

In presenting this theory, I distinguish between aesthetics and philosophy of art. Aesthetics is the narrower discipline; it deals with questions concerning the perception and understanding of works of art. But it does not undertake to answer philosophic questions dealing with the purposes of art, the relation of art to civilization or the status of art genres as symbolic forms in the sense that Cassirer, Malraux, Dewey, or Susanne Langer would approach such matters.* We want to use aesthetics to learn how people understand a language—the language of visual art. By including aesthetics within linguistic study we examine creative expression from two points of view: from the standpoint of the art object regarded as an organization of forms or visual elements; and from the standpoint of the viewer's act of reconstituting these forms in his own consciousness. There is a third way of gaining

*Ernst Cassirer, *The Philosophy of Symbolic Forms, Vol. 1: Language*, Yale Univ. Press, 1953; André Malraux, *The Voices of Silence*, Doubleday, 1953; Susanne Langer, *Philosophy in a New Key: A Study in the Symbolism of Reason, Rite and Art*, Harvard Univ. Press, 1945; John Dewey, *Art as Experience*, Minton, Balch, 1934, especially Chapter XIV, "Art and Civilization."

insight into art as a language, and that is, of course, through artistic performance. Consequently, the art education curriculum has to include creative practices that stimulate awareness of the formal or syntactic traits of art—not that elementary-school children should study the visual elements *apart from what they mean* in a particular work of art. Accordingly, our exemplar curriculum suggests practices in which the visual elements are studied *after the fact*—*after* they have been perceived in the organic relationships of a living work.

Linguistic study is vulnerable to the charge that it tends to become excessively technical, too concerned with the mechanics of expression and hence indifferent to larger humanistic ends. To some extent, this problem is resolved by teaching technique. Skilled and imaginative teachers manage to make even narrowly technical material interesting. Still, it is fair to ask how the structure of a language appeals to the interests of children at the same time that it relates to the fundamental concerns of the humanist. I think the concept of style is the instrument we should use. It is usually considered too sophisticated to be taught in schools except in the most superficial way. But it should be obvious that children already recognize *and are connoisseurs* of styles in walking, speaking, fighting, playing, eating, and so on. The educational problem is really one of bringing this connoisseurship to bear on the visual languages of art. When we do this, there will be a reciprocal reinforcement of the capacity to perceive style qualities in everyday life. And when everyday life is examined for its

stylistic features—its potential for ART—we shall have made an important investment in the improvement of the entire visual and social environment.

MEDIA STUDY

There is a theoretical unity among the several visual arts, and this unity is stressed when we study the language of art. At the same time, there are distinctive features of each art form considered independently. For example, the elements of form may be common to painting and architecture, but these elements appear as oil paint in one case and brick or concrete in the other. The elements of form need to be embodied in specific materials, or media, before we can become aware of them. But a medium is not just a particular material, it is also a *way of using* that material. The *ways* in which materials are used affect what is expressed through them. Consequently, media study is really the study of *the interaction of medium and meaning.**

Among specialists in communications arts, media study involves not only content analysis but also the examination of form/content relationships. Certainly McLuhan has based most of his inferences and insights on the social and psychological consequences of the communications media as forms of meaning in themselves rather than as neutral *vehicles* of meaning. These insights, which have often been received by the public as startling new revelations, constitute in many cases the daily discoveries of

*See my *Art as Image and Idea*, Chapters 11, 12, and 13.

children in art classes. This is said, not to detract from McLuhan's important contributions to media study, but to point out the rich educational opportunities that often remain uncelebrated in art education. It should also be added that media/meaning relationships are accessible to children notwithstanding the fact that they are first pointed out by university professors. Existing theories of art education do not especially notice the role of deliberately examining media/meaning relationships. Clearly, this type of learning should be high on the agenda of any modern educational theory. Furthermore, art education seems uniquely situated to conduct media study within our elementary and secondary schools.

The extraordinary proliferation of nonverbal modes of communication during the past quarter-century threatens much of the curriculum with obsolescence unless it reconstitutes itself as linguistic and media study. So far as art education is concerned, we must look at the several visual art forms as instances of *form taking possession of meaning*. This is the large implication of the media revolution of our time, and educators ignore it at their peril.

Our exemplar curriculum takes up four media: painting, sculpture, architecture, and film. These labels are used only for convenience. Painting should be understood as any kind of two-dimensional imagery. Sculpture embraces all three-dimensional and utilitarian expressive forms. Architecture designates the comprehensive ordering of the environment as well as the design of individual sheltering structures. And by film,

we also imply television, although a different technology creates the TV image. It is not essential that media study in art education include every kind and form of visual expression. What matters is that children have sufficient opportunity to recognize a variety of media/meaning relationships in the visual arts. To do so, they need to draw inferences from their experience with linguistic study. That is, having attended to syntactic relations in linguistic study, they must go a step further by trying to discriminate between media/meaning relations in painting and media/meaning relations in sculpture. These discriminations would take the form of answers to questions such as: What is the difference between making a man in clay and drawing a man on paper? What is the difference between looking at a building and walking through it? Can you tell whether a movie is real or a dream? How can you remind automobile drivers to be careful—that is, how can you convert a verbal command or a moral exhortation into performance with a machine? The answers to these questions—which would entail artistic expression as well as spoken language—require a pupil to perform several mental operations based on media/meaning discriminations.

What is the humanist's interest in media study? It is a matter of recognizing how men are themselves shaped by their forms of communication and expression. A child may not be able to make large-scale generalizations about the effect of glass-walled architecture on human feelings about inside and outside space. On the other hand, if his attention is drawn to the difference be-

OWH! IN SAN PAO, by Stuart Davis. (Collection Whitney Museum of American Art, N.Y.)

THE WALLS COME TUMBLING DOWN, an ad for a television program. (WCBS-TV.)

A picture painted by Stuart Davis in 1951 could anticipate the way many people would see, feel, and think twenty years later. Important artists are prophetic in this sense; somehow they tune in on cultural currents that are destined to become great waves. Because of his fascination with jazz, street signs, mechanical parts, and geometric forms, Davis was able to predict, visually, the developing love affair of today's artist with technology and with the electronic excitation of the senses. He invented his own variation of the form language of Cubism in order to simulate the effect on the senses of urban noise, speed, movement, and rhythm. Today, artists are flirting with the newest technology, trying to simulate the effect on the senses of urban noise, speed, movement, and rhythm. Instead of using hand-painted imagery—like Davis—they employ light projectors, sound amplifiers, photocopying machines, and computers programed to shift, mix, and juxtapose images recorded on film. Although the form language of each succeeding generation may seem bizarre —even absurd—its objective is the same as it was in the past—to tell the world what it feels like to be alive right now. ■

tween mosaics as a pictorial form and stained glass as a pictorial form, he may have some perceptual foundation for discriminating between opacity and translucency in the context of visual communication. This discrimination could be made, of course, in less time than it takes to write about it.

The humanist, then, is interested in media study for the perceptual foundation it provides—a foundation that is essential for making inferences about man's behavior in his own communications environment. Children may not think of themselves as humanists; nevertheless they are almost continuously involved in linguistic and media study, especially outside of school. They *are* humanists, if we will give them the opportunity in school to find it out.

CRITICAL STUDY

The exemplar curriculum stresses critical skills from the beginning—before the child knows that he is engaging in criticism.* We take his natural curiosity about what an object means, or how good it is, or what it might be good for, and involve him in the same critical operations performed by professionals: description, analysis, interpretation, and judgment. A kindergarten child will perform all of these operations spontaneously but in random order. Teaching is

largely a job of systematizing his almost irrepressible desire to talk about art. And talk about art is a defensible definition of art criticism. Critical study is the process of introducing order into the child's natural performance as a critic.

In order to explain critical study, we must first distinguish between the objectives of the educator and the objectives of the citizen who buys art, sells art, exhibits art, or writes about art. The educator is interested in critical study because the operations it entails have a value apart from establishing the rank and worth of art objects. These operations are educationally interesting because they involve the use of human powers of observation, specification, conjecture, intuition, inference, self-correction, risk-taking, and finding out. But these critical operations cannot be seriously undertaken except in the presence of objects which have expressive power—art.

Perhaps you have noticed the inadequacy of some of the systems erected by philosophers and aestheticians for the purpose of judging or explicating works of art. Despite their logical consistency, you may have difficulty in relating them in any authentic way to someone's real perceptions on genuine aesthetic occasions. This happens when a critical *system* becomes a substitute for critical *performance*.† It happens if the system

---

*Unfortunately, the word "criticism" has negative connotations for many persons, and so it may be prudent in some situations not to use it. See my discussion of this problem in "The Critical Act," *Journal of Aesthetic Education*, vol. 1, no. 2, Autumn 1966; also, "Some Adventures in Art Criticism," *Art Education*, vol. 22, no. 3, March 1968.

†In this connection, Professor Sholom Kahn makes the following observation: "The critical reading of a poem is not the same as a discussion of theories of criticism, just as the performance of a moral act is not the same as a course in ethical theory." Sholom J. Kahn, " 'Evidence' in Criticism," *The Journal of Aesthetics and Art Criticism*, vol. 9, no. 4, June 1951, p. 330.

is built around the need to defend assertions about the cost, uniqueness, historical priority, or stylistic influence of works of art. One senses their relevance to a world that teachers and pupils do not necessarily occupy. We look for signs and traces of real encounters with, and real perplexities about, art. We do not seek guidance among philosophers' stones or principles; we want to learn how to *confront* the objects that confront us. You cannot, in other words, learn to be a critic by learning critical principles. You have to *do* criticism.

How do children *do* criticism? They learn criticism the way they learn swimming—by getting into the water. Thus they must have the opportunity to look at art together and to report their findings to one another. It can be "official" art or art they have made themselves. Unfortunately, when a teacher thinks of criticism as the complex pronouncements of philosophers and scholars, he rather doubts that children can do it. The fact is, however, that children are good critics when you consider *the form* of their critical discourse rather than the cognitive reliability of their observations. And cognitive reliability in art criticism comes down to knowing the names of things. (The descriptive stage of criticism, incidentally, is an excellent vocabulary-building device). But notice: It is not "critical" terms the child needs to learn; he needs to arrange his talk-about-art in meaningful configurations. That is, his problem lies in the structure or configuration of his critical talk, not in his knowledge of terms. Critical study is clearly a species of media study. The critic must

make discriminations in one language or medium (speech) which correspond to the perceptions and discriminations he has made in another language or medium (imagery or visual form). If the child or critic knows more about the syntax of visual form than he does about the syntax of verbal language, then he can use his sophistication in one medium to build sophistication in the other. It seems very likely, especially in the case of deprived children, that many youngsters possess better understanding of visual syntax than of verbal syntax.*

Why should teachers struggle with the development of critical skills if such skills merely represent a type of intermedia translation? First, the form of art criticism as a whole is more significant than the form of each critical operation. There is considerable value in the discovery that putting together a set of descriptive, analytic, and interpretive statements confers dividends of meaning retroactively on the separate stages of the critical process. Second, we can teach for transfer of critical learning from the context of art to the context of life. Our general educational aim is to help children to con-

---

*Eisner's study demonstrating weak artistic abilities in deprived children suggests to me that these youngsters do not have "good reasons" for wanting to develop the "appropriate" schema and representational devices which constitute so much of the typical elementary-school art education program. The child who can catch a ride on the back of a moving bus has acquired a very sophisticated understanding of the syntax of a particular medium, and he is well aware of its expressive meaning. Elliot W. Eisner, *A Comparison of Developmental Drawing Characteristics of Culturally Advantaged and Culturally Disadvantaged Children*, Stanford Univ. Press, 1967. Research sponsored by U.S. Department of Health, Education and Welfare.

front life meaningfully. To do so, they must be able to "read" the human situation. Critical study is practice in reading works of art that are microcosms of the human situation. Understanding visual art—or any medium—is more than knowing its various names or labels. Understanding means coping. It is a matter of becoming *engaged with*, or confronting, a system of signs and symbols. Critical study tries to systematize that engagement or confrontation so that the child or youth can extend his insights to the business of living.

Conclusion

I have tried, in this chapter, to paint a large picture of what art education can be. My intention, in formulating educational objectives for a time of enormous ferment and innovation, is to follow the advice of the baseball or golfing coach who urges the beginner to "keep his eye on the ball." The ball in this case is humanism, the study of man. A great deal of wasted effort, busywork, and student apathy can be avoided if teachers periodically remind themselves of their long-range goals, or strategy. When they do, it is easier to formulate short-range goals, or tactics.

A theory is a type of strategic statement. Hopefully, it demonstrates the relevance of certain educational objectives to philosophic assumptions about man, society, the universe, and the life good to live. A theory should also provide the justification for day-to-day teaching practices. It should help us to perceive clearly the connection between what we are doing and what is being accomplished. Finally, a theory should help teachers to select or reject practices intelligently rather than to repeat what has always been done.

Prospective teachers, typically, want to know what to say and do when they are in a classroom. This chapter on theory contains some hints in that direction, but that is not its chief purpose. Its main purpose has been to enlarge the idea of art education that a college or university student gets from his fragmentary perceptions of what teachers do. We have to see beyond art instruction as mixing paint, handing out paper and paste, and displaying children's art products. So far as specific teaching practices are concerned, they are presented in our exemplar curriculum, comprising Chapters 9 through 12. But even then the teacher's imagination and resourcefulness are called for. It is not possible to spell out in the tiniest detail what an art teacher ought to do without insulting his intelligence or implying that he has received no professional preparation.

Assuming that the important strategic questions about art education have been raised and discussed in this chapter, I shall try to deal with tactical questions in the next chapter, *The New Creative Situation*. Here we can come a little closer to the pupil-teacher relationship; we can try to identify some of the features of good quality instruction in an art education program. And we can attempt to identify some of the signs that our educational goals are being achieved.

This chapter is specifically about teaching. It tries to show how to generate learning in a classroom. It tells how teaching practices get born and what happens to them afterward. In short, this is a chapter about methodology—an evil word in some circles.

If you want, you can proceed to Part Four and the exemplar curriculum. There, a number of practices are already set out, and all that is required of the teacher is to adapt and modify them according to particular circumstances. If your conscience is bothered by that sort of procedure, you may call it research. But if you want to know how *to invent or to design* art education practices, and if you want to involve your pupils in your program planning, it would be better to read this chapter. Afterward, Part Four will make more sense.

Why speak of "the new creative situation?" First, we now have an expanded idea of creativity in art education. Teaching prac-tices aim at more than certain kinds of artistic products, they aim at goals employing *any* idea, skill, technique, or process a child can use. Second, the school environment has been transformed by a variety of outside influences: the mass media, the new person-machine teaching combinations, and the increased concern of community groups with the content and effectiveness of teaching. Third, stylistic changes in the official art world are so swift, and news about them is so rapidly disseminated, that they have the effect of redefining art for teachers and pupils almost continuously. Finally, the children we teach are different in important respects from previous generations: They own and use gadgets that did not exist a short time ago; they often have traveled widely; they have seen a lot on television; many have visited museums, or they live in communities with well-run cultural centers. Even poor children have access, through

8

The New Creative Situation

magazines and films, to art and artists working all over the world. It is *difficult* for today's child to be provincial; his culture is world-wide in scope. Naturally, then, it is the child who represents the important new factor in "the new creative situation."

The Pupil-Teacher Relationship

Before you are a teacher of art or science or history, you are just a teacher, which is to say, a person who has a special relation to children. The particular kind of learning you are interested in cannot be advanced if you yourself stand in the way of the relationship that needs to be established. A good relationship does not result merely because you desire it; it grows out of what you do and, especially, the way you respond to what children do. What does a teacher do? What does an *art* teacher do?

Planning

Teachers plan before they meet their classes and they plan with their pupils. Planning can be done in advance, but not entirely. Children today want and are entitled to be included in decision-making about educational goals. Their involvement is a good check on the relevance of your teaching to their needs. In addition, any person makes better progress toward a goal he has had a part in selecting.

Planning with children does not weaken your ability to set in motion worthwhile curricular objectives. If anything, it strengthens the likelihood that you will make real progress toward them. Neither does it mean that you are surrendering your special competence in your field. It means that you are *consulting* children about the way they perceive what you are trying to accomplish. After all, as a teacher you are a leader and initiator. You are the person who marks out the terrain on which planning and learning will take place. It is not a matter of deceiving pupils into accepting your decisions made in advance. Real planning with children involves real freedom for them to decide questions that are genuinely important to them while you retain your freedom to decide questions that have to be your professional concern. Consequently, planning with children calls for you to master a *dialogic technique*: uncovering their needs and your professional concerns in *their* expressions of interest, curiosity, admiration, indifference, enthusiasm, dislike, and desire.

Dialog

To teach art, or music, or anything else, you have to talk with children—not at them. Talking with and being with people constitute dialog. True dialog is not random conversation; it grows out of a special kind of perception: *A teacher has to perceive what the children hear while he is speaking.* But what is it that you try to perceive, or listen to, as you conduct your dialog with children? You listen to, or look for, a spark that can be kindled. You try to build a flame, that is, an intense awareness of something you and the children want very much to know or do.

The tinder is there in the form of "dry stuff" in the child—vaguely perceived feelings, odds and ends of ideas, intuitions, interests, and anxieties. This is the stuff you have to fan into flame, into present awareness. This tinder, when lit, is felt by teacher and pupils as a *confrontation with a real problem. Until you have found that problem you do not start anything else.*

Genuine dialog, then, revolves around the search for a real problem—something that truly concerns your pupils. But what is a real problem? Here is where your curriculum planning, your professional preparation, your experience as someone who once was young, and your ordinary intelligence become relevant. What do you think these children care about right now? How does this connect with your curriculum strategy? That is, how does art—the visual expression of human concerns—combine with a child's present awareness of his being in the world? The answer to this latter question is not known in advance. As an older and more experienced person, you *think* you know the answer, and your intuition about it provides you with the momentum to carry on your dialog. But you do not really know the answer; it can be discovered only in the process of doing and perceiving and interacting. You and your pupils will have this kind of experience together and then you will have an answer that is provisionally valid. You will know and feel something which, for the time being, at least, joins you together as human beings in the world.

The whole purpose of planning with children is to identify real problems, and the technique we use is dialog. One of the delightful results of dialog is the discovery by children that they have "a good reason" or a good place for investing their creative energy.* An organic connection has been built between the existence of a problem and the child's need to confront it creatively, because the problem is real: It has been identified by teacher *and* pupils together. It has not been given or assigned from the outside; it grew from within.

Scope and Sequence

Problems that have been identified, as recommended above, would not seem to present themselves in any logical sequence. And the scope of the art education program would seem to be merely the arbitrary result of a particular set of teacher-pupil interactions. But if the dialogic technique is followed in planning, scope will correspond *in the long run* to the four categories of study described in our humanistic theory, for the theory is comprehensive enough to embrace both the diversity of humanistic concerns and the several ways art can be experienced and created. But there can be no guarantee that classroom interaction in the short run will follow the neat, diagrammatic relation-

*One of the principal points made by Paul Goodman in *Growing Up Absurd* (Random House, 1956, p. 41), is that adolescents often do not have anything worth doing: "If there is nothing worth while, it is hard to do anything at all. When one does nothing, one is threatened by the question, *is* one nothing?" The elementary-school child will build a foundation for feelings of worthlessness too if his schooling does not connect his busy-ness to the perception of real tasks in the real world.

ships of a theory. Furthermore, a theoretical statement has to be discursive or linear; it cannot adequately deal with the simultaneous features of classroom experience. Critical study, for example, is discussed last in Chapter 7, but it should pervade all phases of the program from the beginning.

The scope of the art education program will inevitably include man—what he builds and what he feels about people and things —if the teacher will only let these themes emerge. When you worry too much about scope and sequence, that is, about whether you are covering the right material, and in the right order, it is possible to become rigid and even a little compulsive about "authorized" facts and skills. The truth is, children cannot help being curious about the important human questions; it is the somewhat inflexible teacher who experiences panic and gets "up tight" about coverage, wondering when it is right to teach the color-wheel, whether perspective should be learned, whether watercolor is an appropriate medium in the lower elementary grades, whether it is wrong to demonstrate techniques, and so on. But these problems do not arise for people who have an informed commitment to a humanistic strategy of teaching. Such teachers are too busy—too much engaged in confronting and coping with the shape of reality to become panicky about the shape of scope and sequence.

As teachers and pupils plan together, as they identify real areas of concern, and as they try to work their way through these concerns, the glimmerings of form and sequence *do* appear to be visible in their collaborative effort. It is the teacher's responsibility to be alert to this emerging form in what is being done and learned. And the formal aspect of learning as a whole has value apart from the worth of the parts of each separate experience. A teacher tries to shape the over-all, or comprehensive, form of what is learned. That is, he helps his pupils to perceive a pattern among the parts and types of experience they have had in art. This is accomplished by pausing periodically to review what has been done and discovered, guessing where it might lead, wondering if other things might have been tried, and finally characterizing or giving a name to what has been perceived in the mutual encounter of pupils and teacher.

The form of children's learning often results from a teacher's style. Sometimes it takes years for a teacher to find out what his personal style is really like. A good teacher tries, by any means he can, to gain some insight into his own style and then to build and refine it. The real scope and sequence of what a child learns, as opposed to what is officially stated in course outlines and lesson plans, is often determined by the unique interaction of a particular group of pupils with a particular teacher in a particular place at a particular time. Stated goals and values are important, too, but they are translated into action, into learning, by a teacher acting as performer, questioner, demonstrator. A teacher, in short, can be a very effective audio-visual aid—easily hooked up, always ready for use, rarely in need of repair, and highly adaptable to changes in the classroom climate.

Girl and boy in art classes. (Both photos, The New York Times.)

A moderate amount of disorder. (Photo by author.)

The most momentous philosophical question in art education: how to get kids to clean up. The girl here, protected by a smock, paints on paper taped to the wall. Clean-up is no problem. The wall gets spattered? It can be repainted during the summer vacation. Her smock can be one of her father's old shirts. The point is not to get the youngsters so "up tight" about smears and spatters that they will be afraid to paint.

A boy examines his hands with dismay. He could be Lady Macbeth: "Out, out, damned spot!" The point is not to panic. William Chase said a good painter could work effectively in dress clothes,

and Chase did. In full evening regalia. But children will get messy. No matter. Everything washes out. Children's paints and crayons may not be good to eat, but they are nontoxic. Basic advice: Do not clean up for your pupils. Insist that they do it themselves. Provide enough time for the job. Give specific directions, clearly, about what belongs where. And follow up.

At this point, the school custodian's philosophy of art becomes relevant. He usually has strong views and a strict policy about cleanliness and creativity; you may have a passionate belief in spontaneity, exploration with materials, and the child's right to self-expres-

sion. Therefore, your philosophy and his philosophy might conflict, especially if you and he are the products of divergent philosophies of teacher education. So it would be well if there were a general understanding, established in advance—among you, the school principal, and the custodial staff—about the things children must do in an art program and the standards of classroom cleanliness that can reasonably be expected.

A moderate amount of disorder seems to stimulate some people artistically. Beyond a certain point, however, disorder is a deterrent to creativity. Be alert to that possibility and defend against it. ∎

Cultural and Ethnic Differences

In addition to being older than his pupils, a teacher rarely possesses the same cultural, ethnic, religious, or social background as each of his pupils. That identity would be virtually impossible. The age difference alone —the so-called generation gap—accounts for much of the difficulty in teacher-pupil communication. How can this problem be overcome, especially since most teaching is done with groups rather than on a one-to-one basis? First of all, a teacher in preparation devotes some time to designing questions. Skillful questioning elicits answers; answers create involvement and the opportunity to build communication. But concentration on the form and imagery of verbal exchange rather than its cognitive validity is helpful, too. In other words, a teacher thinks of words as something to paint with and tries not to rely entirely on their logical value. New teachers tend to spend too much time in preparing the organization of cognitive materials or subject matter. As a result, they "overteach" in the effort to "cover" what they have planned. Dialog, which is a self-correcting process, languishes. You need pupil feedback not only to find out whether you are communicating, but also to learn whether your teaching style involves or excludes pupils who belong to groups that employ styles different from your own.

It is a mistake to try to become like your pupils in order to communicate with them or show your affection for them. They will respect you for being yourself. Your fairness, enthusiasm, and good will (or the lack of these qualities) cannot be concealed—not for long. So it is important that you *be* the kind of person your professional role calls for. And this kind of *being*, as contrasted with role-playing, requires self-knowledge as well as commitment to the value of what you are teaching. When there are youngsters you do not understand or cannot seem to like, try to meet them on the grounds of the material you teach. Energy expended on rationalizing your feelings toward certain pupils or coping with your sense of guilt is usually counterproductive. Most human differences can be reconciled within the context of real dialog. And dialog, in turn, is a product of genuinely collaborative teacher-pupil planning. Children who are learning and teachers who are teaching do not have much room for hostile feelings.

But what of the sorely deprived child who comes to your class with already well-developed expectations of failure? What of the child who is bored before you have had a chance to bore him? What of the child whose capacity to learn has been damaged by the culture of poverty? It would be misleading to claim that art education constitutes a panacea for such children. On the other hand, we may justifiably feel that art education as a discipline holds up models of success that are somewhat different from those in other curricular areas. For example, we are not solely interested in "right answers" or in the traditional skills involving information-storage and -retrieval. Our teaching practices can be designed around linguistic and media experiences that do not rely heavily on the types of verbal facility in which deprived youngsters are weak. The next section of this chapter will show how such art education practices can be designed. Fundamentally, it is a matter of building connections between the subculture of the children and the structure of our discipline, art education. We can make progress in this direction by recognizing that the mass media usually constitute the common element in the lives of all children, regardless of the subcultures they come from.

The Anatomy
of an Art Teaching Practice

Let us assume that genuine teacher-pupil planning has taken place, that there has been real dialog, that authentic problems and concerns have been identified: Someone has seen a dead animal that was run over on the highway. An older brother or sister is getting married. A new baby was born. There was a grass fire in an empty lot down the street. A grandfather is very sick. The landlord won't send up enough heat. Fords are faster than Cadillacs. Someone's mother hit him because he and his friends made too much noise. A family bought a color TV.

Identification

These are things that really happen. They are what a child thinks about. They are the sources of his anxiety and delight. The world of a child, the substance of his reality, is made up of materials like those mentioned above. But what do these things have to do with art teaching? First, art is a *by-product* of someone's encounter with the world. If children are asked to make ART directly, the results will be inauthentic. The products may look like art, but they are "teacher art" not "pupil art." Second, art practices have to be derived from the personal encounters of children with reality if the resulting learning is to have any significant humanistic value. Third, we are trying to establish the following idea in the consciousness of each child: *Art is what you do about something that interests, worries, or pleases you.*

Now we are faced with a problem in teaching technique: how to make the transition from the identification of a real concern to the actual practice. This transition is achieved by *expanding* and *elaborating* the theme we perceive in the child's concern. For example, the child has seen a dead dog in the street; there are several potential directions in which this experience, viewed as a theme, can be moved. You try to find out what is problematic to the child about the experience. In the end, you will help him to re-enact or represent its problematic features symbolically. This does not mean he should illustrate what he has seen. For the present, it means that you, as teacher, will encourage the child to discover some of the ways that the death of an animal can be faced, or thought about. To summarize, the first stage in the development of an art education practice is the identification of a real concern. The second stage is expanding and generalizing the concern. What does this mean in behavioral terms?

Expansion and Elaboration

The stage of expansion and elaboration is one in which the child explores the meanings that are latent in his concern. He may have to read, to question his friends, to collect pictures, to write down strings of words, to explore his neighborhood looking for images, to tell a story, to make some drawings. The important point is that the child is *doing* something, and the results of that doing will be made public—to his teacher and his class. A second purpose of elaboration is to extend the period of creative search and form-seeking. We must postpone the impulse to create and display a final art product. Artistic skills are employed during this stage as tools of inquiry. Drawing is a way of recording facts. Acting is a way of rehearsing what happened. Writing is a way of remembering and recording. To make art significant for the child, we have to slow down the rate at which he produces it, while enriching and extending the process during which it is born in him.

The teacher helps during this stage by stimulating the child's fact-gathering, image-collecting, and idea-generating effort. The teacher displays all kinds of art and imagery in the class, playing records or reading poems and short stories related to the work in progress. He might interpret to the class what individual children are doing—giving progress reports, so to speak, and reinforcing the goal-orientation of particular youngsters. He may organize the cooperative effort of several children if they seem to have a similar concern or if they need each other's help. He will have conferences with individual children in which he acts as an audience of one for short explanations of what they are doing. And the teacher continues to ask questions. These are for the purposes of opening up new lines of inquiry and preventing premature closure of a potentially rich experience. Finally, the teacher watches for the ripening of ideas, that is, the child's readiness to say something.

Execution

During the stage of execution, the child tries to find the best possible shape for the ideas, images and feelings he has been gathering. Until now his work has been visible in the form of fragmentary visual-verbal reports to his teacher and the small group he may be working with. He has been storing up little sketches, clippings, short written statements, found objects, quotations. Now the time has arrived when he must move in the direction of commitment to a form of presentation. That is, he needs to make something or do something that can be shown publicly. The role of the teacher is to help the child in making the transition. It is the transition from personal discovery and expression to social exchange or communication.

This transitional phase in the creative expression of children has always seemed traumatic to art educators. There is a certain amount of nervousness in the teaching literature as it tries to steer a course between eliciting art from the child but not showing him how to do it; motivating him to express himself artistically but refusing to demonstrate technique; avoiding display of adult or professional art that might corrupt his naive imagery; hinting at desired formal qualities (large images, free brushwork, overlapping shapes, flat space, exaggerated color) without actually directing the child's effort. It is almost as if teaching were a sort of charade; you know what you want the child to do but you must not directly tell him what it is. It would be easier to walk on eggs.

Conventional art teaching often encourages a sort of masquerade, a lack of candor between teacher and pupils. The following are the reasons some teachers are not as forthright as they might be: The teacher's real objective is the creation of art products exhibiting "appropriate" developmental traits, and the children may suspect as much. (2) The creative process and the creative product are hopelessly abstracted from the reality of the child's existence. (3) The bulk of the pupil-teacher interaction is devoted to execution; the preparatory stages of identification and expansion are omitted or abbreviated in the rush to get out brushes and paint. (4) A general air of mystery surrounds the *purpose* of the child's creative expression. (5) Evaluation and critical explication of creative work are either omitted or confined to perfunctory expressions of approval that are readily perceived as fatuous.

The transition to the stage of forming and shaping will occur naturally and logically and without trauma if the two previous oper-

ations—identifying a concern and elaborating its meanings—have been carried out. Difficulties arise from a premature leap into execution. A teacher can easily recognize a child's readiness through his accumulation of a good body of supporting material, in his expressed desire to start something ambitious, and in a certain amount of restlessness. Every child will not be ready at the same time, and so the teacher can work with individuals, mostly with the intention of building a sustaining fund of ideas. It is important that children understand drawing, for example, as empirical investigation. Little sketches and collected images are for their own use; they may or may not decide to show them in a final presentation. The child should not be self-conscious about the form of his visual fact-finding; and the teacher can help in this respect by creating an intimate, accepting, more-or-less private atmosphere for examining what he has made, written, or gathered.*

Getting into execution is a process of helping the child to select and organize the imagery he plans to present, represent, talk about, write about, explain, combine, offer as a "happening," use in an environment, or display as a collection. He may need the direct sensory stimulation of what he has accumulated in order to get started. Or he may want to rely on recollection. He may attempt a large synthesis—a collective rep-

*It is best to avoid uniformity in materials and format here and to encourage the child to use torn paper, informal sketches the size of his hand, huge brushed paintings on newspaper, cut-outs from magazines, shells, stones, discarded objects—any source of imagery.

resentation of every fragment he has saved. That would be wonderful. Or he may wish to attempt a fresh, nonvisual departure, with his earlier activity serving as a fund of ideas or images in another medium. And that would be fine, too. You *hope* that your work with each child has produced some ability to sustain a creative effort. But if not, and as you see energies flag, it will be necessary to go back to the previous stage of the teaching practice, reinforcing the connection between present execution and the concern or problem that was originally identified.

When is the work done? A child cannot make this decision alone, nor can the teacher make it for him. Hopefully, the decision to stop working will include others if this can be done tactfully. For example, other children can be brought in. When a child is tired, let him have some time to reflect or to change his activity temporarily. The aim is to keep the door open for further elaboration. Most children have a low boredom threshold; they quit too easily. Unfortunately, some adults become their accomplices because they admire the fresh, spontaneous, fragmentary character of child art. But we have an interest, as educators, in helping a child to sustain his creative effort —even if it means "spoiling" the work.

Finally, it is important for the teacher to realize that artistic execution, as we understand it today, embraces a much wider range of forming and organizing activity than it did even thirty years ago. Hopefully, earlier discussions in this book have helped you to recognize the relevance of primitive and contemporary types of artistic expression to creative practices in a modern classroom situation. It is not that we want children to imitate Klee and Dubuffet (who, after all, imitated children). But we can take advantage of the insights into artistic creativity that are evident in the works of these and other modern masters.

Presentation

The culminating stage of a practice is presentation to a group. In this way the individual's concern is united with a social purpose. His act of expression is related to the problem of communication. From the beginning, the child should know that his search for form has two purposes: confronting a crisis, problem, or concern through his own creative effort, and sharing the results of that confrontation with others. The theoretical purpose is that the ritualistic function of individual creativity receives the reinforcement of social witness. It is not enough for the child to relate his effort only to his teacher. What he makes or says has to be informed by the consciousness of a group that cares about, and is involved with, anything he does.

Returning to my earlier example, let us say that a child was upset, really disturbed, about seeing a killed dog on the highway. Suppose he paints some pictures about it and makes up a little story to go with the pictures. This effort cannot truly function as art, that is, it cannot *ritualize* his crisis, unless there are spectators, witnesses, and participants in his confrontation. His presentation *is part of* the act of giving form. We cannot separate the artistic product from the way it is received. Unlike the art gallery world, the world of teaching has to offer an *organic* consummation to the creative process.

The presentational stage of a practice is also a vehicle for critical study. Remember that criticism is "talk about art." Children should be encouraged to "mix" their own feelings with the feeling they see expressed in the presented work. As they respond, they participate, in effect, in a collective act of empathy. The teacher may have to start this response, to give a model of the reactions expected from the group. It is not a good idea, however, to focus strongly on the technical or formal features of what is presented —certainly not in the lower elementary grades—because the natural tendency of young children is to attend to the expressive meanings of urgently felt experience.

How does a teacher know when creative work is ready to be shown? How can he deal with differences in artistic ability? First and most obviously, he realizes that all children are not ready at the same time. Second, the teacher views each creative effort in a combined-arts context. That is, he encourages the child to make his statement any way he can, with emphasis on visual-verbal-dramatic combinations. Where a pictorial effort seems weak, the child can supplement his representational skills by combining them with imagery borrowed from the media—magazines, posters, packages, labels, newspapers, advertising brochures. Here we are adopting the methods of collagists from Picasso to

Rauschenberg. The child who has pictorial facility would have no special advantage over the child who can organize an effective visual-verbal presentation. By "effective presentation," I mean a sensitive account of a person's feelings in connection with something that really happened. The teacher presses for effectiveness by reinforcing ideas and images uncovered during the stage of expansion and elaboration. In the elementary-school art program, therefore, purely artistic skill will be an *outcome* of intensely perceived experience combined with "good reasons" for sharing experience with the group.

Synaesthesia plays a role in the combined-arts strategy of art teaching today. This concept points to the possibility that some persons may experience auditory or tactile sensations when they are stimulated visually. It suggests that the inability to represent visual percepts accurately does not imply inability to make fine discriminations through the other senses. An English writer on art education, Michael Steveni, suggests that Viktor Lowenfeld's "haptics" (persons who have difficulty in representing their experience visually) may be "people that are more gifted in the direction of synaesthesis. Are they, in fact, able to produce a tactile image when presented with a visual sensation and vice versa . . . ?"* Since as much as one-quarter of the population may fall in the haptic group (and haptical tendencies begin to appear around puberty although they may be latent earlier), it seems educationally un-

*Michael Steveni, *Art and Education*, London: B. T. Batsford, 1968, p. 101.

Art class at the Brooklyn Museum. (The New York Times.)

Children painting on floor in art class. (Courtesy Anita Unruh and the Florida Art Education Magazine.)

Above is an arrangement, at the Brooklyn Museum, for training easel painters. It is reminiscent of classes conducted for seven- and eight-year-old Russian children who are beginning their arduous training for the classical ballet. Or the astonishing Japanese children's classes for fiddle players. To become a finished performer, to arrive at the status of "artist," virtuoso, or première danseuse, one must stretch the right muscles early. The analogy is not inexact. Talent must be discovered young and nurtured continuously if we want to produce great performers.

But humanistic education is something else. It is better, perhaps, for producing composers and playwrights and poets—men who invent new forms more than they perfect existing forms. Not so many prodigies result, though. ■

wise to design teaching practices that are likely to frustrate one child in every four. McLuhan is surely an apostle of synaesthesia; he encourages the

process of getting at one thing through another, of handling and sensing many facets at a time through more than one sense at a time. . . . The "common sense" was for many centuries held to be the peculiar human power of translating one kind of experience of one sense into all the senses, and *presenting the result continuously* as a unified image to the mind.*

The isolation and fragmentation of sensory experiences has no place in elementary education. Teaching practices that place a heavy premium on visual performance, isolated from performance in other languages a child can command, represent an invasion downward from the specialized culture of adults into the generalized and synaesthetic culture of children. Children's creative presentations should allow them the opportunity to move fluently among a variety of expressive media. If this idea takes hold, we may look forward to some healthy influence from children's culture as it reaches upward into the frequently arid stretches of adult creativity.

Evaluation

We must move very cautiously in the area of evaluation. It is possible for a misconceived idea of evaluation to penetrate backward into the structure of a teaching practice and ruin it thoroughly. As a rule, art

Understanding Media, p. 67. [Italics mine.]

educators are not guilty of designing their instruction according to the requirements of measuring instruments developed for other disciplines. In fact, it sometimes appears that art teachers do not understand the concept of "progress"—a failing of poets, painters and existentialists. Still, for the purposes of anatomizing an art teaching practice it is necessary to indicate how its educational effectiveness is judged. We might define evaluation in the present context as the process of finding out what children have learned about the human situation.

Until now, I have been discussing what teachers and pupils do together. Does this collaboration end as evaluation begins? No. Evaluation has been implicit throughout the course of the teaching practice. The values of the experience do not become suddenly visible at the end. The practice moves toward a culmination because every experience has an implicit purpose and it has to end eventually. But the children have been learning, we hope, from the beginning. What is the character of their learning and how can it be recognized?

The first thing a child learns about being human is that it requires *courage*. We have asked them to confront their experience honestly, to reflect on its meaning and value, and to report what they have found to the people they most respect and fear—their peers. All of this takes courage, and it is recognized in their ability to live through the art practice. The teacher can evaluate courage in a child according to his ability to identify his real concerns and his willingness to face them. Courage is evident in his willingness to take chances, to speculate about meanings, to explore new realms of expression, to risk failure, and be ready to try again. It is the willingness to undertake a personal search in order to make a personal discovery. All four stages of a practice provide opportunities to display courage, but teachers must be certain to keep the risk-taking options open. The courage children display is related to the freedom a teacher allows them to express.

In addition to courage, children should learn that being human requires making *decisions*. They have to get in the habit of making rational and intuitive choices among the alternatives presented by the tasks they have helped to select. Following directions about what to do and how to do it will result in a more orderly class and more guaranteed "creative" products, but it will not help greatly in forming the attitudes appropriate to citizens of a free society. A child's ability in decision-making will be visible to some extent in the way he opens up options during the stage of expansion. If he is reluctant to explore the meanings of a problem, it is because many alternatives of choice frighten him; he wants to simplify decision-making by limiting intellectual and creative options. A teacher's function, of course, is to enlarge the arena of choice and to prolong the period of deliberation. A child's cooperation with, or resistance to, this process is an index of his development as a decision-maker.

The crucial test of a child's decision-making, however, is the quality of his creative effort. There can be no value in

courage or in decision-making unless their contingent character is recognized by teachers and pupils alike. That is, they have to realize that the process values we have been talking about are dependent upon a real result—the presentation. A phony or inauthentic teaching practice is one that children recognize as having no significant culmination—no relation to life as they understand it. So it is vitally important that we view the presentation as more than an exercise or a preparation for something real that will occur later. An authentic presentation as a goal casts its shadow in advance; it invests present decision-making with serious meaning. Therefore, we have to take the presentation seriously.

From the standpoint of evaluation, how do you take a presentation or artistic effort seriously? First, you pay attention to it, rather than collect or store it. Second, you interpret the presentation to the child *in terms of the quality of the decisions it represents*. That is, the teacher publicly examines what each child has made or presented to the class by describing or explicating the connections between what the class has seen and the creative problems the child has tried to solve. Such explication does *not* entail approval or disapproval. It calls for a sensitive and perceptive response to what the child has done. This phase of the total evaluation process should take place as soon after each presentation as possible. It may be argued that there is not enough class time to perform such an evaluation. But the problem arises only if we encourage children to make more products than we can properly attend to. In other words, we may be trying to avoid evaluation by completely filling the class time with forming activity; as a result we convert the classroom into a cottage industry for the fabrication of art products.

Beyond courage and decision there is *appreciation*, or the capacity to accept and understand what another person has accomplished. Appreciation is a creative and imaginative act—not merely an expression of passivity or tact in a social situation. Some children are gifted appreciators. And all children should be given the classroom opportunity to demonstrate their powers of visual discrimination and interpretation. A resourceful teacher will design practices for those children who seem to have well-developed powers of appreciation. It is their form of creativity and it deserves recognition in a balanced art education program. But appreciation is not mere verbalizing. It is, rather, a type of *intermedia fluency*. What we are trying to recognize is the ability to perceive analogies in form and meaning—the capacity for moving back and forth among experiences and their representations. This capacity may be evident in seemingly absurd correlations of words, constructions, and sounds, or fixed images and moving images, or combinations of objects, light, and motion. Some children may be able to demonstrate their intermedia fluency by creating presentations that exhibit unusual juxtapositions of written, spoken, and represented imagery. If appreciation is indeed a type of intermedia fluency, then it can be evaluated only when it is supported by the total environment of the classroom

(to be discussed in the next section). Here let me say that intermedia fluency would appear to be far more relevant to the creative development of today's children than their mastery of static representational skills.

A Supportive Classroom Environment

From the preceding discussion it should be plain that good teaching is influenced by the classroom as a place and as an atmosphere. Of course, the atmosphere of a place is influenced by its equipment and space for doing things. You will be fortunate, therefore, if you teach in a school that has a specially designed art room. But the typical elementary teacher conducts an art program in the same room where the other curricular areas are taught, a space that is somewhat euphemistically called a "self-contained classroom." From the standpoint of modern multimedia instruction, however, that is not necessarily a disadvantage. Equipment and facilities become more important as the art education program grows more specialized. But specialization can reach a point of diminishing returns in a program of humanistic education. Equipment becomes *crucial* only when you define your objectives in purely technical terms. Not that supplies, tools, space, sinks, storage cabinets, and display areas are nonessential. But it is a pity when teaching and learning are overly defined by what can be done with tools instead of by the human relationships we want to generate and the expressive forms we need to create and organize.

Roof-top children center. (The New York Times.)

Fledgling Dutch artists sketching on street. (Photo, Daniel M. Madden.)

Environments for teaching and learning turn up unexpectedly in a city—on top of and outside of schools.

The roof of a building can be an exciting place for children to learn—not just an overflow area for an overcrowded school. But will the children respond to the visual opportunities and the openness of their improvised classroom? That depends on whether their teachers see beyond its exercise and recreation potential. This roof might be more than an elevated playground; it could be a kind of space platform—a piece of the earth on its way to the stars. Those trusses and girders enclose a magnificent, unobstructed space waiting to be converted into a habitat for human beings. Still, a few of the kids are drawing, just as if they were back in their art room—the dungeon in the basement. The others climb around, just as they would in the school yard. But they have the chance to imagine a new world here—to plan and construct and improvise a fantastic environment. All that energy and power of invention! It needs to be harnessed and translated into humane learning. Doing so would change this roofgarten into something very special. ∎

Building a Model

Before you can think intelligently about physical arrangements for creative work, it is necessary to have an idea about the total *quality* of your workspace. This amounts to forming an image or model of the sort of place that feels comfortable to you and your pupils.

Where do you see yourself, and how do you see the children moving and working in the space you jointly occupy? How immaculate do you want to be? Where must the children go to clean up? How quickly do you need to be able to shift gears and change activity? Where can finished work be displayed? Will you distribute supplies, or will the children learn to get their own? Do you see yourself as the manager of a workshop? The proprietor of a store? The owner of a laboratory? An artist in his studio? The curator of a museum? The operator of a watch-repair business?

In all likelihood you will have to make the best of the room you are given. *Flexible* space is the key. If possible, open it up and place yourself and your pupils inside it. Where you can, break up the traditional classroom grid and arrange seating, benches, tables, storage and supply cabinets around the periphery of a central work space. But if these changes cannot be made, you can often improvise a kind of informal but creative disarray that works as well as more deliberate plans: You can cluster desks together to form temporary tables; you can form an inside quadrangle and put yourself in it; you can permanently appropriate the walls of the classroom for imagery (each wall a gigantic collage!); and you can permanently commandeer the ceiling for kinetic sculpture.

You should try to organize the kind of central space where you and your pupils can look at material together, move out to the edges to work, or move off to a corner to talk privately. It would be fine if there were little three-sided cells, or cubicles, or miniature studios, where a child could go to think and study and paste-up and invent things. To get ideas about workspace, visit a college or university art department and see what art students tend to do with or to their studios. Of course, you need a wall screen for projecting images, a tape recorder, a record player, portable lights, an opaque projector, color reproductions, an enameling kiln, art books, slides, film strips, a typewriter, a photography darkroom, hammers, files, saws and nails, tolerant neighbors, and a good-natured janitor. The list goes on. Art education associations, school furniture manufacturers, art materials representatives, audio-visual specialists and school architects can supplement it further. Getting space and equipment could become a career.

Therefore, you would do well to think of your self-contained classroom, if that is where you must of necessity work, as a base from which pupils and teacher will fan out on a variety of reconnoitering expeditions, hopefully returning with all sorts of ideas and images and information and improvised tools and loot.

Organizing Chaos

It is possible to think of an art room as a three-ring circus with the teacher as ringmaster. This happy thought is intimately related to the "materials approach" in art education—wide-ranging experimentation with all sorts of formal and informal art media—▶ tactile and visual stimulation—▶ accidental, spontaneous, or deliberate discovery of form and meaning—▶ guidance, restimulation, and congratulation by the teacher—▶ personality integration and multidimensional growth because of successful creative expression. And so on. To be sure, this is a caricature of a certain art education philosophy, but its implied image of the art room is a good one. Everyone is "doing his own thing" at his own rate of speed—and without a teaching machine! Such an arrangement permits a teacher to give individual instruction. It does not prevent pulling the group together from time to time to talk about matters of common concern. And it is a sympathetic environment for promoting intermedia fluency. How is it organized?

If every child is expected to produce art like a machine-operator on piecework in a nonunion shop, there will indeed be a tremendous classroom management problem. Supplying materials and storing completed work will be enough to keep a teacher thin and, as Krafft-Ebing used to say, neurasthenic. But it will be necessary, in any event, to move into a three-ring type of arrangement during the stages of expansion and execution. After individual problems and concerns have been identified by the group planning together, it becomes time for breaking down into separate cells to approach problems individually. During this stage, each child has to develop a personal strategy of invention or problem-solving, and he needs individual help. Some children have to go on information- and image-gathering voyages; they will leave the group and return to it. Other children need privacy to think. Some, engaged in a collaborative inquiry, have to huddle and plan how to proceed. Still others need the stimulation of direct work in a medium before an idea will incubate. Organizing a three-ring circus, then, is really a matter of establishing purposes and procedures in advance planning and then turning the child loose to pursue his goal or "do his thing."

It is not desirable, however, for a teacher to determine in advance how the entire class will carry out creative work. When every child executes in the same medium, at the same time, it means that the program has surrendered to logistical or administrative convenience. Artistic execution, as mentioned above, is only *one* stage of an art education practice; it is not the *entire* practice. In a program of real quality, it will be necessary to differentiate the forms of creative expression according to the character of each child's concern and his perception of the best way to confront it. Our objective is to shape an environment that lets the teacher work with the whole class when appropriate, or with individuals when necessary, or with the group again during the consummatory stage of a practice.

GEORGE WASHINGTON, by Gilbert Stuart. (National Gallery of Art, Washington, D.C., Andrew Mellon Collection.)

The Ultimate Environment

What we are looking for is an ambience, an atmosphere, a milieu, in which everything that happens to a child seems to generate insight. If you watch the way artists almost unconsciously arrange their workspace, you will see that they have this same objective. They are professionally engaged in a desperate effort to force their environments to make some kind of sense. In a way, each child is involved in a similar struggle. We help as teachers by trying to arrange a fruitful exchange between the classroom, the school, the community, and the little world a child carries around in his head. If a youngster can show you convincingly that George Washington's face (in the Gilbert Stuart portrait in front of the room) fits into

Why, do you suppose, is the portrait of Washington found in so many classrooms? To inspire patriotism, probably. But the solemn idol Gilbert Stuart painted soon becomes part of the walls or the furniture; no one really sees it.

Our mythic images have to be refreshed periodically; their conventional meanings need to be perceived in new contexts. A fresh examination of an old icon can rejuvenate its imagery. More importantly, it can give children the opportunity to exercise their powers of invention, to build on their fantasies, to create connections between their private imagining and the public world that is supposed to be real.

Since the self-contained classroom is going to be with us for a long time, you must convert it—the whole room, that is—into a learning device. Creative bulletin boards are not enough. Try to see all the objects and images in the room as small electronic transmitters continuously beaming messages that you can juxtapose and combine with classroom talk, textbook language, and children's imagery. First, however, it helps if you can believe in the possibility of objects' and images' changing their location and identity—in other words, occupying imaginary space in a magical world. The children are there already. This, perhaps, is the only chance schools have for competing effectively with the mass media—tuning in on the latent imagery of children and relating it to the goals of learning. Think of the wattage generated by all those little transmitters! ■

GEORGE WASHINGTON (above left), by Horatio Greenough. (National Collection of Fine Arts, Smithsonian Institution.)

GEORGE, by Donn Russell (above center). (Waverly Gallery, Inc.)

GEORGE WASHINGTON (above right), by Roy Lichtenstein. (Courtesy Mr. and Mrs. Leo Castelli; photo, Eric Pollitzer.)

RED, WHITE, AND BLUE (at right), by Sante Graziani. (Courtesy Dr. Thomas A. Mathews; photo, Babcock Galleries.)

the Gulf of Mexico (on your map of the Western Hemisphere) and that Florida would be part of Spain if the Mississippi River did not empty into Washington's hairpiece, then you have an idea of the way surrealist imagery, geological intuition, far-fetched analogy, jazzy historical improvisation, and visual punning can combine in the creative imagination—if the conditions are right. This is the type of multiple perception children are capable of. Hopefully we can foster a classroom environment in which this sort of perception might occur publicly, as it has, no doubt, occurred privately.

The next four chapters represent a departure from the usual way of dealing with curriculum construction. First of all, they are addressed to the student. Through this device I want to remind the teacher of the ultimate users or consumers of a curriculum. Perhaps you can imagine yourself as reading over the shoulders of your pupils. I think you will find yourself reacting to these chapters in several ways: You will try to guess at the reactions of children to the material; you will try to judge the practicality of certain suggestions at particular age and grade levels; you will think of ways to modify the material upward or downward according to the requirements of a specific teaching situation; and you will plan variations and alternative teaching practices that can lead to the objectives of your program as well or better than those I have developed.

A second feature of this curriculum is that it combines the "subject matter" of art with a variety of expressive activities. The practices are not just isolated lessons designed to develop technical skills and creative strategies; each is a part of a sequence in a comprehensive scheme of humanistic study. The theory behind this curriculum has already been presented. Here I want to stress the importance of basing your program on the total curricular sequence rather than scattered pieces of it. Of course, individual practices can be omitted, modified, or replaced by better ideas. But the comprehensive value of the curriculum will not be realized unless your pupils engage in all four types of study through art: cognitive

A

Curriculum

for Art

Education

study, linguistic study, media study, and critical study. You can spread these types of study over a year, a semester, a quarter, or a briefer block of time. But try to give your classes some experience with each mode of learning, and if possible, use the sequence suggested here.

The language of this curriculum is approximately that of junior-high-school pupils. In some cases it may seem appropriate for upper-elementary children, in other cases it may suit high-school students. I have tried very hard not to "talk down" to the reader, no matter what his age, and consequently have not attempted to address elementary-school pupils. For this age group (and for the others to a lesser extent) the leadership and adaptability of the teacher are indispensable for translating the goals of the program into concepts and activities children can understand. A third feature of the curriculum, therefore, is its reliance on the classroom teacher's ingenuity in translating curricular material into usable form for particular pupils. You will not find step-by-step directions here—recipes applicable to each and every teaching situation.

You will also notice that the practices accompanying the curriculum follow the same format: Some Things To See, Some Problems, Some Possibilities, *and* What You Can Do. *It is a format I have found useful, but I offer it only for purposes of suggestion and exploration. As for the practices, I hope you will not feel married to them. Where there are two practices for a particular idea, the first is more elementary and the second more advanced. Each practice has several possible outcomes and is intended to appeal to the wide range of interests and abilities found in any class. I use questions a great deal, and you will notice that their answers are not necessarily known in advance. But the questions are designed to elicit answers that are approximately in the right ballpark for a particular category of study. These answers, incidentally, are not always verbal. More often than not, they will entail investigation, acting out, artistic performance, or interdisciplinary search.*

Let me explain the connection between the teaching practices and the method of teacher-pupil planning advocated earlier. I realize that lessons designed in advance of meeting a particular class seem to anticipate the results of the teacher-pupil interaction. But that is the inevitable impression made by any plan, any curriculum, any systematic set of goals and procedures. Consequently, you must regard these practices as more or less educated guesses about the directions your planning will take. They are designed to be introduced after the concerns of your pupils have been identified. We have to assume that their concerns will be congruent, to some extent at least, with the modes of humanistic study embraced by our curriculum. The practices are flexible enough to allow a teacher plenty of room for improvisation. Furthermore, most teachers can respond creatively to the tensions between freedom and structure within the confines of a curriculum.

Why does the practice format begin with looking at a set of art objects? First, it is a painless way to become familiar with outstanding works of art. Second, children ought to get in the habit of looking at works of art as questions about, and answers to, their problems and concerns. Third, looking at selected works of art is a wonderful device for focusing the attention of a group that has been engaged in a free-wheeling discussion. Fourth, what would you expect to look at in an art-teaching practice?

9

We each know our families, our friends, a few neighbors, and something about ourselves. But the world is much larger than our neighborhood. There are people who live in totally different kinds of places, who work at jobs we never heard of, who do not look like us, who wear different clothes, and have different customs. Still, they all create art. Looking at their art and trying to make sense out of it will tell us something about the individuals who made it.

There is tremendous human variety in this country alone. Right in your own city or town, there are some interesting "characters." All of us meet some strange and wonderful people in this world—sooner or later. And many of us have seen some strange and wonderful places, especially if we have done any traveling (which most Americans do). Among other things, art is a visual record of all sorts of people and places. Just looking at pictures—whether you like them or not—can give you an idea of what people are like. If you have some imagination, you can guess how they might act. They may remind you of someone you know or once met. Since most people are curious about others, they can learn to look at art to find out what they want to know.

This chapter is about two things—people and places, actually *art* about people and places. First, we will look at people by themselves, or as individuals. Then we will see how *groups* of people are represented by art. Finally, we will examine *places* created by art—in other words, the houses and buildings and streets and other kinds of construction that make up towns and cities.

Meeting People

Why do artists paint pictures or carve statues of particular people? What is the

Understanding the World

reason for reproducing someone's face and body in wood, stone, clay or paint? You may remember that you tried to do the same thing when you were a child. Your drawings may not have been very convincing, but at the time you believed they looked exactly like your mother, father, sister, or uncle. No one asked you to create these drawings, you made them voluntarily. It was your way of having friends and close relatives with you whenever you wanted them. And you made those drawings over and over again.

A Person's Image

Not only children, but adults throughout the world create images of people. Today we have cameras, and almost everyone keeps snapshots of persons who are close to him. A man keeps a picture of his children, or a boy keeps a picture of his girlfriend, to remember what they look like. If you are away on a trip, or if you do not expect to see someone for a long time, a picture of that person can give you a great deal of pleasure. A picture or an image of a person can be a substitute for the person when he is gone—that is one reason people make such images.

There is another reason for making images. Suppose you lived at a time when people knew very little about science, very little about health and disease, very little about medicine, about growing food, or about changes in the weather, changes in the seasons, and so on. You would probably believe that all these things are controlled by invisible spirits and demons. Then if it rained too much or not enough, or if someone you loved became very sick, you would want to get help from the spirits who control the weather or health and sickness. But how can you get help from a spirit you cannot see? People who believe in spirits and demons create images of them for several reasons: It gives them someone to appeal to for help when they need it; it gives them a simple explanation—one they can understand—about something as complicated as the causes of rain or the causes of illness. After a while, those images make them comfortable and secure even if they are not facing an emergency.

Preserving Someone's Memory

When a king or a chief dies, one who was considered very strong and very wise, who was the leader of his people for so many years that they grew into the habit of depending on him for protection and advice in any kind of danger—when such a leader dies, his people are unhappy, of course. But they are also very frightened and worried. If there is no one to take his place, or if a young leader arises in whom the people have little confidence, it becomes difficult for them to imagine how life can go on without their wise old chief. In that kind of crisis, the people may ask their best painter or woodcarver to make a picture or statue of the dead chief. After the portrait has been completed and placed in a special house or hut, the people will speak to it on special occasions, give it gifts, and ask for

Avril rayon ad (above left). (ITT Rayonier, Inc., a subsidiary of International Telephone and Telegraph Corporation.)

EGYPTIAN GIRL (above right), by Alexej von Jawlensky. (Courtesy Morton D. May.)

SELF PORTRAIT (at right), by Egon Schiele. (Galerie St. Etienne, N.Y.)

MARGARETHA VAN EYCK, by Jan van Eyck. (Musée Communal Groeninge, Bruges, Belgium; copyright A.C.L., Bruxelles.)

SELF-PORTRAIT, by Leland Bell. (Collection Mr. and Mrs. Marvin H. Brainin; courtesy Robert Schoelkopf Gallery; photo, John D. Schiff.)

You could never meet all these people in real life. If you did, it would not be polite to stare at them. But you can get to know them very well through an artist's image. You can also get acquainted with the artist. That is, you can tell something about him from the way he treats his subject.

Any work of art says at least two things: who or what its subject is, and how the artist feels about that subject. Of course, you have to find out what the work of art is saying. To do this, you have to be able to read the artist's language or style—not too difficult if you make some good guesses and check them against your observations. The important thing is to keep searching until you have made up your mind about the person represented and about the artist too.

You need not feel ashamed of being curious; it's very human to want to know whatever you can about another member of the human race. In the process of satisfying your curiosity, you also learn to read and use visual cues or evidence; they add up to a language—a language you can enjoy for its own sake even when you are not feeling especially curious. ■

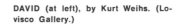

DAVID (at left), by Kurt Weihs. (Lovisco Gallery.)

MRS. METCALF BOWLER (below left), by John Singleton Copley. (National Gallery of Art, Washington, D.C. Gift of Louise Alida Livingston.)

CAPTAIN CHASE (below right), by John Battenberg. (Krasner Gallery.)

advice as they did when the chief was alive. Even the new chief might go to this statue and try to get help with the problems he faces. And when *he* dies, his image will also be placed in the house with the statue of the old chief. Eventually, that house will become a kind of shrine or holy place. It will be decorated with secret signs and markings intended to frighten away evil spirits and enemies of the people. Once again, artists who carve and paint will be asked to make these images. Their work is considered important because the people feel it protects them; it brings good luck; it gains them the help and good will of the invisible spirits hovering all around.

These are just a few of the reasons why primitive people—who do not have scientific explanations of the world—make wood or stone figures of the persons who are important to them. Although we have a better understanding of science and nature than tribal people, we still have similar ideas about images. After all, some of us collect pictures of movie stars or sports figures and act as if we knew them personally. Many people keep statues of saints and other holy figures in their homes or automobiles so they will be reminded of their religious beliefs and obligations. We keep portraits of our ancestors in our homes as a sign that we have not forgotten them. And when anything important happens—like a wedding or a family reunion—we usually take pictures of the event. Picture-taking is so important to us that even a wedding ceremony may be interrupted so that a photographer can get some good "shots." We take pictures not only to have a record of the occasion, but also, probably, because we think a religious ceremony or any event is not really "official" until it is recorded in pictorial imagery. The fact is, images have a kind of magic; they have the power to make us believe or remember something that would otherwise be vague or forgotten.

You may agree that images are important, but what do they have to do with school—with the reason you are in an art class, for example? The answer goes back to the job of learning what life is really all about. The different types of imagery in art are a record of the way life has been seen and felt by different kinds of people. In other words, you can learn through art how men and women express their feelings—their happiness, their disappointments, their hopes, their failures, their successes, their worries, their love, and their hatred.

"Reading" Images of People

In order to learn something about life from art, you have to learn how to "read" a work of art. This task is different from reading words in a book; it is more like what a detective does—looking for clues and evidence and trying to figure out how they add up. The evidence we get from art is visual instead of verbal, but you can still understand it. For example, if you look at an advertisement showing teenagers in a happy mood drinking a soft drink, you know what the ad is trying to say even without reading the words in it: The ad is attempting to say that the soft drink makes people happy. You might notice some other details which suggest that the drink keeps you young; or it helps you to stay slim; or it improves your looks; or the drink is healthy; or it goes with an outdoor, athletic life. These ideas may or may not be true. The important point is, *that* is what the images say to the viewer. If you get these ideas from the ad, you are *reading* the imagery in it.

That advertisement was probably created by a team of artists and designers instead of just one man. And you see it in a magazine or on a billboard instead of in a museum. But it is still an example of visual art—good or bad. You can "read" a famous painting or sculpture in the same way that you read that ad. It is just a problem in collecting visual evidence and deciding what it means.

By looking at images of people represented in art you can learn four things: (1) You can find out something about the person represented in a work of art; (2) you can develop your ability to understand visual evidence; (3) you can become aware of the visual devices used by artists to influence viewers or communicate with them; (4) you can learn something about yourself as you examine the way you feel about what you see.

Conclusion

In this section you have read about one possible explanation of the origin of images of people. However, the original purpose of a statue or a painting does not control the use we make of it today. That is, we do not make human sacrifices to a carved figure because we have had a long spell of dry weather or because the community we live in has had bad luck. But we are still interested in carved figures and painted images. *Our* interest is based on curiosity about the varieties of experience, feeling, and appearance it is possible for human beings to have or think of. After all, it will never be possible for you to see and do everything that is humanly possible. That is why we use music and poetry and art: They introduce us to ideas and emotions we might never know about.

Unlike animals, people can think ahead about things that will happen or might happen to them. We know that we will probably marry, have children, get new jobs, gain weight, make friends, lose friends, have accidents, move around, grow older, get sick, get well, and so on. All of these experiences, and the feelings connected with them, can be found in one form of art or another. In a way, art helps us to get ready for life by letting us know the feelings we are capable of having when we face reality. Art is not separated from life. If you know how to look at it, art can tell you how life really feels.

Meeting People: Practices 1

SOME THINGS TO SEE

Look at *Madonna and Child* by Jacob Epstein, *La Toilette* by Mary Cassatt, *An Old Man and His Grandson* by Ghirlandaio.

MADONNA AND CHILD (above left),
by Jacob Epstein. (The Riverside
Church.)

LA TOILETTE (above right), by Mary
Cassatt. (Courtesy of The Art Institute
of Chicago.)

AN OLD MAN AND HIS GRANDSON
(at left), by Ghirlandaio. (Musée du
Louvre, Cliché des Musées Nationaux.)

SOME PROBLEMS

Each of these works shows a child with an older person. Can you guess what the attitude of the older person is toward the child? Does the child seem to know what the older person is thinking? How old do you think each child is? How can you tell? What is the artist trying to tell us by his use of contrast between age and youth?

SOME POSSIBILITIES

Do you think that the mother in the Epstein sculpture is proud of her son? Why? Does the mother enjoy washing her baby in the Cassatt painting? How can you tell? In the Ghirlandaio painting, does the child think his grandfather is ugly? What makes you believe he does or does not? In addition to portraying individuals, each artist here is portraying a *relationship*. Try to find out how a *relationship* can be expressed without the use of words. For example, if two people walk into a room without saying anything, can we tell if they are brother and sister, boyfriend and girlfriend, employer and worker, strangers or friends? What helps us decide? How do actors use their bodies to show relationships? Listen to *Peter and the Wolf* by Prokofiev. How does the composer use sound to describe the boy, the men, the grandfather? How do artists use shapes to represent childhood, youth, or old age?

WHAT YOU CAN DO

Make up a set of meaningless shapes of about equal size on six sheets of paper and make each shape different. Give a number to each sheet. Then ask the members of your class to write down whether each shape is young or old. Collect the answers and see if there is any agreement among them. If there *is* agreement, how do you explain it?

Make an exhibition for your class based on magazine advertisements showing pairs of people—one older and one younger. Omit or cover up the product and the copy or written material. Label each example by describing the relationship you see.

Can you think of examples from literature in which the hero is ugly? Copy the passages in which the hero's ugliness is described. Would the grandfather in the Ghirlandaio painting fit one of these descriptions? What makes a person ugly? Also, how do people decide what is ugly or beautiful? Write an essay on this subject and illustrate it with pictures from discarded magazines.

In connection with the Cassatt painting, write an imaginary dialog between the mother and her baby (pretend the baby can talk) and read it to the class. Then collect advertisements for baby care products. Cut out the part of the ad that describes what the product will do for the baby. Now rewrite your dialog, substituting the advertising copy for the mother's lines. Read it to the class *after* they have heard your original dialog.

Go on a sketching trip over a weekend, looking for parents and children doing things together. Limit yourself to pairs—mother and son or daughter, father and son or daughter. If you prefer, use a candid camera.

Then, enlarge your most interesting examples and compare them to one of the four works of art shown here. Ask your teacher to set aside about ten minutes for you to tell the class where you gathered your material, how you worked it up and what you think it shows. Show your early sketches or candid snaps as well as the final results. Don't hesitate to include some quotations or something you have written yourself to explain the visual material or tell how you feel about it.

Meeting People: Practices 2

SOME THINGS TO SEE

Look at the following works of art: *Young Man Seated* by William Lehmbruck, *Cain* by Lu Duble, *The Frugal Repast* by Pablo Picasso, and *Man Pointing* by Alberto Giacometti.

SOME PROBLEMS

Each of the individuals represented in these works of art seems to have a personal difficulty; can you tell what it might be? What gave you the clues for your answer? Are you depending on what you know or what you can see in each work? What single visual feature or trait do these works of art have in common?

YOUNG MAN SEATED (top right), by Wilhelm Lehmbruck. (Wilhelm Lehmbruck Museum der Stadt Duisburg.)

CAIN (at right), by Lu Duble. (Collection Whitney Museum of American Art, N.Y.)

MAN POINTING (at right), by Alberto Giacometti. (Collection The Museum of Modern Art. Gift of Mrs. John D. Rockefeller, 3rd.)

THE FRUGAL REPAST (below), by Pablo Picasso. (Collection The Museum of Modern Art. Gift of Abby Aldrich Rockefeller.)

SOME POSSIBILITIES

Find out if there is any connection between a person's body type and his personality. Who would know something about this? Where can you get information on the subject? Do Picasso's people seem to be in love? How do you know? Listen to a recording of Act IV of the opera *La Bohème* by Puccini. Is there any connection with *The Frugal Repast*? Can you think of a poem or contemporary song that goes with Lehmbruck's *Young Man Seated*? Bring it in for the class to hear. Read the story of Cain and Abel in the Bible. How does the Lu Duble sculpture fit the biblical story?

WHAT YOU CAN DO

Invent a new title for each of these works of art and give the class your defense of the new title.

If you are interested in the dance, work up a short dance-narrative based on the Lu Duble sculpture of *Cain*. You might have a team in which one person writes the story, one person narrates, one person plays a musical accompaniment and one person figures out the dance movements and acts them out.

For Giacometti's *Man Pointing*, see how many examples from contemporary literature you can find that deal with the same ideas. Ask a friend to pose and try to model his figure with plastic metal or automobile-body solder in the same style as the *Man Pointing*. Don't copy it. Use a different body position, but try for the same feeling.

Here's a good project for the *Young Man Seated* if you are interested in sketching or photography: Try to find some real-life situations in which people seem to be in a similar position. You might look at athletes resting on the bench, or workmen taking a break, or people sitting in a bus or a train. Do you like rapid sketching? Do a series of seated figures like the Lehmbruck sculpture. Do them fast. Try one or two without looking at your paper. Pick out your best sketch or sketches and work them up into a more finished job. If you are a photographer, enlarge, crop, and mat your better shots and then present a small exhibit of them to the class.

Make up three or four teams of two—a boy and a girl—and take turns doing a pantomime based on Picasso's *Frugal Repast*. Each pantomime should *end* with the boy and girl in the same position as Picasso's couple. But each team should plan a different scene even though the endings will be identical. The idea of the pantomime is to interpret the lives of these people using only the motions of your body. Three members of the class might serve as judges of the pantomimes, giving reasons for their choice of the best performance.

Discovering Groups

A great deal of art is created for groups of people; the most common type is advertising design. It is intended to influence the way large numbers of people feel, think, or act. For example, the cartoon on the editorial page of a newspaper is intended to be seen by thousands of readers. Outdoor statues and monuments are made for groups of people to see, not just individuals. All architecture, including the sculpture attached to it, is meant for public rather than private use. And the advertising art in magazines, on television, and in outdoor posters is directed to millions of viewers. Obviously, all such art would not succeed in selling products or influencing the way the public thinks if only a few persons looked at it. Therefore, in order to communicate with millions of people, such art must emphasize groups—housewives, teenagers, automobile drivers, older voters, unmarried women, sports fans, people with average incomes, people who wear false teeth, men who are overweight, girls who are too thin, and so on. Whenever you look at advertising and communications art, you know it speaks to you as a member of a very large group.

Groups We Belong To

The reason communications art can be effective is that most of us realize even before we reach our teens that we are members of several groups in addition to our family group. You belong to a religious group because of the church you attend, an economic group because of the money you have to spend, a geographic group because of where you live, a racial group because of your skin color, and a nationality group because of the country your ancestors came from. When you get older and begin to vote, you may become a member of a political group. And the kind of work you do will place you in an occupational group. The amount of schooling you get will determine

As soon as you see two or more persons together, you are looking at some kind of group. People have to affect each other, just by being near each other. If an artist represents a group—large or small—he must have a reason for showing them the way he does. Try to discover that reason. Is he mainly interested in the way they influence each other? Or does he want them to influence you, the viewer? You belong to at least one group—your family—and many other groups besides. Which one of these groups is the artist talking to?

Can you enjoy a work of art without liking the people it represents, You can, but it takes practice. You can also dislike a work of art even though you admire the people in it. We have to learn to separate our feelings about art from our feelings about life. Of course, art is always trying to influence your real life through its power over your imagination. After all, art comes from real life—what an artist has seen and done and felt.

As we grow older, we learn to use art to experiment with our emotions. We decide to let art gain power over our thoughts and feelings—temporarily. Then we look back at those thoughts and feelings and try to decide whether we want to keep them, permanently. Do we want to be like the people in "Lawn Party"? Could I become one of Maurer's "Two Women"? Is that possible? Do I have anything in common with the persons in Romaire Bearden's "Sunrise" (p. 228)?

If you can, learn what different groups of people are like—through life and through art; compare them with yourself and your own group; try to discover the artist's attitude toward them; decide whether to make them "your people." ■

TWO HEADS (above left), by Alfred Maurer. (The Michener Collection, University of Texas at Austin.)

LAWN PARTY (above right), by Alex Katz. (The Jewish Museum.)

NEW PEOPLE (at left), by William King. (Courtesy Terry Dintenfass, Inc.; photo, Walter Rosenblum.)

SUNRISE (at right), by Romare Bearden. (Courtesy Cordier & Ekstrom; photo, Geoffrey Clements.)

MOTHER AND CHILD (below), by Alice Neel. (Graham Gallery, Ltd.)

your membership in an educational group. Furthermore, all of us belong to different *combinations* of groups whether we join them purposely or because of the accident of sex or place of birth. Our country is so large that communication is mainly group-to-group rather than person-to-person.

All of the groups I have mentioned, and many more, are real. People really belong to them. And in order to "get along" in our large and complex society, you have to learn what the main groups are, what holds them together, and how they work. But personally you can belong to only a few social groups. And it is not possible to guess what other groups are like just from your own limited group experience. Here, again, art can be useful in the business of learning what life is really like. You can study examples of art

—what I call "social" art—to find out what some of the groups in our society are and how they behave.

Group Life in Movies and TV

As a matter of fact, popular forms of art like motion pictures and television *are* used by young people as a source of information as well as entertainment. All over the world people have had their ambitions shaped and their hopes sharpened by looking at the only art form invented in the twentieth century— movies. And some people watch TV shows for as much as six hours each day. Unfortunately, the ideas we get about group life from television and motion pictures and other mass media are not always accurate, even though they may be convincing. As a result, if you pattern your own life after the group behavior you can see in magazines, TV, and the movies, you may run into conflicts in dealing with life as it really is. For example, there is a lot of killing and beating up of people in television and the movies. Of course, the actors do not really get hurt and you may see the same man killed over and over again. Still, it is possible for viewers to get the idea that killing and brutality are normal, or that being hit over the head with a chair is no more serious than scraping your knee.

Even though the action and violence you see may be exciting, you should always check it against what you personally know about the world and the people in it. Ask yourself if they really act that way. What would the world be like if all arguments were settled the way they are in a typical western movie? What would family life be like if every father were as stupid as the father in many television family comedies? Did you ever wonder what it would be like to be a member of an Indian tribe that is being mowed down by invading frontiersmen or by the U.S. cavalry?

I am not asking these questions to spoil your fun. In fact, you can get *more* enjoyment out of a film or TV show if you learn to look at it skillfully. And looking skillfully or intelligently at visual art is one of the objectives of this book. For example, when you look at a painting or sculpture you should get into the habit of thinking about your reactions to it too. Ask yourself what the artist was trying to make you see or feel or believe. Was he trying to tell you something about nature, about people, about cities, about technology, about love, about beauty? What are the visual clues that let you know what the artist is trying to say? After you have decided what a work of art is all about, then try to decide whether it fits *your* picture of the world. Is it just trying to be spectacular or beautiful or amazing? Does it *try* to change your viewpoint? Maybe it does and maybe it doesn't. Does this mean you should change your idea? Should you decide that the picture or sculpture or movie is not truthful or faithful to reality— that its picture of the world is not one you can believe in? Or should you suspend judgment—should you wait until you have more facts and experience to make a decision?

Immigrants in steerage. (Brown Bros., Inc.)

How Group Art Communicates

There is one other very difficult question you must answer when looking at *any* work of visual art—whether a statue, a poster, a motion picture, a television commercial, a record album cover, a painting, or a magazine advertisement: What group was the work made for? Remember that the artist does not know you personally. Yet he *does* want to communicate with you through his art. Therefore, he tries to imagine what people in your group are like—what you care about, what excites you—and he tries to reach you by "speaking" to you as a member of one or more groups. By looking carefully at what the artist has created, you may be able to tell what group or groups he thinks you belong to. Perhaps he thinks you like pastel colors and flowing curves if you are a girl; or he may think you like jagged lines and strong contrasts of color if you are a boy. Maybe he has decided that older people are attracted by peaceful landscapes and that younger adults are interested in busy scenes showing lots of active people like themselves. All of us are almost automatically attracted by art that deals with our own age group; even babies recognize pictures of other babies. So artists and designers have some fairly good ways of arousing the interest of the groups they want to reach. As a result, you and I see a great many examples of art which were planned for groups we do not belong to. But that does not prevent us from looking at it. Although I am a middle-aged man, I can, for example, look at art created for teenagers; and in that way, I find out what teenagers are supposed to be like. You can do the same thing: learn something about groups you do not belong to.

In a democratic society such as ours it is necessary to know and work with many different kinds of people. Not only is this necessary, it is also a lot of fun—much more interesting than being with people like yourself all the time. Art gets you ready for the human variety you are going to encounter throughout your life. It helps overcome the natural fear of strangers we all have. And since people differ in many ways, we have to learn to enjoy our differences instead of letting them divide us.

Discovering Groups: Practices 1

SOME THINGS TO SEE

Look at photo of steerage passengers, *My Family Reunion* by Louis Bosa, *My Parents* by Otto Dix, and *Handball* by Ben Shahn.

MY FAMILY REUNION, by Louis Bosa. (Collection Whitney Museum of American Art, N.Y. Gift of Mr. and Mrs. Alfred Jaretzki.)

MY PARENTS, by Otto Dix. (Oeffentliche Kunstsammlung, Basel.)

HANDBALL, by Ben Shahn. (Collection The Museum of Modern Art. Gift of Abby Aldrich Rockefeller.)

SOME PROBLEMS

The first three of these works deal with people who look "foreign." Obviously, the immigrants in the shipboard photograph are foreigners, Louis Bosa's *Family Reunion* takes place in Italy, and Otto Dix was a German painter. Shahn's handball players are American youngsters, but they share a certain quality with the foreigners in the other works. What do you think it is? Is there an American "look"? If so, is it a matter of clothing, posture, gesture, hair style, an attitude of confidence? The immigrants represented here are mostly poor. Do poor people look different from those who are comfortable or even wealthy? What can you tell about Shahn's players from the way they are painted? Do the people in the steerage photo seem frightened, hopeful, confused? In Bosa's painting, do the people seem to be enjoying themselves? Why or why not? Why aren't they more graceful? What kind of work do you think Otto Dix's parents did? Has he exaggerated anything in this double portrait? Would you guess that the picture really *looks* like his parents?

SOME POSSIBILITIES

Here again, dramatics is a great help. How do actors or dancers use their bodies to portray poor people? Can you tell if someone has self-confidence from the way he looks or walks? How would you define a peasant? Do we have peasants in the United States? Do these pictures reveal any connection between poverty and freedom? Between poverty and fear? Would you say that Shahn's handball players enjoy the game for its own sake? Or do they want to win very badly? Both Louis Bosa and Otto Dix are telling us something about their family background; Dix concentrates on his parents, but Bosa stresses his very large family. Does that difference give you any idea about the way Dix and Bosa think about themselves? Also, do you think they are being completely honest in the way they describe their families?

WHAT YOU CAN DO

Pick out a figure in each of these pictures and trace it. Then enlarge the tracings very accurately so that each one is the same size —about twenty-four inches high. Make sure the outline is thick enough to be visible at a distance. Then show each figure to students who have not seen the complete pictures that the figures came from. Ask them for a list of half a dozen or more adjectives they would use to describe each tracing. Then make a list of the adjectives most frequently used in connection with each figure. Finally, report your findings to the class and try to explain why certain words were repeatedly connected with each image. If possible, try to narrow down the key line or shape combinations that account for the answers you received.

Try to find pictures of people who are as different as possible from those shown here. Analyze these new pictures and try to specify the visual details that account for the different impression they make on the viewer.

A difficult artistic problem is the representation of crowds. Pick an event, like spectators at an accident, or people in a Christmas shopping rush. Then observe some real crowds. Look at them from a distance and from up close. Also, look at them with half-closed eyes or through the bottom of a drinking glass. Decide whether you want to represent the crowd as a collection of individuals or as a pattern of colors, lines, and shapes. You might want to study the representation of crowds by well-known artists too. What strategies did they follow? Which strategy would be best for your purposes? That, of course, depends on the kind of story you want to tell. Try to paint a crowd picture that communicates a certain feeling or mood and see if your friends can tell what that feeling is without knowing the title of the work.

Discovering Groups: Practices 2

SOME THINGS TO SEE

Look at *Christ and the Apostles* by Georges Rouault, *Night of the Rich and Night of the Poor* by Diego Rivera, *Employment Agency* by Isaac Soyer, and *Mine Disaster* by Berta Margoulies (on pp. 234–235).

SOME PROBLEMS

In each of these works a group of people are together for a different reason. What do these people mean to each other? What do they have in common? What unites them? How does the artist tell you what is going on in their minds? Are these works of art difficult or easy to understand? Why, or why not?

SOME POSSIBILITIES

Perhaps the artists are trying to make you think about certain ideas or encourage your beliefs in a particular direction. Is there anything wrong about that? In *Christ and the Apostles*, what is Rouault trying to tell you about the men who were first attracted to Jesus? In *Night of the Rich and Night of the Poor*, what, according to Rivera, are the main differences between rich people and poor people? In *Employment Agency*, how does Soyer ask you to think about people who are out of work? And in *Mine Disaster*, what kind of reaction does the sculptor, Berta Margoulies, want you to have?

Notice that, with the exception of the Soyer painting, these works show people huddled together. Notice also that most of the people look alike. Only the rich people in Rivera's mural and the unemployed people in Soyer's painting are portrayed as persons you could recognize as individuals. The women in *Mine Disaster* look very much alike. How do you explain that? Also, why are Christ's Apostles painted so crudely? Would you agree that Rivera's rich people are especially ugly? Have you found this to be true in your own experience or observation? If not, then why does Rivera paint them that way?

WHAT YOU CAN DO

Collect reproductions of works of art showing people represented in groups and ask members of the class to write a short statement about each work. On the basis of what they see, ask them to describe the

CHRIST AND THE APOSTLES, by Georges Rouault. (Collection Mr. and Mrs. Jacques Gelman, Mexico City.)

EMPLOYMENT AGENCY, by Isaac Soyer. (Collection Whitney Museum of American Art, N.Y.)

NIGHT OF THE RICH (left) and NIGHT OF THE POOR (right), by Diego Rivera. (Instituto Nacional de Bellas Artes, Mexico.)

MINE DISASTER, by Berta Margoulies. (Collection Whitney Museum of American Art, N.Y.)

age, occupation, educational level, income or class, and general character of the people as they are represented. Also, ask them to mention the visual clues that determine their answers.

Gather a series of illustrations of advertising products used mainly by older people. Then gather a series of ads for products used by teenagers. Now, compare the illustrations visually. Pretend that you know nothing about the products themselves and try to point out the visual features of the illustrations that suggest the character of the product. You might also compare popular music favored by older people and the kind of music your own age group prefers. What are the differences in rhythm, melody, instrumentation, subject matter and lyrics, repetition and variation, volume, choice of harmony, and so on? Do you think similar differences can be seen in the advertising illustrations?

Another interesting research project: Collect the editorial cartoons of one or more newspapers over a period of several weeks. Then notice how the figures standing for political parties, nations, labor, business, government, farmers, union members, generals, consumers, bankers, and diplomats are represented. See if they fit into group patterns. What, would you say, are the traits you are expected to believe each group has? Do you think the editorial cartoonist has been reasonably fair and accurate? Why or why not?

Try to do an editorial cartoon yourself. This could be a project involving several teams. Each team might consist of an editor, an artist, and a reporter. They should have a conference to decide on a subject and its general treatment. Then the editor should write his editorial, the artist should create his cartoon, and the reporter should work up his story. Perhaps the reporter's story is crucial, since it deals with the *facts* that the editor and cartoonist will comment on. If your class is divided into several teams, you might all decide to deal with the same story or subject. In that way, you will be able to make some interesting comparisons of the results. The main purpose of this project is

to find out how you can influence people through combinations of pictures and words.

Exploring Places

We spend our lives in and out of buildings; traveling on streets and highways; riding, flying, and sailing in all sorts of machines; walking or running through town and city spaces; and sometimes resting in the few natural places man has left alone. Almost every place we are in, though, has been shaped and built by man. And that is why our environment and most of the things in it can be considered art, not necessarily good art, but still the work of artists and designers.

Man-Made Communities

The house or apartment you live in, the street where it is located, the hospital where you were born, the stores where you shop, the school where you study, the town or city where they are all located—these did not grow like a plant from a seed. They were planned and built by men according to a design (or probably several designs). Some of the buildings seem to be where they are by accident, indeed, some of them *look* like accidents. But no matter what they look like, they reflect the ideas of architects, engineers, real estate developers, building contractors, politicians, and anyone else who tries to convert nature and land into livable space for people to use.

Whether we know it or not, all of us are

sensitive to the kinds of buildings we live and work in and the kinds of neighborhoods around us. For example, we like streets that we can cross without always worrying about being run over by automobiles. We like to see trees and grass as well as concrete, steel, and asphalt. We like spaces where we can play or just stroll, and benches where we can sit and read or talk to friends. We enjoy looking at reflections in a pond, at fountains, or water running over rocks. It can be fun just to look at shrubs and hedges, fences and gardens, doors and stairs, windows and shutters, streets and alleys, roofs and porches.

Practical Use and Visual Effect

All of the man-made things we see were intended to do a job. That is, the way they are shaped and built results from the combination of purposes they must serve. You might enjoy going up on the roof of your house, or the upper stories of a tall building, to look at all the roofs, chimneys, water tanks, TV aerials, electric cables and smokestacks around you. Each of them has a shape that reflects its purpose: shedding snow, venting smoke, picking up electronic signals, storing water, transmitting electric current, and so on. Even though these objects get their shapes from the jobs they do, you can think about them simply as objects that are interesting to look at. You can study their surface textures, the way light falls on them, the way they cast shadows, the way they form patterns and repetitions, the way they combine into solids or open spaces, the distribution of their colors, the contrasts between heavy, massive shapes and thin, lacy lines and textures. In other words, you get pleasure from seeing things in the man-made environment that were originally intended to serve some practical purpose.

Something else to think about is the material that things are made of. This means more than just making a mental list of building materials you see, such as brick, stone, wood, glass, steel, concrete, and asphalt. Try to see the way they combine. What does a brick wall do to an area of wood next to it? What is the effect of leaf and tree shadows on different surface materials? How do reflections in glass windows combine with the concrete or metal walls of a large office building? Look for the effects caused by wood grain, patterns of brick, poured concrete, roof shingles, metal screens, artificial light, colored accents from plastic panels. Notice the way the colors of cars, signs, lights, foliage, and clothing fabrics look against the textures and shapes of buildings.

After a while, you become good at recognizing certain combinations of shapes and materials in the man-made environment. It seems that they are repeated over and over again. Some of these combinations are pleasing and some are not. Some appear to be planned and some just happened. You should ask yourself why certain combinations look good while others are uninteresting or downright ugly. What kinds of materials and spaces attract you personally? Do some places look good at a distance and become ugly when you see them up close? How can you explain that?

APARTMENT HOUSES. (University of Georgia Department of Art.)

DOWNTOWN SCENE. (Courtesy Oliver Coleman.)

Fire hydrants (at right). (Both photos, Martin Schnur.)

Places are usually interesting because of the people who have built them, lived in them, looked at them, or used them in some special way. That would be partly true of natural as well as man-made places. The moon looks different because we know men have walked on it. An object, too, acquires special interest when we know or can see that it comes from some place that men are concerned about.

Almost any place becomes meaningful as soon as an artist deals with it through his special language. He uses the place to say something he feels is important. Our job is to find out what the artist has discovered.

A place might be beautiful even though you know the people who

UPPER BROADWAY (above left). (New York City Public Schools Bureau of Art.)

THE CITY (above right). (University of Georgia Department of Art.)

AFRICAN VILLAGE (at left). (International Child Art Center, San Francisco.)

live there do not like it. This often happens in art. Why? Why does an ugly place become interesting—even attractive—when an artist represents it in his work? Obviously, he changes it in some way. Does the artist deliberately make a false statement about what he sees? Or has he discovered something valuable that others have not seen? If so, is it just an imaginary value? Do you think the "imaginary value" an artist finds in an ugly place could become a "real" value? What is the process between converting the ugliness or dullness of a place into the beauty or interest an artist finds in it? Is there some way to make artistic discoveries real?

Meaningful action to improve a human environment often begins when art invents or discovers something special in that environment. But art cannot tell us how to convert aesthetic value into practical reality. That is the task of politics. Still, art starts our thinking. It creates the images that practical men pursue. And the reason men pursue aesthetic values is their suspicion that those values are real. ■

Improving the Environment

There is a connection between how much pleasure you can get from seeing a place and how good it is to live in. Naturally, we want to live and work in places that are enjoyable to look at, walk through, and be in. That is why most people work so hard to make their homes attractive. But our communities are home too. They don't *have* to be ugly. Therefore, one of the problems we all face is the problem of improving the visual appearance of our homes and neighborhoods. Of course, there are professional fields like architecture and urban design that specialize in planning attractive, useful structures and communities. But architects working on the design of enormous projects cannot succeed unless the public they work for wants imaginative planning, good construction, and beautiful spaces. The public that pays for and lives in neighborhoods and communities has to *want* good architecture and pleasing surroundings before these things can be created. And before you can want something better, you have to get some idea of what "better" is.

Your art education is not just a job of looking for beautiful places and copying or reproducing them so you can say you have "captured" beauty. Art is also a way of *investigating* places visually. We are interested in things that are ugly or plain or monotonous, too. Our job is to find out what makes them that way. Then we can work intelligently to get them changed. You can explore your community and make sketches or photographs of its public places, not so much because they are beautiful, but in order to bring them back to class for closer study and discussion.

The Art of City Planning

It would be very difficult to give a set of rules that guarantee beautiful buildings and spaces, because every place is different from every other place, if only in small details. But there are some general purposes or objectives that the art of community planning tries to achieve: It tries to provide the best possible arrangements for *living, working, recreation,* and *circulation.* "Living" involves structures like houses, apartments, hotels, motels, hospitals, and, perhaps, schools—wherever human groups are sheltered and have basic needs like eating and sleeping taken care of. "Working" takes place in buildings like shops, factories, offices, laboratories, farms—wherever people make things or have jobs they get paid for. "Recreation" requires theaters, stadiums, parks, skating rinks, bowling alleys, restaurants—any place where people go to have fun. "Circulation" is managed by streets, sidewalks, highways, subways, railways, rivers, canals, bridges—anything that carries people and goods from one place to another.

Putting these structures together—combining them harmoniously—is very difficult. Communities are more or less working at the job all the time, and some have been doing so for hundreds of years. But an invention like the steam locomotive, or more recently, the automobile, can totally change the way communities must deal with the problems of circulation, recreation, working, and living. Unfortunately, the automobile has changed circulation faster than communities have changed the planning of their buildings and spaces. As a result, people still travel by foot on paths that are also used by automobiles, just as they did when transportation was by wagon or horsecar, with the inevitable result that a great many people get killed. It is clear that in a contest between a man and an automobile, the automobile will win. But the people who design our roads and cities cannot seem to learn this simple truth.

There are many other problems involving the organization of space in our cities, although the conflict between the circulation of pedestrians and automobiles is one of the most serious. We have very few attractive squares or plazas where people can assemble on foot just for the pleasure of strolling or being with each other. Residential streets need to be designed so that they slow down cars and present varied views as we travel on them. Houses are more interesting to see and live in if grouped in varied clusters instead of monotonous rows and checkerboard patterns. We have to create more and safer play-spaces for children. Shopping could be a more pleasant experience if stores were grouped around fountains, outdoor sculpture, trees and shrubs, and open grassy areas. And there is no reason why factories and mills cannot be pleasant places for the people who work in them; they can also be attractive to those

who travel by. Finally, we have to find a way to preserve handsome or historically important buildings that are now often torn down because they are not profitable or are in the way of a new superhighway.

These problems are faced by every generation in our society. They are difficult to solve, but the difficulty makes them more interesting. You can begin to improve the world you live in by exploring the places around you and trying to figure out how they could become more attractive—visually and in other ways. At the same time, you will be studying art, because art is a search for meaningful combinations of shape, color, texture, and space in everything we see and **use.**

Exploring Places: Practices 1

SOME THINGS TO SEE

Look at *Landscape Near Chicago* by Aaron Bohrod, *The El and Snow* by Dong Kingman, *Broadway* by Mark Tobey, and the *Midtown Plaza* in Rochester, New York, by Victor Gruen Associates (on pp. 242–243).

SOME PROBLEMS

The first three works of art represent artistic interpretations of places where people live and work. The last illustration shows a place where people shop, stroll, meet each other, and enjoy themselves in the middle of a large city. Why is this plaza so much better than most downtown shopping areas? What do you think causes the kind of scene we see in Bohrod's painting? As you look at Dong Kingman's painting, do you feel ex-

LANDSCAPE NEAR CHICAGO (above left), by Aaron Bohrod. (Collection Whitney Museum of American Art, N.Y.)

BROADWAY (above right), by Mark Tobey, (The Metropolitan Museum of Art, Arthur H. Hearn Fund, 1942.)

THE EL AND SNOW (at right), by Dong Kingman. (Collection Whitney Museum of American Art, N.Y.)

citement or confusion? Can you imagine yourself walking in the melted snow, looking at the signs and store windows, listening to the roar of elevated trains? Is this a good place for people to live out their lives? What is the difference between living here and living in the house painted by Bohrod? From Tobey's painting can you tell why Broadway is called the "Great White Way"? Why do the people in his painting look like white scribbles or like tangles of spaghetti? Do you think the planning of the Midtown Plaza results in a dull, monotonous place? Or does it show a good balance between orderly, regular spaces and interesting little variations of texture and shape?

SOME POSSIBILITIES

We need to find out just what environments are best for people when they are engaged in different kinds of activity. For example, what is best for studying? For having a party? For shopping? For working? Do you think that manufacturers might have information about the best sort of place for working happily and safely? Would an architect or designer have any ideas about the right interiors for a department store, a supermarket, a teen-age center, a bedroom, a family room? Look through some library books on architectural planning. Specifically, find out how an architect decides on the dimensions of a space, what shape it will be, what it will include, how to handle lighting, what surface materials to use, which colors will be most pleasing. Who decides how many signs and lights and posters can be placed on a street as well as their size

Midtown Plaza, Rochester, N.Y., by Victor Gruen Associates. (Midtown Holdings Corporation.)

and location? Do you know anything about the laws governing signs on highways? Do you think they should be changed?

WHAT YOU CAN DO

Write away to some manufacturers of traffic lights, street signs, trash containers, and parking meters requesting illustrated catalogs of their products. While waiting for replies you might go on a sketching trip downtown, making a series of drawings of objects you see—like signs, lights, mailboxes, unusual doorways and entrances, benches, utility poles, fire hydrants, manhole covers, outdoor phone booths, and so on. Then try to redesign some of them so that they will fit harmoniously into a shopping area for your community.

Write a short story telling how the house in Bohrod's painting came to be built. Pretend you are a famous composer, like Brahms or Mozart, who suddenly found himself in the middle of Dong Kingman's picture and describe your feelings.

Imagine that you are producing a TV spectacular based on Tobey's painting, *Broadway*. Write the script, including dialog and dance-movement directions; plan the lighting and design the sets. All of this might be accompanied by music that you have recorded on tape. Finally, of course, put on a performance for the class.

Assume that your community has given you a downtown street to redesign—like Victor Gruen's Midtown Plaza. You can close off traffic, enclose the space overhead, install air-conditioning, resurface the street, and light and decorate the plaza any way you wish. But the stores must remain. And essential services must be provided. You might organize a team to gather all the data, make the necessary measurements and work up the plans. Maybe you can get the advice of some professional designers or planners in carrying out your project. Who knows? The town fathers might decide to put your plan into action.

Exploring Places: Practices 2

SOME THINGS TO SEE

Look at *Room* by Lucas Samaras, the Hanna House (interior) by Frank Lloyd Wright, the Villa Shodan (interior) by Le Corbusier, and the late nineteenth-century American parlor.

SOME PROBLEMS

What do these interiors tell you about the people who live in them? Does any one of them remind you of a cave? Or a tent? On the basis of the nineteenth-century parlor how would you define interior decoration? What would you say about the interior decoration of Wright's Hanna House? Can you explain the lighting in Le Corbusier's Villa Shodan? If you object to the Samaras *Room*, is it because of the way it looks or for some other reason? Finally, do you see any similarities between the Victorian parlor and the Samaras *Room*?

SOME POSSIBILITIES

Try to find out where ornament and decoration come from. Herbert Read would be a good source. Also, look into the way ornament has been affected by mechanization. You might try to explain why some people prefer busy, richly decorated surfaces, while others prefer simple surfaces with a minimum of ornamentation. Does this have anything to do with feelings of being protected by a room or space? Compare the interiors of early and modern automobiles. What caused the changes? You can get illustrated material on this subject from the major auto manufacturers in Detroit.

Le Corbusier's Villa Shodan is in India, a very hot country. Do you think the materials (mostly reinforced concrete), the spaces, and the window openings reflect something of India's climate and culture? Should a house reflect the traditions and customs of the region where it is located

ROOM (above left), by Lucas Samaras. (Pace Gallery.)

Hanna House (interior) (above top right), by Frank Lloyd Wright. (Courtesy Paul R. Hanna.)

Villa Shodan (interior) (above right), by Le Corbusier. (Courtesy Lucien Hervé.)

Late nineteenth-century American parlor (at left). (The Granger Collection.)

or should it primarily suit the personal needs of the individuals who live in it?

What types of interiors do you associate with various professions—medicine, law, business, the ministry, engineering? It would be interesting to find out what connection there is between a person's place of work or business and how he thinks of himself.

WHAT YOU CAN DO

Plan an office for a business executive. First design it as you think Frank Lloyd Wright would have done it. Then do the office in the style of Le Corbusier.

Build a real living room in the style or spirit of the Samaras *Room.* Then use the living room as the set for a dramatic skit in which performers either sing or recite home-made poems about their housekeeping problems. You might introduce a character representing a magazine like *Better Homes and Gardens, House Beautiful,* or *Good Housekeeping.*

Look around your community for some examples of Victorian architecture. You can make line drawings of the wooden gingerbread decorations. And if possible, try to see some of the interiors. Report to your class on the history of Victorian furniture and decoration. Do you know any families who live in Victorian houses? How do they like it? If you know something about building construction, explain why we no longer build homes as they did in the nineteenth century.

Someone should give an illustrated report on the prairie houses of Frank Lloyd Wright. Contrast his houses with those of Ludwig Mies van der Rohe. Ask your classmates to say which architect they prefer and why. Then each member of the class might design a vacation house in the style of the man whose work he admires most. But before starting this project, you should have some clear ideas about how to create satisfying and useful space. This does not mean you must know as much as an architect. It means that you should become familiar with the varieties of surface and space that can be created with today's building technology.

In the last chapter you studied examples of art dealing with people and places. You also gained experience in "reading" art—looking for visual evidence and trying to decide what it means. Of course, reading any new language is difficult. But you have been using your eyes to get along in the world almost from the day you were born. So understanding what you see is not as new as it seems. Still, there must be more to "reading" art than using your common sense. There *are* other ways to get at art: you can study the concepts, or *visual elements*, artists use; you can study the way artists plan, or *design*, their work; you can study the families, or *styles*, of art; and you can study what happens in the mind *during the act of seeing* a work of art. That is what we hope to do in this chapter.

People who plan to become artists must study the language of art just as future composers must study the language of music.

But if you do not plan to be an artist, why should you learn the language of art? To answer this question, we have to return to the main reason you are in school—so you can become a complete, reasonably happy, and effective human being. In school you can grow and learn less painfully than if you had to find out everything by yourself. You can learn what people are like, how they communicate, what they think is important, how they respond to new feelings and ideas, and which events in the past shaped the world as we see it today. Art deals with all these things. But you will hardly recognize them unless you learn the *language* of art. It is just like watching professional football on TV: You have to know the rules and strategy of the game if you want to enjoy it completely. Otherwise, you will see what everyone else sees; however, like *some* viewers, you will lose track of the ball.

10

Learning
the Language of Art

Think of all the different materials in a large building. Then think of the different shapes and dimensions these materials must have so they can fit together and work. Finally, think of the spaces and surfaces that result when the right materials, with the right dimensions, are correctly put together. Obviously they don't put *themselves* together; someone has to plan and organize the whole process. That someone is an artist —an architect or a designer. He does not actually erect or fabricate the building himself; he makes plans for technicians and construction workers to read and follow. The architect's design is his intention, or purpose, which is visible in the form of his drawn plans. When the building contractor and his workmen see these plans they understand them as directions. If you asked an architect what he does, he might reply that he plans and organizes the way materials will be shaped and put together so that they form a building.

The same thing could be said about a composer. He writes notes on paper that musicians read as if they were directions for making certain sounds. The written music, or score, represents the composer's design; it indicates his intention as the architect's plans indicate his. And the musicians carry out the composer's intention almost as faithfully as the builder carries out the architect's design.

Similarly, a playwright types out dialog and stage directions that actors and a director will translate into the actual performance you see. Of course, the director *interprets* the playwright's written script just as a sym-

phony conductor interprets a composer's musical score. Builders, however, have less room for interpretation when they are working from an architect's plans. The important point is that in each case there cannot be a completed work of art unless there is first a plan of organization, or a design—a design that takes the form of an architect's plans, a composer's score, or a playwright's script.

Painting and sculpture are a little different. A painter may plan or design his work, but he also executes it himself. The sculptor does too, although, if the work will be cast in metal, he must rely on workers in a foundry to make the final statue from his wax or plaster model. But most artists design and *execute* their own work. As a result, they can make changes in their plans while carrying them out. In fact, some artists start to work with little or no plan at all, and they make their design decisions as they go along.

Whether an artist works with clay, stone, paint, plaster, concrete, or wood, he must remember what his materials are capable of doing. He has to know the kinds of shapes and spaces and colors he can make with them. If he works with words or sounds or dance movements, he must also know the limitations of his medium—that is, the possibilities of the materials that will be formed into a poem, a painting, a play, a ballet, a song, a building, or a sculpture. He has *to think* about what he is going to do or what others are going to do in following his directions. The thinking that any artist must do in advance of execution is what I call design. Even if an artist plans his work *as he goes along*, he still thinks or designs a little bit ahead of actually painting his picture or writing his poem. No matter what kind of artist he may be, he must be a designer, too—someone who thinks about changing materials into shapes, spaces, and rhythms; someone who worries about how those shapes and spaces should be organized; and finally, someone who tries to predict how others will react to what he has made.

The Visual Elements

If you spent a long time as a wood carver, you would probably know a lot about the grain of wood, about keeping your tools sharp, and the best ways to avoid splitting or breaking the wood as you worked on it. We expect a good wood carver to be very skillful and to know a great deal about his tools and materials. But a really good wood carver—one who is truly an artist—knows more than how to keep his tools sharp or how to prevent wood from splitting. He knows how to think about the forms he can create with his tools.

Wendell Castle perched on the end of his serpentine desk. (Lee Nordness Galleries; photo, The New York Times Studio.)

A double chair by Wendell Castle. (Lee Nordness Galleries.)

This is furniture that doubles as sculpture. It shows that usefulness can be combined with expressiveness. It also demonstrates visual language in action: Man-made shapes that look as if they were alive, wood grain used for texture and color, lines moving in and out of deep space, a style of curved forms that excludes all right angles. What could be the reason for making furniture that has no straight lines? Would you like to sit in a chair that seems to be growing? Would you prefer rather to look at it? Does a desk top resting on a serpent make sense to you? ■

As an artist gains practice and experience, he develops special ways of thinking about his materials and techniques. These ways form a kind of artistic shorthand, convenient mental devices for planning what to do with wood, paint, plaster, clay, and so on. In the visual arts—painting, sculpture, architecture and all their variations and combinations—this artistic shorthand has turned out to be very much the same for thousands of years: Whatever the material is, the artist usually has to think of what he will do to change its shape, color, light pattern, and volume. He thinks about how his changes will form lines and spaces and patterns of light and dark. We can call these mental devices *the visual elements of design* because they help the artist to think about and organize the work viewers will see.

The elements of design are mental, like the numbers used by a mathematician. For example, the number "three" exists only mentally; it becomes something real when you see or touch three *oranges* or three *apples*. Similarly, the name of the color "red" exists mentally and becomes real only when we see a red apple or a red balloon. But the artist has to use ideas, or mental devices, such as *red, curved, rough, smooth, light, dark, square, round*, and so on, to plan or design his work in advance. Otherwise, he wouldn't know what he was doing until after he had done it. By then, he might have spoiled the effect he was trying for.

If the artist uses the elements of design to think about the organization of his work, *we* too can use them to understand his work after it is completed. That is, we can try to discover what decisions he has made about shape, color, volume, and so on, to create the final result. This effort will help us find out what he was trying to do. If something about a building or a picture bothers us, we may be able to find out what it is by examining the way it was designed. Or, if a work is judged to be very good, its excellence may be due to its design. For these reasons it is useful to know something about the elements of design and the way they operate in works of art.

Line

A line really has width, but it is so much longer than it is wide that we usually think mainly about its length and direction. Still, a line can also be light or dark, thick or thin, curved or straight, smooth or jerky, simple or complicated or any combination of these things. You have made many lines, especially when writing, so you know that a line almost always suggests motion because it starts at a point and seems to be going somewhere. Your eye follows a line just as your hand guides it when making the line in the first place. It is difficult for a line to be vague or uncertain. Even a scribble gives a definite idea of the motions that made it. As a result, working with lines forces the artist to make up his mind. Of course, some lines are more definite than others, but usually a line announces where it has been, where it is going, and how it expects to get there.

Another thing about line is its personality. As you know, everyone's handwriting is different because of different ways of holding the pencil, different pressures applied to it, and different ideas about how the letters should be formed. The same differences are found in the artist's use of lines, except that he may create these differences purposely. There are so many variations possible with line that like palm-readers we can read meanings into them, even when they are not intended to represent anything. We discover eventually that lines, like people we know, can be lively or dull, formal or informal, direct and purposeful, or indirect and unpredictable.

In addition to handwriting, we get some of our ideas about line from nature—from the line made by the horizon or by trees against the sky; from the grain of wood; from the veins of marble or of leaves; from strands of straw or seaweed; from the lines of tree branches, flowers and weeds, spider webs, falling rain, water ripples, lightning, sun rays. And in the man-made world we see lines in TV antennas, telephone poles and wires, jet trails, road maps, railroad tracks, cement cracks, brick joints, bridges, fishing poles, kite strings, boat rigging, plumbing systems. When we see lines in art we often connect them with similar lines we have seen in nature or in the man-made world, and from these connections get some of their meaning. Remember that artists live in the same world you live in, and therefore they get their ideas from the same places and experiences you get yours.

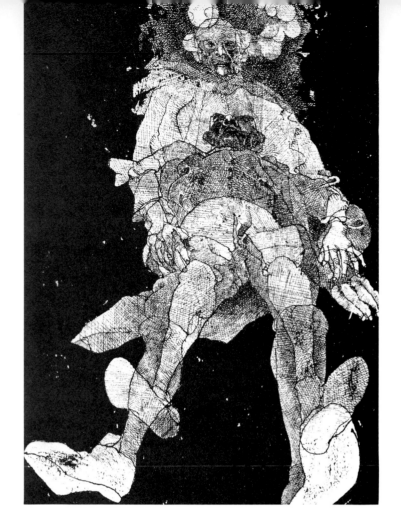

Illustration (above) by Alan E. Cober from "Mr. Corbett's Ghost" by Leon Garfield. (Pantheon Books.)

EZRA POUND (at right), by Wyndham Lewis. (Redfern Gallery, London.)

These are some of the things you can see in two examples of visual language at work: Line used to create texture, line used to foreshorten the figure, distortion created by an unusual angle of vision, emotion stimulated by fantasy, natural forms treated as geometric shapes. Why did the artists use these devices? ■

Shape

We could say that shape is just the result of a line connected with itself—in other words, a line that encloses an area creates a shape. But shapes are also made without lines. For example, a shape is formed all at once when you get up from a fall in the snow, or from sitting in the sand, or when you walk on the floor with wet feet. An artist can create shapes by drawing them in line and then filling them in with color or tone, making a kind of silhouette. But he can also create a shape directly with a large brush if he uses the brush to make the area and the boundaries of the shape at the same time. In a way, that is what you do when you make a shape in the sand with your body, assuming your seat is a kind of brush. You might say that Line is an ice skater gliding over a surface and Shape is a skier who has taken a spill.

When you look at a shape you have the choice of watching its boundaries or exploring its area, its inner space. Sometimes the artist wants you to pay attention to the color or texture of the area; other times he does not seem to care about what goes on inside and he clearly wants you to watch the outline. Usually, you can tell which is most important for getting the meaning of the whole work. If the shapes are vague there may be a reason for the vagueness, and that reason may help you to read or interpret the artist's design.

Something else to remember is that there are shapes in sculpture and architecture too —in fact, everything we see has shape, even a thin line. Although a building has *depth* as well as length and breadth, we see it as a practically flat shape because of the relative flatness of the retina in our eye where the shape's image is reflected. Having two eyes and what is called binocular vision, we can often guess how thick or deep an object is, but the first thing we usually notice about an object is its more or less flat shape. That is the quickest way for human beings to identify what they are looking at. You can often recognize a particular automobile or a tree from its shape alone, without knowing anything else about it. A person who is color-blind, for example, can usually see well enough for most purposes and can get along almost as well as someone with normal vision. Artists depend heavily on shape to communicate information to viewers.

What can art tell you through shape? It can tell you what a shape was formed with, what tools and motions and processes the artist used to produce the shapes you see. Sometimes, shapes tell you mainly how they came to be created—fast or slow, spontaneously or deliberately, freely or through measurement. Shapes are also used to remind you of experiences that look or feel the same. For example, shapes can suggest pointed, jagged, dangerous objects. They can also remind you of objects that will or will not bend, that will or will not float, that will roll or stand still, that will break or crack, that feel rough or smooth. Naturally, these shapes will not mean much to you unless you have bent a wire, spilled a glass of milk, floated a boat in the bathtub, dropped a bag of groceries on the floor, cracked a dish, sailed a kite, cut yourself with broken glass, and so on. But almost everyone has had good and bad luck of this sort, so almost everyone has had real-life experience with shape. In fact, you don't have to cut yourself with a sharp object to know what certain shapes mean. You can tell whether something is safe or not just by looking at it. And that is what the artist relies on: He knows that human beings respond to shapes visually; they get feelings and thoughts just from looking at combinations of shapes.

Shapes communicate whether they are made by men or by nature or by machines. A tire track in the mud is made by a machine, a leaf shape is made by nature, a picture of his mother is made by a man.

NIGERIAN RAILSPLITTER. (Photo, Ken Heyman.)

Ad for art exhibition. (Hemingway Galleries, N.Y., designed by the gallery directors.)

Two examples of shape at work: One is abstract and the other is recognizable. But the shapes in the abstract painting could be real; they might be biological organisms seen under a microscope. And the body of the Nigerian worker looks almost like an abstract shape; it could be a flat pattern cut out of black paper. It seems that artists like to make living things look dead and dead things look alive. Or do they think everything is alive? ■

In addition, men can imitate the shapes made by nature and machines. In that way they enlarge the vocabulary of visual language. And now that technology enables us to see into the nucleus of a cell, to look at the earth from outer space, to "see" the surface of the moon and to see what is going on inside a nerve or blood vessel, a tremendous range of new shapes is available to artists for the expression of their ideas and emotions.

Light and Dark

Light is what permits us to see. That is, the pupil of the eye admits light energy and the eye uses that energy to send messages to the brain. But we need the absence of light—darkness—to create *patterns of light and dark* so that the brain can make sense out of the messages it gets from the eye. If the world were totally light or totally dark we wouldn't be able to see anything at all. The lines and shapes I have been talking about can only be seen as patterns of light and dark. You cannot see a white line on a white piece of paper or a black line on a black sheet of paper. It is the difference, or *contrast*, between light and dark that makes vision possible.

An artist can fool your eye by drawing or painting shadows on a light surface, which makes you think you are seeing real light. Or he can paint light areas on a dark surface, which makes you think you are seeing shadows cast by real objects. So, whether he is working with dark on light or light on dark, the artist has to think about their com- bination or patterning in order to create illusions of reality. Sculptors and architects, however, do not create *illusions* of forms, they build *real* forms. But they, too, plan the patterning of light and dark that the viewer will see. Their work is made to be seen as well as touched or occupied. Sometimes the change from light to dark is very sudden; there is no area of half-light or half-shadow. That might be the case when a geometric solid, like a cube, is seen in a strong light; there is a sharp contrast when the plane changes abruptly. On curved surfaces, however, the change from light to dark is usually very gradual. In fact, that is how you can often tell a surface is curved—by the gentle changes in its light-dark patterning.

As with lines and shapes, we get a variety of ideas and feelings from light and dark. Part of it is inherited from our culture and part of it is biological. For example, we are inclined to turn toward the sun or any source of light rather than away from it. That is why lights are used to attract attention as traffic signals, as decoration and as advertising. Darkness in nature usually means night, the absence of the sun and its warmth. People who have lived in cold climates for generations almost worship the sun and the warmth it brings. Think of the passion for sun-bathing that seems to overcome whole cities in Sweden when the long winter is over. On the other hand, people who have lived in tropical climates value the coolness of shadowy places away from the blazing heat. In general, we prefer a balance between light and dark, between warm and cool—not too much of either. The half-tones are very pleasant. And people look better in a light which is not so intense that it shows their defects and not so weak that it is difficult to recognize their features. Even food is more appetizing when served in a soft light. The meals you get in some fluorescent-lit cafeterias would taste much better if they were eaten under soft lights, because their color would be improved and color affects taste.

Certain color pigments at full saturation (when they are pure, or undiluted) are naturally light or naturally dark. For example, pure yellow almost becomes sunlight, and blue seems to resemble the shadows of evening and night. As a result, we associate gaiety, sunshine, and optimism with yellow; pure blue suggests sleep, mourning, or a sad kind of thoughtfulness. These associations are based partly on the amount of light, or energy, a color reflects. But colors also symbolize other ideas and feelings based on their age-long use in human communities. Something as basic as night and day has a great deal of influence on your thoughts when looking at light-and-dark combinations in art.

Since man has known how to create artificial sources of light, beginning with man-made fires, he has been able to interpret the objects he sees according to the way they are illuminated. For example, most of us can be frightened by a face lit from below, because we normally expect light to come from above—from the sky. Presumably, an evil spirit would be lit from below. Flickering lights from candles or fires create a mood that must go back to the base camps of hunters in prehistoric days when men used fire to frighten off wild animals. The flickering firelight stood for safety, warmth, family life, and comradeship. But lights that flash on and off or blaze suddenly remind us immediately of modern show business, photography, gun blasts, explosions, getting hit on the head and seeing stars, or a burnt-out television tube. In other words, we react to them with a mixture of fear and excitement.

It may seem that I have left the discussion of art, but all of these observations about light and dark constitute tools that artists use when they want to influence the way people see and respond to their work. By shaping lights and shadows, mixing them, sharpening their contrast or blending their edges, emphasizing light or dark pigments, showing more sky or less earth in a picture, and through dozens of other devices that involve light, the artist tells you much more than the name of the objects he may be representing. He uses light and dark to reach into your most fundamental social and biological feelings. When designing with light the artist is really designing with human emotions.

Color

Color is a tremendous source of pleasure and meaning. Physically it is light. It is caused by surfaces that absorb part of the light spectrum and reflect the rest. The color we see is the reflected light. But emotionally, color seems to be a language all by itself. You already know that it affects the taste of food. It also reflects our state of health. It symbolizes the nation in the flag; it governs the movement of traffic, tells us when a melon is ripe, announces holidays like Christmas or Easter, attracts babies, is added to the food we buy and the faces ladies wear. Without color, needless to say, it would be a very gray world.

For artists, color comes in the form of pigments and sometimes in dyes. And artists have ways of thinking about color that would be useful for nonartists to know. For example, the name of a color, like red or green, is called its *hue*. There are, of course, dozens and dozens of variations of a simple hue like blue, but we have to have words for the hues when we talk about them even though these word-labels cannot describe the color we actually see. Our memory for colors and our words for colors are not very close to the colors we see, but the words are convenient for practical purposes like stopping on *red* and going ahead on *green*. Artists' pigments have special names to identify colors more accurately—names like Cadmium red or Venetian red or Alizarin crimson—all of which look different but are still called red. When an architect gives directions about color to a building contractor, for example, he rarely depends on the ordinary name of a hue; instead he gives the builder a sample of the colored material he wants to use, and in that way there are fewer misunderstandings.

The *value* of color refers to its lightness or darkness. By adding white or some other light color to a hue, you *raise* its value; by darkening a hue you lower its value. If someone suggests that the value of an area in your picture needs to be raised, you know he means that it ought to be lighter. Of course, there are many ways to raise or lower the values of color areas once a decision has been made about them. The point is, we need special words about color to give directions, to teach, to criticize, or even to talk to ourselves—that is, to think about color.

The *intensity* of a color refers to its purity—not chemical purity, but the absence of any admixture which would make it less clear, rich, or less saturated. Artists' pigments do not always come at full intensity; the artist must decide which colors to mix with them to get the intensity he wants. He can "kill" the intensity of a color by adding a great deal of white or black or by adding a color that is very different—a *complementary*, or opposite, color. Complementary colors strengthen each other when placed side by side, but they usually produce a muddy gray if they are mixed. In fact, thousands of interesting grays can be created by mixing complementary colors and adding white. Examples of color complementaries are red-green, yellow-purple, and orange-blue. Of course, these are just the hues, or names of color complementaries; you would have to see and work with them to discover how they actually affect each other.

We talk about *warm* and *cool* colors mainly because of associations with things like blood, fire, the sky, the ocean, and so on. But a color becomes warm or cool only in relation to another color. For example, you might think red is warm, but it can be cool next to a yellow-orange. Violet is usually cool, but it would be warm next to a blue-green. So you should rarely make a decision about a color by itself. Always try to see the way it is affected by the colors around it. That, of course, is what the artist must do, and his color problems become very complex as the many parts of his work build up.

When color is combined with line, shape, and light-and-dark, the possibilities for expression become tremendous. Some artists try to limit the possibilities by simplifying shapes and colors in order to get greater control over their work. Other artists do not care if their work is very complicated and hard to control. After all, the world is also complicated, and they feel art should reflect that complexity. In nature, the range and variety of color are very wide and many of our ideas about harmonious color combinations come from nature. But man has created colors through chemistry and he has invented color patterns through his imagination that have never been seen in nature— not in the most brightly plumaged bird or the richest tropical forest. And now artists can arrange shapes and combinations of color that make us calm, excited, dizzy, happy, depressed, hopeful, disappointed, or satisfied. In addition to becoming a very gaily colored bird himself, man today can use the art of color to communicate an enormous range of ideas and to control his different moods as never before in history.

Summary

Other design elements could be mentioned, such as texture, volume, and motion.

Certainly artists use these concepts in planning their work. But texture is something we originally discover through touch. When we "see" a texture, we really interpret a surface from its patterning of light-and-dark and color, and we guess at what it would *feel* like. Volume and mass refer to the bulk and weight of objects in space, but, once again, the eye sees these things as shapes in a more or less flat visual frame. As for visual motion, we can think of it here as the result of seeing many fixed images in rapid succession. More, however, will be said about motion in art in Chapter 11. The important point to remember is that most of the visual effects artists create result from organizing and combining the varieties of line, shape, light-and-dark, and color.

The Visual Elements: Practices 1

SOME THINGS TO SEE

Look at *Family Walk* by Paul Klee, *The Hostess* by Alexander Calder, the Thonet rocking chair, *Flower Garden* by Konstantin Milonadis, and *Pool Parlor* by Jacob Lawrence (on pp. 258–259).

SOME PROBLEMS

These examples were chosen to demonstrate the use of only one visual element— line. Do you see how line can have a personality of its own? Do you see any lines that create suspense? How? Are some lines funny? What makes them funny? Which lines are shaped like lines in nature? Which ones are shaped like ideas? Where do people get their ideas about what lines mean?

257

FAMILY WALK (above left), by Paul Klee. (Permission COSMOPRESS 1969 by French Reproduction Rights, Inc.; photo, Kunstmuseum, Bern.)

THE HOSTESS (above right), by Alexander Calder. (Collection The Museum of Modern Art. Gift of M. M. Warburg.)

Rocking chair by Gebruder Thonet (at right). (Collection The Museum of Modern Art. Gift of Café Nicholson.)

POOL PARLOR, by Jacob Lawrence. (Courtesy Dintenfass Gallery; photo, The Metropolitan Museum of Art, Arthur H. Hearn Fund, 1942.)

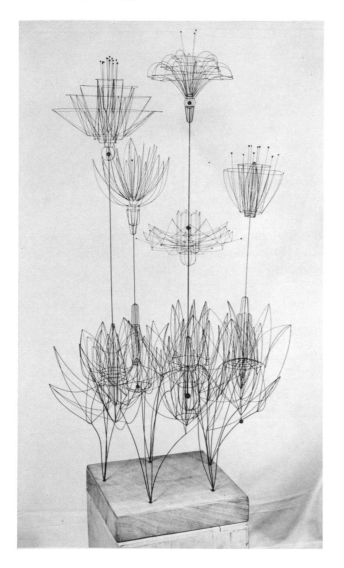

SOME POSSIBILITIES

There seems to be a connection between the lines and shapes in Calder's *Hostess* and the Thonet rocking chair. Does *The Hostess* look like a rocking chair? Why or why not? Do people ever look like things? Have you ever seen anyone who looked like an apple tree? Or an unmade bed? Do automobiles look like people? Look at the cue sticks in the Lawrence painting. Trace them or copy them alone on a sheet of paper. Now try to decide what they might mean by themselves. Could you make up a poem about those lines without the people in the picture? Turn your paper so that the lines are horizontal. Why has their meaning changed? Could gravity have anything to do with it? Do you think Milonadis was foolish to represent flowers with metal rods? Write down a list of the traits of flowers. Which ones has Milonadis represented? Which did he omit? Would you say *Flower Garden* is beautiful? Why or why not? How do you know the people in the Klee picture are walking? In which direction? Is this connected to the way we read lines of print?

WHAT YOU CAN DO

Collect a group of objects no larger than your hand and bring them to class. Now draw the pattern of the lines inside each object, but don't show the outside shape. Give your teacher these drawings and ask her to place a number on each one and then to display them. Everyone in the class should then try to list the names of the objects he can recognize. Which people got the highest scores? Is this because they are good observers? Or good guessers?

Trace the line pattern of a picture you like. Just keep the most important lines and leave out the shapes and small details. Then put aside the picture and make an enlargement of your tracing. Now do some exploring: Can you find a different place or a different set of objects that fits your pattern of lines? If you can't find something that fits, make an arrangement on a table. Use any combination of objects you like. After you have set up this arrangement, shine a light on it to make an interesting light-and-dark pattern. Then draw or paint a picture of this new arrangement based on the original line pattern. When you are done, show your finished drawing together with the line pattern you traced and the original picture you started with. Have you proved anything?

Try this athletic experiment in the school yard. You will need a smooth, dirt surface. Mark out a rectangle about ten yards square. Then run a single football play in that dirt area; use two players on each side. Then chart the paths each player took as well as you can, using footprints when they are clear. Make a number of these charts and bring them back to class. Now transfer the lines on your chart to a larger sheet of paper and strengthen the lines. Give a different color to each team. Work out a code for each enclosed area or shape. For example, a certain color or texture might stand for places where there was blocking; another might stand for passing or running. This same chart approach could be used for other games. When the "charts" are finished, show them to the class and see if they can tell what they represent. The pictures that result might be given titles like "End Rush," "Lateral Pass," "Quarterback Sneak," and so on. The purpose of this project is to show how patterns of lines, colors, and texture can be based on something real without looking like a photograph. Also, this gives you a chance to show how line combinations can give information and make a picture at the same time.

The Visual Elements: Practices 2

SOME THINGS TO SEE

Look at *Spectre of Kitty Hawk* by Theodore Roszak, *Star* by Jean Arp, *Blue Horses* by Franz Marc, the photograph of spiny lobsters, and *Pomegranate* by Douglas Pickering (on pp. 262–263).

SOME PROBLEMS

Here we see a strange combination of shapes. Do they have anything in common? Would you have guessed from the Arp sculpture that a star is in outer space? Does it matter? Do you know anything about Kitty Hawk, North Carolina? What does Roszak's creature have to do with Kitty Hawk? Where do its shapes come from? What do the lobster shapes remind you of? What letter form do you see in Franz Marc's horses? Do those horses look as if they have bones? What causes the shapes in Pickering's *Pomegranate*? Could you get the same thing with an apple, a melon, a squash, or a pumpkin?

SOME POSSIBILITIES

Find out what ancient people thought about stars. Did they believe stars were people? Can you find an ancient representation of a star, the sun, or the moon which looks like Arp's *Star*? What makes a shape look safe or dangerous? It might be interesting to read what the Swiss psychologist Jean Piaget has to say about the way children react to shapes. You could also watch your baby brother or sister play with square blocks or with a smooth, round rattle and describe the differences in the way he handles them. To understand what Franz Marc has done, try to draw a jelly jar, a milk bottle, or a soda bottle from the end instead of the side. How do you make things look as if they go back in space when you are drawing them on a flat surface? Can you think of any musical work that *Blue Horses* reminds you of? By the way, have you ever seen a blue horse? Or a purple cow?

WHAT YOU CAN DO

Collect some paper shapes by cutting out objects in magazines like *Life, Look,* or *The National Geographic*. After they are cut out, turn the shapes over so that you cannot see what is inside them. Next, pick out two or three shapes that interest you most and give them names, like George or Gwendolyn. Then paste George and Gwendolyn on a sheet of colored construction paper, adding details in paint or crayon that will make them look the way they should. Finally, write out what George and Gwendolyn are saying to each other.

Pretend you are a person from another planet where everything is transparent, so that you can see what is inside of everything. But you cannot see surfaces, you can only see the outlines. Now make some large drawings of the following objects as if they were seen by this man from outer space: a watermelon, a lobster, a cat, a horse, an automobile, a refrigerator, a television set, a house, a hospital, a small boy after a party.

Make a picture of the shapes between things. For example, pretend you are an ant and draw all the in-between shapes you

SPECTRE OF KITTY HAWK (above left), by Theodore J. Roszak. (Collection The Museum of Modern Art. Purchase.)

STAR (above right), by Jean Arp. (Photo Étienne Bertrand Weill, Paris.)

BLUE HORSES (at right), by Franz Marc. (Walker Art Center, Minneapolis.)

Spiny lobsters. (New York Zoological Society.)

POMEGRANATE, by H. Douglas Pickering. (Courtesy the artist; photographed for The Museum of Modern Art by Soichi Sunami.)

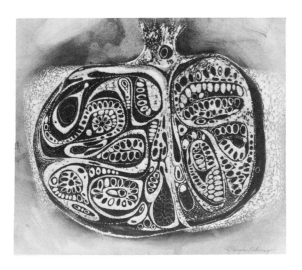

would see from the floor. Give them different colors but leave the chair legs, feet, table legs, shoes, fallen objects, and so on blank. Or cut out the in-between shapes and paste them up on construction paper to make a new picture. Suppose the in-between shapes were solid and the legs, tables, shoes, and so on were empty spaces. Suppose all the solid things and all the empty things in the world became reversed. What would your classroom, your home, or your community look like? Could you paint a picture of such a place?

Find or build a box about twelve inches square. Make a peep-hole in the side of the box and cut a small hole in the top. Crumple several pieces of paper into different-sized shapes and place them in the box. Pretend that the crumpled papers represent people or buildings. Then shine a flashlight on the crumpled shapes so that you can control their shadows. Then open up the box and paint or decorate its inside walls so they will combine better with the shadow shapes. Try shining the light into the box from different angles. If you can remember some of the better light-and-dark and shape patterns, you can use them for pictures you want the class to see. You could invent a title for your pictures; it will be hard to believe that you got your idea from pieces of crumpled paper in a box.

Organizing the Elements: Design

If we took a work of art apart, we would see that it is made up of lines, shapes, light-and-dark patterns, and colors. But you may have had sad experiences in taking apart a complex object—like a clock, for example. The question is: How is it put together?

Many people think there are rules or principles that tell us the best ways to put the visual elements together. These principles are sometimes called *unity, balance, rhythm,* and *proportion,* and artists often try to design their work with these principles to guide them. But where do the rules or principles come from? Who decided that effective works of art follow rules? The answer is that no one enacted these rules as if they were laws; they were just discovered by artists as they tried to learn how people react to what they see. Don't forget that art is an attempt to communicate ideas and feelings through vision. So it is natural that artists, over the centuries, would experiment with the most effective ways to influence people visually.

Their experimentation seems to prove that we want—even crave—unity, balance, rhythm, and proportion in everything we see. So, no matter what purpose a work of art serves, or who makes it, or where it is used, or what it is made of, it will usually follow these principles of design if many people are expected to pay attention to it.

Unity

Unity is the property of an object that allows you to see it completely and as a whole. Looking at a work that lacks unity is like listening to a conversation while other people are interrupting, the radio is playing, an auto horn is blowing, and you have a sore toe. In other words, *disunity* in an art object prevents you from paying attention or concentrating on what interests you. Unity lets you enjoy, understand, and benefit from what the artist is saying. But the artist faces two types of problems when he seeks unity: one, he may wish to include so many different things in his work that he cannot pull them together; second, he may simplify his work so much in the effort to unify it that he creates something dull and monotonous. For example, he might paint a picture that consists of nothing but a dot in the middle of the canvas. The picture would certainly be unified, but no one would want to look at it for very long.

Unity is not easy to achieve—not if you are also interested in variety. When there are many lines, shapes, and colors in a work of art, the artist tries to unify them in a variety of ways: He uses *similarity*—the colors, shapes or textures all resemble each other; *dominance and subordination*—one of the shapes or colors is larger or stronger than the others; *convergence*—all the lines and shapes seem to be directed toward a single "unifying" center; *proximity*—many different parts are clustered together so they are seen as a group instead of separately.

You can see that these devices for achieving unity are intended to help the viewer find *coherence,* or a sense of *belonging together,* in the work of art he is looking at. Of course, the act of seeing itself gives unity to what is seen. But that unity comes from the viewer and it may not be the unity the artist wants. For example, if you write a play and people laugh at the sad parts and cry at the funny parts, you are not a very good playwright: The audience is creating its own places of climax or unity, not the ones you intended. In an effective work of art, the unity that the viewer sees or feels is very close to the unity that the artist intended. As with a play or a complex musical composition, there can be several unified centers, but all of them together must also create a *larger* sense of unity. When this happens, we usually feel very good and we are grateful to the artist for making such feelings possible.

Balance

The word "balance" might suggest a tight-rope performer in the circus, a spinning top, an experienced oarsman guiding his canoe through rough water, or the moment before a diver jumps into space. No matter what it suggests, we have all had basic training in balance because we learned to walk long ago, mastering a problem of being able to balance on two legs instead of crawling on all fours. Because of that experience we associate balance with security, with *not* falling, with being unhurt. And these same attitudes toward balance carry over into art.

We also seek balance visually because, at an early age, we learned that our bodies exhibit symmetry. Of course, we did not know what symmetry means. But we did discover that people, including ourselves, are divided visually into a right half and a left half and that these halves are practically identical. Later on, it came as a surprise that the left side of a person's face is similar but not always identical to the right side. In other words, we had become accustomed to seeing symmetry or balance everywhere —in people, in the man-made world, and in nature too. And when balance is not actually present in something we see, we tend to project it—to imagine that we see balance where it doesn't exist—or we shift our vision until we *do* see it.

Like unity, balance gives the viewer a kind of pleasure, a feeling of completeness and security. That is why artists try to balance their work optically—that is, to the eye —so that viewers will not be frustrated or made uneasy in their search for visual wholeness. We can get tense if we do not feel complete fulfillment in a work of art, that is, the balancing out of all its weights, directions, colors, shapes, and areas of interest. Suppose you were watching an old tree fall and it stopped falling halfway down to the ground. You would be expecting a crash that never comes: The result is suspense with no let-up. Life provides many instances of that kind of suspense, disunity, and lack of balance. But art should be fair to your feelings; it can use imbalance and it can build up tensions, but it should satisfy your visual interests and expectations after it has aroused them.

The simplest type of balance is symmetrical, or bilateral, *balance*—where both halves of what we see match each other. Your eye will tolerate very difficult and complicated arrangements of shape and color provided they are paired. But such mirror-image types of balance can grow monotonous and your

Everson Museum of Art. (I. M. Pei & Partners; photo, Ezra Stoller.)

Design from an employment ad. (Westinghouse Electric Corporation.)

Design principles in action—in the clean, calculated balance of massive rectangles; or in the casual balance of precise, geometric shapes. One type of balance is in a physical structure; it shelters people and works of art. The other is in a visual image; it tries to attract the attention of architects and designers. The balance we see in the museum is almost symmetrical; it encourages contemplation—feelings of confidence and calm. The Westinghouse image suggests an aerial view of buildings and roads; or a plan view of furniture and functional areas in a workspace. It represents the process of problem-solving with spaces, volumes and shapes—the kind of game designers like to play. ■

eye gets bored; it wants balance *plus* variation. Nature taught us to look for variation. Take a look at the outline of one side of your arm, for example. You will notice that the outline of the opposite side is similar to it but not identical.

Asymmetrical balance resembles two children on a seesaw balanced by one heavy adult. The two halves of the seesaw do not look alike but they act alike. This type of balance introduces the idea of *weight*—not the specific gravity of colors, shapes, and textures, but their optical weight. Some colors and shapes *look* heavier than others. For example, dark colors, coarse textures, and rough edges are heavier optically than light colors, smooth surfaces, and even edges. An artist or designer has to consider all these factors as he tries to unify and balance his work.

There is also a type of balance that depends on *interest* instead of weight. If you are curious about something small and seemingly insignificant, your curiosity may give it enough weight to balance a large, bright, heavily textured area. Balance by interest is really a type of psychological balance. It might be compared to looking for something you lost in a crowded drawer, or seeing your brother in a swimming pool full of kids, or hearing the instrument you happen to play while the whole orchestra is going full blast. The artist knows how to make an apparently insignificant area much more interesting than it deserves to be. And in that way he balances it against mightier visual forces.

Rhythm

In music, rhythm is a repeated beat or stress, and in art it amounts to the same thing—repetition. A visual element or combination of elements is repeated in a regular order or pattern. For example, the rows of windows in an office building set up a visual rhythm, a series of trees along an avenue may constitute a rhythm, even fence posts or the ties in a railroad track establish visual rhythms. Of course, these are simple repetitive rhythms involving almost identical elements repeating themselves at almost identical intervals. There are also more complex and interesting visual rhythms, just as there are more interesting musical rhythms than simple one-beat repetitions. Why is rhythm something we find in art, music, poetry, dance—in all the arts? Because rhythm is part of life and art often echoes life. We see it in planting and harvesting, giving and receiving, loving and being loved.

In part, rhythm reflects man's desire to see similarities and order in his environment. If you look at a bag of beans or a box of nails, you do not examine each bean or nail to see if it is identical to the others; you assume they are all more or less alike. When you cross the street while cars are still moving, you assume they will continue to move at the same rate. In other words, you have to believe there is a certain amount of order and regularity in the world if you are going to be able to survive in it. That order and regularity—whether it is regularity in space,

SHEEP, by James Lloyd. (Collection Mrs. Emily M. Wilson.)

WINTER PATTERN (below right). (Photo, James Carroll.)

Rhythm through repetition—but notice that the repeated elements are not monotonously alike. Little variations in size, contour, and placement allow us to see the sheep or the cars as separate units; yet we are very much aware of them as a group made up of almost identical entities. An effective work of art always creates some tension between unity and variety; first we are aware of one, then the other. In James Carroll's photograph, tire tracks in the snow constitute a powerful linear device for dramatizing ordinary rows of parked cars. The tracks look like lines drawn with a felt-point pen. They show how abstract lines can grow out of real events in the real world. Would you have trouble in "reading" those tire tracks? ■

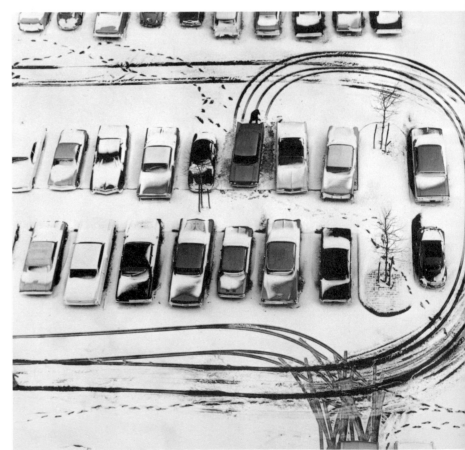

motion, acceleration, sound, shape, or quantity—is rhythm.

Men probably became aware of rhythm in nature and in animals during the New Stone Age, about twelve thousand years ago. Mostly they saw it in the breeding cycles of animals and in the time between planting and harvesting. New Stone Age, or Neolithic, art makes great use of repetition; Old Stone Age art does not. Modern culture is much more complex and so we have developed more complex types of rhythm. Older rhythms might have been based on the human heart beat, or the rhythms of men working—pulling and pushing in unison. Today we see and hear strange new rhythms in machines, electronic computers, submicroscopic energy paths, auto traffic, and the words, letters, and lights of the urban scene. And because technology creates new materials like plastics, reinforced concrete, and molded plywood, we see new rhythms in the varied shapes, surfaces, and textures they can assume at man's command.

Visual rhythms can be classified as repetitive, alternating, progressive and flowing. You already know what repetitive rhythm is. *Alternating* rhythm involves the addition of one more element. For example, instead of a continuous band of windows, we see *a window followed by an area of brick followed by a window followed by an area of brick*—visual alternation very much like the verbal alternations in this sentence. *Progressive* rhythm uses repetition *plus* a consistent change, like the number series X plus 1, X plus 2, X plus 3, X plus 4, and so on. The artist might set up a series of identical shapes and then vary their color or value regularly as the viewer's eye scans the series. Or he might introduce the variation in the shapes, keeping the color constant. *Flowing* rhythm tries to move the viewer's eye along a continuous path very much like the path of a sailboat bobbing up and down in the water but still carried forward by the wind. Because there are no breaks, no sudden changes of direction in flowing rhythm, it is very pleasing and soothing. It reminds us of the action of a really good swimmer, or an accomplished ballroom dancer, or maybe a dream in which you float effortlessly over the landscape.

You can see that rhythm is usually a pleasurable visual quality. It comforts the viewer because he sees what he has been led to expect. There may be surprises but they are small surprises, not shocks. Rhythm makes us feel that the world is appealing and friendly—adjusted to our needs for change and regularity or interesting sameness.

Proportion

It is almost impossible not to see proportion. If you look at a man, you immediately see whether he is tall or short, stout or thin, broad-shouldered, short-legged, long-nosed, or whatever. You see whether his head is too large or too small for his body. With a girl, you decide whether her hairdo is too high above her head, whether her heels are too high, whether her eyebrows are too thin, or her ankles too heavy. All of these are judgments about proportion—about the *size relationships of parts to a whole*.

Although there are no absolute rules about "correct" proportions in people or things, most of us still see and speak as if such rules existed. We get our ideas about "the right" proportions from everyday life, from looking at ourselves (we usually prefer our own proportions), from people and things we admire, and from the opinions we hear others express. It is also possible that we behave like very efficient calculators —our eyes "measure" what they see and then we rapidly but unconsciously figure out how something compares to the average dimensions of all the people and objects we have ever seen. This would explain how we seem to know immediately that someone is too stout or too short.

An artist rarely decides on the size of a shape by itself; it is always *the relationship* of that shape to other shapes, to the size of the canvas, the *volume of space* in which a building will be seen, the *location* of the shape in his total visual scheme, and the *order*, or *sequence*, in which the shape will be seen. Most of us feel large objects are more important than small ones. So if we see a large area next to a small one, we decide that the small one is insignificant. That may be exactly the idea the artist is trying to express. Or he may want to stress the significance of the small area and the emptiness of the large one. To do so he would have to compensate for the effect of the proportion by manipulating color, light, or shape to make the small area seem more important.

In painting a face, an artist could emphasize the importance of the eyes or the mouth without making them larger but simply by using very intense colors to describe them while keeping the surrounding areas subdued in color. But that would not be using proportion, since size is not involved. It *would be* a use of dominance and subordination. By manipulating size relationships, however, he could accomplish the same thing—perhaps in a more obvious way. The result is to express the artist's intention by controlling what the viewers see.

Proportion is crucial in architecture. Some of us think of buildings in the same way we think of our bodies, and we want buildings to have the same proportions as our bodies. Since the head is the most fascinating center of interest in the human figure, we attach tremendous importance to the tops of buildings. We locate all kinds of decorative and massive shapes there so that our houses and state capitols, for example, will not look "headless." Even when the technology of building construction changes, we often seem to require special roof emphasis to avoid a feeling of emptiness on top.

When an artist wants to create new or original relationships, he has to remember that they will be seen by people who have definite ideas about what good proportions should be. As a result, he can surprise and disappoint them, or he can please them by designing size relationships they have grown accustomed to expect. The decision he makes will depend on many factors: whether he is working on a large and expensive scale, as in architecture, or on a small scale as in printmaking; whether he wants to change the viewers' habits of seeing or *use* the viewers' habits to communicate an idea easily and quickly; whether his audience is small and well educated or large and intolerant of change. Whatever he decides, proportion will be one of his most powerful tools for expressing ideas or feelings without using words.

Design: Practices 1

SOME THINGS TO SEE

Look at *The Anatomy Lesson* by Rembrandt, *Caligraph K.C. III* by Herbert Ferber, The Cathedral of St. Basil in Moscow, and *Christina's World* by Andrew Wyeth (on pp. 272–273).

SOME PROBLEMS

These works of art solve the problem of unity in different ways. Can you tell how unity is achieved in each case? What is the purpose of unity in a work of art? Do you see how the artist or architect can create a feeling of unity without letting the work become monotonous? Think about monotonous things you have seen or done. What makes them that way? Do you like variety in food, clothing, music, natural surroundings, entertainment? Or do you prefer uniformity and consistency? How can you tell when there is too much variety in your life —in your diet, your clothing, your hobbies and recreation? How can you tell when you need more variety?

SOME POSSIBILITIES

Sometimes unity results from what you see; sometimes it results from what you know or remember. Is the Ferber sculpture united visually?

Does unity depend on someone or something being "in charge"? Most works of art have leaders and followers. When you are looking at a picture like *The Anatomy Lesson* or a building like St. Basil's Cathedral, how can you tell what is supposed to be important and what is meant to be unimportant?

What is harmony in music? Is musical harmony the same as harmony among the members of a family or a classroom? Does everyone have to agree in order to have harmony or unity?

WHAT YOU CAN DO

One way to develop your creative power is to organize a variety of unconnected things so that they make sense, so that they are unified visually or as ideas. Here are some challenges to your creativity:

Ask three different friends to draw a shape on a piece of cardboard and then give it to you. Cut out each shape and arrange it with the others on a large sheet. First try to unify these shapes just by moving them around in relation to each other. Then try to unify them by making additions of your own with line, texture, or color.

Repeat this same problem with the following changes: Ask a fourth person to suggest a word, an adjective. Now try to unify the shapes so that they have the feeling or quality of that word.

Pretend you are a cook. You have to make an interesting dish out of the following ingredients: two eggs, one ballet dancer,

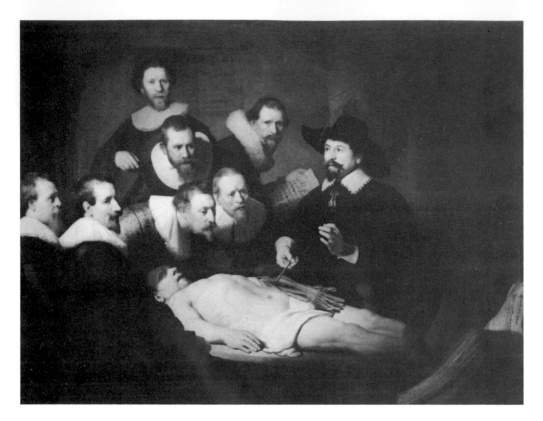

THE ANATOMY LESSON OF DR.
TULP (above), by Rembrandt van
Rijn. (Mauritshuis Museum, Holland.)

CALIGRAPH K.C. III, by Herbert
Ferber. (Courtesy the artist.)

Cathedral of St. Basil, Moscow (at
right). (Air France.)

CHRISTINA'S WORLD, by Andrew Wyeth. (Collection The Museum of Modern Art. Purchase.)

one French horn, one sliced tomato, a pair of old shoes, salt, pepper, and paprika. Paint a picture of the dish you prepare and try to make it look good. Then write a menu for a meal including a description of your dish.

Play this game with some friends. Ask each person to write any word on top of a piece of paper. Fold it over, and pass it on to the next person. When you have about two dozen words, read them to everyone. Do the words make sense? What can you do with them so that they will mean something? Would the addition of small drawings or cut-outs help? Perhaps you will find out that things which seem crazy or wild at first can become meaningful if you work on them a bit.

Design: Practices 2

SOME THINGS TO SEE

Look at *Liberation* by Ben Shahn, *Spring Blossoms* by Alexander Calder, *Royal Bird* by David Smith, *Seated Woman* by Bruno Lucchesi, and *Flowering Trees* by Piet Mondrian.

SOME PROBLEMS

All of these works show a type of balance. Yet none of them is absolutely symmetrical. Can you explain how each artist balanced his work? Suppose he did not balance the work; how would that affect you? Can you think of a reason why a picture or sculpture would be deliberately unbalanced? Why do you think absolute symmetry was avoided?

Does Calder work against nature, or does he cooperate with nature, or does he do both at the same time? Could you build a realistic painting on the foundation of Mondrian's *Flowering Trees*? Make a diagram of Shahn's painting showing how it is balanced. Does balance have anything to do with *the idea* of a picture? What does balance have to do with the idea of the Lucchesi sculpture?

SOME POSSIBILITIES

A good way to understand what balance means is to describe its opposite. How do

LIBERATION, by Ben Shahn. (Collection Mr. and Mrs. James Thrall Soby.)

SPRING BLOSSOMS (top left), by Alexander Calder. (Pennsylvania State University.)

ROYAL BIRD (center left), by David Smith. (Walker Art Center, Minneapolis.)

SEATED WOMAN #2 (bottom left), by Bruno Lucchesi. (Forum Gallery.)

FLOWERING TREES (below), by Piet Mondrian. (Nieuwenhuizen Segaar Art Gallery.)

you feel when you are off balance? How do spectators react when they see someone or something fall? Can you explain their reactions? Did you know that walking is a process of losing your balance and regaining your balance?

Ask a biology teacher to explain how people know they are in balance. Ask a science teacher to explain how a gyroscope works. He might also tell you something about levers or seesaws. Does the action of a lever tell you anything about balance in a picture or a sculpture?

Watch athletes try to keep their balance: skiers, skaters, running backs, boxers, divers, and others. Notice how important balance is for a really good athlete.

WHAT YOU CAN DO

Try to paint a picture in which a very large, heavy, or bright area is balanced by something which arouses your curiosity.

Make a still-life arrangement on a table in your classroom and try to arrange the objects in it so that the whole set-up will appear balanced no matter where you happen to be when you look at it.

Copy the pattern of veins in a leaf on a sheet of paper. Then try to build an imaginary picture around this pattern. Does the leaf help you to balance your picture? Is it symmetrical balance or were you able to introduce asymmetrical variations to create interest?

Study the role of balance in making mobiles. Then make a mobile in which you get balance by changing the sizes of the same basic shape. Build another mobile by balancing different kinds of objects and shapes. The first mobile might be monotonous; the second mobile may lack unity. What can you do to these mobiles to give them unity as well as variety?

The Handwriting of Art: Style

What makes your handwriting recognizable? Why is it that people who have seen your writing can often tell it is yours without reading what you've written? Probably because there is something unique and personal about the way you shape and connect your letters, end your words, dot your *i*'s and cross your *t*'s. From your handwriting people can get an impression of you that does not depend on the words and sentences you use. They react to your handwriting *style*.

The same can be said about works of art —they exhibit style. What *is* style in art? First of all, it is a family likeness that you can see in many works of art: They are slightly different but they look alike. Or it is something in a group of works that causes each one to affect your feelings in a similar way. You might say that style is the "look" or the "feel" of a work of art.

Style is part of the *language* of art. You get impressions and meanings from style the way you do from handwriting—without considering what it is **about**. Two artists might paint the same ocean and convey totally different feelings about that ocean because they use different styles of expression. Of course, the artists may not intentionally set out to work in a certain style. It's just that they cannot help working that way, because of their personalities or their training. Sometimes, the same style is used by several artists because they studied together, or they were taught by the same teacher, or they admired the same masterpieces. At other times, artists arrive at a common style independently—because of the way they see things. No matter what causes the artist to work in a certain style, we are interested in what his style can tell us. In other words, a style is a way of working which tells you something about the creator of a work of art—his time, his environment, his country, and his way of seeing, thinking, and feeling.

If you learn to "read" style, you can get ideas from art that could not be discovered by knowing the artist's name or where he lived or who influenced him. In a way, style is an involuntary language. That is, it com municates things the artist may not have intended or was not aware of. It is a little like saying one thing in words but meaning something else by the tone of your voice or the expression on your face. Studying style in art might provide you with clues about style in other areas of life—in conversation, in dress, in the way people move, in eating, in sports, in almost everything we do or watch.

The styles of art can be compared to four different persons: the first likes *accuracy*, the second admires *order*, the third prefers *emotion*, and the fourth favors *fantasy*. Although it is possible for the same person to like order *and* emotion, we usually find that people who prefer one do not like the other. In other words, when you look at a work of art, *one* of these four traits will usually be stronger or more outstanding than the others. After a while, you will be able to see the dominant style of a work as well as its minor variations. But even if you see styles mixed and in combination, it would be a good idea to discuss each style separately so you can get a clear idea of what it is.

Accuracy

Visual art often imitates what we see. Sometimes the artist changes reality, adds to it, or leaves things out. At other times, he tries very hard to reproduce exactly what he sees. Even though he has a good camera, the artist may want to represent reality with his own eyes and hands. Why does he do this when photography is so much more accurate and complete? Because imitating what he sees gives the artist a feeling of power over what he represents. He wants people to recognize two things—the *object* he has seen and his *skill* or *power* of representation. The artist may also feel that honesty in art—"telling it like it is"—means the most accurate possible recording of everything he sees. If art is a language, then it can be used truthfully or untruthfully. Finally, some artists believe that accuracy results from thoroughly *knowing* or understanding what they see. They believe that inaccurate representation is the result of ignorance.

Viewers also value accuracy in painting and sculpture because they get a thrill out of recognizing the artist's original model.

They also enjoy discovering some fault, something the artist failed to observe or to record. It almost seems as if they are testing their eyesight and visual memory against the artist's. But usually viewers do not want to compete with the artist, they want to be convinced of the truth of his representation. They want to believe in the illusions a man can create. Even if a camera can do a more accurate job, they still admire the ability of a man rather than a machine to *re*-present a piece of the world.

There are many ways to imitate reality without actually showing every detail a camera would record. That would be "photographic" realism. We are more interested in the "look" of reality after it has been filtered through the eyes and mind of an observant and sensitive person—the artist. We want to see what he thinks is important, the way his personality "screens out" certain details, and makes changes and additions in others. To get the feel or look of reality without mindlessly copying it, the artist will often combine accuracy with simplification. For example, he may very accurately reproduce the shapes and outlines of what he sees, but use simple, flat color within the shapes. Or he might employ very accurate color combined with free, more-or-less distorted shapes. And the artist can greatly simplify his light-and-dark patterns, eliminating the half-tones and thus creating a bold, crisp series of forms—forms that look even more solid than the real ones they represent.

Focus is another device for controlling accuracy. When we see something sharply we believe it is closer than an object whose edges are blurred. By varying the sharpness or softness of the edges he paints or models, then, the artist can create the effect of distance; he can also force you to see the sharply focused object first. Color helps too, because warm colors seem close, cool colors more distant. As objects recede, their lights and shadows become cooler and less distinct. The painter can imitate these effects on a flat canvas and in that way create optical impressions of depth and distance.

Perspective is the whole science of representing objects on a flat surface and making them appear to move back in space. Mainly it uses diminishing size of objects and converging lines to imitate the way objects are observed by our eyes. If the artist combines the converging lines of perspective with accurately drawn contours, control of focus, warm-cool color transitions, and careful rendering of light-dark patterns, he can create a remarkably convincing and accurate type of visual art.

Perspective, which was discovered during the Renaissance, is probably the single most important device employed in the style of accuracy, for it shows the world, not as we know it, but as we *see* it. According to the laws of perspective, a house might be represented as large as an apple in order to show that it is located far in the distance. Once artists learned to use this device, they were able to create the illusion of real space. It was an invention equivalent to the banker's discovery that he could create money by lending his depositors' savings over and over again. The device works. But it depends on your willingness to believe the money will always be in the bank when you want it, or your wish to believe that a certain arrangement of lines on a flat surface really represents distance.

Order

The sense of order in art does not depend on accuracy of drawing or the creation of illusions. Order is a feeling you get from the *abstract* arrangement of things. For example, whether you leave your room orderly or disorderly has nothing to do with *the things* in your room; it is the way they are left or located that matters. Your mother looks at your room and knows *instantly* that it is a mess, or "out of order." How does she know? What makes one arrangement "messy" and another one "orderly"? To answer these questions we must first discuss an idea mentioned above—abstraction.

Abstract shapes and forms rarely look like real objects but they often *feel* like real objects. For example, a triangle resting on its base feels like a house although it only looks like part of a house—the roof. A circle does not look like a human face, but most of us would accept it as a face rather than a tree trunk. These simple shapes can stand for or symbolize objects they do not really look like, objects they resemble only in part, because you sense that they share a common quality—roundness, or slantingness, or sharp-cornered-ness. Because of what they have in common, we can say that a circle is an abstraction of a face. That means all the recognizable features of a face have been abstracted—taken away—and only the quality it shares with a circle has been kept—its roundness.

In order to create an abstraction of a face or a house, the artist has to think about what he believes is their most typical quality. He hopes you will agree, when you see his abstraction, that it is connected in some way with the object it came from. Abstracting involves thinking about an object more than *seeing* it and reproducing what is seen. The abstract symbol of a house, to be effective, has to remind you of many houses, not just a particular or unusual one. It has to deal with the essentials, not the details that might change from city to city, from builder to builder, or from owner to owner. You might say that abstraction is a process of finding forms that represent the *permanent* qualities of something real.

Permanence is one of the most important traits of the style of order. When the parts of a work of art seem to be permanent, stable, or motionless, we say it is an orderly work. Nothing is there by chance. Everything is located where it is by choice and calculation. Now do you see why someone can tell instantly whether your room is "in order" or not? It is just a matter of seeing whether your shoes were dropped, thrown, or *placed* where they should be. The phrase "where they should be" tells us a lot about abstraction and order. Some objects get their location accidentally, that is, thoughtlessly. Others are located where they are *for a reason*: convenience, safety, appearance, pride, display, and so on. Similarly, there are works of art that are created impulsively, spontaneously, and thoughtlessly—the way you drop your socks on the floor. Others are created carefully and thoughtfully—the way you fold your socks and put them in a drawer.

Another trait of the style of order is stability, or absence of motion. Of course, most pictures and statues do not move (although some, called mobiles and kinetic art, *do* move), but even if the shapes and colors hold still, they may *look* as if they are about to move. They suggest motion because their lines and shapes lead your eye *beyond* themselves. Stable, orderly works always keep your eye *within* the picture space or the sculptural form. Motion, on the other hand, suggests change and change is the opposite of permanence. The artist who is interested in permanence and order is likely to use forms that are associated with stability: vertical lines, horizontal lines, triangles resting on their bases, squares and rectangles resting on their sides, symmetrically balanced shapes, repetitive rhythms—anything that avoids the unexpected.

Do not think that the style of order is better or worse than other styles. It just reflects the way many people—artists and viewers—feel about the world. Some of us want life to be less hectic, more carefully planned and lived. Usually, older people prefer order in art and in life, but not always. There is in each of us a desire for the kind of permanence and perfection that an art of order strives for. Sometimes it is called the classic style because it is especially associated with the art of Greece during the fourth and third centuries B.C. But even

when you are young, energetic, and almost continuously in motion, there are times when a little peace and quiet would be welcome. Remember, too, that in these moments of stillness we may feel related to the largeness and wholeness of the universe. The feeling that we get from classical art—that the world is not always and completely chaotic—is very welcome at times and men seem to return to it again and again.

Emotion

The style of order is based on the idea that the world and everything in it is arranged according to a plan. The artist's job is to find evidence of that plan and make it visible to everyone. He tries to see the hidden order that lies beneath everyday objects and places. But the style of emotion is different. It reflects the attitude of another kind of personality. For this personality, having strong feelings and expressing them to others is the most important thing in the world. This is the style used by artists who want to lift you out of your ordinary routine, to give you, for a moment at least, an intense feeling of dread, joy, hope, despair, or exaltation.

How does visual art manage to communicate such strong emotions? We know what it does *not* do. It avoids evenly measured shapes and spaces, precisely formed objects, carefully balanced arrangements, motionless figures, and dominant vertical and horizontal lines. These are order-producing devices. Their opposites, however, can give the viewer a feeling of losing himself, of forgetting where he is, of thinking only about the present moment instead of yesterday or tomorrow. Objects with indefinite shapes and exaggerated colors tend to arouse your feelings because you have trouble recognizing and locating them. They make you feel uncertain or slightly confused. And when that happens to a human being, his basic instincts are alerted—he gets ready to run or fight. This is what the artist wants. To succeed he must get you to respond with your instincts instead of your mind. Instead of thinking, you are supposed to *feel*.

Sometimes it is not wild shapes and colors that cause emotion, it is subject matter. Naturally, art dealing with violence stimulates human emotions because we cannot help feeling as if we are involved in the violence. Paintings of the kill at a wild animal hunt, or of the climax of a ferocious battle, or of natural catastrophes like hurricanes and floods are typical subjects of the style of emotion. And people enjoy them for many reasons. But they do not enjoy seeing soldiers butchered or animals torn apart by hunting dogs. What people enjoy in this type of art is their own sense of excitement. You probably enjoy horror movies for the same reason—they give you a chance to be really terrified, to feel the sort of danger and fear that civilized living does not often present.

A very frequently used device in emotional art is *distortion*. When people and objects are represented in a twisted, stretched, or exaggerated manner, we become quickly aroused, because any departure from what we expect to see creates tension within us. Distorted forms are not necessarily ugly, however. Sometimes they are used to express grace, delicacy, and refinement. But usually, distortion is upsetting. It sends signals to the nervous system that make us feel that something is wrong. It makes us look harder and try to decide how to react or what to do. Once again, the artist has us hooked; he gets us passionately involved in his work.

Distorted photo. (The Upjohn Company.)

Distortion used by a pharmaceutical manufacturer to convey the feeling of sickness or nausea. No words are needed; the image speaks for itself. Does it make you feel uneasy? Why? Perhaps you make yourself a little dizzy in the process of looking at this photograph. Now do you know what perception through "bodily imitation" means? ■

In our time, the style of emotion has been much more popular than the style of order. You can imagine why. But both styles are potentially present in all times, although individual artists tend to be drawn toward only one of them. Right now, many people are interested in having strange new emotions and in experimenting with all the feelings it is humanly possible to have. Sometimes they look to visual art for stimulation; perhaps they hope to be shocked into wonderful, trance-like states. Some persons want visual art to have the same effect on them as jumping into an ice-cold shower. They want to get an emotional and even a physical jolt out of art. This search for extreme emotions—in art and life—is called Romanticism. For Romantics, everyday life often seems unspeakably dull. But a life of intense and violent emotions can grow stale, too. Besides, it becomes exhausting sooner or later. When that happens, the pendulum swings; strong emotion seems to be in bad taste, and people grow interested in art that is classical, orderly, peaceful, and serene. In moderation, however, emotional or Romantic art is a wonderful antidote to the sameness and monotony that can creep into anyone's normal existence.

Fantasy

You remember that the style of accuracy is based on visual realism—on telling the truth about what the artist sees. The realistic artist feels it is wrong or dishonest to represent objects and places that do not exist. At least they should look as if they *might* be real. But the fantastic artist enjoys creating unreal places and things. And often he tries to make you believe they actually exist. For him, fantasies are as real as anything else; they are things he has truly imagined. And these imaginings become part of the real world when the artist gives them visual form.

Why do we enjoy looking at fantastic art and why do artists create it? First of all, it is very difficult to draw a sharp line between reality and imagination. Certainly it is difficult for children to do so. All of us can recall dreams or nightmares that seemed, if anything, more real than our waking lives. Also, we remember the fairy tales and myths of our childhood with a great deal of pleasure. We were reluctant to give up believing in them. Adults, too, believe in myths although they do not usually admit it. There is really no way to avoid fantastic ways of thinking and imagining because the human mind seems to require fantasy to explain the mysteries it cannot understand.

Fantasy is not something you grow out of. You just replace the fantasies of childhood with the myths of maturity. Much of art consists of creating visual fantasies—that is, representing strange worlds and creatures that would otherwise be imagined privately. You must have looked at the clouds, at frost on the windowpane, at wallpaper patterns, at the grain of wood, and at marble veins and seen all sorts of things. Your capacity for visual fantasy was at work. Leonardo da Vinci claimed that he could get ideas for his paintings by looking at cracks in plaster walls. Apparently, the act of seeing is creative or inventive; we can all see things that aren't there.

The fantastic worlds that artists and writers create are not always impractical. Many of our ideas for the future—in architecture, technology, and social relations—come from fantastic thinking. Probably the real world we live in now would seem fantastic to people living only fifty or sixty years ago. Good ideas for improving the world often begin as imaginative fantasies. Then practical men find ways to make them work.

As we grow older we hide or become ashamed of our tendency to daydream—to imagine ideal places and wonderful times. We are forced to live in the world as it actually is. The real world, however, is hard to change. Only fantasy shows the way it might be. Unfortunately, our ability to imagine and to fantasize seems to grow weaker and weaker. That is why the style of fantasy in art is so important: It preserves the life of imagination for many of us who have lost it. The artist and the poet are permitted to be dreamers. They can violate the rules of "common sense" and get away with it—in their art, at least. So we look to them for images, colors, forms, and visions where our eyes and minds can travel without worrying about the requirements of reality.

There are visual fantasies for every taste; no single "look" characterizes the style of fantasy. Its only common denominator is the absence of everyday logic, everyday usefulness, or everyday appearance. A fantastic work of art usually creates its own rules or logic or reality. As a result, it can be shock-ing. People and objects exchange identity the way they do in dreams and folk tales. The law of gravity may be repealed. Animals speak. Machines have emotions and feel pain. Objects pass through each other. Solid substances become transparent. Rocks learn to fly, and thoughts become visible. Men and trees seem to be brothers. The world is surrendered to magic.

Of course you cannot live in a fantastic world always. That would be sick. But some fantasy is healthy because it is a kind of vacation from reality that returns you to the real world as a more creative, more "balanced" person. And most of us need a vacation from reality once in a while. Besides, science and technology have made the real world so fantastic that our daydreams seem tame by comparison. In fact, technology changes the world too fast; as a result we create scientific fantasies to help adjust our thinking to our rapidly changing environment. The next time you see a far-out work of art, you might consider whether it helps you to understand the new supersonic, interstellar, submicroscopic, continuously exploding, infinitely receding, extra-galactic worlds of curved space and antimatter that science and technology are engaged in discovering.

Style: Practices 1

SOME THINGS TO SEE

Look at *House by the Railroad* by Edward Hopper, *Church of the Minorites* by Lyonel Feininger, *The Cardplayers* by Paul Cézanne, and *Man with a Guitar* by Georges Braque.

HOUSE BY THE RAILROAD (above left), by Edward Hopper. (Collection The Museum of Modern Art.)

CHURCH OF THE MINORITES (above right), by Lyonel Feininger. (Walker Art Center, Minneapolis.)

THE CARDPLAYERS (at right), by Paul Cézanne. (Musée du Louvre. Cliché des Musées Nationaux.)

SOME PROBLEMS

Although all of these works belong to the style of order, two are naturalistic and two are abstract. What makes the naturalistic works orderly? How would you defend your opinion? Which of these works of art seems very personal, very individual in style? Why? Could you paint a picture of someone and make it look like the Braque painting? Could you imitate the Feininger painting? Would a photograph of a Victorian house like the one in Hopper's painting show the same traits of order and stability? Can you tell the difference between light and space and solid materials in Feininger's picture? Does the Cézanne painting tell you anything about the card game or the men who are playing cards? What is the picture *really* about?

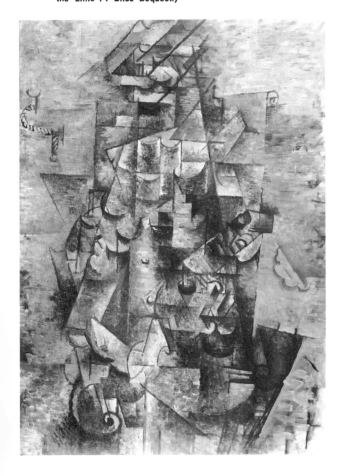

MAN WITH A GUITAR, by Georges Braque. (Collection The Museum of Modern Art. Acquired through the Lillie P. Bliss Bequest.)

SOME POSSIBILITIES

It would be interesting to photograph subjects similar to those shown in these four pictures: an old Victorian house, two people playing cards, a Gothic church in the city, and a man holding a guitar. If you compared the photographs to the paintings you might be able to guess at the changes the artists made in what they actually saw. Then you could try to decide why they made those changes. Suppose Hopper included more details in his picture—what would happen? How do you know the Braque painting is not of a woman with a guitar? Compare Monet's *Cathedral (in sunshine)* on p. 356 with Feininger's *Church of the Minorites.* Cover the left half of Cézanne's *Cardplayers* and then do the same to the right half. What happens to the picture?

WHAT YOU CAN DO

Cut an eight-by-ten sheet of black paper into different-size rectangles. Do the same with a sheet of white paper. Then arrange these black and white rectangles on a larger sheet of gray paper, keeping them either vertical or horizontal. Try to make the arrangement look like a picture of a place or of some people. When you have worked out the best picture you can, paste the rectangles down and sign your name on the back. Your teacher can collect the pictures, mix them up, and then hang them on the wall. Now you can try to tell who made each picture. Can you tell which ones were done by boys? Or by girls? Can you recognize anyone's "handwriting" or style? How? Did anyone get curved, circular, or diagonal effects just by using rectangles? Is that possible? Do you think you could convert Hopper's picture into an arrangement of black and white rectangles?

Empty everything in your pocket or purse on your desk. Now arrange these things so that they are orderly but dull. Then arrange them so they are orderly and interesting.

Make a list of words which stand for things that don't move. Then try to find some of these things in magazines. Cut them out and arrange them in a picture. Now write a poem or story about stillness, based on your picture.

Style: Practices 2

SOME THINGS TO SEE

Look at *Death and the Mother* by Käthe Kollwitz, the Los Manantiales Restaurant by Felix Candela and Joaquin Ordoñez, *The Rebellious Slave* by Michelangelo, and *The Starry Night* by Vincent van Gogh.

SOME PROBLEMS

Emotions of many sorts are expressed in painting, sculpture, and architecture. Sometimes the artist cannot help showing how he feels. But how do we find out what those feelings are? What makes a work of art look sad, mournful, angry, excited, or happy? Is happiness expressed in art the same way it is expressed in life? What do you do when you feel very good?

SOME POSSIBILITIES

Try to find out how people act when they have strong feelings about something. Do they show their emotions through their bodies? Would a Frenchman show his emo-

DEATH AND THE MOTHER, by Käthe Kollwitz. (Courtesy Erich Cohn.)

Los Manantiales Restaurant, Xochi-milco (at left), by Felix Candela and Joaquin Alvarez Ordoñez. (Courtesy Felix Candela.)

THE REBELLIOUS SLAVE (below left), by Michelangelo. (Musée du Louvre, Cliché des Musées Nation-aux.)

THE STARRY NIGHT (below right), by Vincent van Gogh. (Collection The Museum of Modern Art. Acquired through the Lillie P. Bliss Bequest.)

tions like an American? What would be the basic difference between someone who is calm and someone who is excited? What happens to people who keep their emotions "bottled up"? Does an artist show his emotions because he can't help it, or does he want you to feel the same way he does? Can a building express emotion? What about a chair, a pair of shoes, a tree—any object?

WHAT YOU CAN DO

Write a story telling what happened up to the time of the events shown in *Death and the Mother.*

Stage a debate based on the proposition: Resolved that van Gogh's *Starry Night* could only have been painted by someone who was delirious from a high fever or was suffering from a bad dream.

Study *The Rebellious Slave* and try to figure out if any other title would fit this sculpture. Can you get into the same position as the statue? Make up a list of words like ambition, memory, anticipation, disappointment, and so on. Then invent body positions you can act out which stand for these words. You might report to the class on what you have found out about the connection between emotions and body position, muscle tension, balance, imbalance, hand gestures, and facial expressions.

Draw the main lines of the window opening in the Los Manantiales Restaurant. Then draw or paint a picture around these lines, but do not copy the restaurant. When you have finished, collect all the pictures in the class and hang them up. Now answer these questions: How many are "happy" pictures?

Are any of the pictures sad? How did the basic lines affect each type of picture? Have you ever seen a giant clam shell? Why does it resemble the Los Manantiales Restaurant? What makes a line happy or sad?

Bring to class some photographs or drawings of buildings in your community and try to convince the class that they express certain emotions.

Cut out magazine advertisements and try to combine them with pictures of buildings in your community. Use the words in the ads but not the pictures. Then reverse the process: Cut out some advertising messages and try to find buildings in town which express the same feelings as the ads.

Find at least one instrumental record that expresses the main idea of each of the four works of art illustrated above. Play the record for the class without giving its title or telling which work it goes with. After everyone has written down the answers, discuss the answer that most of your classmates picked: What quality in the music connects with the main quality of the art object? What is the over-all mood of the record? Can people *see* things when they listen to music? Can they *hear* things when they look at art?

Explaining How We See: Aesthetics

Optics deals with vision—in human beings, in animals, or in machines like cameras, microscopes, and telescopes. Aesthetics as it is used here deals with the way people *use* their vision. So we are not talking about how light enters the eye and creates images on the retina, although that is important. We are mainly interested in the way your mind does things to the visual impressions it receives. We are not even talking about the human brain, which is also very important in vision. Your mind is more than your brain and sense organs, it is the way they work together. A mind is not a thing, it is a process. Although we talk about "your mind" as if it were an object inside you, like your liver, we really mean a process that goes on as long as you are alive.

The process called mind has habits—typical ways of behaving. We want to study the way these habits affect the business of looking at art. Since this chapter is devoted to the *language of art*, we ought to know how that language is understood. So far we have studied the parts of the language, the way they are organized, and some typical ways of using them. But we have not examined the way they affect the people who "listen" to the language. It is possible to know what art is made of and still not know how and why people react to it the way they do. Aesthetics, then, is an attempt to explain human reactions to what they see—especially what they see in art.

Empathy

Empathy means "feeling into" whatever you are looking at or listening to. By feeling into a work of art or a musical performance you almost become what you see or hear; you identify with the object that interests you.

This may sound strange: How can anyone feel into something he listens to or sees? How can he "become" anything except himself? Part of the answer comes from looking at some real-life situations. Perhaps you have noticed how your friends react to the characters in a movie they are watching. They seem to behave as if they themselves were the actors or actresses on the screen. They flinch or duck when the hero is about to be hit; they become happy and excited when the heroine gets her man; their eyes fill with tears if one of the characters is suffering. For some persons it is very difficult to hold back their feelings as they watch a dramatic or musical event. Have you noticed that they may even cry while listening to music, even though no words are spoken and nothing real can be seen?

Something else worth watching is a group of teenagers who are listening to music they really like. They often snap their fingers, keep time with their feet, sway their bodies, shout, hum, scream, close their eyes, laugh, jerk their heads, twitch, and so on. All of these sometimes strange, sometimes funny, actions are caused by empathy. The individuals whose behavior we can see and describe in this way have been receiving "signals" from a work of art, and those signals "turn them on."

To be "turned on" by a work of art, or to be "tuned in" to it, means becoming very interested, deeply involved. To be involved is to have empathy: We get involved not only with our minds and emotions but also with our bodies and senses. In fact, our senses get the signals first and our emotions and thoughts follow. You can think of a painting or a poem as a small transmitter that sends out electronic signals when you are paying attention to it. Your body acts as a receiver that may or may not be tuned in to the wavelength on which the transmitter is broadcasting. When your body *is* tuned in, its components go to work like the resistors, condensers, transistors, batteries, coils, and wires of a standard radio receiver. Your body converts artistic signals into feelings and ideas the way a receiver converts radio waves into sounds.

But how do the sounds of music or the colors of painting get a person to respond by swaying his body or closing his eyes? The answer is very important for understanding not only art but human nature as well: *People imitate what they see and hear.* We imitate with our bodies everything our senses can detect. Even though you may not be aware of it, you imitate colors and lines and shapes with your body, starting with the openings in your eyes, the muscles controlling your eyeballs, your nervous system, your large muscle and skeletal system, your glandular system, your skin, and even your internal organs. That is why ancient people thought certain emotions were located in specific organs like the heart, stomach, liver, spleen, and so on. Even we locate love in the heart. The ancients realized that our bodies are involved when we witness drama, music, poetry, and painting, and they thought an emotion was in the liver, for example, waiting to be turned on. That old-fashioned idea is still good, so far as it goes. But we need the concept of empathy or bodily imitation

to explain how you can "feel into" colors and sounds and images. What really happens is that you become aware of your body as it tries to imitate what your senses detect in a work of art. That awareness becomes a thought or an emotion, depending on the kind of motor activity (foot-stamping, finger-snapping, teeth-clenching, nose-wrinkling, eye-blinking, shoulder-swaying) you are engaged in.

Another problem remains. We can understand bodily imitations or motor activity when someone listens to music. But usually people sit or stand very quietly when they are looking at art. This inactivity, however, is deceiving. You may want to feel a sculpture you are looking at in a museum, but the guard is watching, so you obey your parents' or teacher's instructions, and you do not touch. Similarly, in looking at paintings, you have been trained not to show your feelings or make any unusual gestures—just to say the right words. But persons from another culture—individuals who have not been trained as we have been—might react by jumping, dancing, or swaying, just as teenagers do when music gets through to them. In other words, because of our upbringing, we often suppress our normal desire to respond with large-scale bodily movements to what we see in art. Nevertheless, we respond with many outwardly invisible, small-scale movements. And these tiny neuromuscular motions are experienced as ideas and feelings. Empathy, then, is a concept that describes your *inner imitation* of what you watch and listen to in art. It shows how the emotions you see expressed in art are really caused by awareness of your own bodily feelings. But of course these bodily feelings do not start by themselves; they are set off or triggered by the lines, colors, shapes, sounds, and rhythms of a work of art.

Psychic Distance

Empathy explains how we get involved with a work of art. *Psychic distance* goes one step further: It describes what happens when we are either too involved or not involved enough.

By psychic distance we mean how close or far away you feel you are in relation to works of music, painting, drama, or sculpture. This idea does not refer to your distance measured in inches, feet, or miles; it means your mental and emotional distance from the work. For example, if you are so involved with the hero of a movie that you scream "Watch out!" when the villain is about to shoot him, you have no psychic distance from the movie at all. That is, you have forgotten that the movie is a type of make-believe; you act as if it is real life instead of a form of art you are watching. But we do not really enjoy art if we forget that it isn't real. Part of our enjoyment depends on knowing that the actors in a play are pretending, that the fruit and vegetables in a picture are made of paint, that the images and feelings described in a poem are made of words.

But suppose you see a movie and do not believe, even for a second, that the actors are the people they pretend to be. In that case, you cannot get interested in the film; you do not care *what* happens to the characters or *how* the story turns out. You have too much psychic distance from the movie and, as a result, it bores you. Maybe you are bored because of bad acting, bad direction, poorly written dialog, or lack of understanding of the story. Whatever the reason, you have too much distance, and that prevents you from enjoying what you see.

Obviously, the ideal amount of psychic distance is somewhere between the extremes of no distance (or complete identification) and maximum distance (or total boredom). To get the most out of a work of art, it would be best to have as little distance as possible *without completely losing yourself*. In that way you can concentrate on the art object and your own reactions at the same time. Now, what controls the amount of distance you actually feel?

Realism or naturalism in art is probably the strongest way of reducing distance, that is, getting the viewer deeply involved with what he sees. On the other hand, abstraction increases distance; it is simply easier to become involved in a painting that closely resembles a real object. This does not mean that a realistic work is superior to an abstract work; it is just easier to understand and therefore to become emotionally involved with it. But, as mentioned above, there is danger in too much realism: You might forget you are looking at art. Therefore, realism has to be combined with some abstraction —*some* simplification or some use of symbols and signs to express the artist's intentions without spelling out every single detail.

Music that sounds exactly like your heartbeat would be very realistic, but it would probably make you feel you were going mad. You may be interested in the sound of your heartbeat when you are examined by a doctor, but a work of art which sounds exactly like what he hears in his stethoscope would be too close for comfort. On the other hand, a musical composition woven around the human heartbeat *in a disguised way* could be emotionally and intellectually powerful. So there are two things that control the amount of psychic distance between you and a work of art: One is the blend of realism and abstraction in the object; the other is your personal ability to remember that you are watching or listening to an imitation of life.

Children have trouble telling the difference between art and reality. As a result, adults often try to control the stories they read or the pictures they see so they will not be frightened by artistic fantasies or get distorted ideas of what life is really like. But as we grow older, we usually learn to create psychic distance between ourselves and the various kinds of art in our environment. It is fairly easy to maintain your distance from architecture and abstract paintings; but the human figure seen in dancing, in sculpture, in drama, the films, and television has tremendous power to reduce your distance because it is so real, so much like your own body. Everyone is intensely interested in the human figure, especially in its sexual traits. That is entirely normal. Consequently, art that shows the figure, either dressed or undressed, may cause some people to act as if they were looking at real life. If they cannot maintain their psychic distance in such instances, it is possible to get art and life mixed up. Sometimes community groups, acting as censors, try to protect young people from this type of confusion. But it is very difficult for them to control what people see or read or listen to. Therefore, one of your most important objectives in growing up is to learn to control your psychic distance from art by yourself. One of the best signs of your maturity will be the ability to tell whether a very realistic book or play or movie has presented a basically honest picture of life as you know it to be. That is when art becomes a genuinely important part of life. Because then you will be testing your perceptions–what you know and have seen—against the vision of reality presented by the art forms which are constantly being created. Then psychic distance —how much to believe, how strongly to feel, how far to let yourself go—becomes a sign of your manhood or womanhood.

Funding and Fusion

If you read a book or see a play and a friend asks about it, you can usually say whether it was pleasant or exciting, depressing or funny, whether it made you feel satisfied and optimistic or angry and disappointed. You can sum up your feelings about a complicated experience in a sentence or two—even in a word. After seeing a play you can remember the single impression it made even though it consisted of many different details. That single impression lasts because our minds add up, or *fund*, all the details of a work of art and *fuse* them into a single, unified feeling or quality. Afterward, when we think about those details, they seem to be permeated with that fused, over-all feeling. As a result, you can often sum up an entire work in a few words by describing its unique quality—the dominant feeling that all its parts seem to have.

What causes the fusion of feeling in a work of art and why is it important? In part, fusion is created by the artist's attempt to unify his work. You may remember that he tries to make it possible for the viewer to feel that all the parts of a painting are related or connected to each other. They should seem to belong to each other. This belonging together encourages the viewer to see the work as a whole. But even if he feels the wholeness and togetherness an artist has built into a painting, the viewer himself has to do the work of funding and fusion in order to sense the single impression of the picture on him. So there are two sources of the fused feeling: One is the art object itself, the other comes from the spectator.

Every time you look at a picture you get dozens of separate ideas of what you are seeing. It might help to think of yourself as a movie camera whose shutter is opening and closing so fast that it seems to be open all the time. The longer you look, the more you receive different ideas and impressions of the work. Just as the movie camera builds up film footage while it is being used, you build up a fund of ideas and images when a picture holds your interest for any length of time. But our minds cannot tolerate too many different impressions of an object or event. A point is reached where your mind

tries to sum up and to fuse these separate ideas. A multitude of impressions is perplexing; it prevents you from deciding whether you like what you see, whether you agree with the point of view expressed, whether you would like to own the object, whether you would prefer not to look at it any more, whether you understand the meaning of its symbols, and so on. As a result, you are forced to choose *one* of your impressions and to decide that its qualities and traits apply to all the others. This happens without your conscious effort, but when it does happen, you suddenly notice that the picture begins to "make sense." That is, all the parts seem to fit into a single pattern of feeling. It may not be a pattern you enjoy, but nevertheless you now can see or feel the dominant, controlling, *fused* quality of the work. The tension you built up in trying to fund or fuse your different impressions is relaxed. You are able to move on to other things.

Fusion is a process that seems to take place without your knowledge. That is, your mind will sum up and unify its impressions of a work of art whether you want to or not. What you *can* control, however, is how soon the process takes place. There is a skill in looking at works of art; it consists of trying to delay the moment when a single feeling seems to dominate all the parts of what you see. To do this you must avoid becoming too fascinated with any particular detail early in your experience of the work. With visual art you should try to *keep looking,* that is, encourage your eyes to search and rove over the entire object. That roving gives you a chance to discover places of interest that you might have missed. Then, when fusion *does* take place, it will be based on a rich set of impressions instead of a short, superficial examination.

The ability to search a work of art thoroughly increases with practice. It makes you a more discriminating person—someone who knows how to look for what he wants. People who immediately like or dislike what they see make a great many mistakes: They overlook many satisfying things and they buy or accept what later turns out to be worthless. The habit of looking at works of art carefully and searchingly has practical advantages. You learn to choose and decide for yourself in a world that seems to be telling you what to like or do or own or enjoy.

Aesthetics: Practices 1

SOME THINGS TO SEE

Look at *Nude Descending a Staircase* by Marcel Duchamp, *Europa on a Cycle* by Richard Stankiewicz, *Lion Hunt* by Peter Paul Rubens, and *Migration to Nowhere* by Rico Lebrun.

SOME PROBLEMS

We want to find out how these works of art send visual signals that affect our feelings. We also want to know what we, as viewers, do with the signals sent out by the art object. Does the subject of a painting cause you to react in a certain way, or is it the way the subject is presented? How much of your reaction depends on your attitude? That is, can you prevent yourself from having any feelings when you look at these works of art? Is it possible for you to be indifferent?

NUDE DESCENDING A STAIRCASE, NO. 2, by Marcel Duchamp. (Philadelphia Museum of Art: The Louise and Walter Arensberg Collection.)

Could you ignore a marching band if it was playing outside your window? Can you look at a TV commercial without being affected? What happens if you turn off the sound?

SOME POSSIBILITIES

It would be a good idea to carry out a really thorough investigation of human vision. Find out how the human eye works.

EUROPA ON A CYCLE (above left), by Richard Stankiewicz. (Courtesy of the artist; photo, Stable Gallery.)

LION HUNT (above right), by Peter Paul Rubens. (Alte Pinakothek, Munich.)

MIGRATION TO NOWHERE (at left), by Rico Lebrun. (Courtesy Mrs. Rico Lebrun.)

It would also be useful to study how a camera works, and then to compare the photographic process with human vision. If possible, invite a psychologist to class and ask him to explain the origin of human emotions. Could you get a doctor or a nurse, perhaps, to tell how organs and glands affect our feelings, or how our feelings affect our organs and glands? Does Duchamp's *Nude* send signals to your muscles? Could you do a pantomime of the Rubens *Lion Hunt*? If you start looking at Lebrun's painting by seeing the soles of feet first, what is the chain of feelings and thoughts that follows? When reacting to the Stankiewicz *Europa on a Cycle*, do you think your own sense of body balance is affected?

WHAT YOU CAN DO

Try to find out which of the following affects people the most: a picture of a tree, a song about a tree, a poem about a tree, or a real tree; a picture of a mountain, a picture of a dog, or a picture of a man. You might run an experiment and report your findings back to the class.

Compare the reactions of people to a house, an igloo, a teepee, a tent, a mud hut, and a marble palace. Find or make pictures of each dwelling and ask different people the same question about each picture. The objective is to discover whether previous experience with a certain kind of dwelling affects the way we see it.

Draw a picture from memory of someone you know very well. Then draw a picture of a person you have seen only once or twice. Now compare the two drawings. Which drawing was easier to make? Why?

Using modeling clay, make a portrait head of one of your friends. Next, draw a picture of your friend. Then, draw your friend's picture by looking at the clay model you made. Compare the drawing you made from life with the drawing you make from the clay model. What caused the differences you see?

Aesthetics: Practices 2

SOME THINGS TO SEE

Look at *Number 1* by Jackson Pollock, *Essex* by John Chamberlain, *Report from Rockport* by Stuart Davis, and *The Ravine* by Vincent van Gogh.

NUMBER 1, by Jackson Pollock. (Collection The Museum of Modern Art. Purchase.)

ESSEX, by John Chamberlain. (Collection The Museum of Modern Art. Gift of Mr. and Mrs. Robert C. Scull and Purchase.)

REPORT FROM ROCKPORT, by Stuart Davis. (Collection Mr. and Mrs. Milton Lowenthal.)

RAVINE, by Vincent van Gogh. (Museum of Fine Arts, Boston. Bequest of Keith McLeod.)

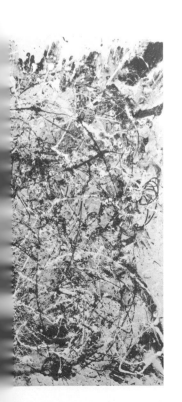

SOME PROBLEMS

Each of these works of art deals with movement in a special way. But it is imagined movement because each picture or sculpture is motionless. The questions that have to be answered are: What causes the movement I am looking at? Does the movement suggest places, people, events, or emotions? Is there any single feeling or idea that seems to govern the whole work of art? Are my reactions influenced by the materials I see, by their lines and shapes, by the way the materials have been used, or by my discovery of feelings I didn't know I had?

SOME POSSIBILITIES

Think of processes or things or happenings that the Pollock painting reminds you of. Then explain what they have in common. Ask yourself what the Stuart Davis painting *almost* looks like. Does it remind you of any kind of dancing? Why? Roll a sheet of paper into a tube and look at the van Gogh painting through it. Get close to the picture so that you cannot see its edges and move the tube around. Do the same thing with the Pollock. As you look at these pictures, do you feel you are being drawn into them? Does that feeling frighten you? Is there any kind of connection between Chamberlain's *Essex* and Davis's *Report from Rockport*? What would you have to do to imitate the Chamberlain sculpture?

WHAT YOU CAN DO

Make an accurate tracing of the outlines of the shapes in the Stuart Davis painting. Then strengthen these outlines and transfer them to the kind of musical graph paper used by composers. Next, try to write down the notes you believe come close to the visual shapes. Be sure to consider the silent periods or rests between the phrases or shapes or note clusters. Perhaps you can get someone to play this music. If so, does the music sound like the picture?

Look at the Pollock painting through a magnifying glass. Make an enlargement of what you see through the glass. Then, pretend your enlargement is the map of a community. Locate the most likely places for streets, buildings, residential areas, shopping centers, sports and recreation areas, traffic, industrial buildings, and so on.

Get a photograph of a natural scene near where you live. Then, using the van Gogh painting as a guide, make a picture based on the photograph. But do not use paint. Use pieces of twine and paste them down on a heavy sheet of cardboard. Make the picture with curves, spirals, and concentric circles. See if you can avoid straight lines and sharp angles. Finally, ask your friends to shut their eyes and pass their hands over your finished picture. Can they recognize the place represented in your picture?

Stage a crash between two empty milk cartons. Separate the crashed cartons and cut them open. You might also tear as well as cut the cartons apart. Then arrange and reassemble the torn carton parts on a cardboard sheet painted a dark or intense color. Finally, write a description of the construction as if it represented a battle between prehistoric monsters.

The language of the visual arts takes many forms: painting, sculpture, architecture, films, the crafts, and the various types of visual communication. Naturally these forms change throughout history. One of them, motion pictures, did not even exist until this century. And the visual images used to provide information or to sell products today are richer and more varied than ever before. It almost seems impossible to study the full range of visual art when you think of how quickly it changes, the many different materials it uses, the variety of purposes it serves, and the difficulty of understanding some of its new experimental forms. But we have to try because our environment is shaped by artists and designers more than it is by nature.

Although we cannot study all the varieties of visual language in one chapter, we can examine the fundamental traits of its major forms. You have been able to learn how artists think and organize their ideas; and you know something about the way viewers respond to their work. So you are prepared to look at the specific traits of painting, sculpture, architecture, and film. We can learn where they are similar or different, and we can examine the way the artist's tools and materials affect what he is able to say with them.

Two-Dimensional Images: Painting

Making marks on a flat or curved surface may be the oldest form of human creativity. It could have begun when men noticed the patterns left on bones by their crude knives after they had scraped or cut away the meat of killed animals. Or painting may have started when men dipped their hands into colored mud and then pressed them against the stone walls of their caves. In one case

11

Studying Varieties
of the Language

the image is a set of lines, in the other, a filled-in shape. Over a long period of time these lines and shapes were given names, were combined, arranged, simplified, decorated, and copied. There were accidental resemblances to real objects. Early artist-hunters learned to create those "accidents" purposely. Some of the markings could be used to tell stories, to give directions, and to serve as maps and records.

At first, men made pictures of what they loved and feared most—animals. When they learned to raise crops, build houses, and breed animals for food, men began to tell more complicated stories with their pictures. This activity required small, concentrated images that could carry a great deal of information. Picture-writing developed. Then followed letters—images that stood for the *sounds* of spoken words instead of seen objects and events.

The creation of images that stand for sounds—phonetic letters—marked the separation of spoken language from visual language. Now we get information from both languages, but in the middle of this century we began to depend more on visual images and less on printed letters and spoken words for our information. The reason may be that we began to create more information to learn (and read about) and therefore had to get this information faster. Letters and words have to be arranged in a special sequence and spread out along a line in order to be understood. This takes more time than looking at a picture which can be seen and understood almost at once. Furthermore, we use only *part* of our visual capacity when we read writing, but we use all of it when we look at pictorial images. Of course, the meanings of pictures are not as exact as the meanings of words (which you can look up in the dictionary). But sometimes exact meaning is not important in communication —only the general meaning. And by adding motion to images—motion pictures—even more information can be carried and transmitted. When telephones carry the image of the person you are talking to, there will be many changes in spoken and written language. Although we may lose some of the exactitude of written and spoken expression, we will make up for it by the tremendous amount of visual information we can exchange. So two-dimensional images—no matter how they are made, reproduced, and transmitted—will become more and more important in carrying information, in expressing ideas and feelings, and just giving pleasure.

Line and Mass

There are two fundamental ways to think about flat images. One is to think about the lines and boundaries that form the shapes and separate the colors from each other. Another is to think about the areas or masses of color themselves. Some people naturally search for boundaries and others naturally explore what is inside the boundaries. Artists create images in the same way: They draw lines or they arrange masses.

From your own artistic experience you know that the materials you happen to have affect your approach also. For example, a pencil or any pointed tool almost forces you to draw lines. A brush or a thick stick or crayon or chalk makes you work in areas or masses. But natural objects are rarely made of lines, they are usually made of surfaces. Representing these objects in line forces the artist to find *out*lines that separate different surfaces from each other. These outlines are not real, they are devices artists have to use. Thinking about objects and representing them with lines—especially outlines—is usually called drawing. Drawing encourages you to measure things with your eyes, to look for the places where different colors, textures, and materials meet. When you draw you have to make up your mind about how things are shaped. It is difficult to be vague or indefinite when you are working with line. As a result, drawing forces the artist to think and measure and plan ahead.

Representing objects in mass calls attention to their surfaces. But the surfaces of real objects are hardly ever perfectly flat—as flat as a sheet of paper or an artist's canvas. So the artist must think about making an area or mass look like the surface of the object it represents. Since he doesn't depend on outline, he must concentrate on the inside or area of a shape. Usually, he can represent a surface by controlling its color and its value (its lightness or darkness). This type of control is easiest to get by mixing colored pigment and flowing it onto a surface with a brush. That is why working in mass is usually thought of as painting, whereas working in line is usually called drawing.

Actually, the art of painting involves both line and mass. And it is possible to make lines with a brush and areas with a pencil. But I have been talking about the easiest and most natural ways to use these tools. Also, people seem to be divided temperamentally or psychologically into groups that prefer one or the other way of thinking about images. Of course, all painted images are not intended to represent real objects; many are invented. Nevertheless, our habits of seeing and representing reality carry over into the painting of imagined as well as real things.

Many artists combine drawing and painting. They use line to plan what they are going to do and they use mass to represent large surfaces and textures. It is difficult to cover a large area with lines. And getting a sharp, accurate line with a brush full of paint is also difficult. As a result, subjects that call for a great deal of fine detail are usually handled with a linear technique. The painter uses small, pointed brushes and probably makes a careful drawing or sketch in advance. In fact, he may make several preparatory drawings or studies. These are not meant to be seen by others; the artist uses them to work out his problems before beginning to paint. Drawing is really a way of investigating and solving problems with line. Lines can be easily changed or erased, but masses of color are harder to change. As a general rule, then, when line and mass or drawing and painting are combined in a single picture, the drawing of the lines usually comes first and the painting of the masses follows.

Indirect and Direct Painting

There are almost as many different approaches to painting as there are painters. Some artists have a very definite idea of what their picture will look like. Others prefer to be surprised. Some plan ahead very carefully, and, as mentioned above, make many drawings or studies in advance. Others, who are searching for a fresh, spontaneous look, avoid planning ahead. But all the different approaches fall roughly into one of two classes–the indirect and the direct.

The indirect method has been partly described already. It involves a gradual build-up from drawing to painting to glazing in separate layers for each stage. Glazing is painting with semitransparent color, that is, a paint film that lets most of the form underneath show through. This technique involves mixing the artist's pigment with varying amounts of varnish. Glazing darkens a picture surface slightly and changes the color of what you see very much the way sun glasses do. It permits the painter to deal with one thing at a time: first, drawing; then modeling or arrangement of patterns of light and dark; finally, glazing or coloring the light and dark patterns without changing their distribution. Glazes also give the picture a sort of inner glow because of the way they trap light and reflect it back to your eyes. That is why paintings by the traditional masters, who usually preferred the indirect method, often have a rich luminous glow, especially in the dark areas.

You can see that the indirect method calls for very sure knowledge of what the final result will be. Otherwise the painter would not know what to do at each stage of the process. There is room for some minor changes, but usually the major decisions are made early—during the drawing stage. Glazes cannot alter the shapes because glazes are translucent. And painting the light and dark masses will not change the basic composition that has been firmly established by the drawing. As a result, some of the old masters, like Rubens, could permit their assistants to paint in backgrounds, minor figures and details because the master controlled the drawing. He was like a playwright who entrusts the director and actors with certain adjustments in the performance provided the lines are not rewritten.

Direct technique allows the painter to go after the final effect immediately. It also lets him paint a picture by groping or "feeling" his way. He does not have to start out with a definite idea of what he wants. Often, the artist bypasses the drawing stage (which would commit him to a plan) and begins to paint from the start. He combines modeling with color and shape in a single process. To do so he usually must apply paint more thickly: He covers over or wipes out areas he wants to change. Fortunately, modern pigments will cover an earlier film of paint without letting it show through. But the paint used by the masters would eventually "bleed" through, another reason why they preferred indirect technique.

Today, artists value freedom and spontaneity—the opportunity to change their minds whenever they want to, and a final look of "no hesitation," "no afterthought." And viewers enjoy seeing signs of spontaneity in the picture surface; they like the vigorous brushmarks, the smears and drips and splashes of paint. These are the traces and evidence of directness—like the honesty of someone who immediately says what is on his mind instead of pausing to figure out how people will react to his ideas.

Because modern paintings do not often represent objects as we normally see them, our attention is directed to how the pictures were produced. We look for the performance instead of the object. Direct technique is ideal for showing the physical process the artist went through. And the colors, thickly applied and often mixed on the canvas, create a terrific spectacle. By comparison, indirect technique looks cautious and tame. And it is. The masters *built* a painting the way engineers build a bridge. You would not want to travel on a bridge that was spontaneously designed by its engineers. Of course, no one travels on a picture, but the traditional attitude toward pictures and the craft of painting implied that a picture was composed and executed as soundly as the objects it represented. All this has changed. Emphasis today is on the expression of feelings and ideas as directly as possible. The painstaking reconstruction of real objects is a thing of the past.

Collage and Assemblage

Images are not always made with paint. They have been created with colored pieces of stone as in mosaics, with colored glass divided by lead strips as in stained glass, and with colored plaster as in fresco murals. Men have formed images in magnificent woven tapestries, embroideries, rugs, wood, marble and ivory inlays, high-fired enamel—with almost any available material that an artist could control. Primitive or tribal artists have worked with shells, beads, colored sand, seeds, animal skins, stones, horn, bone, hair, grass, and leaves. And when they use pigments or dyes, a brush is only one of many ways of applying them. But we who can buy manufactured paint conveniently packaged in jars or tubes tend to forget how many different methods there are for coloring a surface and creating an image.

Today glues and plastic adhesives are so strong and cheap, there is virtually no material that cannot be included in a "painting." In this way image-making has regained some of its primitive variety. We can make just about anything stick to a surface—and permanently. Early in the century, Picasso and his colleagues, Braque and Gris, began to glue pieces of printed paper into their pictures, thus beginning the modern departure from the brush-and-paint idea of image-making. They were mainly interested in the textures they could get by working areas of real print into their compositions. The letters and words or wallpaper designs weren't as important as their shapes and textures. This type of picture-making was called *collage*, from the French expression, *papier collé*, glued paper. It started the movement away from brush and paint—a movement that is today almost a stampede.

They're all great deals until you bring the car back.

Ad for car rental. (Courtesy Kinney Rent A Car.)

What are the reasons for deserting painting as we normally think of it? First, technology provides wonderful adhesives, as mentioned above. Second, technology also provides a tremendous variety of new materials with fascinating colors and textures; it may be that artists don't believe they can create surfaces of equal brilliance, complexity and interest by using paint. Third, artists no longer feel they have to imitate the look of reality. Giving up realistic representation has opened up an enormous range of color, texture and shape for the artist. Brush and paint were ideal for representing objects and for imitating nature under varying light and atmospheric conditions. But photography has largely replaced these functions of painting. As a result, painting concentrates on the organization of real materials on real surfaces, and paint is only *one* of those real materials.

In this advertisement employing collage technique to get its message across, there is no striving for subtle aesthetic effect—just shrewd exploitation of the attention-getting power in little pieces of torn newsprint, pieces announcing the same theme.

Collage is, in many ways, the most characteristic type of image-making used by painters today. It is a way of creating new imagery by assembling pieces of material that already carry words, textures, colors, shapes, and pictorial fragments. Perhaps painters have been driven to the collage method because of the superabundance of printed and manufactured visual material that all of us receive, examine at a glance, and throw away. Why make images by hand if they can be so easily borrowed from the printed media? Each fragment sounds its own note and tells its own story. The artist sees his role, increasingly, as that of the conductor of an orchestra: He organizes the separate little sounds made by the musicians into a large new sound that reflects his own judgment and intention.

For schools, collage technique is also a tremendous new asset. It permits children and adolescents to create images at a fairly sophisticated level without having to fashion the constituent pictorial imagery by themselves. No need for cameras, computers, or photocopying machines (although they are useful). The finest printers, engravers, painters, photographers, letterers, and designers are instantly at their disposal through the mediation of the printing press, the United States mail, and the corner drugstore. ■

Assemblage was the logical follow-up of collage. Instead of just glueing pieces of paper to a surface, painters began to assemble and attach almost anything they could glue, nail, weld, solder, or bolt to a surface. Their materials became heavier and bulkier. Many materials were interesting because of their own identity, not just for the textures, as in Picasso's early collages. And as the surface of a picture was built up, it became more three-dimensional. The difference between painting and relief sculpture began to disappear. Today assemblage—making images by putting together real objects–is practiced by painters *and* sculptors.

All of these developments took place after painting surrendered some of its functions to photography: keeping records, making accurate descriptions, imitating nature, and illustrating literature. The camera, which is a light-recording machine, can do some things better than a man. But at first, photographers tried to make pictures that looked like paintings. Years later, photographers began to realize that they could create a new and separate art of the camera instead of trying to imitate forms made of paint. Similarly, as if photography did not exist, many painters continued to create exact, detailed images; this shows that people often do not understand how an invention will affect their lives or work. But as the consequences of photography began to be felt during this century, painting rediscovered itself as an art of expression in line, shape, color, texture, and light-and-dark. These elements can be created with bits of cloth, paper, metal, plastic, and glass as well as pigment. When paint *is* used now, it no longer pretends to be skin or sky or water; it is just paint.

Today, when we look at images—no matter what they are made of—we do not usually expect them to imitate something we have seen. They may suggest something we have done or felt or seen, but they do not especially look like what they suggest. The images of the painter have become like the sounds of the composer: They do not sound like an automobile engine or water running through a pipe but they are capable of reminding you of these sounds and of arousing the feelings you have in connection with them. And now that the viewer's eye has been trained not to expect visual imitation, it is possible that artists will return to making images—realistic and abstract—with paint. It is still a flexible and versatile medium.

Painting: Practices 1

SOME THINGS TO SEE

Look at *Monsieur Boileau at the Café* by Henri de Toulouse-Lautrec, *Broadway* by Mark Tobey, *Nighthawks* by Edward Hopper, and *Woman, I* by Willem de Kooning (on pp. 306–307).

SOME PROBLEMS

Two of these paintings emphasize line and two of them emphasize mass; they create shapes either by outline or by applying areas of color. Can you tell which is which? Which paintings are closest to drawings? In your opinion, what kind of artist prefers to use masses of color instead of

MONSIEUR BOILEAU AT THE CAFÉ
(above left), by Henri de Toulouse-
Lautrec. (Cleveland Museum of Art,
Hinman B. Hurlbut Collection.)

BROADWAY (above right), by Mark
Tobey. (The Metropolitan Museum of
Art, Arthur H. Hearn Fund, 1942.)

NIGHTHAWKS (at right), by Edward
Hopper. (Courtesy of The Art Institute
of Chicago.)

WOMAN I, by William de Kooning. (Collection The Museum of Modern Art, Purchase.)

Hopper's method or style of painting helps him to express the lightness or heaviness of things? Does it express noise or silence? How? Does Toulouse-Lautrec aim at a beautiful picture or does he try to report what he sees? How does de Kooning's brushwork express his attitude toward his subject? What decision do you think each of these artists made *before* he started to paint, and what decisions did he make *after* he began to work?

WHAT YOU CAN DO

Set up a still-life in front of the room and try to represent it in line using string or thread glued to a colored sheet of paper or cardboard. Then represent the same still-life by using only torn pieces of colored construction paper glued to a sheet of paper or cardboard. After the members of your class have completed both kinds of picture, make another picture, this time using tempera paint. Then make up a questionnaire for each student to fill out. It might have questions like the following:

Which technique is easiest for you?
Which technique is best for telling the truth about what you see?
Which technique is best for expressing your own attitudes?
How does the linear technique make you look and think?
How does the "mass" approach make you look and think?
Are some subjects better suited to line or mass? What are they?
Could you invent a new "mass" approach? What is it?
Could you invent a new "line" approach? What is it?

filling in outlines? What sort of person would he be? What kind of person would rather draw his shapes first and color them afterward?

SOME POSSIBILITIES

Try to figure out what advantages Mark Tobey found in using a type of scribbled line to make his picture. Do you think that

As an experiment, take a panel of a comic strip like "Barney Google" or "Peanuts" and try to translate it into enlarged areas of colored construction paper. Do not use lines in any way, just large shapes cut or torn by hand. When you are done, try to decide whether the panel was hurt or improved. Maybe both. How was the meaning or idea of the strip affected? Were there any artistic gains? Defend your point of view.

Cover design for *Fortune* Magazine (1952), by Alvin Lustig. (Courtesy Time, Inc.; photography by Sandak, Inc., N.Y.)

Painting: Practices 2

SOME THINGS TO SEE
Look at *Fortune Magazine* cover by Alvin Lustig, *Sacco B.* by Alberto Burri, *Old Models* by William Harnett, *My Cart, My Garden* by *Jean Dubuffet*, and *For Kate* by Kurt Schwitters.

SOME PROBLEMS
Old Models is an oil painting that looks like an assemblage—a collection of objects attached to a surface. The other pictures are combinations of paint, cut paper, burlap, printed letters, postage stamps, ruled lines, and so on, glued to a surface. But paint is

SACCO B., by Alberto Burri. (Courtesy Mrs. Alberto Burri.)

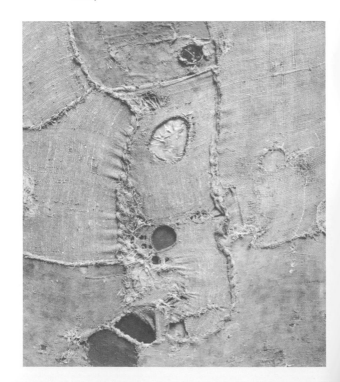

OLD MODELS (above left), by William Harnett. (Courtesy Museum of Fine Arts, Boston, Charles Henry Hayden Fund.)

MY CART, MY GARDEN (above right), by Jean Dubuffet. (Collection Mr. and Mrs. James Thrall Soby, New Canaan, Connecticut.)

FOR KATE (at left), by Kurt Schwitters. (Courtesy Kate T. Steinitz.)

a type of glue, too. These works of art show that a picture can be made of almost anything. What happens when people look at real materials instead of painted or photographed imitations of real things? Does it please you to know that the objects in *Old Models* are painted, not real? Can an artist say more with paint than with collage? Can he say less? What would your reaction be if you touched each of these pictures? Do you think pictures are meant to be touched or only seen?

SOME POSSIBILITIES

Why does so much of Dubuffet's painting (about two thirds) show the ground? Do children spend much time looking at the ground? What do they hope to find there? Is it really a garden? Do some people save what others throw away? Why doesn't Schwitters paint his own picture instead of pasting up drawings or paintings by others? Is it possible that he would rather make art out of reproduced images than by starting "from scratch"? Why? Do we always know when we are looking at a reproduction of a picture instead of the picture itself? Why do the shapes in Lustig's *Fortune* cover fight with the words? Do the words make visual noise? How? Do they make a texture too?

WHAT YOU CAN DO

Write a poem or a short story of one or two paragraphs. Then type your poem or print it in ink or paste it up, using letters and words cut out of magazines and newspapers. Finally, with Lustig's cover as a model, design some shapes that express the main idea of your poem or story. Fill in the shapes with words you printed or pasted up.

Go on an expedition hunting for old gum and cigarette wrappers, flat pieces of metal, things that have been run over by autos, discarded match covers, tin can labels, and so on. Collect them as you find them and don't change their shapes. Then try to compose a picture with these "found materials." Think of them as shaped areas of color and texture; try to "paint" with them. Try to work what they are into the meaning of your painting.

Stretch a sheet of coarse burlap over a wooden frame and place it on the floor. Then stand on a chair and drop some thinned out paint on the burlap; let it splash any way it wants to. When the paint is dry, study your burlap canvas. You can stab the burlap or tear it, burn small holes in it, sew on patches of colored fabric, or glue on some things you have found; or do any combination of these. There is only one rule: The result has to make sense. That is, you have to explain to the class what your picture is supposed to mean.

Three-Dimensional Forms: Sculpture

During the past twenty-five years, painting and sculpture have come close together. But for most of human history they have been separate . . . because they are fundamentally different. Even after the invention of photography, painters continued to create illusions. But sculptors have always had to build the forms you see. During the Renais-

In the park...or in the schoolroom:

People are looking at art, or making it, almost all the time, almost everywhere.

Art-room still life (above). (Courtesy Oliver Coleman.)

Art in a park (right). (Floyd Jillson.)

HENRI CALET, COSTUME ROUGE
(left), by Jean Dubuffet. (Collection
Ossorio/Dragon.)

THE MADWOMAN [detail] (below
right), by Chaim Soutine. (Courtesy
The National Museum of Western Art,
Tokyo, presented by Mr. Tai Hayashi,
1960.)

Through visual art we can see a wide range of
human feelings and conditions. We discover
that the image and the medium of expression
cannot be separated.

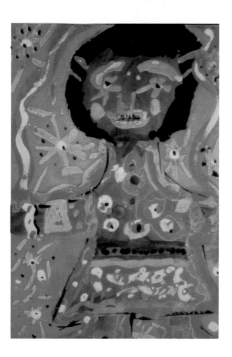

Three portraits of children by children (left). (University of Georgia Department of Art.)

Child looking out a window (below). (Courtesy Bergstrom Paper Company.)

Urban forms and textures:

This is the imagery that must, increasingly, find its reflection in the creative expression of children and adolescents.

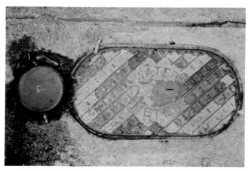

Urban ''sculpture.'' (Photos by Martin
Schnur and the author.)

Machine imagery.

For today's youth, the man on the motorcycle may be the equivalent of yesterday's equestrian statue. The two-wheeled monster symbolizes a wonderful masculine power and strenuous grace. The functional parts are exposed in a motorcycle. Perceptions of the mechanical action, the roaring exhaust, the acceleration jolt merge with the mythic image of the cowboy on his horse. But to ride such a machine is to own the power of dozens of horses—to be a modern hero.

When Orozco painted his "Mechanical Horse," he followed the ancient tradition of conquerors on horseback. The vision is that a feudal man on foot, simultaneously admiring and hating the armed and mounted horseman, seeing the power of the machine turned against himself. But our adolescents, the children of an industrial society, know they can own and ride these machines. Motorcycles are painted by our young as familiarly as Constable painted a haywagon. The machines belong to their environment. They are placed as unerringly among drugstores and Coca-Cola signs as Verrocchio's Colleoni monument stands in a square in Venice. This student work is authentic because it represents an authentic situation. First there must be a truthful perception of life, then art has a chance.

Student work on motorcycle theme (left and facing page left). (Courtesy Mrs. Mary Hammond.)

THE MECHANICAL HORSE [mural detail] (top right), by José Clemente Orozco. (Hospicio Cabañas, Guadalajara.)

HONDA A GO-GO (center right), by Claudia Cook. (The National Art Education Association.)

COLLEONI MONUMENT (bottom right), by Verrocchio. (Art Reference Bureau, Inc.)

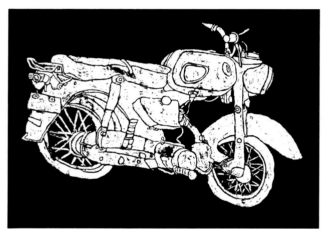

A bicycle changes the status and self-image of a boy; he becomes a mounted rider instead of a pedestrian. No longer a walker, he uses his legs to generate mechanical power. He is amazed when he discovers, personally, that a machine can multiply organic effort.

BICYCLE I (left), by Kendall Shaw. (Courtesy the artist.)

BICYCLES (below), by Robert Vickrey. (Collection Mr. and Mrs. F. Richards Ford; courtesy Midtown Galleries, New York.)

sance, painters developed perspective and modeling with light and dark to fool the eye, to create an imitation of space and volume that was not really there. The sculptor, however, had to work harder—at least physically—because his forms and volumes had to be real.

Originally, a sculpture was a model, an effigy of a man or an animal. It was a substitute for that man or beast. But it is hard to know whether early men realized that a sculpture-substitute wasn't really the creature it represented. They probably thought that if it looked even slightly like a real individual, then it was. We know that early sculpture was almost always painted to make it look more real, that people talked to statues, gave them gifts, and even worshipped the figures we call idols. This worship was part of the magic practiced by men who needed statues to remind them that their gods and ancestors were still with them.

As always, art became involved in the question of what is real and what seems to be real. Painting claims to be real because it can fool your eyes. Sculpture claims to be real because it occupies real space and can be touched and carried, like any real object. Even abstract sculpture has these qualities and makes you believe that it truly exists. What are the basic processes for creating sculptural reality?

Modeling

If you have ever played with mud or clay you know what modeling is. Fundamentally, it is the creation of forms by squeezing, slicing, stretching, and hollowing out a soft, pliable material like clay or wax. These materials join with themselves easily and quickly so that modeling also involves adding lumps and bumps to build up forms There is probably no material as responsive to the human hand as modeling clay or one of its plastic imitations. You can *think* in clay because it becomes the shape you want so quickly. That is the reason many sculptors do their advance planning in clay—before executing a final sculpture in marble, wood, or stone. Just as the painter uses drawing to plan his full-scale work, the sculptor uses clay modeling before he begins to face the problems he may have to solve in a harder, more permanent, and expensive material.

The disadvantage of clay is that it is not strong. It cannot be made permanent unless it is fired in a kiln, which makes it as hard as stone. But it would be impractical to build a kiln large enough to fire a life-size clay figure. A clay sculpture as large as a human figure would need a large metal or wooden armature to hold it up. An armature is a type of skeleton that the sculptor builds to hold the weight of the clay. Without the armature, extensions like arms and legs would break off. Even smaller clay sculptures need an armature to give structural strength to the soft modeling material. As a result, most works that are modeled in clay or wax are cast in bronze, which faithfully reproduce the soft, pliant clay in hard, shiny metal.

Very small modeled sculptures—about the size of your hand—were among the earliest art objects created by man. They could be sun-baked and painted, like primitive pottery, and carried by wandering tribesmen for good luck or as models for the larger paintings and figures they would make when settled in a cave for a few weeks. The softness of clay, its availability in most any river bank, and the simplicity of using it make it the warmest and friendliest of sculptural materials. And since fired clay is watertight, early sculptures were often combination vase-figures—little, hollow vessels in the form of a human or animal body. These pottery figures show that clay was thought of as a type of skin that can hold human and animal spirits as well as water and other liquids. If you think of it in this way, clay is a magical material. The sculptor or potter who uses it often gets the feeling that he is making spiritual containers. Proba-

bly that explains why so many people today make or collect pottery which they do not use to hold anything. They are satisfied just to see the empty vessel, to enjoy its surface decoration, and to think about its outer form and its inner space. Many primitive people thought that the human soul was a liquid substance. So you can see how the materials and processes used by sculptors affect our ideas of what life and reality are made of.

Carving

Although clay can be cut, sliced, and hollowed out, it is mainly used by building up or *adding on* material. Modeling, therefore, is an *additive* process. But carving is subtractive. Whether carving wood, stone, ivory,

---

Three modes of sculpture. The Indian work tells us that skill in carving was sufficiently specialized among the tribesmen of British Columbia to justify social and artistic recognition. Carving in stone makes strenuous visual and intellectual demands. It is more difficult than modeling with clay because the final form emerges indirectly. It may seem that the sculptor just cuts away the unnecessary material; to do that, however, he needs to see what is essential with his mind's eye.

Agostini's sculpture celebrates the plaster-casting process—its amazing capacity to transform ordinary objects into a marvelous,

hard, superwhite substance. Something mysterious happens when bottles and fruit change material without changing form. It is a mystery that was probably discovered by Neolithic artist-magicians, like the mythological Daedalus. Today, exact duplication is a common industrial event. But sculpture has long been separated from physical utility. Often, the sculptor's purpose is to eliminate any vestige of practical function. He prefers to focus our attention on the transformation of materials. As a result, we are encouraged to look at form alone—a type of perception that characterizes the late stages of a culture.

Lily Harmon's work grows out of construction and assemblage techniques, with a minimum of direct forming. Some of its parts may have been cast, stamped, turned, or extruded. Fundamentally, however, the sculptor builds with discarded industrial products —debris. The process is simple even though manufactured materials are used to express a satirical concept. As with collage, the creative method yields sophisticated results while drawing on relatively simple skills. For school art programs the advantages are plain: genuine aesthetic potential combined with a minimum of technical preparation. ■

SHELF STILL LIFE (above), by Peter Agostini. (Collection Joseph H. Hirshhorn; courtesy Stephen Radich Gallery.)

Haida Indian figure holding a mallet and chisel (far left). (Photo, courtesy Museum of the American Indian, Heye Foundation.)

THE GENERALS (near left), by Lily Harmon. (Courtesy the artist.)

or marble, the sculptor starts with the shape given by nature and then tries to cut away what is not essential. To do this, he must have an idea of what the final work will be. He cannot make drastic changes whenever he wants to, like the modeler. He must worry about the grain of the wood, stone, or marble he is carving, and he must be sure that he does not crack or break off parts of the sculpture by striking weak points with his mallet and chisel. Like a diamond cutter working on a valuable gem, or a dentist drilling someone's tooth, the sculptor who carves is engaged in a nerve-wracking process, especially as the final form is approached.

Overcoming the technical problems in carving gives this kind of sculpture some of its special qualities. First is permanence. Stone and marble will last almost forever if they are not mutilated. Wood may warp, crack, or burn, but with reasonable care and control of temperature and humidity it is extremely durable. A second asset of carving is the direct control it allows the sculptor. The final surface can be exactly what he wants it to be since no workmen and no technical process stand between him and the completed work. Finally, there is the beauty of the carved material. Few people would claim that clay is attractive; it is just a type of mud. But carved and polished marble, stone, ivory, jade, or wood present beautiful surfaces to the eye—surfaces with individual variations in color or texture that add to the interest of the sculptural forms.

When we look at carved sculpture, the skill and magic of the sculptor is never far from our thoughts. We know that a man with only sharp cutting tools to help him has made a formless, inert substance come to life. We know the stone or marble is hard and resistant to the artist's wishes, unlike clay which responds so easily. And we know that the sculptor's vision has somehow penetrated his material so that he could see the "hidden" forms within. At the same time that he is cutting material way, he must be thinking about what he wants to leave. That is what seems to be magic—the ability to see what an almost shapeless substance can become. It is something like the magic of the medieval alchemists who tried to turn worthless materials into gold. At heart, sculpture is an act of turning dreams or visions into reality. And when that reality is as hard, solid, and permanent as marble, sculpture generates a very quiet, powerful, almost reverent excitement.

Casting

Metalworking is one of the earliest arts of civilized man, beginning about ten or twelve thousand years ago. Extracting ore from rock, smelting and combining it with other ores, shaping it by casting and forging processes—these inventions caused an enormous advance for men who had been using tools of stone, wood, and bone. Not only were metal weapons sharp and strong, they were also capable of taking complex shapes: They did not break easily; they were often more lethal; and they had their own special beauty. Remember how King Arthur loved his sword, Excalibur. And think of the ancient legends about swords with magical powers. This may give you an idea of how wonderful cast and forged metal weapons seemed to the earliest men who used them.

The art of casting enables easily broken wax or clay sculpture to be made permanent. And once a mold is cast, the same modeled forms can be duplicated over and over again, as with metal coins, for example. Casting also permits the sculptor to create long extensions that will not break the way wood, stone, or fired clay might. A casting is so strong that it can have many openings or perforations without becoming much weaker. These openings reduce the weight of the sculpture and create opportunities for decoration shaped around the perforations. Perhaps that is why casting was such a high art among nomadic peoples: All their weapons and tools and household implements had to be light to be carried along on their continuous treks. In the form of a bronze casting, a clay model can be changed into an almost indestructible figure with thin but strong walls, a smooth surface, and a warm gold or dark green skin color—depending on how it is burnished, aged, or treated with chemicals.

Modern industry has carried casting to a very high art. Not only do we cast the older metals, like iron and bronze, gold and silver, but also steel, aluminum, titanium and, of course, plastics. Think of the tiny metal and plastic parts in a transistor radio. Most of them have been formed by a casting or stamping process. The plates and false teeth a dentist makes are also produced by a casting process. In fact, a number of the operations a dentist performs—drilling, cutting, scraping, carving, filing, and casting—are the same as those done by a sculptor. It is not surprising, therefore, that some dentists have become sculptors.

Casting brings a complex technology to the art of the sculptor. Like printmaking, it places a series of processes between what the artist originally forms and what the viewer finally sees. Very few sculptors do their own casting, they rely on professionals working in a foundry. The work is heavy and hot; it requires close teamwork and careful timing. The well-trained modern sculptor can usually cast his own plaster molds and from these he can make plaster of Paris casts. But metal castings are usually made by professional founders. Jewelers often do their own casting, but the small scale of their work does not create the problems of handling large amounts of molten metal and carrying off potentially explosive gases during the cooling process.

Industry creates and discards so many varied metallic objects and materials that today's sculptor is more and more attracted to them as sources for the shapes and textures of his work. In this way he can use forms created by extremely complex and expensive manufacturing processes. To be sure, they are not forms he himself has invented, but by rearranging and reassembling them he makes them his own. In addition, his sculpture gets a contemporary look automatically because we can see and often recognize the everyday origin of some of the forms. By making automobile-bumper sculpture, for example, a sculptor uses the great factories of Detroit for his foundry. Like the painter who discarded his brush, the contemporary sculptor depends on the industrial environment for his materials.

Sculpture in Motion

Assemblage, you remember, is practiced by painters *and* sculptors. So the contemporary sculptor can employ this technique along with his traditional skills of modeling, carving, and casting. But he must know how to use many modern constructional and fastening techniques—welding, brazing, soldering, and riveting—in order to combine and assemble the extraordinary variety of objects and materials that have been added to the traditional wood, stone, and bronze. On the other hand, some sculptors confine their work to a few design decisions. They have been known to draw specifications for a sculpture and then turn them over to a metal or plastic fabricating shop for final execution. This may seem similar to giving a clay model to a foundry for casting or using a marble cutting machine which can carve a large marble sculpture from a small, plaster figurine. But the cast or carved sculp-

ture of the past closely followed its physical model. Today's artist is often trying to find out how far he can get away from the actual process of making. Some painters have learned to program or instruct a computer that then executes their pictures. The computer becomes an extension of the artist's hand and eye, like a pencil, a brush, a power loom, or a printing press. Our technology is so capable and versatile that artists are tempted to give it more and more of the work they used to do by hand.

Because machines play such a large role in our lives, art inevitably reflects their influence. Some sculptures look like machinery although they may not work like machines. And recently, sculptors have introduced motion into their work, calling the result "kinetic sculpture." It may be battery-powered, driven by electric motors, or moved by random air currents. Stationary sculpture is not obsolete, but moving sculpture opens up a vast new element for artistic expression. Of course, dancers use motion to express ideas and they have the almost infinite variety of the human body as their vehicle of expression. The sculptor, however, would be foolish to build mechanized imitations of

From real life to art. Three stages in the evolution of reality; beginning with an accident—an unplanned crash; moving to a neat package of planned industrial destruction; and culminating in artistic form—a sculptured assemblage that sums up the automotive life cycle. The meanings we get from Chamberlain's "Essex" depend, partly, on knowing about or seeing auto wreckage. But torn, twisted, and crushed metal forms also speak directly, because they em- body processes we have already encountered in other materials, other contexts. Old metal, discarded machinery, useless parts— what do they tell us about the quality of life in the last half of the twentieth century? ■

very now and then a VW runs into a little trouble at the factory.

Volkswagen ad (above left). (Volkswagen of America, Inc.)

ESSEX (above right), by John Chamberlain. (Collection The Museum of Modern Art. Gift of Mr. and Mrs. Robert Scull and Purchase.)

Racing driver being freed from car crash (at left). (Wide World Photos.)

the human figure—like the robots you can see in amusement parks or holiday store-window displays. The artistic objective is to show how motion, combined with sculptural form, is capable of conveying meaning and emotion.

We can think of animated cartoons and motion pictures as two-dimensional images plus motion. In other words, one branch of painting developed into photography, added motion, and became cinema. Similarly, a branch of sculpture has developed strong mechanical traits, added motion, and has emerged as kinetic sculpture. With different kinds of power, and the use of electronic programing devices, kinetic sculpture may become as richly expressive as movies. Who would have predicted the modern art form we know as motion pictures on the basis of the early photographs taken by the Frenchman Daguerre?

We know from the way actors and dancers use their bodies that motion has enormous aesthetic potential. Think of the movement of natural objects as well as man-made things. Then imagine sculpture that imitates and elaborates their movement without imitating their appearance. The possibilities for creating great sculptural spectacles combining motion, lighting, and sound are tremendously exciting. As sculpture begins to resemble the theater and as the dance borrows from painting, we can see a new coming-together of the arts—a unity of sight, sound, form, and movement that was visible only in the magnificent cathedrals of the Middle Ages.

Sculpture: Practices 1

SOME THINGS TO SEE

Look at *Ceremonial Mask* by Samuel Laroye, *Head of Joseph Conrad* by Jacob Epstein, *Veiled Beggar Woman* by Ernst Barlach, *Human Concretion* by Jean Arp, and the *Head of Eustache de St. Pierre* by Auguste Rodin.

SOME PROBLEMS

Can you tell which of these sculptures was modeled and which was carved? Can you tell what material each work is made of? How is the surface of a sculpture affected by carving? How is its total form affected by carving? As you look at the *Head of Joseph Conrad*, what tells you it was created by an "additive" method? On the basis of the Rodin sculpture, would you say that modeling increases or decreases the sense of movement? How do you think Arp was able to make his sculpture so smooth? Can you explain the meaning or purpose of the *Ceremonial Mask* created by Samuel Laroye?

SOME POSSIBILITIES

If you were a sculptor and you wanted to "freeze" the action of a figure, would you model or carve? If a sculptor had to represent a tree, what medium would be best? If a sculptor were carving a hand, would it be better to show the fingers outstretched, or would it be better to use the form of a fist? Notice that the veil on Barlach's *Beggar Woman* looks more solid than a veil should be: How does this solidness affect the mean-

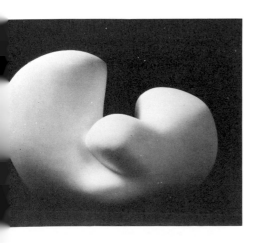

Ceremonial mask (above left), by Samuel Laroye. (Marc and Evelyne Bernheim from Rapho Guillumette.)

HEAD OF JOSEPH CONRAD (above center), by Jacob Epstein. (Courtesy Joseph H. Hirshhorn Foundation.)

VEILED BEGGAR WOMAN (above right), by Ernst Barlach. (Private collection, New York; courtesy, Galerie St. Etienne, N.Y.)

HUMAN CONCRETION (far left), by Jean Arp. (Collection The Museum of Modern Art. Gift of the Advisory Committee (by exchange).)

Head of Eustache de St. Pierre (near left), detail of THE BURGHERS OF CALAIS, by Auguste Rodin. (Permission S.P.A.D.E.M. 1969 by French Reproduction Rights, Inc.; photo, Musée Rodin.)

ing of the sculpture? Even though the Arp sculpture represents something fantastic, why does it seem to be real? Does the sculptor's technique make you believe it is alive? How? Suppose the Arp sculpture were flesh-colored instead of white; would it be more or less believable?

WHAT YOU CAN DO

Answer these "crazy" questions: What would happen if a clothespin were made of clay? If a candle were made of wood? What happens when clay is carved? Can you carve a turkey? Can you carve mashed potatoes? How does soup get its shape? Can you cast ice? Do people squeeze wood? Why shouldn't stones be nailed together? Why are cookies so thin? Would mud be better than sand on the seashore? Did you ever model with peanut butter? Did you ever paint with jam?

Make a hamburger with modeling clay. Then make a hot dog on a roll. Cut the hamburger and the hot dog in half with a knife. Put them on real plastic plates with real mustard. Then set a table with knives, forks, paper napkins, and so on. Is this ridiculous? Why or why not?

Pretend that you are a sculptor eating an apple. You are going to carve an apple core. Explain how this is done without ruining the "sculpture." Then model an apple core in clay. Do the same thing by eating a slice of watermelon—"inside" sculpture. Now write a story about the difference between carving and modeling.

Sculpture: Practices 2

SOME THINGS TO SEE

Look at *The Stove* by Claes Oldenburg, *Nantucket* by Gabriel Kohn, *Sculpture Picture* by César, *Royal Tide I* by Louise Nevelson, and *Chow* by Edward Renouf.

SOME PROBLEMS

Can all of these objects really be sculpture? None of them were made by modeling,

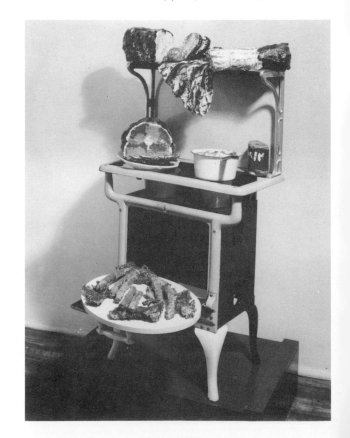

THE STOVE, by Claes Oldenburg. (Collection Mr. and Mrs. Robert Scull; photo, Eric Pollitzer.)

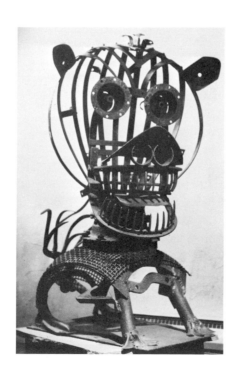

NANTUCKET (above left), by Gabriel Kohn. (Photo, Rudolph Burckhardt.)

SCULPTURE PICTURE (above right), by César (Baldaccini). (Collection The Museum of Modern Art. Gift of G. David Thompson.)

ROYAL TIDE I (far left), by Louise Nevelson. (Photo, Rudolph Burckhardt.)

CHOW (near left), by Edward Renouf. (Courtesy the artist.)

carving, or casting. Instead, they were nailed or welded or glued together. *The Stove* is a real, old-fashioned stove, with painted plaster food on it.

Do you think we need a new definition of sculpture? Why not make up a definition that would fit all of these objects plus other sculpture you have seen? Can you think of everyday objects that look like these sculptures? Nantucket is an old whaling port in New England; why did Gabriel Kohn give that name to his sculpture? Were the old whaling boats made of wood or metal? What about their anchors? Are you supposed to know what the objects are in Mrs. Nevelson's boxes? Do you think the metal parts of Renouf's *Chow* were made for the sculpture of a dog? Why didn't Renouf make the dog's head solid? Would you rather not look at Oldenburg's sculpture?

SOME POSSIBILITIES

Think of the advantages a sculptor gets when he doesn't have to copy what he sees. Do words look or sound like what they describe? No. They just give you ideas or *mental* images about objects, places, and happenings. Well, sculptural forms can give you ideas and mental images too. In looking at these sculptures, try to put together strings of words that have almost the same meaning, *when they are put together* like each of the objects. Some of the words come from imagining what the sculpture would feel like if you could touch it. Other words come from thinking about your inner feelings while you are looking. There are times when sculpture has the power to make

you want to do something. Could you act out or write out your reactions to that *Chow* dog, for example?

SOME THINGS TO DO

Bring to class one of the following objects: an old mailbox on its post, an old door, last year's automobile license plates, a discarded metal garbage can, some broken children's toys, an empty olive oil can, an old highchair, a broken doll. Now try to make a visual poem with the object you have. Add things to it. Paint or write on it. Nail it to something, or nail something to it. Glue on little quotations, or photographs. When you present your "sculpture-poem" to the class, try to frame or isolate it: You might use artificial light, a drapery background, or play a record while people are looking at it. You could also read something you or someone else has written. Try to create a definite mood or atmosphere with your work.

See if you can make another "poem" by driving different-sized nails into a block of wood. Use old and new nails; use some screws; try painting the wood. Paste a picture on the wood block before you drive the nails. Add little rags, flags, or pennants to the nails. Now make another poem-construction by nailing objects to a block of wood: clothespins, spools of thread, sticks, odd-shaped pieces of metal, pieces of cardboard boxes, crumpled match book covers, empty cigarette packs. But make sure your construction is unified by a single, dominant idea; give a hint of your idea in the title.

Sheltering Structures: Architecture

Men painted pictures and made sculpture while they were still living in caves—before they built their own shelter. Perhaps they had the ability to build simple huts but were prevented from doing so by the need to keep moving in search of food. At any rate, man-made shelter probably appeared seven to ten thousand years *after* the earliest-known examples of painting and sculpture. Therefore, men were already on the way to civilization when they took their first steps toward architecture. The ability to imagine space they could live in and the skill to assemble materials to shape that space was a major achievement of New Stone Age men. Many architectural principles still observed by builders were invented by these early tribesmen—people we would probably call natives.

Today buildings of all sorts are designed by specialists called architects or engineers and constructed by all kinds of skilled workmen under the supervision of a builder or contractor. And because civilization creates many complex needs, our buildings are varied and complex too. Primitive life required only a few basic houses: houses for families to live in, houses for the men to meet in, houses for storing food, and houses for the dead—a combination of what we would call tombs and houses of worship. For these different purposes the same building vocabulary was often used. But we have so many different building materials and ways of construction that our architectural designers can choose the combination that seems best for the function or purpose of any particular building. The enormous number of combinations results in the architectural variety you can see on the main street of any American city or town. And that variety creates a rich and sometimes bewildering spectacle.

We use buildings by living and working in them. But we also look at them. When looking at a building we try to enjoy or understand it, and that requires knowledge of its materials and structure. It is like looking at an automobile or a sailboat or an airplane: You can begin to understand what you see if you know something about how an internal combustion engine works, or how a boat's hull moves through the water, or the aerodynamic principles that shape a plane and make it fly. Somehow the form of an airplane wing makes more sense when you understand how it is designed to solve the problem of lift. Building, too, results from the solution of technical problems—problems of space, materials, and structure. You and I can enjoy the solutions by trying to figure out what the problems were.

In addition to the technical problems, there are social problems in architecture too. The spaces of a building and their arrangement determine how groups of people will use them and work with each other. Also, we get a *feeling* from a building: It seems to stand for an idea or an institution, like a school or a church; it becomes a symbol as well as a container for people and equipment. For example, large apartment house developments not only create shelter for thousands of people, but they also establish patterns of living for those thousands. Furthermore, houses and apartments cost money to build and maintain—costs that must ultimately be paid by the people who live in them. Therefore, the expensiveness of housing greatly influences who can live where and what kinds of equipment and special features a home will have. Money spent on rent or mortgage and taxes is money that will not be spent on other things. In many ways, then, architecture influences family behavior—through space for eating, sleeping, preparing food, entertaining friends, and in the costs the family must pay for these facilities. You can see that an architect works with more than bricks and mortar. The way he does his job shapes the way we live our lives.*

The Traditional Materials of Architecture

Buildings have to be made of materials, but materials are not equally distributed in all the places where people live. Therefore, geography influences how men build: It determines whether wood, stone, marble, or brick will be available for architectural purposes; and geography is responsible for the climate, which affects the way men think about shelter. In the ancient world, trans-

*"Architecture is not merely an art, more or less badly done; it is a social manifestation. . . . Our buildings are an image of our people. . . . Therefore . . . the critical study of architecture becomes . . . a study of the social conditions producing it." Louis Sullivan, *Kindergarten Chats*, Scarab Fraternity Press, 1934.

porting building materials over a long distance was usually impractical and so people used what was near at hand. Their methods of building were mainly based on the local materials that nature had provided in abundance. And, of course, before modern technology created steel, concrete, plate glass, plywood, plastics, and metal alloys, building materials were used in a form very close to the way they are found in nature. At a very fundamental level, therefore, architecture could be defined as the conversion of available raw materials into specialized spaces for living.

STONE

Stones were the earliest material of architecture, probably because men were used to stone shelter in caves. A simple type of hut was built by digging a shallow, circular hole in the ground and then piling flat rocks on top of each other around the edge to make a wall. The roof was cone-shaped and was made of tree boughs filled in with grass. A hole in the roof let out the smoke from a cooking fire. Although early men had no mortar, they probably stuffed mud and grass between the rocks to hold them firm and to keep out the wind. Since they kept some livestock, they must have hung up hides to dry on the outside of the hut and then discovered that, like clothing, the hides helped keep the hut comfortable. From this experience with hides they may have learned to build a tent of wooden poles and animal skins—something like the American Indian teepee. This structure was especially practical for hunting people who moved a lot and needed light, portable shelter. In some ways, the modern house-trailer solves the same problem for people who want to carry their housing with them.

Although stone is used as a building material today, it is usually found in combination with other materials. Stone is strong and durable but it tends to transmit moisture and therefore it keeps a house damp. Also, stone walls—or masonry walls—have to be joined together with mortar by skilled masons, and their work is slow and expensive. Dry masonry—stone walls built without mortar—is still used for fences and for outdoor garden decoration, but, of course, it will not keep out the weather. Nevertheless, we like the solid, durable feeling we get from rock surfaces and so we often use stone masonry as a veneer—as an outer skin that covers an inner structure of wooden timbers or concrete blocks. Fireplaces are often built of stone (around a core of brick and steel) because stone seems to make people feel warm and safe. Perhaps they still have dim, unconscious memories of sitting around the fire in a cave or in a low-walled, stone hut. That might explain why our houses are so often a blend of practical and sentimental building techniques.

WOOD

Wood, another ancient building material, was used by early forest dwellers or by people near a river they could use to transport logs. Inhabitants of arid and desert regions—like the American Southwest, or North Africa, or the Middle East—being denied wood and stone, developed brick masonry. Mud suggests bricks just as wood suggests posts and beams. Just looking at a tree tells you something about slender strength combined with grace. And perhaps the idea of using columns to support great overhead weights came from seeing clusters of tree trunks in the forest.

The major disadvantage of wood is that it burns. Remarkable ancient buildings—palaces in China, churches in Russia and Scandinavia—are lost because they were built of wood and burned. The earliest Greek structures were built of wood, but the Greeks converted to marble (Greece still has magnificent marble) because wood burns, and as they grew rich and powerful, the Greeks could afford to build with expensive and durable marble. Still, many details of their building technique were based on construction with wood. Hundreds of years later, when steel became available, European engineers used it the way they were accustomed to use wooden timbers in bridge and building construction. Wood is so light and strong for its weight that it is ideal for roofing over great spans. But again, the wooden roofs of Romanesque churches burned too easily and Gothic stone masonry vaulting was developed to solve the problem.

Most of our single-dwelling houses have wooden skeletons called balloon frames. The balloon frame method gives great strength and flexibility of space arrangement. But you will notice, if you watch carpenters put up a house, that our stud walls and roof rafters are covered with fire-resistant sheathing and noncombustible insulation

materials. Interior walls of plasterboard and exterior walls of brick, aluminum, or asbestos siding combine to create a complex "wall-sandwich" that is almost fireproof. Even so, modern houses burn. But we use wood because it is cheap and abundant and fast to cut and assemble.

Whether it is used in sculpture or architecture, wood is appealing because of its beautiful color and grain. Interior walls are

Airport hangar at Orly, France, by Eugène Freyssinet. (Photo, copyright of Dr. Franz Stoedtner.)

Framework of Huron longhouse. (Ontario Department of Tourism and Information.)

The beauty of a building is often visible in its bare bones—before its skin or fabric has been completed. There is a special sort of pleasure in seeing a rhythmic system of arches, posts, and braces built of timbers that still resemble the trees they came from. We seem to have the best of natural and man-made forms. This tribal, communal shelter could be compared with the famous airport hangar at Orly, France, designed by Eugene Freyssinet. The Indian builder created a remarkably open interior space and a beautifully functional exterior form by exploiting the elasticity of tree timbers—much as today's designers use steel and prestressed concrete or laminated wood arches. They seem to have needed interior posts and braces to give rigidity to the arch system; otherwise, the longhouse would represent thoroughly modern architectural thinking. How would it look with a skin of translucent plastic? Almost ready for the next World's Fair. ■

often surfaced with wooden boards or plywood panels to create warm, natural decorative effects. The development of plywood panels has greatly increased the use of wood, as both a structural and a surface material. Plywood overcomes the tendency of wood to warp; it is consistent in dimension and strength and extremely strong for its weight. The process of manufacture permits inexpensive and flawed sheets of wood to be used for inner layers while a thin outer veneer can be a fine, beautifully grained specimen. The advantages for furniture-making and architectural interiors are plain. Plywood is an example of what happens when an ancient raw material is transformed by the creativity of modern technology: The advantages of the new product are gained without sacrificing the special qualities of the old.

BRICK

Bricks are a type of man-made stone. As mentioned above, they were used mainly by people who had little or no wood or stone for building. Probably, bricks originated in ancient Mesopotamia, where they were made from sun-dried blocks of mud or clay. Modern adobe, as used in Mexico and the American Southwest, is not much different. It would be impractical in a region of heavy rainfall. But brick walls do not burn, they are wonderful insulators against the hot sun, and they can support very heavy weights. As with stone masonry, brick masonry requires a great deal of slow, hand labor. Of course, in the ancient world, with its slave labor, this factor was not crucial.

Being small, bricks would not bridge over wide spaces, a disadvantage that led to the development of the arch (to be discussed below). To prevent erosion from rain and cracking from cold, clay bricks had to be kiln-fired, a process that makes them as strong as stone and, of course, more uniform in shape and dimension than stone. But while the manufacture of good, strong brick is not costly today, building with brick is expensive because of all the hand labor it requires. That is why walls of solid brick are very rare in modern building. Instead, brick is used decoratively, as a veneer, the way fine wood panels are used. Also, brick, like stone, is heavy and expensive to ship: Therefore, you find brick masonry used only where there is a good local supply of clay and plenty of skilled masons.

The permanence and stability of brick- and stone-masonry construction depend mainly on their weight—the effect of gravity —and the strength of their mortar joints. But architecture, especially in modern times, is an effort to defy gravity—to develop materials and designs that can enclose or bridge over space without being bound to the earth. And the modern cost of labor makes the intricate and painstaking masonry of the Gothic builders too slow and expensive. Of the old materials, only wood has the strength combined with lightness to serve modern structural needs. Increasingly, therefore, we move to metals and plastics to serve as the bones and skin of our buildings. Stone, brick, tile, and marble are rarely used to support anything. They are surface materials now. We "paint" with them.

A World of Glass, Steel, and Concrete

Early builders were limited to the use of local natural materials and brick, the only man-made material. But modern building materials are almost always manufactured, and they can be transported more easily than in the past. As you look around at the new buildings near you, what do you see most? Glass, steel, aluminum, concrete, and wood. These materials are made by most of the world's great nations, and those who cannot manufacture steel or aluminum can buy it from those who do. As a result, there are very few differences among modern buildings wherever you travel. Architecture is one of the most powerful forces for making this planet look like one world.

GLASS

In the form of bottles and jars, glass was used thousands of years ago in Egypt, but large, thick sheets of plate glass are very recent. Glass today is so strong that it can be used in areas large enough to fill an entire wall. And by using double panes of glass with a partial vacuum in between, heat and cold are prevented from passing through. Thus, you can have more than a large window in your room; you can have doors of glass; glass partitions can separate spaces without turning them into small, dark cubicles. This flexibility permits you to have protection from bad weather and still see as much of the outdoors as if you were actually there. In other words, plate glass can let nature into the house or it

can make the house seem to belong to the space around it.

Of course glass is not a structural material, except in the form of glass bricks. Plate glass areas still need wood or metal framing to do the work of supporting weight and holding the building parts together. But instead of thick stone or brick walls to hold up weight, we use thin, strong posts made of wood, metal, or reinforced concrete. Then the areas between the posts can be filled-in with "curtains" of glass. As much as ninety per cent of the surface of a large building might be glass. From the outside, the spectator sees continuously changing patterns of light, shadow, and color in the reflecting surfaces of our huge, glass-walled sky-scrapers. This effect gives a building the feeling of lightness and delicacy you might see in a many-faceted crystal or a tall sculpture made of thousands of mirrors. From the inside there is a wonderful flood of light. People feel open and free instead of confined or trapped; yet with soft, textured drapes to frame their window-walls and tinted glass or blinds to control the sun's rays, they can still feel protected against the outside world.

STEEL

In the past, walls had to be thick and windows had to be small in order to make strong buildings. That was because their strength depended on the weight of one stone or brick piled on top of another. Large window openings would weaken a masonry wall. Wood, although light, was not as safe as stone: It might burn or warp or split.

Stone and brick arches and columns limited the height of a building because their weight becomes tremendous as a structure goes higher. Only metal could support a tall building. Its walls would not have to be ten or fifteen feet thick. At first, that metal was cast iron. Brick or stone masonry was combined with a cast iron framework that was sturdy and rigid. Large windows were then possible; again that was especially useful for factories, offices, and large stores. But cast iron is also very heavy (although not as heavy as stone) and it can crack under stress. Buildings made of cast iron sections bolted together could rarely be taller than twelve storeys. And much higher buildings became necessary as our cities grew in the nineteenth and twentieth centuries and the cost of downtown land became enormous. Maximum strength and lightness (and therefore great height) could only be achieved with steel. Today's steel-framed skyscraper has very thin walls and very large windows without sacrifice of strength. Unlike cast iron, steel is flexible. When there are strong winds, a building can bend slightly without cracking its metal framework. Tremendous heights become structurally and financially practical.

Prefabricated framework for large buildings, which began with cast iron, reduced the number of operations performed and the amount of space needed at the building site. Today, steel girders for a building are manufactured to the correct size and shape at the steel mill and then shipped to the building site where they are assembled by bolting, riveting, or welding. In this way, the supporting structure of a very large and complex building can be put together in a short time. While construction workers are building the upper storeys of a skyscraper, plumbers, electricians, carpenters, sheet metal workers and many others can be working on the lower storeys. High-speed elevators make it possible for workers and building material to be carried directly to the point where they are needed. In fact, the skyscraper is impossible without the modern, high-speed elevator. Today, passengers can travel vertically faster and more comfortably than they can travel horizontally by street vehicles. If you consider air-conditioning, heat and humidity controls, quiet carpeted interiors, harmonious lighting, and freedom from noise and penetrating automobile exhaust fumes, the inside of a modern office building is superior to anything around it.

CONCRETE

Concrete, like brick, is a type of man-made stone. Like stone, it is fireproof and very heavy. It can support tremendous weight and it can be given almost any shape because it is cast in wooden forms on the building site. But concrete posts and beams will crack and break unless they are reinforced with steel rods. Combined with steel, concrete becomes a new material, an ideal building material called *ferroconcrete*. The steel rods buried inside a concrete post or beam prevent it from cracking and the concrete itself will not be crushed or twisted by weights and stresses that steel could not take.

Ferroconcrete shows its advantages over steel in buildings that will have unusual, especially curved, shapes. Steel girders are used best in straight-line combinations because of the way steel beams are rolled in the mill. But concrete is cast on the site in any shape the architect wants. Sometimes, concrete parts can be prefabricated, increasing the efficiency of construction. Steel framework has to be covered with brick, ceramic tiles, or concrete to make it fire-resistant and also to give it a more attractive finish. But ferroconcrete is often left the way it was cast in order to create interesting textures. If you watch ferroconcrete buildings as they are being constructed, you will notice that their framework takes longer to build than a steel cage type of frame. But after the concrete frame is done, the rest of the building is finished more quickly. In general, however, the steel-framed building goes up faster, even if it is more expensive because of the high cost of steel per pound. Therefore, steel frames are used in preference to ferroconcrete where speed of construction is a vital factor.

The aesthetic problem facing architects is how to build with steel *or* concrete without having to cover them with expensive and deceptive surface materials. It is difficult to make naked steel look attractive. And some people feel that exposed concrete is too coarse—in a hotel lobby, for instance. But that rough surface is often a good textural contrast next to great areas of mirror-like glass and thin strips of stainless steel, bronze, or aluminum. By shaping and arranging the wooden forms for the concrete, some bold sculptural effects have been achieved together with rich light-and-shadow patterns.

Ferroconcrete engineering is so advanced that huge "eggshell" vaults and domes can be made of thin, light shells of concrete reinforced with a fine mesh of steel wire and rods. These shell structures have no joints: They distribute their loads and stresses over their entire surfaces, creating great strength with a minimum of materials. Beautiful curving bridges, sports stadiums, airport terminals, and other major public buildings can be constructed through the imaginative use of ferroconcrete. Although it has many of the advantageous properties of steel and stone, ferroconcrete is beginning to be used like a plastic—a material that gets much of its strength from its shape and the accuracy of its engineering.

The steel-cage skyscraper is the most spectacular building of our age—especially when clustered to form our man-made canyons. But the future will probably see more and more use of ferroconcrete because of its flexibility, the wide range it gives to the designer's imagination. Steel-framed, box-like buildings make the most efficient use of their space, and so they are favored in a commercial civilization. But when we want buildings that appeal to the artist's imagination rather than the realtor's purse, we seem to turn to concrete. It is the kind of material that combines engineering with architecture the way Gothic stone masonry did in the great medieval cathedrals. A rich and powerful society needs such structures to inspire and unite its citizens as well as serve their physical and commercial needs.

Principles of Building

The materials of building had to come first. Putting them together depended on their size, shape, and natural advantages. Then methods of construction were invented based on the materials men had. These methods were improved and perfected until the shape of a roof or the building of a wall seemed as natural as putting on your clothes.

Living in one place all their lives, and traveling very little, people did not realize there were other ways of building. Sometimes they continued to use traditional materials and methods of construction even after new materials and engineering techniques had been developed. Familiar ways always seem safe, and people are unwilling to accept change in architecture—especially in home design—despite the changes in their work, transportation, communication, recreation, eating habits, and so on. Nevertheless, architecture in this century has produced several fundamentally new building principles. And today people are more willing to try new architectural ideas; in fact, they are often eager to be the first to use a new device or own a new product—from household appliances to whole houses.

New building principles are new solutions to architectural problems that have remained basically the same. That is, people still need protected space for living and working. They want comfort, safety, privacy and convenience. They want buildings to be strong and durable without being wasteful.

They also would like beautiful architecture so they can enjoy living and working in any building they happen to be in. These needs and desires are satisfied by a few basic building devices. When you know what they are, you can begin to understand buildings that vary greatly in appearance and purpose.

POST-AND-BEAM

You remember that the earliest building involved piling up rocks. Perhaps you also remember playing with building blocks as a child: The problem is to get them to stay on top of each other; it is much more difficult with rocks since they are unequal in size and rarely have perfectly flat surfaces. Early men learned that a large flat rock would stay put if it rested on three huge stones; they could build a sort of artificial cave that way. The flat rock on top acted as a beam and the supporting rocks acted as posts. Children make this same discovery when playing with blocks without going through the heavy labor of erecting boulders the way Stone Age men did.

The post-and-beam is the simplest of all building principles. It depends on a single, horizontal member, called a beam, resting on two or more vertical members, called posts. The weight of the beam is enough to keep it in place if it is made of stone. If the beam is wood, it can be nailed or bolted to the posts. Posts can be made of stone, wood, marble, stone and brick masonry, or cast iron and steel. These materials can be mixed. That is, steel beams may be set on stone masonry posts. This combination is common because masonry is strong in compression: It resists crushing. But a stone beam might break of its own weight because stone is weak in tension, that is, it tends to tear apart or crack. As a beam becomes longer in order to span a wider space, the tension within it increases. But steel is very strong in tension, so it is the ideal material for long beams, for bridging over very wide distances.

The inside space created by the post-and-beam is, of course, rectangular, the basic shape of the living space in houses, hotels, offices, stores, schools, hospitals, and so on. But you will notice that building an auditorium or gymnasium by the post-and-beam method is impractical because extremely long beams would be required. If posts were located inside the gym to support a series of short beams, the space would no longer be usable. The area has to be unobstructed if you are going to play basketball, for example. In order to enclose very large spaces without using interior columns or posts, the truss was developed.

THE TRUSS

A truss is a triangle or a system of triangles that functions like a very long beam. It can be made of wood or metal, and it is very light for its strength. This strength is based on the geometric fact that no side of a triangle can be changed without changing the other two sides. In other words, the three sides and the three angles of every triangle in a truss cooperate to resist any force that wants to change their shape. In order to break the truss, it would be necessary to stretch its wood or metal sides. And

although wood and metal will bend, it is almost impossible for them to stretch. This resistance to stretching and tearing, which is strength under tension, makes the truss ideal for bridging over large spaces that would be ruined by interior walls and posts.

The gable roofs of most houses are formed by a series of trusses arranged side by side. The bottom edge of each truss helps form the interior ceiling. The sides form the roof slopes that shed rain and snow. And the space in between the trusses can be used for storage or for additional living space. By now you realize that the attic of a typical gable-roofed house is space created by trusses. Cape Cod houses, very much used in Colonial American days, are still being built today because of their space economy: the same arrangement of trusses that forms the roof and ceiling of the main living space is also usable for extra rooms and closets. By cutting openings in the sloping sides of the roof and building little roofs over these openings, the builder creates *dormers*—built-out windows for letting light and air into the attic space.

Imagine a triangle of solid wood or metal. It would function like a truss and would be very strong. But solid wood or metal would add weight without increasing the strength of the truss. And, of course, the usable inside space would be reduced. The main advantage of a truss made of a system of triangles is the great strength it obtains with a minimum of material. Now, with the development of high-tensile steel, trusses of amazing lightness and supporting power can be constructed. When you see them in the form of beams on bridges and elevated highways, you get some idea of their strength despite their lacy look.

Unlike the post-and-beam, which might have been found accidentally in nature and then imitated by man, the truss is an example of the capacity of men to think abstractly. But it was not the result of a course in geometry. Instead, men probably learned some of the abstract principles of geometry by building trusses. Through experience with real materials, real weights, and real stresses, they were able to gain real knowledge of the properties of triangles.

THE ARCH

Like the truss, the arch is an answer to the problem of bridging over the space between two posts. How would you cover over that space if you had only bricks (or stones) to do the job? The arch is an ingenious solution. It consists of bricks (or stones) arranged between the two posts so that they seem to *squeeze* each other. As you know, bricks and stones are very strong in compression (squeezing) and so they resist crushing under great weight. By cutting the stones or shaping the bricks so that they are narrower on the bottom and wider at the top, they can be arranged in a semi-circle between the posts. In the center of the semi-circle is a stone or brick called the *keystone* of the arch; it receives the squeezing pressure from the bricks or stones (called *voussoirs*) on either side of it. As weight is applied to the arch from above, it grows rigid and strong. Then it transmits its load to its supporting posts or columns.

A beam resting on columns sends its weight straight down. So does a truss. But an arch transmits its weight in two directions —outward and downward. The outward thrusts would knock the posts over unless they were very thick and heavy, or were themselves buttressed by additional posts, or were part of a row of arches arranged side-by-side, or were surrounded by solid walls. In practice, all these ways of counteracting the sidewise thrusts of an arch are used. The result might be a solid wall with arch-shaped openings at various intervals; a wall of arches side-by-side, called a colonnade; or a row of arches arranged behind each other and buttressed by one or more rows of extra posts.

In many ways, the arch is more graceful than the post-and-beam or the truss. Rows of arches behind each other create a high, curved ceiling that feels more like the curve of the heavens than the straight, flat ceiling formed by a series of beams or trusses. But the arch is difficult to build. It begins to work only when it is completely finished; it will not hold itself up while it is under construction. Therefore, temporary wooden scaffolding called *centering*, has to be built to hold the stones or bricks and mortar in place until the arch is finished.

Because arches require very skilled masonry work, they are slow and expensive to build. Still, they were a principal building device of the Roman empire and were used in every type of architectural and engineering project. Once it is in place, the arch is very stable. It lasts and lasts. The great cathedrals of medieval Europe show what magnificent structures can be created by systems of arches. It is hard to believe they evolved from the mud-brick architecture of the Sumerians and Babylonians two thousand years earlier.

VAULTS AND DOMES

A series of connected arches, one behind the other, form a vault, sometimes called a barrel vault because it looks like a barrel cut in half lengthwise. If you can imagine an arch rotating around a vertical line drawn through its keystone, you understand the ancient idea of a dome. It looks like a tennis ball cut in half, but it was made by a series of half arches radiating around a single point. Both of these heavy masonry structures were the solutions of the ancient Mediterranean world to the problem of enclosing very large spaces. They needed such buildings to conduct the business of government, for law courts, for great public baths, for temples, churches, and mosques. Unfortunately, the thick walls which made these vaults strong also made them dark. Openings cut in the sides of the barrel vault would weaken it. A dome could have an opening at the very top, called an *occulus*, but the dome presented other problems because it had a circular rim that had to be supported on a square base. There were two solutions to this problem: one was the *dome on pendentives*—resting the rim of the dome on the tops of four arches rising from each side of the square; the second was the *dome on squinches*—little quarter-domes in the corners between the four arches instead of the curved, triangular shapes between the

arches, called pendentives. The squinches really break the corners of the square base and convert it into an octagon. The pendentives formed a more elegant geometrical solution while retaining the unobstructed square shape of the supporting base.

The difficulty with the barrel vault was that it was too heavy. But it grew lighter when it was developed into a cross-vault— two barrel vaults intersecting at right angles. The points where they crossed were reinforced and called groins. In effect, the groin was a half arch to which most of the weight of the vault could be transferred. With the weight concentrated in the groins, the rest of the vault could be made of lightweight, fill-in masonry. Eventually, additional groins called ribs would be added to the original four groins and then the fill-in material in the roof of the vault would become even lighter. Weight concentrated in the ribs was then carried down to the ground in compound posts or columns called piers. It was no longer necessary to support a heavy masonry vault with thick, solid masonry walls. The walls were opened up. Instead of stone, they could be glass, stained glass. Colored light flooded into the building that had once been a Roman *basilica* or law court and had now evolved into the Christian cathedral, the architectural triumph of the Middle Ages.

You can see that weight is one of the big problems of architecture. The ancients did not know how to achieve strength without heavy, massive shapes. Progress in building involved finding ways to reduce weight without sacrificing strength. And this became possible when the medieval builders gained more accurate ideas about the location of invisible stresses and strains. But real accuracy and precision in design was difficult to get by their trial-and-error methods. Mathematics had to become a more important tool of building, and when it did, the men who could use mathematics—engineers—began to dominate the art of architecture. Architects remained responsible for the outside appearance—especially the ornamentation—but engineers really determined how the space would be organized and how the structure would work.

Architects today are trained in engineering as well as art and design. They must also understand the social sciences because their work involves planning for whole communities, not just individual families. Although they collaborate with engineers, they design much more than the facade, or outside surface of a building. They develop its basic concept—its inner space, its feeling, its look. The contemporary architect must be a very versatile person. Part artist, part poet, part engineer, part philosopher, and part businessman, he must be a dreamer and a doer at the same time.

Architecture: Practices 1

SOME THINGS TO SEE

Look at the interior of the *Villa Shodan* by Le Corbusier, the interior of *Taliesin East* by Frank Lloyd Wright, the interior of his *Glass House* by Philip Johnson, and the interior of the *Hanna House* by Frank Lloyd Wright (on pp. 336–337).

SOME PROBLEMS

Each of these houses creates a mood or an atmosphere because of its materials, light, and space. What is the distinctive mood of each interior? Does this mood depend on what the architect has created, or does it depend on furnishings? What kind of person, do you think, would prefer to live in each house? Can you see any disadvantages in any of these houses? Were these houses designed to fit a "style"? After looking at these interiors, how would you define a house?

SOME POSSIBILITIES

It would be helpful to conduct some experiments about the influence of inside spaces on human emotions. This could be done in class by using large cardboard packing crates. For example, you could make some spaces shaped like a cone, or an Indian teepee, an igloo, a tent, a cube, or the inside of a pyramid. You might vary the height of the ceiling, slant the ceiling, or cut openings in the ceiling. You could also cut openings in the walls—locating windows at different heights and giving them different shapes. Every member of your class should sit in each type of space alone for a few minutes; and then he might write down his reactions and read them to the class. Don't try to build spaces like the ones in your own home. Experiment with something different to see how it makes you feel.

Conduct another series of experiments with artificial lighting. Find out what happens when a lamp or other source of light

Villa Shodan interior (above left), by
Le Corbusier. (Courtesy Lucien Hervé.)

Taliesin East, interior (above right),
by Frank Lloyd Wright. (Hedrich-Bles-
sing photo.)

Hanna House interior (at right), by
Frank Lloyd Wright. (Courtesy Paul
R. Hanna.)

Glass House interior, by Philip Johnson. (Courtesy the architect; photo, Ezra Stoller.)

comes from below your eye level, when it is at your eye level, and when it is above your eye level. Compare lighting that comes from one side with lighting that comes from two opposite sides. How do people and objects look?

In a third series of experiments, study the artificial light on wall surfaces. Use a single lamp to light a dark-colored wall, a light-colored wall, a cool-colored wall, a warm-colored wall, a patterned wall, a rough wall, a wood-textured wall, a shiny painted wall.

Bring an object to class: a rock, a tree branch, a vase, a toy, a plant, a bird cage—anything. Then build an environment for it.

Build something around that object to make it "happy." Give it a home.

Sit inside a large cardboard container. Then cut a small hole in it from the inside. Then another, and another. Change the shape and size of one of the holes. Bring a small night light into the box with you. Bring in a leaf or a stone or a small piece of wood and place it where the light will shine on it. Go outside the box and cut a small peephole from the outside. Now do whatever you can to control the atmosphere and mood inside the box. When you are completely satisfied, invite your friends to look at it.

Architecture: Practices 2

SOME THINGS TO SEE

Look at the *Guggenheim Museum* by Frank Lloyd Wright, the *Pan Am Building* by Walter Gropius and associates, *Lever House* by Skidmore, Owings and Merrill, the *Yale Art and Architecture Building* by Paul Rudolph, and also at the *Chapel at Ronchamps* by Le Corbusier.

SOME PROBLEMS

Can you tell what is done in these buildings by looking at them? Can you tell what materials they are made of? Why is *Lever House* more successful than the *Pan Am Building*? Would the *Yale Art and Architecture Building* make a good museum? Would the *Guggenheim Museum* make a good department store? Does the *Chapel at Ronchamps* remind you of a ship or a fish? What does that have to do with a church? Would the *Pan Am Building* look better in another location? Why doesn't *Lever House* use more of the vertical space on the site it occupies? What makes Paul Rudolph's building look masculine? Which of these buildings look as if they were designed by engineers?

SOME POSSIBILITIES

Try to guess what the inside of each building looks like just by seeing its outer form. Which tells you most—the shape or the surface? If you had to make a model of each building in clay or cardboard, which ones would you make in clay? What does

Guggenheim Museum interior, by Frank Lloyd Wright. (The Solomon R. Guggenheim Museum.)

Pan Am Building, by Walter Gropius and others. (Photo, H. Rinehart.)

Lever House (above left), by Skidmore, Owings, & Merrill. (Courtesy Lever Brothers Company.)

Art and Architecture Building, Yale University (above right), by Paul Rudolph. (Courtesy Yale University News Bureau.)

Chapel at Ronchamps (at left), by Le Corbusier. (Courtesy Lucien Hervé.)

that prove? Try to define the problem each architect tried to solve. Do you suppose it is harder to design a building with curved shapes than straight-line shapes? Which of these buildings looks like a fortress? Which looks like a castle? Which of these buildings could be called Romantic? Which of them could be called Classic?

WHAT YOU CAN DO

Conduct a survey about architecture among your friends. Ask them which of the following things is most important in a building: strength, beauty, or convenience. Ask them to give their answers in order of importance. Figure out a way to score the answers and then report your scores to the class. Try to explain your findings.

Look for examples of "buildings" made by nature: nut shells, a cow skull, sea shells, a pea pod, a turtle, a crab or lobster shell, or an egg shell. Now choose one of these "buildings" and make a large model of it. Then organize the space inside the model for performing some everyday activity: eating, sleeping, reading, watching TV, playing, or anything else you like. Try to use the special features that nature has built into her structures.

Pretend that your classroom is a city and that the objects in it are buildings, garages, streets, shopping centers, theaters, and so on. Then pretend that your "city" is being attacked from outside. How would you reorganize the city? Now pretend the attackers have been driven away and your "city" is being rebuilt because the people are not afraid of invasion. How would your "city"

look when everyone feels safe? Make a model of the new city or paint some pictures showing scenes of everyday life in the city before and after it was attacked.

Imagery plus Motion: The Film and Television

Much of our time is spent watching moving images—on television and in the movies mainly. In addition, we travel in vehicles a great deal and only rarely on foot. This means that even reality is seen at speeds anywhere from fifteen to seventy miles an hour. Those who fly glimpse a world that cannot be imagined by earth-bound creatures. So motion is a factor in everyday vision as well as in films and television. Nevertheless, the still image is not obsolete, but we see it with eyes that have been affected by machine speeds and machine types of acceleration.

Moving pictures do not really move: Their motion is an illusion created by projecting as many as twenty-four still images on a screen each second. Our eyes cannot see the blank screen between these rapidly changing images. Each picture lingers as an afterimage in the eye of the viewer beyond the instant when it appeared on the screen, and as a result we think we are seeing continuous motion. From the standpoint of theoretical physics, it is quite possible that there is no such thing as continuous movement, just the *illusion of continuity* created by our perception of separate states of matter. For practical purposes, however, films make us believe we are seeing continuous action—a tremendous technological achievement. This achievement, however, opens up even greater artistic possibilities: the visual manipulation of space, time, and motion.

Films are so fascinating because they give man the illusion of magically controlling reality; he can convincingly reverse time, take apart matter and put it together again, and move at supernaturally slow or fast speeds. Motion picture imagery, combined with faithful sound, spectacular color, luxurious seating, controlled temperature and humidity, and shown in a softly darkened room, is perhaps the most soothing, pleasurable, and gratifying art form man can experience. The film experience almost rivals the perfect comfort and instant satisfaction of the prenatal state.

Film Realism

Motion has always fascinated artists. Even the cave painters of the Stone Age attempted to depict running or leaping animals. In their desire to capture the complete aliveness of a creature, they must have felt terribly frustrated by the fixed, static image imposed by painting. Throughout the history of art we see any number of ingenious attempts to make the fixed picture or sculpture suggest movement. But only with motion pictures did a breakthrough actually occur—the truly convincing representation of movement. This breakthrough was technological at first, but it had important and largely unforeseen artistic results.

As films were technically perfected, especially with the addition of synchronized sound and accurate color, the representation of reality was carried beyond the ambitions of the most competent artist. A medium was developed that could make dreams appear real. Still photography was superior to painting, of course, in the accurate representation of visual reality. But the absence of motion meant that people looked at photographs as if they were skillfully executed paintings. That is, they thought of photography in terms of hand-made pictures. Motion, however, compelled belief in the truthfulness, the reality, of film imagery. The picture frame disappeared and the viewer began to "live" in the space-time of the film.

The first principle of film art, therefore, is realistic representation. Even when fantastic events are shown, the film has the capacity to make you believe in it. Have you noticed that small children enjoy a film no matter how bad we think it is? That is because they cannot tell the difference between their dreams and film imagery. Just as dreams fascinate and occasionally frighten the dreamer, films fascinate and frighten the child. Adults "know" that a film is not real, but they forget or lose this intellectual knowledge while they are watching a motion picture. As a result, they respond to the reality of the film the way they respond to the reality of life. Motion pictures then become part of life, part of everyone's living experience, and they mix with the rest of our experience on an equal basis. Have you noticed that people talk about places they have seen or events they have witnessed in films just as if these were places and events they had actually seen?

The realism of the film explains its educational value and its entertainment value. Through documentary and historical films, we can have experiences and feel we have seen events very far away in space or in time. Instead of reading about Eskimos in Canada or Aborigines in Australia, we visit them through films and see what their daily life is like. Not only is this an easier way to get a genuine feeling about people and places, but it also is more accurate and vivid than reading about them. The viewer can form his own conclusions about what he sees. He can imaginatively live with what he studies. There is the danger, however, that the film will distort its subject. Errors of fact and misleading emphasis are possible in any medium of communication, of course. But while we do not believe everything we hear or read, we are inclined to believe everything we see. Partly, this is because we have had a long time to develop critical skill when responding to printed or spoken forms of communication. Our lack of film literacy, however, means that it is possible for cinematic realism to convince viewers that what they see is true when, in fact, it isn't. The only defense against deceptive and misleading types of artistic realism—whether in films, television, plays, novels or pictures —is the development of critical distance, which is a factor in your over-all personal maturity. That is, you must learn to examine art experiences reflectively and analytically; you need to distinguish between types and levels of reality; you must learn to avoid

"snap" judgments and give yourself a chance to relate, compare, and interpret what you see. The next chapter in this book offers some help in developing these critical skills —not only with films, but with all the other visual art forms.

The entertainment value of the film comes from its ability to make you forget *your* reality and live in *its* reality. People need to forget their problems and frustrations now and then. Sleep and dreams do this for most of us; however, films resemble dreams and so they can give us an extra "vacation from reality"—an extra vacation from daily life. That is why you often feel good when coming out of a motion picture theater even though the film was about a sad or frightening subject. Perhaps the reason children enjoy films so much is that real life is so much more frightening to them than to adults. Therefore the film dream (notice how children love television cartoon fantasies) helps drain away the fear they have accumulated in real life and gets them ready to face reality again. You can see, of course, that six or seven hours of television viewing per day by a small child might have the opposite effect: It might destroy his capacity to deal with real situations—situations that are not plotted in advance by a screen writer.* In general, however, the artistic form of even

*One psychiatrist points out the possible harmful effects of too much TV viewing as follows: "If a child watches enough television, he will *automatically* become violent, because he has nowhere else to go with his normal aggressive energy that he should be working off in creative activity." [Italics mine.] Dr. Lawrence J. Friedman, senior faculty member of the Los Angeles Psychoanalytic Institute, quoted in *Saturday Review*, April 12, 1969, p. 69.

bad films is an aid to the young child in his struggle to understand the world. It accustoms him to look for the structure or "plot" of real life instead of being dazzled, confused, or overwhelmed by the patternless complexity of living events.

Film Time and Space

The technical ability to *represent* motion in films also results in the ability to *manipulate* motion. Motion can be speeded up or slowed down; it can be squeezed or expanded. This means that time and space, as we usually experience them, can also be squeezed or expanded. You are familiar with some of the film devices for expressing the passage of years in a few seconds of viewing time: the falling of calendar leaves, successive shots of season changes, quick views of people aging or growing up, shots of equipment as it wears out and is replaced. Short time lapses are shown by watch dial readings, changes in light and shadow patterns, the movement of vehicles, or the completion of a process like the disappearance of food from a table set for dinner. The illusion of crossing a great distance, of covering a vast space, can similarly be created by a series of very brief shots showing different stages of a journey. The viewer crosses the continent effortlessly, in a few seconds, and is fully convinced of the psychological duration of the journey.

Conversely, the film-maker can make an event of only a few seconds' duration last for an hour. He does this by photographing the event simultaneously from many angles and positions and then cutting-in many of these views in his final version. In addition, he may photograph the reactions of witnesses to the event he is portraying. This, too, takes viewing time although it is interpreted as taking place at the *same time* as the central event. The result is a spreading out or expansion of real time.

In addition to these essentially psychological devices for manipulating space-time, there are also mechanical devices available to the film-maker. Slow motion, for example, really gives you "more time"—more time to see what could not normally be seen. A dancer tries to slow down or expand time when he leaps by seeming to arrest his motion at the top of his leap. To do this, he must train his body to take certain positions which make it appear to *pause* in mid-air. But he only creates an illusion. Motion picture photography actually slows down time by photographing motion at a much higher rate of speed than it will be projected; it increases the number of separate states of matter that we see and therefore it expands time's duration for the viewer. In addition, zoom and telephoto lenses collapse space, bringing us closer to things than we could go with our own bodies and eyes. The split screen lets you see at one time several actions occurring in different places simultaneously or at separate times. Television sports reporting is a good example. Instant replay and stop action shots almost replace the use of memory. Wide screen can create a vivid and believable illusion of your own body moving through space.

Three stills from 2001: A SPACE ODYSSEY (above), a film by Stanley Kubrick. (© 1968 Metro-Goldwyn-Mayer, Inc.)

Two stills from THE MAGICIAN (below), a film by Ingmar Bergman. (Courtesy Janus Films, Inc.)

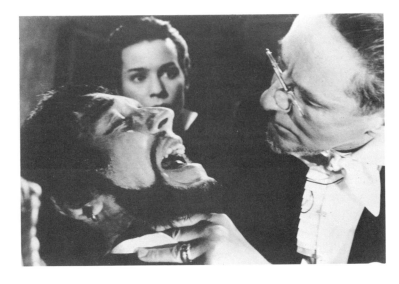

Projecting film backward has the effect of reversing time. You can see people back into a room; combined with slow motion, backward projection can show a flower become a bud. Such effects may seem to be only tricks, but they reveal the capacity of motion pictures to play with time in a believable way. When time and imagery are moving normally, the cinematographer can suddenly stop or "freeze" the action of his film, thus creating the impression that he has stopped the movement of time.

Motion pictures show how often psychological and aesthetic effects depend on technical devices. Color and sound and wide screen are just tricks if used to display mechanical cleverness, however. In the hands of an artist, they can become tools of significant expression. Slow motion may help

Because the motion picture illusion of reality is so convincing, the film experience enables us to live simultaneously in many worlds: the everyday world of everyday people, places, and events; the dream world of terror, pleasure, and magic; and the fantastic world of the future envisioned by science and technology. ∎

us analyze a complex football play; but it can also convert a broken field run into magnificent, dance-like motion.

Movies as History

There is another kind of time that film makes alive—historical time. It is especially visible in old movies. Such "out-of-date" films revive the past, of course, although that was not their original purpose. Historical movies deliberately revive certain periods, events, and personalities just as a historical novel does. But an old film that was originally designed for contemporary entertainment compels you to live for an hour or two in the period of the actors, writers and directors who made the movie. It forces the viewer to feel the difference between his own time and the time he is living in temporarily. It is not an artificial revival of the past, as when a modern writer or painter tries to recreate an ancient period. In that case, we never really lose our moorings in the present; we see an earlier time through the eyes of a contemporary man. Motion pictures *compel* belief in ways that

painting and sculpture can only suggest. Old films, however, remain the same even though we are changed. The contrast between their sameness and our different-ness creates a peculiar awareness of historical change—a type of change which film permits you to feel emotionally and not just cerebrally.

Once again cinema creates a special awareness of time. It is not the passage of time as historians deal with it in their books. It is the creation of a package of time that belongs forever to a particular set of reels of film. And yet it is a time that the viewer can automatically share. It would not be inaccurate to call the cinema a time machine.

To get a feeling for historical change from films, it helps to see many motion pictures. The same is true of painting, sculpture, and architecture. They, too, were made for contemporary audiences or viewers. We learn to see the transmission of style and influence in *sequences* of works of art. This is especially true when you are looking at the expression of change through the convincing fantasy of filmed images. But it is easy to become overly fascinated with styles of acting, directing, and photography. Then you can lose sight of the historical substance of a film: the kinds of ambitions people had during the Depression of the 1930s; the way people used to think about love and romance; what kind of behavior was considered disgraceful; ideas about comfort, luxury, and convenience; standards of masculine and feminine beauty; the status of businessmen, public officials, policemen, army officers; opinions about ethnic groups, immigrants, foreigners, manual laborers, and factory workers. You can see interesting changes in attitudes toward age groups—toward children, adolescents, teenagers, young and old adults. At first, these changes seem funny, even hilarious. It is hard to imagine that our parents and grandparents could have been so stupid, or unimaginative, or dull. Then you realize that your dreams will also seem quaint to your grandchildren. And that is the beginning of wisdom.

Film and TV: Practices

SOME PROBLEMS

What is the difference between the time it takes to do something in the movies and the time needed to do the same thing in real life? When you watch a film do you think you are sitting still or do you think you are moving? When a movie close-up makes an object larger and nearer, what is it doing to the space around the object? Can a motion picture camera "stretch" or "squeeze" space? Can it squeeze objects? What is the difference between a motion picture and a cartoon strip? What is the difference between a motion picture and an animated cartoon? Can you explain how animated cartoons work?

Are there any important differences between movies and television? Do you prefer to eat, talk, do homework, or play while your television set is on? Would you do these things while watching a movie? Would you pay more attention to a leaf falling off a twig if you saw it in a movie instead of in real life?

What is the difference between watching people dancing and watching a film of people dancing? What is a flashback? What makes movies seem like dreams? Why do people enjoy seeing cartoons in which dogs and cats talk, or trees and houses dance? Why do we enjoy seeing a cat squashed flat by a steamroller and then enjoy seeing him pop back to his normal shape?

How can you tell the difference between the hero and the villain in a movie? Is it the way he looks, what he wears, his way of talking, the way he moves? Do you like happy endings? Why? Why do some people enjoy horror movies? Do they like to be frightened? Why? Who is most important in making a film—the actors? the screenwriter? the photographer? the director? the producer? Do you ever read what critics write about movies? Do they help you decide which movies to see or not to see? Do they give reasons for liking or disliking the movies they write about?

WHAT YOU CAN DO

Watch one of your favorite television shows with the sound turned off. This makes it almost like the old-time silent movies. Ask your friends or classmates to watch the same show with the sound turned on. Then tell them what you think happened. How important are words, sounds, and music when you are watching images in motion?

Watch some TV commercials with the sound turned off. Does this make them better, easier to take? Are they more entertaining or less entertaining? Why?

Watch your favorite television show with the sound turned on but with the picture tube turned black. Can you imagine what is happening? Is it the same as listening to a radio broadcast? Suppose a comic strip had no words. Have you seen some strips that have *practically* no words? Make up a comic strip using pictures cut out of magazines. Try to tell a story or a joke using the comic-strip technique.

Get a reproduction of a painting or a photograph you like very much. Then roll a sheet of paper into a tube and look at your picture through the tube. Move close to the picture so that you cannot see its edges. Now pretend that you are a motion picture director or photographer who is going to film that picture through the tube. You are going to make a whole movie out of that single picture. Plan the parts of the picture that should be seen first, second, third, and so on. Also, decide how many seconds to spend looking at each spot. Plan the path of the camera as it moves over the picture

surface. Make a tracing of the picture and then plot or diagram the path of the tube-viewer across the picture, marking the amount of time to be spent in each location. Use arrows to show directions and a color code to show length of time. Remember that you can return to a spot you have already seen. Also, your movement can be slow, wavy, fast, zig-zag, smooth or jerky. Finally, lend your diagram to other members of the class so that they can see your "movie."

If possible, organize a movie-producing team in your class. Buy, rent, or borrow a sixteen millimeter motion picture camera. Perhaps you can buy some film—color or black and white—through Army surplus sources. You might plan to do a documentary based on school life. You could use recorded sound and music instead of spoken dialog. Find someone in your school or community who can give you technical advice about film-making. It isn't as hard to make a movie as you may think. Many school children have made some really fine motion pictures.

12

Just seeing films and paintings and buildings is not enough. People want to talk about what they have seen. They want to compare their likes and dislikes. Talking about a work of art with friends frequently leads to the discovery of something that was missed. Often, we want to know if we are getting the same message as others. Or we want to persuade someone to agree with our opinion about a work of art. But whatever the reason for talking about art, everyone does it in order to share experiences.

Art criticism can be defined as talk—spoken or written—about art. It is not necessarily negative or destructive talk. It can include praise, comparison, description, and explanation as well as disapproval. Naturally, some people are better critics than others. They can see more in art than others can see, and so their reports about it are more interesting. In fact, a good critic's report about a work of art can add a great deal

to your enjoyment of it. He can help you to see things you would not have seen alone. But eventually, you must learn to be a good critic yourself so that you do not become too dependent on "official" opinions. One mark of an educated person is the ability to recognize and evaluate excellence independently. This ability, however, does not come from memorizing lists of so-called masterpieces. It comes from developing sound procedures for analyzing and interpreting art and then applying those procedures as well as you can. This chapter, therefore, will be devoted to explaining some techniques or procedures that you can use to develop your ability as a critic.

Attending to What We See: Description

There are two ways to draw attention to a work of art you are going to criticize: the

Mastering the Techniques
of Art Criticism

first is to identify the work; the second is to describe it. I prefer to emphasize description because that immediately involves us in using our eyes and minds to understand what we are looking at. There are four stages of criticism—description, analysis, interpretation and evaluation—and when they have been completed, the viewer will have a *critical* identification of the work. This identification is very valuable from an educational standpoint. But there is also the standard, scholarly identification which the critic should know: the title of the work, the artist who made it, the date when it was created, the place where it was made, and, if possible, the medium or materials it was made of. Not all of this information may be known with certainty. In that case, the critic proceeds on the basis of the facts he does have. Usually, art historians or archaeologists have identified a work of art as accurately as they can and the critic can rely on their best judgment. A disagreement among historians about the date of a work, or about who created it, should not seriously affect a critic's interpretation, however. The critic should proceed with the help of the facts that scholars *are* able to bring out. That is, knowing the country an artist lived in or the period in which he worked can give the critic some clues about the original purpose or use of the art object. Nevertheless, as critics we are mainly interested in the *present* meaning and purpose of a work of art. We want to know how it affects our lives and our world outlook right now. The historical function of a work of art is useful to us, as critics, only when it points to significant features of life as it is now understood and as we feel it must now be lived.

The most common mistake made in art criticism is jumping to conclusions—deciding too quickly about the value or meaning of what is seen. We have to give ourselves time to see as much as can be seen in a work and then we can decide what it means and is worth. You get this time by *describing* what you see, that is, by listing what the art object seems to be made of. Making a list, or an inventory, does two things: It slows you down, and it forces you to notice things you might have overlooked. This process of listing is *description*.

The words you use in description are like pointers; they are not intended to be the exact equivalents of what you see. Instead they draw attention, or *point to*, something worth seeing. They force you to pause in your race to a conclusion and they help you to notice or attend to inconspicuous details of the art object. A description also gives the critic a chance to get the agreement of a group of people about what they are looking at. One of the reasons why the public may disagree with a critic's judgment is that they have not been looking at the same work of art; they are really noticing different features of the same art object. By describing what he sees, the critic gets his audience or public to examine the same work that he plans to judge. Later on, when he tries to form an interpretation, he can be reasonably sure that he is talking about something his audience has really observed.

In some descriptions, you can get agreement about the *names* of what you see.

That is, you can say that a picture shows a man, a tree, a lake, grass, children, animals, sky, and so on. But sometimes, it may not be clear whether you are looking at men, for example, or women. The forms may be too indistinct to enable you to make that decision. In such a case, you should say you see some people. Your objective is to describe only what you are reasonably sure of. Perhaps other details will enable you to decide, later on, whether you see men or women, children or adults. Right now, during the stage of description, you are more interested in a complete and neutral inventory than in certainty and precision. We would prefer to be vague about some detail rather than take the chance of making an error that might throw off the final interpretation.

Traditional works of art show many recognizable persons and objects—making the job of description easier. (But even recognizable persons and objects may present problems if they are part of a complex system of symbols, as in medieval art. In that case, it is necessary to be a student of iconology in order to know the *original* meaning and function of the work.) Contemporary abstract and nonobjective works rarely show us things that have common or proper names, so we have to describe the shapes, colors, spaces, and volumes we see. Remember that the purposes of a description are to point out what can be seen (regardless of names) and to slow down the viewer's tendency to form conclusions too quickly. Therefore, the critic has to adjust his language to the level of what he sees: the more

abstract the forms, the more general the words he uses to describe them. Fortunately, we have words that call attention to the specific properties of very general things— words like vertical, round, oval, smooth, dark, bright, square, horizontal, and so on. As these adjectives are combined and attached to general nouns like shape, space, and volume, we add precision to our description of a work of art without judging or interpreting it too early.

Another phase of description is technical. That is, the critic tries to describe the way the art object seems to have been made. He discusses the way the paint was brushed on, the kind of tools or manipulation used to create a sculptural surface, the way a building's walls were erected and supported. Naturally, the critic's own experience as an artist or as a person who has studied artistic methods will be very useful in technical description. Technique is important for criticism because it is just as expressive as the shapes and forms we see.

Describing a work of art can be done publicly, just by telling a group of people what you see; or it can be done privately, by telling yourself what is there. But the important feature of a good description is its neutrality. That is, your list or inventory contains only the things other people would agree are there. A description does not have any conclusions about the excellence or the meaning of what you see. It is an impartial inventory.

In order to be impartial or neutral, you have to watch your language, avoiding loaded words or expressions that reveal feelings and preferences. Assume that you are going to be challenged whenever you use adjectives that might suggest your point of view—words like strong, beautiful, harmonious, weak, ugly, disorderly, funny-looking, and so on. Instead use words like straight, curved, small, large, rough, smooth, light, dark. You can use the names of colors in description, too, because colors are neutral until judged in relation to surrounding shapes, sizes, textures, and other colors. Of course, the word "red" may not be an exact description of the particular color you see; it is just a way of saying that a certain area is more like red than some other color. A viewer is affected by the way something seems to be made as well as by what it is; he imaginatively repeats the operations the artist carried out, especially if the artist employs a style that does not cover up or conceal his technique. Your ability as a critic will obviously be increased if you study artistic processes and procedures. You can get more enjoyment out of a film, for example, if you can detect the director's control of acting style, lighting, composition, cutting, camera angles, focus, fadeouts, montage, and so on. It is a mistake to believe that art and technique are separate. One way you can discover ideas in a work of art is by studying the technique that created the art object in the first place.

Description: Practices 1

SOME THINGS TO SEE

Look at *Hide and Seek* by Pavel Tchelitchew (along with the two photographs of children in trees), *Carnival of Harlequin* by Joan Miró, *An April Mood* by Charles Burchfield, and *Woman Combing Her Hair* by Julio Gonzales (on pp. 352–353).

SOME PROBLEMS

These works were selected to give you practice in identifying and describing what you see. They are complex works of art. That is, there are many things to see in them. You may recognize some familiar things very quickly, but you will not see everything at once. You have to search each work carefully to make sure you are not overlooking something important.

When you look at Burchfield's trees, you must also describe their shapes, their size, and the way they are lighted. *Hide and Seek* shows a tree, but is it also something else? What about the spaces between the tree branches? Do the photographs suggest any visual metaphors that may have inspired the artist? *Carnival of Harlequin* is a real party; but you have to know who the guests are if you expect to enjoy the party. *Woman Combing Her Hair* is a humorous work, like *Carnival*, but the humor is not obvious. You must first be able to see how the woman's posture is described by metal shapes.

SOME POSSIBILITIES

Have you ever heard of tree-worshippers called Druids? Can there be any connections between tree-worship and Burchfield's painting? How would you explain the combination of leafless trees and the traces of vegetation in *April Mood*? How does the mood of the blossoms combine with the

Children in trees (right, top and bottom). (Both photos, The New York Times.)

HIDE-AND-SEEK (below), by Pavel Tchelitchew. (Collection The Museum of Modern Art, N.Y., Mrs. Simon Guggenheim Fund.)

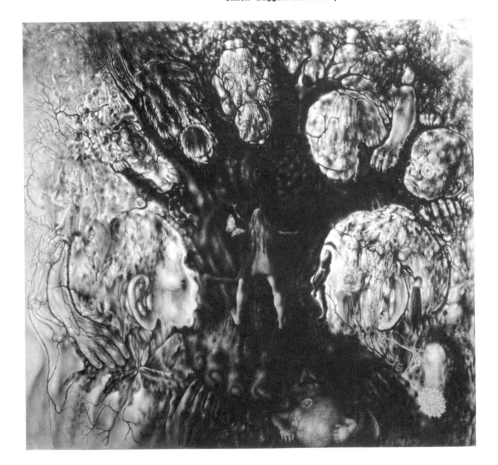

CARNIVAL OF HARLEQUIN (above left), by Joan Miró. (Albright-Knox Art Gallery, Buffalo, N.Y. Room of Contemporary Art Fund.)

WOMAN COMBING HER HAIR (above right), by Julio Gonzales. (Collection The Museum of Modern Art, N.Y., Mrs. Simon Guggenheim Fund.)

AN APRIL MOOD (at left), by Charles Burchfield. (Collection of the Whitney Museum of American Art. Gift of Mr. and Mrs. Lawrence A. Fleischman.)

mood of the dark clouds? *Hide and Seek* also deals with a mysterious tree. What is the difference between this tree and Burchfield's trees? Surely you have played hide-and-seek: What does that game have to do with the meaning of this picture? To understand the Miró painting you should know who Harlequin is. You have to find out something about the popular Italian street dramas called Commedia del'Arte because Harlequin was a character in those plays. Then you will have some clues about what the insect-like figures are doing in the Miró painting. The problem in the Gonzales sculpture is to figure out how the woman is combing her hair; you need to describe the motions she is making in the sculpture and compare them to the motions made by a real woman who is doing the same thing. Study the shapes and lines that the figure makes as it goes through an everyday task like brushing teeth or tying shoelaces.

WHAT YOU CAN DO

Write a description of your backyard on a rainy day. Try to be very specific. That is, tell what happens to the objects in the yard as they get wet. Do they begin to look different—unlike themselves? Mention the way puddles form, and describe the way water builds up, splashes, or runs off. How do the rain clouds affect the outdoor light? What happens to the shadows? Do you notice any changes in colors, sounds and echoes? Finally, how do these changes affect you? What do they make you want to do?

Watch some children playing a game—any game. But pretend you do not understand the game because you are a person who comes from another planet or someone who lived during another century. Now describe what the children are doing—write it down—according to what you see instead of what you know about the game. Read your description to the class and let them guess what was "really" happening.

Cut out a large picture from a magazine or the newspaper. Next, make a cardboard picture mat with an opening about four by five inches large. Then frame a part of your picture with the mat so that you cannot recognize what it is supposed to be. Exchange your framed picture with someone else in the class. Then tell the class what the lines, shapes, textures, and colors in the picture you have are supposed to be.

Ask your father to paste a red piece of tape to his index finger while he is smoking a pipe or shaving or lighting a cigarette. Or ask your mother to do the same thing while she is sewing or putting on earrings. Watch the motion of the red dot. Then describe that motion in space with wire that is soft enough to bend and stiff enough to hold its shape. You might suspend this construction inside a cardboard box by tying it to black threads attached to the walls of the box. Painting the inside of the box and lighting it from within might make a dramatic work of art out of the performance of an ordinary, everyday act.

Description: Practices 2

SOME THINGS TO SEE

Look at *Seated Man with Owl* by Leonard Baskin, *Gallas Rock* by Peter Voulkos, *Cathedral (in Sunshine)* by Claude Monet, *The*

Generals by Marisol, and the *Kalita Humphreys Theater* by Frank Lloyd Wright (on pp. 356–357).

SOME PROBLEMS

To understand these works of art, you must first describe them technically, explaining the way they seem to have been made. Technical processes carry meaning just as well as the names and identities of things. Can you tell how the clay was shaped and assembled to create *Gallas Rock*? Is it possible to guess what materials were used to make *The Generals*? Does the material and the way it was shaped affect your feelings about Baskin's *Seated Man*? From looking at the bold concrete shapes in the *Humphreys Theater* do you get any ideas about the kinds of space inside the building?

SOME POSSIBILITIES

Watch a ceramist "throw" a pot on the wheel. Also, watch him make a pot by building its walls with clay slabs. Try to analyze the connection between the potter's technical methods and the pot's shape and surface. Watch a carpenter or a cabinetmaker at work and try to imagine how he would make a figurative sculpture using his regular building and constructing methods. Is there any connection between painting a picture like Monet's *Cathedral* and creating images through weaving, embroidery, or making mosaics? Examine a magazine color reproduction under a very strong magnifying glass and compare it with the Monet. Then explain how your eye sees these images. If possible watch workmen put up a reinforced concrete building. Notice especially how they build the wooden forms, place the reinforcing rods, pour the concrete, and remove the forms. Finally, try to shape a block of wood using a mallet and chisel. Do not use sandpaper or a file.

WHAT YOU CAN DO

Bring a collection of ordinary manufactured objects to class: a broom, a dish, a pot, a salt cellar, a napkin, a shovel, roller skates, a ladies handbag, some fabric, bookends, or a baseball bat. Study each object, especially its surfaces. Then try to describe the forming or shaping processes that gave the object its final appearance. Pretend that the salt cellar is a sculpture and the fabric is a picture. Imagine these objects in a frame or on a pedestal. Describe them as if they were works of art.

Place a sheet of newspaper on the floor. Ask a friend to walk back and forth over the newspaper a few times, so that his footprints overlap each other. But don't watch him as he does this. When you friend is finished, tack the newspaper on the wall or on a drawing board and outline all the combined shapes. Then describe the actions that produced the shapes. If you wish, turn the newsprint into a picture, coloring the positive and negative shapes. Give it a name based on the action it expresses.

Build a little house or a bridge out of toothpicks and glue. Then crush the building flat by stepping on it or pounding it with a heavy board. Place a sheet of paper over the crushed building and make a "rubbing" by going over it with a soft lead pencil or a crayon. Write a description of what you see in the "rubbing" and read it to the class.

SEATED MAN WITH OWL (near right), by Leonard Baskin. (Smith College Museum of Art.)

GALLAS ROCK (far right), by Peter Voulkos. (Courtesy the artist.)

CATHEDRAL (IN SUNSHINE) (below left), by Claude Monet. (Musée du Louvre, Cliché des Musées Nationaux.)

THE GENERALS (below right), by Marisol. (Albright-Knox Art Gallery, Buffalo, N.Y. Gift of Seymour H. Knox.)

The Kalita Humphreys Theater, Dallas, by Frank Lloyd Wright. (Messina-Dallas.)

Observing the Behavior of What We See: Analysis

In the first stage of art criticism we named the things we saw. We tried to make a complete list of the objects and forms everyone would agree are visible in a work of art. Now we must go one step further and try to describe the *relationships* among the things we see. This whole process is *formal analysis*.

In this stage we want to find out what the forms do to each other—how they affect or influence each other. Imagine two circles side by side, and two identical circles, one above the other. Although the forms are the same in each case, their relationships are different. One is a horizontal and the other is a vertical relationship. Obviously, these relationships have a different effect on the viewer. The way forms are located, then, is one of the things we try to notice in the formal analysis.

Size relationships are very important. We do not see shapes and objects in isolation, we see them in pairs, groups, or clusters. We notice the largest or the smallest shapes; or we notice whether the sizes are about the same. In any event, comparative size is significant because it gives us clues about importance (large shapes usually seem more important, they seem to have higher "rank" than small shapes). In addition, size is a clue to location in space if you are looking at a picture in which spatial depth is represented.

Shape relationships reveal a great deal, too. What happens when curved shapes are next to each other, or when they are next to square or pointed shapes? How do jagged shapes affect smooth ones? Shape also calls attention to the quality of an edge. There are hard and soft, even and uneven edges. You can study their combination in the same work of art and get valuable evidence for deciding what the total work of art means.

Color and textural relationships should also be described. You have to notice whether the colors of related shapes are similar to, or different from, each other; whether they vary slightly or contrast strongly. You will want to mention their value relationship—whether a color area is lighter or darker than a nearby area. Perhaps the colors are different while the values are the same. That observation may be useful later on when you try to interpret the entire work of art.

Textural and surface relationships are things we notice in everyday life. For example, when you go out on a rainy day, you

357

High-school students looking at a painting by Conrad Marca-Relli at the Georgia Museum of Art. (Photo, Al Wise, University of Georgia Office of Public Relations.)

can usually tell from looking at surfaces whether you are about to step in a puddle, walk on a wet but firm sidewalk, or possibly slip on a thin coat of mud. You can often tell whether a metal surface is dirty or clean, wet or dry, perfectly new or old and bruised, or even whether it is hot or cold. We make the same kind of observation when analyzing the surface qualities of a work of art. Once again, this type of observation helps us discover the emotional qualities as well as the ideas conveyed by the art object.

Somewhat more difficult than describing shape, size, color, and textural relations is

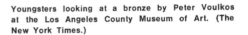

Youngsters looking at a bronze by Peter Voulkos at the Los Angeles County Museum of Art. (The New York Times.)

People seem to be passive when attending to works of art. And frequently they are, because our conventional model of the art appreciation situation assumes that someone—a teacher, a museum curator, docent, or other "expert" —should tell them what the work is all about. There is the difficulty! How can viewers learn to analyze and interpret works of art if the job is already done for them? The appropriate role of teacher or museum docent is to design a strategy of commentary and questioning that will stimulate descriptive, analytic, and interpretive operations by the viewers. Otherwise, the guided museum tour is like visiting a restaurant where someone else dines on the food and tells you how good it is. ■

analyzing space and volume relationships. In painting, we look for clues to the location of forms—not only *on* the picture plane, but also in depth, in the *implied* space that the artist creates by using perspective, size, color, or light-and-shadow relationships. We want to find out whether this implied space is indefinite, seemingly open and endless, or whether it has limits and is enclosed. It is important to know whether the painter's forms seem to rest on the surface, crowd around each other in shallow space, or move far back into the picture's depth. We also want to learn to see the shapes of the empty spaces—the so-called negative shapes—as well as the positive forms or volumes that constitute the art object.

For the artist or designer, negative space must be organized and controlled just as much as positive shapes and volumes. The way a sculptor, painter, or architect treats negative space may offer useful clues to the total meaning of his work, because an artist's space conception is often the controlling factor in his creative expression. He may not be aware of the way he thinks about space. Nevertheless, his space conception—one way or another—will be represented in his work. Consequently, a critic should look for signs of openness or density, clarity or obscurity, darkness or light, and flatness or depth in the over-all treatment of space.

When the description and formal analysis are completed, the critic has probably been able to describe most of the visible features of the art object. These two critical operations accomplish the following purposes:

1. They encourage as complete an examination of the object as it is possible for the viewer to make.

2. They slow down the viewer's tendency to jump to conclusions.

3. They help build skill in observation—a skill that is vital for understanding the visual arts as well as for general personal development.

4. They accumulate the visual facts that will form the basis for a critical interpretation.

5. For public criticism, they help establish a consensus about which features of the art object constitute the subject of interpretation and judgment.

Analysis: Practices

SOME THINGS TO SEE

Look at *Painting* by Georges Mathieu, *Blast II* by Adolph Gottlieb, *The Prophet* by Emil Nolde, and *Girl in Doorway* by George Segal (on pp. 360–361).

SOME PROBLEMS

Each of these works of art represents a solution to a problem—the problem of creating meanings by arranging textures, lines, shapes, colors, and light-and-dark patterns. You discover these meanings by analyzing the arrangement, the *organization* of these elements. In *Blast II*, how do the two shapes affect each other? Does their placement tell you anything about their identity? How would you analyze the black-and-white patterning in Nolde's *Prophet*? Does the shape of the doorway in Segal's work affect the way you see the girl who is standing by the door? Notice how the rectangular glass panes contrast with the rounded, lumpy

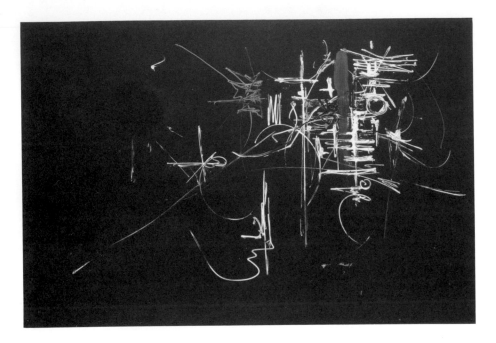

PAINTING (above), by Georges Mathieu. (The Solomon R. Guggenheim Museum, N.Y.)

BLAST II (far right), by Adolph Gottlieb. (Joseph E. Seagram & Sons, Inc.)

THE PROPHET (near right), by Emil Nolde. (National Gallery of Art, Washington, D.C., Rosenwald Collection.)

GIRL IN DOORWAY, by George Segal. (Collection of the Whitney Museum of American Art, N.Y.)

looking at the moon's surface, where it is safe to land? Is it possible to locate underground water or oil by looking at aerial photographs of the earth's surface? Do you know how military photo interpreters detect camouflaged areas when they are searching for bombing targets? Ask a geologist to tell you how he identifies rocks just by looking at them. Ask a radiologist to tell you how he analyzes X-ray photographs. If you saw a fly, a bee, or a hornet buzzing around in your room, could you tell if it was trapped, looking for food, angry enough to sting, or just wandering around? If you are about to cross the street, and cars are coming from the left and the right, how do you know whether it is safe to cross? When looking at objects in the distance, how do you decide which ones are closer to you?

WHAT YOU CAN DO

Bring an automobile road map to class and cut out a nine-by-twelve-inch section of the map. Next, pick out any three cities or towns on the map and look up the population of each town. Then cut out three two-inch squares of construction paper and paste them on the map where the three towns are located. Now your problem is to do something to each square (without writing on it or changing its size) which will show how large the towns are in relation to each other.

Mark out a rectangle on the floor of your classroom. It could be as large as four by six feet. Next, place several good-sized objects inside the rectangle and cover them with a sheet or a blanket. Then ask a member of the class (who was not watching you do

shape of the girl's figure. What kind of motion do you think the Mathieu painting describes? Have you ever seen anyone or anything that moves that way?

SOME POSSIBILITIES

Suppose you were an astronaut planning to land on the moon. How can you tell, by this) to identify the objects underneath. In addition, he should try to describe what they are doing together or what they seem to be doing *to* each other. It might help if he stood on a chair so he could see the whole area. Also, you could light the blanket from one side to create a more mysterious pattern of light and dark. If you get an arrangement you like very much, try to reproduce it on a smaller scale, using cheesecloth and plaster, or papier-maché, or any other technique that would work.

Giving Meaning to Works of Art: Interpretation

This stage of art criticism is the most difficult, the most creative, and the most rewarding. It is the stage when you have to decide what all your earlier observations mean. Of course, your intelligence and sensitivity are needed; but especially important is courage. You must not be afraid to risk being wrong, that is, making an interpretation that does not fit the facts immediately. You can change or adjust your interpretation until it does fit the visual facts, so there is no harm in being wrong or wide of the mark at your first try. It would be bad art criticism only if you changed or ignored a great many facts to make them fit your interpretation. Just what is an interpretation and how do you go about making one?

A critical interpretation is a statement about a work of art that enables the visual observations we have made to fit together and make sense. In other words, what single, large idea or concept seems to sum up or unify all the separate traits of the work? Please notice that an interpretation does not describe the object (we have already done that); and it does not try to translate visual qualities into verbal combinations. We use words now to describe ideas—ideas that, in turn, explain the sensations and feelings we have in the presence of the art object. An interpretation might also be regarded as an *explanation* of a work of art.

Sometimes an interpretation is a statement of the problem that the work seems to be trying to solve. We pretend that the art object—like a person—has aims and purposes, that it "wants" or "tries" to reach certain objectives. The evidence we have been gathering in our description and analysis seems to point toward those objectives, and as critics we try to state what the objectives appear to be.

In describing the objective or goal of the work, we are often guided by our own artistic experience. We can recognize the technical signs that an artist is trying to solve a certain problem because it is a problem we might have struggled with ourselves. A knowledge of art history and artistic styles is also useful because it helps the critic to recognize problems that artists have persistently tried to solve—problems of meaning or form or social function.

In stating what the goal or aim of the work of art is, we are not necessarily saying what the artist's purpose was. We do not really know the artist's purpose. It is possible that he does not know his purpose either. The artist may *believe* he knows what he was trying to do, and he may also think he succeeded in reaching his objective. (It is very difficult for any artist to be objective or impartial about his own work.) But as critics, we state only what the *visual* evidence seems to point to, or mean, regardless of the artist's intentions. Sometimes, an artist's statement about his work is useful in suggesting good places to look for visual information. However, it is an important rule of art criticism that your interpretation and judgment be based on what you have seen and felt in the work—not on what someone says about it. After all, you are judging images, not words.

From what has been said, it follows that no one is an absolute authority about the meaning or value of any work of art—not the artist and not any critic. When the artist talks about his work, or the work of another artist, he becomes a critic and is subject to the same errors as other critics. Some critics, however, are better than other critics because their interpretations are more persuasive and illuminating than others. Therefore, their conclusions about a work of art —especially if they are shared by other good critics—tend to be understood as standard or authoritative judgments. Naturally, we do not want to ignore the ideas and opinions of respected and well-qualified persons. But we must remember that as times change, ways of feeling and thinking change too. Critical interpretations, therefore, will not be the same for all times and places.

Although critical interpretations vary, we should not make the mistake of thinking that *any* interpretation of a work of art is as good as any other. The best interpretation would be one that (a) makes sense out of the largest body of visual evidence drawn from a work of art and (b) makes the most meaningful connections between that work of art and the lives of the people who are looking at it. Now this second trait of a good interpretation is the one which calls for a very creative critic. Of course, he must know enough about the language of art to observe and describe the art object sensitively and completely. But also, he must know enough about people—those who are viewing the work—to understand what interests or concerns them and how a particular work of art meets those interests and concerns. If I tell you things about art that you really do not want to know, I may be speaking truthfully, but not relevantly so far as you are concerned. Therefore, the good critic must be able to persuade people of the relevance or significance *for them* of the observations and meanings he has found in a work of art.

Now how do we build an interpretation? As suggested earlier, it is difficult to be right at the first try. In fact, being wrong—missing the target—is very helpful in arriving finally at a convincing explanation. Testing an idea, even if it doesn't fit all the visual evidence, helps you decide which adjustments to make in your explanation, which visual features are controlling and which are subordinate, which guess or intuition is promising and which looks like a dead end. This process is what I call forming an hypothesis. It is very similar to what scientists do when they have accumulated a body of observations that needs to be explained—except that in art we rely more on our feelings than in science. A scientist can run experiments to test out his hypothesis about a phenomenon. In these experiments he is very careful to separate his feelings from his observations. But an art critic is not pursuing the same kind of truth as a scientist. Instead, he is looking for a statement or explanation that satisfies his *feelings* about a work of art as well as his observations of it. That is, the critic is not looking for the *cause* of his feelings, he is looking for an idea that will *connect* his feelings to each other, and also, connect them with the observations he has been making about the object.

Since feelings are so important in art criticism, we try to pay special attention to any impression that seems to suggest itself while we are interpreting a work. Usually, such impressions come to us in the form of "looks like" and "feels like" reactions. They may be funny, illogical or absurd, but do not reject them. Try to *use* your far-out impressions. The way to employ these strange, even weird, ideas is to ask yourself what they have in common with the relationships you were able to describe in your formal analysis. Perhaps your "looks like" or "feels like" reaction can be modified so that it fits some or all of the formal relationships in the work of art. Your "looks like" reaction is often a very shrewd response to the work except that it does not sound like what an art critic should say. But if you work on that response —sharpen it, say it in a more general way— you can retain its fundamental insight and sensitivity without sounding silly or stupid.

This method of forming an interpretation is nothing more than a way of trusting yourself—your observations, your hunches, your intelligence. During the stages of description and analysis, your mind and imagination were working more than you realized. But you kept them "quiet" and under control in order to concentrate on a full description of the art object. Now, during interpretation, you can draw on those impressions. They are much more useful now because there has been time for them to interact with your whole personality. Your intuitions are richer because you have given yourself a chance to combine them with a greater variety of thoughts and observations.

Clearly, we have been building to the stage of interpretation. This is the stage where you give expression to your natural desire to respond to an experience as completely as possible. Perhaps you thought that a truly complete and intense human response is possible only when another person is involved, as in love, for example. But if you have carefully governed your examination and search into a work of art; if you have tried to see it and feel it and know it; if you have learned to focus your imagination and search into a work of art; then you have discovered what it is like to have an aesthetic experience. You have been able to let a *thing*—an art object—enter your life and become part of you. Your mental and emotional powers have transformed that thing—that work of art—so that it is yours in a very unique and special sense.

Interpretation: Practices 1

SOME THINGS TO SEE

Look at *Family Group* by Henry Moore, *Pies and Cakes* by Wayne Thiebaud, *Three Women* by Fernand Léger, and (on p. 366) *The Feast of Pure Reason* by Jack Levine.

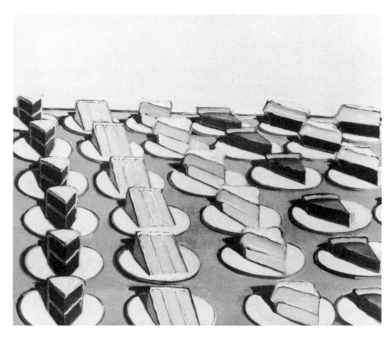

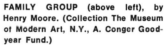

FAMILY GROUP (above left), by Henry Moore. (Collection The Museum of Modern Art, N.Y., A. Conger Good-year Fund.)

PIES AND CAKES (above), by Wayne Thiebaud. (Collection of the Whitney Museum of American Art, N.Y.)

THREE WOMEN (at left), by Fernand Léger. (Collection The Museum of Modern Art, N.Y., Mrs. Simon Guggenheim Fund.)

THE FEAST OF PURE REASON, by Jack Levine. (On extended loan to The Museum of Modern Art, N.Y., from the United States WPA Art Program.)

SOME PROBLEMS

These works of art show persons and objects that are easy to recognize, but telling what each work means is not so easy. You must describe and analyze each work and then think of an idea that explains it. Is Wayne Thiebaud trying to show how realistically he can paint slices of pie and cake? Is he complaining about the food in restaurants? Or something else? Does Henry Moore's *Family Group* seem to be frightened, proud, confident, ashamed, or lonely? How would you defend your answer? Do Léger's *Women* look a little like their furniture and dishes? Can you explain why they also look alike? What is a "feast of pure reason"? Is that an accurate title for Levine's painting? Do you know what sarcasm is? Do the characters in Levine's picture represent anyone or anything? Can you guess how you are supposed to react to them?

SOME POSSIBILITIES

Two of these works seem to be monotonous—the same all over. Is the artist *trying* to get that idea across? How does an artist make living things look dead? Does Moore tell you very much about each member of the *Family Group*? Or does he concentrate on the group instead of the individuals in it? Can you tell whether a picture is boring because of the things in it or because the artist tried to make it interesting but failed? Would Levine's picture be convincing if the characters in it were young men? Do you think he enjoyed painting their coarse features, their heavy jowls, and their pudgy hands? Should artists concentrate on pictures of better-looking people or beautiful scenes?

WHAT YOU CAN DO

Select a reproduction of a painting or a sculpture you like and conduct a survey among your friends and relatives about what it means. Write down what each of them says in a sentence or two. Remember that you are not trying to find out if they *like* the reproduction; you just want to know what they think it means. Report your findings back to the class. Was there much agreement? Did some of the people say the same thing using different words to say it?

Compare the interpretations made by different types of people when they look at the same work of art. For example, you might compare artists and nonartists, men and women, young people and old people, people who live in the city and people who live in the country.

Look at a work of art you have never seen before and write down or tell your class what you think it means. Ask other members of the class to do the same thing. Then find an art book which discusses the same work of art. Compare what the book says with your interpretations. Did you discover some things that the author of the book missed? Or did you miss some good ideas? Are all of you right even though your interpretations are different?

Ask a classmate to interpret a picture you have painted. But do not tell him what you were trying to do. Try to share his point of view and look at your picture "through his eyes." Does his interpretation make sense even if it differs from what you thought you were doing?

Cut a photograph out of a picture magazine. Do not include the written caption. Then pass the photo around your class and ask each member to write an interpretation in only two sentences. Afterwards, read these statements aloud in class. Although the photograph is an accurate type of representation, people will interpret it differently. Does this mean they do not see correctly? Or do they differ in ability to *report* what they see? Or do they somehow change what they see? Try to explain what happened in this experiment.

Interpretation: Practices 2

SOME THINGS TO SEE

Look at *Little Hands* by Arman, *Secretary* by Richard Stankiewicz, *The Beware-Danger American Dream #4* by Robert Indiana, and *Merritt Parkway* by Willem de Kooning (on pp. 368–369).

SOME PROBLEMS

Sometimes a work of art "asks" you to compare it with something that it may resemble in real life. But it does not look exactly like real life. You have to concentrate on two things: what it seems to look like and *the difference between what it is and what it looks like*. In *Secretary*, the title tells you what those metal parts are being compared to. But how do you explain that typewriter in the secretary's midsection? What do you think the doll hands glued into a wooden drawer are being compared to in the Arman construction? Robert Indiana's painting seems to be made of carefully lettered signs. Do you know where the words may have come from? Is the painting itself a type of sign or billboard, or is it *about* signs and billboards? What would de Kooning's splashy brush strokes have to do with a highway? Do they describe the landscape? The cars? The drivers? An accident?

SOME POSSIBILITIES

Maybe Stankiewicz is poking fun at women who are secretaries. What do we say about people when we are making fun of them in a friendly way? Do we use words

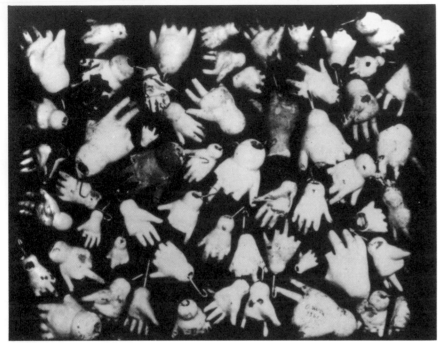

LITTLE HANDS (above), by Arman (Fernandez). (Collection Mr. and Mrs. Robert C. Scull.)

SECRETARY (above right), by Richard Stankiewicz. (Collection Mrs. Martin Cannon, Jr.)

THE BEWARE-DANGER AMERICAN DREAM #4 (at right), by Robert Indiana. (The Joseph H. Hirshhorn Collection.)

MERRITT PARKWAY, by William de Kooning. (Collection Ira Haupt, N.J.; courtesy Sidney Janis Gallery, N.Y.)

to exaggerate their defects? Do we make up tall stories about their work, their clothing, their posture, speech, and so on? What is your first thought when you see a part of something which you are accustomed to see whole? Why would anyone exhibit a collection of dolls' hands arranged inside a drawer? Notice that Indiana's lettering looks as if it were stenciled. Do you know how that is done? Who makes use of stenciled letters? Could you give a serious definition of "the American dream?" Is that the "dream" in Robert Indiana's painting? De Kooning's painting deals with motion. What

kind? Whose? What types of energy and feeling are involved?

WHAT YOU CAN DO

Choose an occupation you want to make fun of and interpret it in a construction like the Stankiewicz *Secretary*. (But don't choose the occupation of teacher.) Try to say something about the kind of work your subject does and show how this work affects what he looks like.

Bring your favorite *Beatles* record to class. If possible, get copies of the lyrics of the songs and read them silently while listening to the record. Then cut about a dozen color areas out of a magazine without paying attention to their shapes. Pick out about three of those color areas and arrange them in a combination of circles, squares, triangles, and rectangles on a sheet of construction paper. Try to make your arrangement suggest the main feeling of the *Beatles'* song. When you are satisfied, paste the colors down, mat your work, and display it with a title chosen from the song lyric.

Bring a small box or cardboard carton to class—about the size of a cigar box. Next, collect some discarded objects to be placed in the box. Line the walls of the box with paper, cloth, or magazine cut-outs. Then arrange the objects inside carefully so that they seem to be related to each other. Glue them into place. Now exchange boxes with someone in your class. Your assignment is to make up a story based on what you see inside the box and tell it to the class. Give yourself some time to look at the box before you tell everyone your story about it.

Deciding about the Value
of an Art Object: Judgment

From the discussion of interpretation you can see that a viewer or critic puts a lot of himself into the examination of a work of art. That is, if he is serious about it and wants to get something out of the experience. But our time and energy are not endless. We cannot have really close relationships with everyone we know, for example. Life is too short—or so it seems. And for the same reason, we cannot become deeply involved in every work of art we happen to see. Some will mean more to us; some will seem less valuable; some we would like to own, or at least, see again; some appear to be worth talking about; and some are best forgotten.

For many of us, deciding whether a work of art is worth serious attention is one of the most important problems of art criticism. Some people collect art, however, and for them the decision is complicated by the fact that they will risk their money and much of their time on their judgment. That is, they may buy a work because it satisfies them in some way and they expect it to continue to be satisfying. Whenever a collector, dealer, or critic says that a work is

---

The theologians have mined a rich vein in the "Peanuts" mother lode; now it is time to prospect for "Peanuts" wisdom in art criticism.

Lucy initiates the drama by offering a critical judgment before Linus has finished his work. She judges on the basis of the intention Linus is foolish enough to declare. Linus, who epitomizes the naive artist, is instantly trapped by Lucy's unsolicited judgment; he proposes changes to meet her objections. Lucy remains adamant. As critic (and imperialist) she can control the creative situation through her definition of art; she makes Linus believe he is trying to create ART. By the fourth frame, Lucy has concluded that Linus will not be able to solve the ART dilemma by himself; she jumps into the creative act with specific directions for success. Linus, by now thoroughly enthralled, carries out Lucy's instructions. Intoxicated with creative ardor, Lucy issues more elaborate instructions. In the sixth frame, like a good teacher, she explains to the artist what he has achieved (with her sympathetic guidance). In the climactic seventh frame, Lucy abandons her collaborative role and reverts to her original calling as critic. Her conditions have been met; Linus has created ART! He is appropriately astonished. Her mission accomplished, Lucy leaves the scene with a wry comment about the importance of lay criticism.

Aside from the demonstration of Lucy's well-known domineering tendencies, the episode richly illustrates several theoretical and **practical problems** of art criticism. First, the critic confuses the definition of art—which should be descriptive—with her critical standards—which can be normative. Second, she criticizes an incomplete work and—even worse—judges on the basis of the artist's words instead of his imagery. Third, she commits the critical sin of declaring, in effect, how she would execute the work. Fourth, Lucy passes judgment on a work in whose creation she has participated; she lacks judicial impartiality. Finally, Lucy convinces herself that aesthetic catastrophe —while not inevitable—is distinctly possible without critical intervention. Still, although Lucy's methods are high-handed, the artist seems to need a critical presence as he works. If not, why does he put up with that female? ∎

PEANUTS, cartoon by Charles Schulz. (© 1968 United Feature Syndicate, Inc.)

good, he is saying, in effect, that it has the power to satisfy or please many viewers for a long time. Naturally, a museum or a private collector would like to own works of this quality.

Most of us do not have enough money to buy really famous works of art, although many of us can afford to own work by artists who are good but not well known. Nevertheless, we seem to be interested in knowing which works are considered outstanding or excellent. Sometimes, we are curious mainly about the cost of a masterpiece—a curiosity that reflects an interest in money more than art. Or we are interested in "great artists"—an interest in the lives of certain men rather than their creations. But usually we want to know if a work is important so that we can decide whether to examine and study it seriously. If we have gained any experience in art criticism, we can make this decision by ourselves. If not, we tend to rely on the word of authorities. But authorities do not always agree, especially about new works that have not been discussed in print. The student of art should take steps toward becoming his own authority, his own guide to artistic excellence.

To become a "judge" of excellence, it is helpful to know how good "judges" or critics decide whether a work is poor or excellent. In other words, you must know the reasons good critics give for their opinions about art. If a critic gives no reasons—directly or indirectly—then he is not a good critic. If he asks you to rely on his judgment because he is famous, important, well traveled, well educated, well acquainted with artists, and so on, then he is not giving good reasons. The reasons for judging a work excellent or poor have to be based on a philosophy of art, not on a man's personal authority. Fortunately, we have a choice of several philosophies of art for justifying critical judgments. You may prefer one or the other, but at least you have some freedom in choosing the philosophy that suits you best: You need not depend on someone's unsupported opinion. And, if you are resourceful, you can develop your own philosophy of art as a basis for judging the merit of any work that interests you.

Formalism

As the word implies, formalism is a philosophy that stresses the importance of the formal or visual elements of art (as discussed in Chapter 7) and especially the way in which they are put together. The formalist is not interested in the view's associations or memories about what he sees. He does not care about how you intend to use the work of art, or whether it influences your social, political, and religious thinking. The formalist wants the experience of art to be devoted to contemplation of the relationships of the parts to the whole in a work of art. In some ways, he is satisfied by a very thorough formal analysis as described in the second stage of art criticism. Interpretation, he feels, would not really be necessary if the viewer has truly and deeply perceived the relations among the visual elements. They should be perfectly adjusted to each other. Each part should enhance the quality of the parts around it. It should not be possible to change a single element without changing and therefore spoiling the whole work of art. Perhaps without being aware of it, the formalist believes art should demonstrate successful cooperation among all the parts of a work the way all the parts of a living creature cooperate to keep it alive.

The best signs of successful cooperation in a living creature are its general health, ability to grow, reproduce, fight illness, work, and so on. What are the signs of successful cooperation in a work of art? How do we know that each part has been perfectly adjusted to every other part? It is usually in our feeling that there is no excess and no deficiency in any quality that the work of art brings to our attention. The artist is responsible for introducing certain forms and colors and qualities in his work; the formalist expects him to carry each of those elements to its ideal potential for harmony and sensuous appeal. The viewer should not be aware of too much or too little of any emotion or sensation as he experiences the work of art. When eating a good meal, for example, we experience a variety of tastes and textures, but too much sweetness, saltiness, crispness, or sogginess would be displeasing. The same is true of excellent art according to the formalist. But how does he decide how much is too much or too little? Here there is no logical rule the formalist can use. He must depend on a psychological observation. He has to say that there are people who have moderate but refined appetites—whether for food or anything else—and they can recognize the perfect blending and cooperation of the elements in any experience, in any work of art they encounter. The perfection in the work of art should somehow echo the perfect adjustment of interests, appetites, and desires in the normal person—the person of moderate feeling. Perfect art communicates its perfection to people who have managed to develop all their potential interests—not to a maximum degree but to an ideal degree.

The trouble with formalism lies in its dependence on the reactions of a certain type of person as the test of artistic excellence. It would be better if we had an *im*personal rule that we could use regardless of the feelings of individuals, no matter how well adjusted they are. After all, who is to judge which individuals are well adjusted or well balanced in their interests and desires? Of course, society does operate *as if* some behavior is wrong or illegal and other types of behavior are desirable. Probably, then, there are agreements—understood rather than written—about what constitutes a normal appetite or the expression of normal feeling. It also seems that artists keep adjusting and polishing their unfinished work as if they believed they were trying to please a person of very discriminating taste. Perhaps artists often imagine themselves *in the place of* a person of perfectly developed feelings. That would explain the mysterious little modifications they make as they work; it would also explain how they know when to stop. Obviously, the artist who is a formalist believes he is communicating with viewers who are formalists too. He knows that when he is pleased or satisfied, his pleasure or satisfaction will be shared by other men who feel the way he does.

Formalists want our pleasure in art to come from the art object itself—its surfaces, its colors, its stimuli, and combinations of sensation. They have had a healthy influence in directing attention to the basic materials and forms that constitute the art object instead of sentimental, literary and social associations. Perhaps the less desirable influence of formalism has been its tendency to separate art from life. Sometimes, it seems, formalists encourage the independent, autonomous development of art. To be sure, artists are greatly stimulated by the work of other artists. Accordingly, they try to refine and perfect the forms and styles they have inherited. At the same time, of course, they must recognize that great art has always served the needs of people who are not artists. The ideal and perhaps the greatest artist, therefore, would be one who could satisfy the somewhat specialized aesthetic interests of formalists as well as the broader human needs of the general public.

Expressivism

The formalist is probably interested in that old-fashioned idea, beauty—the sort of feeling we get when the visual elements of any object cooperate harmoniously. The expressivist is more concerned about the depth and intensity of the experience he has when he looks at art. For him, an excellent work of art could even be ugly. Art should communicate ideas and feelings, he believes, and no matter what they are, they should be communicated forcefully, with conviction. Formalists also believe that art communicates feelings and ideas. But they want these feelings and ideas to depend only on the way the artist shapes his materials. They do not admire art that relies on symbols, or on subject matter, or on the viewer's experience with represented places and objects. The expressivist, however, does not care *how* a forceful or (to him) truthful idea is communicated. If a work of art can reach him emotionally, or intellectually, then he concludes it is successful. He feels the formal and technical organization of the work has to be good, otherwise it would not be able to affect his feelings.

You can see that expressivism is not very particular about how the art object is organized so long as it manages to be effective. How, then, does the expressivist critic decide that one effective work is better than another? Basically, he has two rules for judging excellence: (1) That work is best which has the greatest power to arouse the viewer's emotions, and (2) that work is best which communicates ideas of major significance. These two rules are related, because the expressivist believes that the power to arouse emotions (1) grows out of the forceful communication of an important idea (2). He does not think that beauty, by itself, can result in great art. Beauty would have to be associated with a great idea, like the force of sexual desire, or the serenity of nature at rest, or the ability of a building or container to do a certain kind of job. In other words, beauty does not exist unless it is visible in places and objects that eloquently declare their connection to human needs and interests.

The expressivist also likes to feel that a great work of art has grown out of an experience the artist *had to* communicate. Art should look and feel as if it is based on reality, not other works of art. Art can be abstract, but abstraction should be a tool the artist uses to *intensify* his expression of life's meaning. Great art should not look calculated, it should seem to be the *inevitable* result of what an artist has seen or felt deeply. Therefore, the expressivist judges a work according to whether it looks believable, true to life. Does it really grow out of something that changed the artist? How can we tell? We cannot know whether the artist was, in fact, moved by an experience that made him create what we see. Perhaps the artist is just skillful in making us *believe* he has really felt an emotion or had a particular experience. Actors, for example, do this all the time. For the expressivist, however, the genuineness or actuality of the artist's emotion does not matter. What matters is the artist's ability *to make the viewer believe in what he sees.* The viewer has to feel emotion before he will believe that the artist also felt and expressed it.

We might sum up expressivist art criticism by saying that it expects art to be convincing, real, and emotionally effective. It should also deal with feelings or ideas that penetrate deeply into some human concern. Formalists prefer art that removes the viewer from everyday hopes and cares. But expressivists want art to make everyday life more meaningful and profound. They want to be involved in life rather than detached from it. To gratify this need for involvement, they seek art that reaches out and stirs them: It tells them a truth they did not know; it makes them aware of new emotions; it connects them indirectly with a great personality who happens to be an artist. Expressivists are not content with the passive contemplation of organized form. They want a more active experience and a more massive response from art. You might say the expressivist wants to exercise his mind and emotions through art's signs and symbols. Therefore, forms that empty out his old associations are bad; forms that heighten his experience by combining old associations with new sensations are good.

Instrumentalism

If the formalist is interested in beauty and the expressivist is interested in depth or intensity of communication, the instrumentalist is interested in art's effectiveness for a purpose. And he wants art to serve purposes that have been determined by persistent human needs working through powerful social institutions. Art should serve the interests of the church, for example, or the state, or business, or politics. According to the instrumentalist, art fails when you are aware only of visual forms and their interrelations. You should be made conscious of certain religious teachings, or the obligations of citizenship, or the superiority of a certain political philosophy. When art is at its best, in this view, it helps to advance some cause that will, presumably, advance the interests of humanity.

You can see that instrumentalists are not very sympathetic to the formalist position. Art that depends on art or grows out of art seems to them decadent. Art should always be a servant of man, not an independent language that prides itself on elegance and perfection of form. Indeed, the instrumentalist believes that forms can be perfect only when they perfectly embody a great idea in the service of a major force or institution. For example, great religious art heightens a viewer's awareness of the sacredness of certain symbols, the holiness of certain persons and events. It should lead to more perfect acts of faith and more effective commitment to the symbols of holiness.

The excellence of a work of art, according to instrumentalist standards, would be measured by its capacity to change human behavior, if possible in publicly visible ways. Great political art results in greater allegiance to a party, or greater conviction as to the truth of a political or social point of view. Great art in the service of commerce and industry should help sell merchandise, or encourage favorable attitudes toward certain corporations or industries and their activities. The pleasure we get from harmonious or striking combinations of forms should seem to be connected to the institution that caused these forms to be created and displayed. A beautifully proportioned industrial plant should encourage the viewer to see that industry as a necessary cause of the building's beauty. A powerful, attention-getting outdoor poster should not only divert the viewer's attention from his normal business, it should also make him want to own the advertised product at the same time that he sees it described in the poster.

Instrumentalists may seem aggressive in their demands on art, but history supports them: Most art *has* been created to serve purposes that artists themselves did not define. The artist may have been free to decide how best to express the teachings of the church, the magnificence of a king and his court, or the respectability of a group of businessmen, but he could rarely support himself by creating art that served no patron. Only in modern times–that is, since the French and American revolutions—has art been free in the sense that it has had no official sponsorship. Even so, an enormous amount of commercial and industrial art is created today. We would be foolish to say that it is not art because it is influenced by the people who pay for it. If that were true, some of the greatest works in history could not be considered art because sponsors or patrons exercised considerable control over their creation.

What the instrumentalist is really saying is that great art comes into being only when it serves a great cause: He believes he knows the *motivation* for great art. The technical and imaginative gifts of the artist need to be organized by an idea that is greater or more important than the private emotions of the artist. Excellent technique applied to trivial purposes will result in mediocre art. This view is similar to that of expressivists who are also distrustful of purely formal or technical displays of facility. But an expressivist would be satisfied by dazzling technique combined with profound emotional impact on the viewer; the instrumentalist would still insist that technical facility, emotional impact, and formal harmony be enlisted in the service of a cause that is larger than the individual artist or viewer.

After many years have passed, the cause or purpose for which a great work of art was created may be forgotten. Nevertheless, the art object may continue to be considered a masterpiece. Why? A formalist would say it is a masterpiece because of its perfect visual organization and technical execution. An expressivist would say it is great because its forms still have the power to communicate strong feelings and ideas although they are different from those originally communicated. The instrumentalist would say that the work we still consider great could never have been created if not for a purpose of overriding importance or the patronage of a great and powerful institution. The instrumentalist, therefore, claims to see the greatness of a work in the greatness of its purpose. It is not because he knows the purpose of the work in advance, he *sees* its purpose embodied in its forms. He has to interpret the word "purpose" as the social, political, moral, or economic meanings he can discover in the art object. If he cannot discover the purpose of the work in its forms, then it is a bad work of art. If the meanings he *does* find are not good or "correct" meanings, then no excellence of form will save the work; it is mediocre. If the meanings are noble and generous, then no deficiency of form can deny some value to the work. If the meanings of the work are good and expressed through perfectly organized forms, then the work is a masterpiece. By "perfectly organized forms" the instrumentalist would mean the closest possible connection between the appearance and the social intention of the work. If the viewer sees this connection, and, furthermore, *acts* as if he sees it, then the work is both excellent and effective.

Conclusion

Justifying your opinion about a work of art can be done with several different arguments, it seems. This does not mean that the value of a work depends on the cleverness of a critic. It means that a truly great work has the capacity to be found valuable by several different kinds of critic. Each is looking for certain conditions to be satisfied; and each finds those conditions satisfied in a work of genuine significance. But there is

a warning I should give the new critic. Do not *start* the examination of a work of art by asking whether it meets your conditions for excellence. That is the last question you should ask. Begin, as I have suggested, with identification and description and work your way through analysis and interpretation. By then you will know which type of judgment, which philosophy of art, is most appropriate for the work you are examining. It is better to use these philosophies interchangeably, according to the character of the art object, than to stick rigidly to one philosophy alone and thus lose discovering some excellence the work may have. The goal of art criticism is not necessarily to demonstrate how consistent you are in your final judgments. The real goal is to increase the sum of values and satisfactions you can get from art.

Judgment: Practices 1

SOME THINGS TO SEE

Look at *Echo of a Scream* by David Alfaro Siqueiros, *Portrait of a Young Man* by Bronzino, *Minotauromachy* by Pablo Picasso, and *Chapel at Ronchamps* by Le Corbusier (on pp. 378–379).

SOME PROBLEMS

Each of these is an outstanding work of art; we have to decide why. Or perhaps you do not agree. Then you must give your reasons. Let us assume that each work has been described, analyzed, and interpreted; we know that *Echo of a Scream* tells us about a child who is suffering. Is that important? Do you respond to the idea of suffer-

ECHO OF A SCREAM (above), by David Alfaro Siqueiros. (Collection The Museum of Modern Art, N.Y. Gift of Edward M. M. Warburg.)

PORTRAIT OF A YOUNG MAN (above right), by Bronzino. (The Metropolitan Museum of Art. Bequest of Mrs. H. O. Havemeyer, 1929. The H. O. Havemeyer Collection.)

MINOTAUROMACHY (at right), by Pablo Picasso. (Collection The Museum of Modern Art, N.Y. Purchase.)

ing? Or to the way the idea is expressed? Or both? Bronzino's *Young Man* is very handsome, beautifully dressed, confident but not arrogant. Is this painting a great work of art because we admire the young man portrayed in it? Or do we admire the way Bronzino has organized all the parts of the picture and the way he has executed the painting? Or is it interesting because of the clues it gives about Renaissance habits and attitudes? Does Picasso's etching frighten, confuse, and excite us for any special reason? Does it have anything to do with an experience, dream, or memory you have had? Le Corbusier's *Chapel* is both architecture *and* sculpture. Is it a great building because of its unusual or original shape? Or because of the feelings the shapes and volumes arouse in us? Why is it so difficult to put those feelings into words? Would this difficulty be a clue to the greatness of the structure? Is it important to know the connection between the building's forms and what is done and witnessed in the *Chapel*?

WHAT YOU CAN DO

Make a list of the most important things in the world. Give them a rank in order of their importance to you. Next, take the five most important things on your list and write each one down on a separate sheet of paper. Then think of as many things as you can which are connected to each of these five words, and write them down. Now look through this book and write down the titles of ten works of art which are connected to the things and ideas on your lists. Finally, combine the titles of the works of art with the words on your list and read them to the class.

Pretend that you are the king, queen, or dictator of America. You control what people read in books and see on television and in the movies. You also control what artists create because you do not want the people to get ideas that would lead to your loss of power. Go through this book and list at least five works of art that you would not allow the people to see. List five works you would let them see. Explain your lists.

Suppose that someone you know has had a long illness and is feeling very depressed. You are going to visit this person and you would like to give him a present—a picture that would cheer him up or take his mind off his troubles. Which picture in this book would you give? Why?

Chapel at Ronchamps, by Le Corbusier. (Courtesy Lucien Hervé.)

Judgment: Practices 2

SOME THINGS TO SEE

Look at *Nude Descending a Staircase* by Marcel Duchamp, *Six Persimmons* by Mu Ch'i, the interior of the Guggenheim Museum by Frank Lloyd Wright, and *Torso of a Young Man* by Constantin Brancusi.

SOME PROBLEMS

In these great works of art, form is dominant. That is, the ideas expressed and the functions performed are less important than visual qualities by themselves. Therefore, Brancusi's *Torso* does not tell you very much about a young man's anatomy. What is the sculpture really about? I believe *Six Persimmons* is a masterpiece, but not because it tells me anything new about persimmons. What is crucial in this painting? If you are looking for nakedness in Duchamp's *Nude*, you will not find it. The picture deals with motion. When you recover from your disappointment, answer this question: What makes the picture beautiful? Wright's Guggenheim Museum is a type of interior sculpture. It may not be a very good place to display art, but what makes the building itself a great work of art?

SOME POSSIBILITIES

Do you think the world we see is made of unreal shells and surfaces covering up truly real, underlying forms—forms that are usually invisible? If so, does the Brancusi *Torso* reveal the invisible form of a young man's body? Or could it be the model on

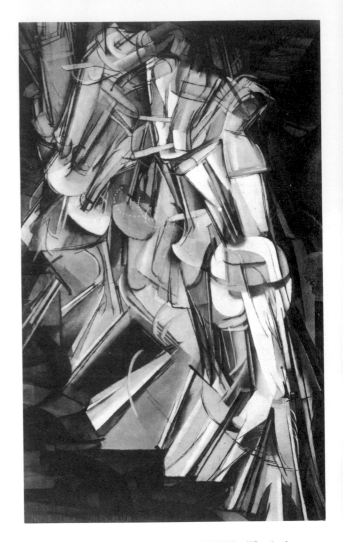

NUDE DESCENDING A STAIRCASE, NO. 2, by Marcel Duchamp. (Philadelphia Museum of Art. The Louise and Walter Arensberg Collection.)

which all male torsos are based? Does Mu Ch'i call attention to the persimmons or to his skill in composition and execution? The painting looks simple, but it isn't. We are looking at a perfect performance of a limited task. Is that enough to create a masterpiece? Does Duchamp's study of motion

SIX PERSIMMONS (left above), by Mu Ch'i. (Daitoku-ji, Kyoto.)

Guggenheim Museum interior (left below), by Frank Lloyd Wright. (The Solomon R. Guggenheim Museum.)

TORSO OF A YOUNG MAN (near left), by Constantin Brancusi. (The Joseph H. Hirshhorn Collection.)

remind you of Brancusi's study of form? He has tried to eliminate the female-ness of the woman and has painted only her motion. But her motion is very feminine. Perhaps moving forms are more beautiful than static forms. Do the forms of Wright's Guggenheim interior get their power from the ability to symbolize something larger than a building? Or do they stand for nothing more than themselves? Try to explain the effect on the viewer as he looks up at the museum balconies and into the skylight.

WHAT YOU CAN DO

Collect statements by critics of movies, plays, music, and art. You can find them in newspapers and magazines. Underline the parts where the critic is judging something. What do critics say when they want to praise a work of art or when they think it is poor? What reasons, if any, do they give for their judgments?

Visit a department store or a furniture store with a friend and try to pick out a good chair for watching television. List the advantages of the chair you think is best. Ask your friend to do the same thing. Compare your chair and your list with those of your friend.

Which is the finest public building in your community? Make a drawing or a photograph of it. Then tell the class why you think it is best.

When you and your classmates have finished an art project, be sure to remind your teacher to save time for the whole class to see what was done and to discuss the completed work. The person who painted a picture, for example, might tell what he was trying to do; others could tell him what they see in his picture; someone might give suggestions for a different approach the next time the class works on a painting project. You should collect reproductions and search them for ideas that you or someone else can use. If there is a museum or gallery in your community, plan a visit to see specific works of art there in order to study artistic quality in the original.

Conclusion

At this point, I should attempt to summarize the main argument of the book: The education of children and adolescents takes place through what they see and hear as well as what they read. Many of the things they see, hear, and make deserve to be called art although they may not be of professional quality. Regardless of quality, however, children need to be able to deal with the visual environment effectively since so much of what they learn and become depends on seeing intelligently, sensitively, and pleasurably. The organized effort to learn about man and the world by studying art is an integral part of aesthetic education. Learning to confront the world meaningfully by creating art is also part of aesthetic education. It is not possible, however, to learn or to teach in such a program without reference to specific instances of looking, making, listening, and understanding in the presence of specific works of art. In other words, aesthetic education has to be approached through concrete examples of human creativity rather than the general principles that presumably underlie all types of creativity.

A child's aesthetic education can be gained through studying music, dance, drama, art, literature, or a combination of these. But it is not essential that a child be a finished performer in each of the arts in order to deal successfully with his environment. Indeed, he need not be a finished performer in any of them provided the distinctive language of at least one of the arts is available to him as an instrument of understanding and delight. What matters is not the way a child gets his insights so much as the fact that he does get them. Teachers may need to have a specialty, but children do not.

General classroom teachers are rarely expert artistic performers. It is unreasonable, therefore, to expect their teaching in the realm of aesthetic education to be based on artistic competencies they do not have.

On the other hand, we *can* expect the general classroom teacher to know how to organize learning according to broadly humanistic principles of aesthetic education. In other words, we can rely on a teacher's experience as a person in the world, his command of some language of expression that he prefers, his insight into the needs and interests of pupils, and his compassion for people trying to be persons. That is the specialty of teachers—using their own humanity to make others human.

More of us are artists than is generally realized. And all of us are shaped by art. Once we step outside the narrow world of narrow definitions, so far as art is concerned, many things become possible. Work and study, teaching and learning acquire a visible form. A teacher becomes a medium for translating behavior into art and art into meaning. His relationships with pupils exhibit style and content. Then teaching itself emerges as an art and the truly human person as its distinctive product.

Bibliography

The Nature of Art

ABELL, WALTER, *The Collective Dream in Art*. Cambridge: Harvard University Press, 1957. ACKERMAN, JAMES S., and RHYS CARPENTER, *Art and Archaeology*. Englewood Cliffs, N.J.: Prentice-Hall, 1963. ADAM, LEONHARD, *Primitive Art*. Baltimore: Penguin, 1949. BERNDT, RONALD M., editor, *Australian Aboriginal Art*. New York: Macmillan, 1964. BURKITT, MILES, *The Old Stone Age*. New York: Atheneum, 1963. *CARPENTER, EDMUND, Eskimo*. Toronto: University of Toronto Press, 1959. CAUMAN, SAMUEL, *The Living Museum: Experiences of an Art Historian and Museum Director: Alexander Dorner*, Introduction by Walter Gropius. New York: New York University Press, 1958. CHILDE, V. GORDON, *Man Makes Himself*. New York: Mentor, 1951. DEWEY, JOHN, *Art as Experience*. New York: Minton, Balch, 1934. FELDMAN, EDMUND B., "On the Necessity of Fusing Two Views of Culture." *Arts in Society*, Winter 1959. FISCHER, ERNST, *The Necessity of Art: A Marxist Approach*, tr. by Anna Bostock. Baltimore: Penguin, 1964. FRASER, DOUGLAS, *The Many Faces of Primitive Art: A Critical Anthology*. Englewood Cliffs, N.J.: Prentice-Hall, 1966. HADDON, ALFRED C., *History of Anthropology*. London: Watts, 1949. HARRIES, KARSTEN, *The Meaning of Modern Art*. Evanston, Ill.: Northwestern University Press, 1968. HAUSER, ARNOLD, *The Philosophy of Art History*. New York: Knopf, 1959. HOWELLS, WILLIAM, *Back of History*. New York: Doubleday, 1963. HUDNUT, JOSEPH, *Architecture and the Spirit of Man*. Cambridge: Harvard University Press, 1939. INVERARITY, ROBERT BRUCE, *Art of the Northwest Coast Indians*. Berkeley: University of California Press, 1950. KAVOLIS, VYTAUTAS, *Artistic Expression—A Sociological Analysis*. Ithaca: Cornell University Press, 1968. LIPMAN, MATTHEW, *What Happens in Art*. New York: Appleton-Century-Crofts, 1967. LOMMEL, ANDREAS, *Shamanism: The Beginnings of Art*. New York: McGraw-Hill, 1967. LYNES, RUSSELL, *The Tastemakers*. New York: Harper & Row, 1954. MEIER, NORMAN C., *Art in Human Affairs*. New York: McGraw-Hill, 1942. MUENSTERBERGER, WARNER, *Sculpture of Primitive Man*. New York: Abrams, 1955. NEUMEYER, ALFRED, *The Search for Meaning in Modern Art*. Englewood Cliffs, N.J.: Prentice-Hall, 1964. PANOFSKY, ERWIN, *Meaning in the Visual Arts: Papers in and on Art History*. Garden City, N.Y.: Doubleday Anchor, 1955. POWELL, T.G.E., *Prehistoric Art*. New York: Praeger, 1966. RADER, MELVIN, *A Modern Book of Aesthetics*. New York: Holt, Rinehart and Winston, 1960. READ, HERBERT, *The Grass Roots of Art*. New York: Wittenborn, 1947. *Icon and Idea: The Function of Art in the Development of Human Consciousness*. Cambridge: Harvard University Press, 1955. *The Origins of Form in Art*. New York: Horizon Press, 1965. SCHENK, GUSTAV, *The History of Man*. Philadelphia: Chilton, 1961. SCHMALENBACH, WERNER, *African Art*. New York: Macmillan, 1954. SCHMITZ, CARL A., *Oceanic Sculpture: Sculpture of Melanesia*. Greenwich, Conn.: New York Graphic Society, 1962. SHAHN, BEN, *The Shape of Content*. Cambridge: Harvard University Press, 1957. SMITH, RALPH A., "The Structure of Art–Historical Knowledge and Art Education." *Studies in Art Education*, Vol. IV (Fall 1962), pp. 23–33. TEJERA, VICTORINO, *Art and Human Intelligence*. New York: Appleton-Century-Crofts, 1965. TISCHNER, HERBERT, *Oceanic Art*. New York: Pantheon, 1954. Photographs by Friedrich Henricker. WAAGE, FREDERICK O., *Prehistoric Art*. Dubuque, Ia.: William C. Brown Publishers, 1967. WELLER, ALLEN S., *The Joys and Sorrows of Recent American Art*. Urbana, Ill.: University of Illinois Press, 1968. WÖLFFLIN, HEINRICH, *Principles of Art History*, tr. by Mary D. Hottinger. New York: Dover, 1950. *The Sense of Form in Art: A Comparative Psychological Study*. New York: Chelsea, 1958. WOOLEY, SIR LEONARD, *The Beginnings of Civilization*. New York: Mentor, 1965.

The Character of Learning

BETTELHEIM, BRUNO, *The Children of the Dream: Communal Child-Rearing and American Education*. London: Collier-Macmillan, 1969. BLOOM, BENJAMIN S., et al., *Taxonomy of Educational Objectives, A Classification of Educational Goals, Handbook I: Cognitive Domain*. New York: McKay, 1956. BRACKMAN, JACOB, "Onward and Upward With the Arts: The Put-On." *The New Yorker Magazine*, November 26, 1966, p. 34 et seq. BUBER, MARTIN, *Between Man and Man*. Boston: Beacon, 1955. COMBS, ARTHUR W., *The Professional Education of Teachers*. Boston: Allyn and Bacon, 1965. ERIKSON, ERIK H., *Childhood and Society*. New York: Norton, 1950. FELDMAN, EDMUND B., "The Educational Value of Aesthetic Experience." *The Harvard Educational Review*, Vol. 21, No. 4, Fall 1951. FREUD, SIGMUND, *Civilization and its Discontents*. Garden City, N.Y.: Doubleday Anchor, 1958. FRIEDENBERG, EDGAR Z., "Sentimental Education." *The New York Review of Books*, Vol. XI, No. 9, November 21, 1968. FROMM, ERICH, *The Art of Loving*. New York: Bantam, 1963. GOODMAN, PAUL, *Growing Up Absurd: Problems of Youth in the Organized System*. New York: Random House, 1960. "The Present Moment in Education." *The New York Review of Books*, Vol. XII, No. 7, April 10, 1969. HAYES, BARTLETT H., JR., "Ideas at My Fingertips." *The Harvard Educational Review*, Vol. 16, No. 4, Fall 1966. HERBERG, WILL, ed., *The Writings of Martin Buber*. New York: Meridian, 1956. KAELIN, EUGENE F., "Aesthetics and the Teaching of Art." *Studies in Art Education*, Vol. V (Spring 1964), pp. 42–56. KAPLAN, ABRAHAM, *The Conduct of Inquiry*. San Francisco: Chandler, 1964. KELLOGG, RHODA, *What Children Scribble and Why*. San Francisco: N-P Publications, 1959. KRATHWOHL, DAVID R., BENJAMIN S. BLOOM, and BERTRAM B. MASIA, *Taxonomy of Educational Objectives, A Classification of Educational Goals, Handbook II: Affective Domain*. New York: McKay, 1964. LEVI, ALBERT WILLIAM, *Philosophy and the Modern World*. Bloomington, Ind.: Indiana University Press, 1959. LEVI-STRAUSS, CLAUDE, *The Savage Mind*. Chicago: University of Chicago Press, 1966. MUNRO, THOMAS, *Art Education: Its Philosophy and Psychology*. New York: Liberal Arts Press, 1956. PHENIX, PHILLIP, *Realms of Meaning*. New York: McGraw-Hill, 1964. READ, HERBERT, *Education Through Art*. New York: Pantheon, 1945. RIESMAN, DAVID, *Constraint and Variety in American Education*. Garden City, N.Y.: Doubleday Anchor, 1958. SCHAEFER,

ROBERT J., *The School as a Center of Inquiry*. New York: Harper & Row, 1967. SCHRAMM WILBUR, ed., *The Effects of Television on Children and Adolescents*. New York: UNESCO, 1964. SELZ, PETER, *New Images of Man*, prefatory note by Paul Tillich. New York: The Museum of Modern Art, 1959. SMITH, RALPH, ed., *Aesthetics and Criticism in Art Education*. Chicago: Rand McNally, 1966. TILLICH, PAUL, *The Courage To Be*. New Haven: Yale University Press, 1963. WHITEHEAD, ALFRED NORTH, *The Aims of Education*. New York: Mentor, 1949.

The Creativity of Children

ALSHULER, ROSE H., and HATTWICK LA BERTA, *Painting and Personality*, 2 vols. Chicago: University of Chicago Press, 1947. ARNHEIM, RUDOLPH, *Art and Visual Perception: A Psychology of the Creative Eye*. Berkeley: University of California Press, 1965. BOWRA, C.M., *Primitive Song*. Cleveland: World, 1962. BRITTAIN, L. LAMBERT, and KENNETH BEITTEL, "A Study of Some Tests of Creativity in Relationship to Performances in the Visual Arts." *Studies in Art Education*, Vol. 2, No. 2, Spring 1961. BRUNER, JEROME, ROSE OLIVER, and PATRICIA GREENFIELD, *Studies in Cognitive Growth*. New York: Wiley, 1966. CAMPBELL, JOSEPH, *The Hero With a Thousand Faces*. New York: Pantheon, 1949. CULKIN, JOHN M., "A Schoolman's Guide to Marshall McLuhan." *Saturday Review*, March 13, 1967. EISNER, ELLIOT W., *A Comparison of the Developmental Drawing Characteristics of Culturally Advantaged and Culturally Disadvantaged Children*. Stanford, Calif.: Stanford University Press, 1967. ENG, HELGA, *The Psychology of Children's Drawings*. New York: Harcourt, Brace & World, 1931. FELDMAN, EDMUND B., "Research as the Verification of Aesthetics." *Studies in Art Education*, Vol. 1, No. 1, Fall 1959. "On the Connection Between Art and Life." *School Arts Magazine*, January 1963. "Engaging Art in Dialogue." *Saturday Review*, July 15, 1967, p. 60 *et seq*. FREUD, SIGMUND, *A General Introduction to Psychoanalysis*, tr. by Joan Riviere. New York: Garden City Publishing Company, 1943. FREUND, PHILIP, *Myths of Creation*. New York: Washington Square Press, 1965. GASTER, THEODORE H., *Myth, Legend, and Custom in the Old Testament*. New York: Harper & Row 1969. GIEDION, SIGFRIED, *Mechanization Takes Command*. New York: Oxford, 1948. GRAVES, ROBERT, *The Greek Myths*. New York: Braziller, 1959. HARRIS, DALE, *Children's Drawings as Measures of Intellectual Maturity*. New York: Harcourt, Brace & World, 1963. JAENSCH, E.R., *Eidetic Imagery and Typological Methods of Investigation: Their Importance for the Psychology of Childhood, etc*. New York: Harcourt, Brace & World, 1930. KELLOGG, RHODA, and SCOTT O'DELL, *The Psychology of Children's Art*. New York: Random House, 1967. KOFFKA, KURT, *Principles of Gestalt Psychology*. London: Routledge & Kegan Paul, 1935. KÖHLER, WOLFGANG, *Gestalt Psychology*. New York: Harcourt, Brace & World, 1935. KRIS, ERNST, *Psychoanalytic Explorations in Art*. New York: International Universities Press, 1952. LANGER, SUSANNE K., *Philosophy in a New Key: A Study in the Symbolism of Reason, Rite and Art*. New York: Mentor, 1949. McLUHAN, MARSHALL, *Understanding Media: The Extensions of Man*. McGraw-Hill, 1964. MORRIS, CHARLES W., *Signs, Language, and Behavior*. Englewood Cliffs, N.J.: Prentice-Hall, 1946. PHILLIPS, WILLIAM, ed., *Art and Psychoanalysis*. New York: Criterion, 1957. PIAGET, JEAN, *The Child's Conception of Space*. London: Routledge & Kegan Paul, 1956. SEITZ, WILLIAM, *Art of Assemblage*. New York: Museum of Modern Art, 1962. STRAUS, ERWIN, *The Primary World of the Senses: A Vindication of Sensory Experience*. London: Collier-Macmillan, 1963.

A Curriculum for Art Education

ANDERSON, DONALD M., *Elements of Design*. New York: Holt, Rinehart and Winston, 1961. ARNHEIM, RUDOLPH, *Toward a Psychology of Art*. Berkeley: University of California Press, 1966. BARKAN, MANUEL, and LAURA CHAP-MAN, *Guidelines for Art Instruction Through Television for the Elementary Schools*. Bloomington, Ind.: National Center for School and College Television, 1967. BOAS, GEORGE, *A Primer for Critics*. Baltimore: Johns Hopkins Press, 1937. CATALDO, JOHN W., *Words and Calligraphy for Children*. New York: Reinhold, 1969. FELDMAN, EDMUND B., "Works of Art as Humanistic Inquiries." *The School Review*, Vol. 72, No. 3, Autumn 1964. "The Critical Act." *The Journal of Aesthetic Education*, Vol. 1, No. 2, Autumn 1966. "Some Adventures in Art Criticism." *Art Education*, Vol. 22, No. 3, March 1968. GOODMAN, PAUL and PERCIVAL, *Communitas: Means of Livelihood and Ways of Life*. New York: Vintage, 1960. GREENE, THEODORE M., *The Arts and the Art of Criticism*. Princeton: Princeton University Press, 1947. HASTIE, W. REID, editor, *Art Education: The Sixty-fourth Yearbook of the National Society for the Study of Education*, Part II. Chicago: University of Chicago Press, 1965. JANIS, HARRIET, and RUDI BLESH, *Collage: Personalities, Concepts, Techniques*. Philadelphia: Chilton, 1962. KRACAUER, SIEGFRIED, *Theory of Film: The Redemption of Physical Reality*. New York: Oxford, 1960. LOWENFELD, VIKTOR, *Creative and Mental Growth*, fourth edition. New York: Macmillan, 1964. MARGOLIS, JOSEPH, *The Language of Art and Art Criticism*. Detroit: Wayne State University Press, 1965. McFEE, JUNE K., *Preparation for Art*. Belmont, Calif.: Wadsworth, 1961. MONTGOMERY, CHANDLER, *Art for Teachers of Children*. Columbus, Ohio: Merrill, 1968. MORMAN, JEAN M., *Art: Of Wonder and a World*. Blauvelt, N.Y.: Art Education, Inc., 1967. PEPPER, STEPHEN C., *The Basis of Criticism in the Arts*. Cambridge: Harvard University Press, 1949. PRALL, D.W., *Aesthetic Judgment*. New York: Thomas Y. Crowell, 1967. RASMUSSEN, STEEN EILER, *Experiencing Architecture*. Cambridge: M.I.T. Press, 1959. STEVENI, MICHAEL, *Art and Education*. London: B.T. Batsford, 1968. WILLIAMS, HIRAM, *Notes for a Young Painter*. Englewood Cliffs, N.J.: Prentice-Hall, 1963.

Index

Page numbers in italics indicate illustrations.